A Tree of Life

THE LITTMAN LIBRARY OF
JEWISH CIVILIZATION

For the love of God
and in memory of
JOSEPH AARON LITTMAN

"Get wisdom, get understanding:
Forsake her not and she shall preserve thee"

March 13, 1985

Louis Jacobs

A Tree of Life

Diversity, Flexibility, and Creativity in Jewish Law

Louis Jacobs

Published for
THE LITTMAN LIBRARY
by
OXFORD UNIVERSITY PRESS
1984

Oxford University Press, Walton Street, Oxford OX2 6DP

London New York Toronto
Delhi Bombay Calcutta Madras Karachi
Kuala Lumpur Singapore Hong Kong Tokyo
Nairobi Dar es Salaam Cape Town
Melbourne Auckland

and associated companies in
Beirut Berlin Ibadan Mexico City Nicosia

Oxford is a trade mark of Oxford University Press

Published in the United States
by Oxford University Press, New York

British Library Cataloguing in Publication Data
Jacobs, Louis
The tree of life.—(The Littman library
of Jewish civilization)
1. Jewish law
I. Title   II. Series
296.1'8   BM521
ISBN 0-19-710039-2

Printed in Great Britain
at the Alden Press, Oxford

For my grandchildren—
Daniel, Paula, Ziva, and Noa

"It is a tree of life to them that grasp it (Proverbs 3:18). R. Banaah used to say: Whoever busies himself in the Torah for its own sake, his Torah becomes for him an elixir of life."

Taanit 7a

"The benediction recited after the reading of the Torah is: "Who has given us a Torah of truth"—this refers to the Written Torah—"and has planted eternal life in our midst"—this is the Oral Torah." *Shulḥan Arukh, Oraḥ Hayyim* 139:10

Contents

Introduction:
Halakhah and Aggadah

The central thesis of this book is that the Halakhah—the legal side of Judaism—far from being entirely self-sufficient and self-authenticating, is influenced by the attitudes, conscious or unconscious, of its practitioners toward the wider demands and ideals of Judaism and by the social, economic, theological, and political conditions that occur when the ostensibly purely legal norms and methodology are developed. Our chief concern is with the post-Talmudic Halakhah, though the earlier Halakhic developments are also discussed. No investigation of the river's course is possible without an examination of the spring from which it emanates.

A superficial glance at the Halakhic literature may give one the impression that the Halakhah is a closed system; the Halakhists appear to operate as if theirs were an exact science, a discipline that can and should be approached objectively on its own terms. A deeper understanding of the Halakhic process demonstrates, however, that the Halakhists were by no means disembodied intelligences, working with and on bloodless abstractions. They are real human beings of individual temperaments and dispositions whose theories and decisions are not infrequently governed by the needs of the people for whom they are legislating. The thrust of this study is to show how other than purely Halakhic considerations have been determinative both in the original formulation of many of the laws and in their subsequent development; that, in other words, there is a history of the Halakhah.

Chaim Tchernowitz (1871–1949), who wrote under the penname Rav Tzair ("Young Rabbi"), tells, in his delightful autobiography,[1] how his essays on "The History of the *Shulhan Arukh*" *(Toledot ha-Shulhan Arukh)*, published in the journal *ha-Shiloah*, were received with hostility by the majority of traditionalist rabbis. In part, their objection was based on the fact that the editor of the journal, Ahad ha-Am, was seen by the rabbis as a notorious unbeliever. In addition, they faulted the essays themselves, not so much for any particular errors that might have been perpetrated but because the rabbis recoiled in horror at the very thought of the *Shulhan Arukh*, the standard and hollowed Code of Jewish law and observances, having a *history*. When Tchernowitz was appointed Rabbi of Odessa, a rabbi protested that a scholar who had produced a study in which he had surveyed the history of the *Shulhan Arukh* is thereby automatically debarred from serving as a rabbi, since his investigations into how the laws of the great Code have developed are bound to inhibit him when he is called upon, as a practicing rabbi is, to render decisions on the basis of that Code. Tchernowitz's somewhat disingenuous reply is, "This rabbi seems incapable of appreciating that it is possible for a judge to render a decision on the basis of an accepted Code of Law even though that judge may not personally agree with that law or may lack belief in its sanctity." The reply raises significant questions, not the least of which are: whether a historical approach really does destroy, in some measure at least, belief in the sanctity of the law and whether there is not something schizophrenic, not to say dishonest, in such a dichotomy between theory and practice? These and similar questions must be faced, and in the following chapters we throw some light on a way in which they can be answered. For the moment all we have to note is that the researches of Tchernowitz and other modern scholars show conclusively that the Halakhah has followed the lines of development common to all human institutions, even though, at times, the Halakhic giants were looked upon by teachers of a later age as beings of a superhuman stature, genius, and sanctity.[2]

It will not do to exaggerate. Like every other legal system, the Halakhah has its own characteristic methodology. The overt aim of the Halakhist is not to declare what the law should be but to discuss and eventually to state what the law is. The Halakhist seeks far more to apply the established rules than to function as a legislator. He is guided in his decisions by precedent, accepting in toto the authority of the Talmud, his final court of appeal, and he generally has complete deference toward the *rishonim* ("early ones"), i.e., to the teachers who flourished before the codification of the law in the

Shulhan Arukh, compiled in the sixteenth century, even though he may be less deferential to the *aharonim* ("later ones"), the post-*Shulhan Arukh* teachers. Moreover, the Halakhist's viewpoint is based on the belief that the Torah is divinely revealed in all its details—the Written Torah of the bible as well as the Oral Torah as recorded in the Talmudic literaure. *Hazal* (from the initial letters of *hahamenu zikhronam li-verakhah*, "our Sages of blassed memory"), the Talmudic rabbis, are, for the Halakhist, infallible teachers, at least in matters of Halakhah, whose decisions may never be countermanded except when they themselves have provided the necessary machinery for change or abolition. New circumstances, demanding the need for legislation where there is no direct guidance in the Talmudic sources, can only be approached by the use of analogy, except for the *takkanot* (rabbinic or communal enactments), the scope of which is limited and the right to enact that is itself given in the Talmudic sources. A major portion of the vast Responsa literature is concerned with applying Talmudic legal principles to problems the solutions for which cannot be found explicitly in the Talmud.

Nevertheless, there is sufficient evidence to allow us to reject as one-sided the conventional picture of the traditional Halakhist as an academic lawyer who, when he sits down to investigate his sources dispassionately and with complete objectivity, never knows beforehand what his conclusions will be. In many instances, even when the Halakhist follows the accepted Halakhic methods, he knows full well, before he begins his investigation, that only one conclusion is acceptable, not because the sources he is about to examine will inevitably lead to that conclusion but because his general approach to Judaism compels him to come up with a conclusion that must not be at variance with Jewish ideas and ideals as he and his contemporaries or his "school" sees them. Any neat distinction between Halakhah and Aggadah (the nonlegal side of Judaism) is untenable. Behind the most austere Halakhist there sits the passionate, easily moved, poetic Aggadist. As Rabbi A. I. Kook once said: just as there are laws of poetry there is poetry in laws. The Halakhist obeys the rules and plays the game according to them. In order to arrive at his decisions the Halakhist must use the acceptable legal ploys. He has always to demonstrate that the law really is what he declares it to be and that his decision has been reached on Halakhic grounds. Yet, especially when the problem he confronts is of vital religious or ethical concern, he knows only too well that some conclusions are ruled out from the beginning even if these appear convincing from the point of view of abstract logic and pure legal theory.

Against this is the alleged quotation from the Jerusalem Talmud, "One does not learn (i.e., for the purpose of legal decisions) from the Aggadah," suggesting that no legal rulings are to be derived from Aggadic passages in the Talmud so that there is, in fact, a complete and total distinction between the prose of the Halakhah and the poetry of the Aggadah; the former objective, the latter subjective, the former binding, the latter optional, the former applying to all Jews categorically, the latter only to the individual and with qualifications.[3] Two actual parallel passages in the Jerusalem Talmud clarify the matter. The first of these from tractate *Peah*[4] reads: "One does not learn from the *halakhot* or from the *haggadot* or from the *tosefot* but only from the *talmud*." The other passage in tractate *Hagigah*[5] reads, "One does not render decisions from the *halakhot* or from the *aggadot* or from the *tosefot* but only from the *talmud*." Apart from the differences in spelling—*haggadot* and *aggadot*—the two texts are identical except that in the first the term used is, "One does not learn" *(eyn lemmedin)*, whereas in the second the term is, "One does not render decisions" *(eyn morin)*. It is obvious that "One does not learn" in the first text means, "One does not render decisions," as in the second text. The statement, odd at first glance, that the law must not be decided on the basis of the *halakhot*, becomes intelligible if, as the commentators note, the reference is to earlier formulations of the law. The meaning then is that it is the law (the *halakhah*) as recorded in the Talmud (i.e., by the Amoraim) which is decisive not that recorded in the Tannaitic collections whether in the form of *halakhot* or of *tosefot* ("additions"). The basic question is whether the Jerusalem Talmud (where, incidentally, the author of the statement is the Babylonian Amora, Mar Samuel) really means that no legal decisions are to be based on the Aggadah as found in the Talmud and the Midrashim. Some authorities understand the passages as implying precisely this. Yom Tov Lippmann Heller (1579–1660), in his Commentary to the Mishnah, *Tosefot Yom Tov*,[6] remarks that the law must never be decided on the basis of rulings or statements found in the Aggadic Midrashim. R. Akiba Eger[7] (1761–1837) refers in this connection to the observation of Hezekiah da Silva (1659–1695) that the rule only applies where the Midrashim state that the rule is according a particular authority and where such a ruling is not found in the Talmud. It certainly does not mean that laws cannot be based on

Aggadic statements. Zevi Hirsch Chajes (1805–1855), who has treated this whole topic comprehensively,[8] plausibly suggests that the reference in the Jerusalem Talmud is not to all Aggadah but only to popular sermons which are for edification and were never intended to lay down the law. Be that as it may, Chajes has no difficulty in pointing to numerous authorities who did derive rules of conduct from the Aggadic passages in the Talmud and from the Aggadic Midrashim. To quote one example among very many, all the laws regarding the mourner's *kaddish* are based on statements in the Aggadic Midrash.[9]

A warning against any attempt to allow pure Halakhic reasoning to become infected with extralegal notions was issued by the great Halakhic authority R. Moses Sofer (1762–1839). In an aside, the *Hatam Sofer* (as he is called, after the title of his works) writes:

> Your honour does well, in rejecting the arguments of your opponent, who quotes from the writings of the *Ari*. [The *Ari* is R. Isaac Luria, the famous sixteenth-century Kabbalist of Safed]. As you write: "I do not enter into the mysteries." I am fond of saying that whoever mixes Kabbalistic topics with the established *Halakhah* is liable because of the law against sowing mixed seeds "lest the fruit of the seed which thou hast sown, and the fruit of thy vineyard, become sanctified" [Deut. 22:9, taking *tikdash* as "sanctified," i.e., the sacred mysteries of the Kabbalah, if used in an Halakhic context, introduce the supernatural into the very realistic and natural Halakhah]. On the other hand, whoever mixes words of logic [*higgayon*, here referring to rationalistic philosophy[with matters of Torah offends against the law of: "Thou shalt not plough with an ox and an ass together" [Deut. 22:10]. And if he is a leader [*manhig*] in Israel he is guilty of leading diverse kinds [i.e., a pun on "leader" and the prohibition of "leading" two different species].[10]

Leaving aside what might be considered a mere quibble—that this very statement of the *Hatam Sofer* is itself an example of the introduction of his general philosophy of Judaism into the Halakhah—the statement cannot possibly be taken at its face value as the total rejection of philosophical, theological, and Kabbalistic considerations in questions of Halakhah. As we demonstrate in this book, both philosophical and Kabbalistic opinions have had a voice in determining the Halakhah. The Hasidic master and Halakhist R. Hayyim Eleazar Shapira of Munkacs (1872–1937), embarrassed by the *Hatam Sofer*'s rejection of the Kabbalah having a voice in the Halakhah, though, evidently, quite happy about the other remarks on philosophy, observed:

When he states that whoever mixes Kabbalistic topics with *halakhot* is liable because of sowing diverse kinds etc., God forbid that this righteous Gaon, of blessed memory, should have intended it to be taken literally. Were, then, our master the *Magen Avraham*, whose notes to the *Shulhan Arukh, Orah Hayyim*, are replete with references in many places to the writings of the *Ari*, of blessed memory, and in connection with the Halakhah, and our master, the *Bet Yosef* (Karo) and the other Codifiers who quote in their works, for the purpose of actual practice, from the holy zohar and from the *Ari*, of blessed memory, were all these guilty, God forbid, of sowing diverse seeds! But, begging his forgiveness, genius and righteous as he was, it was a slip of the pen, and was intended solely as a literary pun for the sake of his conclusion, because he wished to castigate those who mix philosophy and enlightenment ideas [*haskalah* i.e., the rationalist movement founded by Mendelssohn] as is evident from that Responsum. We are bound to explain it in this way.[11]

In fact, the *Hatam Sofer*, in many of his Responsa, did try to avoid much influence of the Kabbalah on the Halakhah.[12] But there is no case here for the thesis that Halakhah is always "pure" and "unadulterated," never affected or influenced by non-Halakhic categories.

The foremost exponent in this century of complete Halakhic autonomy is J. B. Soloveitchik in his famous essay *"Ish ha-Halakhah"* ("Halakhic Man"). In this lengthy and justly admired essay, Soloveitchik describes the ideal Halakhist as possessing the characteristics of both "the man of God" and "the man of science." The ideal Halakhist is religious and totally dedicated to God's service but, at the same time, he is concerned with the Torah for men on earth. Like the scientist he sits down before the Halakhic facts, which he examines in detachment, refusing to allow his enthusiasms to affect his deliberations in any way. For the pure Halakhist there is no difference whatsoever between one *mitzvah* and another. Not for him are such things as listening to the *shofar* on Rosh ha-Shanah in a spirit of extra awe and dread. This day is judgment day for the whole world, and in this sense some special awareness seems to be called for, but whatever special attitudes are to be cultivated when the shofar is sounded on this day have to be cultivated because this is what the Halakhah demands. Even in the heavenly Yeshivah, the topics of the discussions, for the Halakhist, are, as the Talmud states, not the divine mysteries but the subtle definitions and profound legal theories of the earthly Halakhah. Soloveitchik's essay calls for careful study and can serve as a caution against too hasty generalizations, but it does not affect our basic thesis. Soloveitchik himself observes right at the beginning of his essay that his "Halakhic Man" is only an abstraction like "Economic Man." The Halakhists were complex personalities not stereotypes. This book hopes to show that even in the Halakhic processes other influences are not infrequently at work.

At times the Halakhists state explicitly that their decisions in particular instances are not based on the strict *din* ("law") but are given because to decide otherwise would lead to undesirable consequences. Occasionally, when this kind of motivation is recorded in the work of a renowned Halakhist, the decision based on it comes to enjoy Halakhic authority, despite its acknowledged extra-Halakhic basis, precisely because it has been recorded and accepted by that Halakhist. When this happens the theory is that since a Halakhist of undisputed rank has allowed this kind of extra-Halakhic motivation to govern his final decision this becomes a *legal* motivation to be applied in analogous circumstances. For instance, Levi Ibn Habib (d.1545) states[13] that it is wrong to teach in public such Kabbalistic doctrines as the belief in reincarnation not because there is any strict law forbidding this but because people unaccustomed to the doctrine will find it bizarre and this will tend to bring Judaism into disrepute. Centuries later, Abraham Steinberg (1847–1928), rabbi of Brody in Galicia, states[14] that although there is no strictly legal objection to using a former brothel as a synagogue, it is forbidden, nonetheless, on the grounds that people will find it exceedingly odd for such a thing to be allowed and he quotes Ibn Habib in support. Another example of nonlegal motivation becoming part of the Halakhah is the statement by R. Moses Isserles (d. 1572), the *Rama*, [15] that although a *mamzer* ("the issue of an adulterous or incestuous union," Deut. 13:2) is not disbarred by law from occupying a position of trust in the community and can even serve as a judge, yet even a doubtful *mamzer* (a *shetuki*) should not be appointed as a judge because to make such an appointment offends against the dignity of the Torah; that is, he should be disbarred from serving as a judge on extra-Halakhic grounds. The *Hatam Sofer*[16] concurs with this ruling. This authority observes that although, as the rabbis say, a scholar who is a *mamzer* takes precedence over the aristocratic high priest,[17] if the latter is an ignoramus, yet to appoint a *mamzer* to be a rabbi can only result in disrespect for the Torah since, because of the man's base origin, people will refuse to abide by his decisions. The *Hatam Sofer* continues in what is clearly a non-Halakhic vein; "How much more so in our generation when, for our sins, the glory of the Torah has departed so that people say even to those of aristocratic birth: "Remove the beam from thine own eye," how much more so to one of base parentage."

More frequently, however, the other than purely Halakhic motivation is implicit, rather than explicit as in the examples given. Here, whatever the Halakhist may appear to be saying on the surface, the historian of the Halakhah is often able to uncover the attitudes of a particular Halakhist and to note the background of the times in which particular decisions were rendered in such a way as to demonstrate that the Halakhist, granted his circumstances, can have done no other than arrive at the conclusion he has recorded at the end of what appears to be a purely Halakhic argument.

The interaction between Halakhah and Aggadah as two complementary aspects of Judaism is not only found in particular laws founded on what might be termed Aggadic motivation. There is an important instance of a whole new Halakhic field of inquiry that began as Aggadah, the treatment of the concept *Taryag* (613) precepts in the post-Talmudic Halakhah. In the Babylonian Talmud[18] there is found the preachment of the third-century Palestinian Amora, R. Simlai, that 613 precepts were given to Moses: 248 positive precepts, corresponding to the "limbs" of the human body, and 365 negative precepts, corresponding to the days of the solar year. Despite assertions to the contrary,[19] it is unlikely that the concept of *Taryag* was known to the Tannaim. But even among the Amoraim it is obvious that the concept belongs to Aggadah. It is a homily intended presumably to convey the thought that the precepts of the Torah embrace all man's bodily life and the whole of his temporal span on earth. The 365 days of the solar year determine the number 365 for the negative precepts. The number 248 for the "limbs" of the body is similarly quite independent of the 248 precepts. It is as clear that these two sets of numbers are prior to R. Simlai and were used by him with reference to the precepts. If there had been, say, 400 days of the solar year and 200 "limbs" of the body, R. Simlai would have "discovered" 600, not 613, precepts. It is inconceivable that R. Simlai actually counted the precepts to find that there were 248 positive and 365 negative ones conveniently to coincide with the number of the "limbs" of the body and the days of the year. In the whole of the Talmudic literature there is not a single attempt to list the actual 613 precepts, although, there are numerous references to this or that precept being an *aseh*, "positive precept," or a *lo taaseh*, "negative precept."

That any such attempt must in the nature of the case contain a strong element of artificiality can be seen from the great debates among the post-Talmudic authorities[20] as to how the 613 are to be determined; i.e., which precepts of the Torah are to be considered primary to be listed and which are to be considered secondary to be omitted from the list, since there are, in fact, far more than 613 commands in the Torah. Yet out of this Aggadic statement there has developed an immense Halakhic literature of much influence on Jewish life and thought.[21]

In the following pages an attempt is made to demonstrate that in a number of areas Halakhists throughout the ages allowed other considerations than those of pure legal theory to influence their decisions or, at least, that such influences were present even when they went unacknowledged. Moreover, as we have already noted briefly, these other than purely Halakhic considerations tend to become part of the Halakhic process. The extra-Halakhic motivation is generally invoked for the purpose of developing or reinterpreting the law, not for the purpose of its abolition. When the Halakhists apply to their legal theories arguments based on considerations that stem from general Jewish values, they are saying in so many words, such-and-such must be the law for, if it were not, this or that significant idea or principle of Judaism would have been overlooked or set aside. This would have been something quite intolerable to the Halakhists who, after all, are not only academicians and theoreticians but believing Jews alert to the demands that Judaism makes on the whole of life. For the Halakhists, the Torah is a tree of life and Jewish law, the Halakhah, affords scope for diversity, flexibility, and creativity.[22]

NOTES

1. *Pirkey Hayyim*, pp. 185–91. On the question of the historical as opposed to the static view of the Halakhah, see Federbusch; *bi-Netivot ha-Talmud*, chapter 1: "The Scientific Study of the Talmud" (Hebrew), pp. 9–30. Federbusch, p. 10, observes that among traditional Talmudists, nurtured in the Eastern European yeshivot, there is the strongest resistance to any "historical" interpretation of the Halakhah on the grounds that this destroys its permanent binding force, whereas many Talmudic scholars, nurtured on *Jüdische Wissenschaft*, tend to conclude from their historical researches that the foundations of the Halakhah have been underminded. On p. 11 he remarks:

The negative stance adopted by Orthodoxy towards scientific inquiry stems from its religious attitude toeards the Talmud. According to the traditional outlook, Talmudic law is obligatory for the Jew throughout all generations just like the Torah given at Sinai.

Consequently, the Orthodox saw this historical interpretation as undermining the sanctity of the Talmud and as a kind of contradiction to the force of its obligatory character throughout all generations. If the emergence of the Halakhah depended on temporal causes or its outcome based on the views of the particular sage who formulated it, its binding power is weakened because you are then able to argue that this or that law was only intended for a particular generation or is the fruit of an individual theory and has no binding power for all time and in different circumstances.

2. Boaz Cohen, *Law and Tradition in Judaism*, preface, pp. viii–x, remarks that there is a five-fold tradition in Judaism: (a) the Halakhic; (b) the *ethical;* (c) the *theological;* (d) the *philosophical;* and (e) the *mystical;* and he rightly notes that whereas the Halakhic tradition is primary that tradition itself can only be understood and observed in the framework of the other four traditions. Cf. K. Kahana, "The Connection Between Law and Other Branches of Knowledge." Kahana refers to two theories of law: "logically formal rationality," exemplified in Roman Law, and "substantive rationality," exemplified in English Law. The first theory is that law proceeds on the assumption that there can be a scheme of detailed rules rising out of a conscious and systematic arrangement of concepts.

3. On this subject see ET, vol. 1, p. 62; Heschel, *Torah Min ha-Shamayyim*, introduction, pp. i–lix; Jacob Katz, *Exclusiveness and Tolerance*, p. xiii, note 1, who makes the interesting observation that all the sources limiting the authority of the Aggadah, quoted in ET, date either from Gaonic times or from Spain, i.e., and that the medieval French and German teachers would never have discarded any part of the Aggadah as representing merely an individual opinion; Elon, *ha-Mishpat ha-Ivri*, pp. 144–46; Kahana, *Mehkarim*, pp. 1–7. On the interweaving of Aggadah into the Halakhah of the Mishnah see A. Arzi's article, "Interweaving etc." The idea is a sound one but some of Arzi's illustrations are questionable.

4. *Peah* 2:4 (17a), cf BT, *Bava Batra* 130b.

5. *Hagigah* 1:8 (76d).

6. Commentary to *Berakhot* 5:4.

7. Notes to Mishnah *Berakhot* ad loc., no. 36.

8. *Darkhey ha-Horaah*, chapter 2, in *Kol Sifre*, pp. 243f.

9. See *Rama*, SA,YD 376:5.

10. Responsa, *Hatam Sofer*, OH, no. 51.

11. *Minchet Eleazar*, II, no. 78 end.

12. See, e.g. *Hatam Sofer*, OH, nos. 15 and 16.

13. Responsa, nos. 8 and 75. See my *Theology in the Responsa*, pp. 142–44 and 305–6. In this book I have tried to show, and it is relevant to our theme, that many of the Halakhists were by no means averse to examining purely theological questions with the same precision they resorted to in their dicussions of the Halakhah proper.

14. Responsa, *Mahazey Avraham*, vol. 1, no. 27. CF. SA,YD 242:10 that it is wrong for a rabbi to render a decision that seems grotesque even if that decision is otherwise correct.

15. *Teshuvot Rama*, no. 24.

16. *Hatam Sofer*, EH, Part II, no. 94.

17. Mishnah, *Horayot* 3:8, see *infra*, pp. 35, 262.

18. *Makkot* 23b. In M. Friedmann's critical edition of tractate *Makkot*, pp. 62–64, the variant readings in the passage are recorded; e.g., some texts do not have "at Sinai" and some simply have the numbers 248 and 365 without reference to positive and negative precepts.

19. See Y. M. Guttmann, *Behinat ha-Mitzvot* who argues for a Tannaitic origin of the concept and the note of S. W. Baron, *A Social and Religious History of the Jews* vol. 6, note 103, pp. 371–72. Similarly Chavel, *Maimonides: The Commandments*, vol. I, Foreword, p. viii, says: "An early tradition dating as far back as the Tannaitic period lays it down that the number of Commandments in the Torah is *taryag*"; and Gersion Appel, *A Philosophy of Mizvot*, p. 26,

says, "This tradition, which is apparently of long-standing since it is also found in the earlier Tannaitic literature, was generally accepted as the legal frame for the codification of Jewish law." Both Chavel and Appel, p. 204 note 3, refer, in support of their contention that *Taryag* is Tannaitic, to *Mekhilta* to Exod. 20:2, cf. *Sifre* to Deut. 12:23. But, see Guttmann, *Behinat*, p. 25, that the reading *Taryag* is not found in the Munich ms. of the *Mekhilta* and see Weiss's edition of the *Mekhilta* (*Yitro* 5 note 5a, p. 75). Weiss notes that the reading *Taryag* in both the *Mekhilta* and the *Sifre* is very suspicious and that this number for the precepts is never found among the Tannaim. As for the passage in *Shabbat* 87a, referred to by Chavel, this is the Gemara commenting on a Tannaitic statement so that it is an Amoraic not a Tannaitic source. Appel's note also refers to E. E. Urbach, *The Sages: Their Concepts and Beliefs*, p. 302 for the view, undoubtedly correct, that the concept is Amoraic. Urbach refers to *Pesikta de-Rav Kahana*, ed. Mandelbaum, vol. 1, p. 202: "248 positive precepts and 365 negative precepts. 248 positive precepts corresponding to man's 248 limbs, each limb saying to man: I beg you, perform with me a precept." And 365 negative precepts, corresponding to the days of the solar year, each day saying to man, "I beg you, do not commit a sin on me." The number 248 for the "limbs" of the body is Tannaitic and independent of R. Simlai, see Mishnah *Ohalot* 1:8. On Talmudic anatomy in this connection see Katzenelleonbogen, *ha-Talmud ve-Hokhmat ha-Refuah*, pp. 234–303. Cf. Urbach, *The Sages*, p. 302, note 97, in support of the view that the number 613 in the *Mekhilta* and the *Sifre* is an interpolation and the further remarks of Urbach on pp. 302–3.

20. See Maimonides, *Sefer ha-Mitzvot* and Commentaries.

21. The totally observant Jew is frequently referred to as one who keeps the *taryag mitzvot*. Cf. the oft-quoted pun: "I sojourned (*garti*) with Laban and yet I kept the *taryag* precepts," Rashi to Gen. 32:4 and *Midrash ha-Gadol* p. 561, to Genesis, and the Halakhic literature on the details of the 613 for example, in Joseph Babad's *Minhat Hinnukh* and the *Sefer ha-Hashlamah* to this work.

22. On the Halakhah as an inexact science see the interesting remarks by Nahmanides in the Introduction to his *Milhamot*. This work was compiled by Nahmanides in defense of R. Isaac Alfasi, the *Rif*, against the strictures of Zechariah ha-Levi. Nahmanides, in his humility, writes,

"And you who peruse my book do not say to yourself that all my refutations of R. Zechariah, of blessed memory, are conclusive in my eyes, compelling you to agree with them despite your stubborn opposition so that you can boast to anyone who is doubtful about them: "Do not bother to enter the eye of a needle to refute his arguments." It is not so. For every student of our Talmud knows that where its commentators disagree with one another there are no absolute proofs and no definite refutations. For this science does not possess any clear methods of proof as, for instance, there are in the theorems of mathematics or the demonstrations in astronomy. But we must use all our judicious powers in every debate so as to reject one of the two contending opinions by means of convincing arguments, urging against the opinion the views found in the sources (*ha-shemmuyot*), giving preference to the rival opinion because that is what is suggested by the plain meaning of the *halakhot* and the logic of the *sugyot* in accordance with sound reasoning. This is all we can do and is the sole intention of every scholar and God-fearing man engaged in the science of the Gemara.

A Tree of Life

[1]

The Talmud, Source of the Halakhah

For traditional Halakhists, from the immediate post-Talmudic period, the sixth century, down to the present day, the Talmud has always been the final court of appeal in matters of practical Halakhah.[1] This is axiomatic for all the Halakhists so that the Halakhic debates, at least on the surface, are always over whether or not the Talmud rules in this or that way, never on whether the Talmudic rule constitutes authority. This applies to the Jerusalem Talmud (the Yerushalmi, the Palestinian Talmud) as well as to the Babylonian, except that where the two are in conflict the Babylonian Talmud is generally followed.[2] If, however, we are to do justice to the idea of the Halakhah as a developing system, it is essential to note that the Talmud itself has to be seen as the end product of a very lengthy process. The notion of development is built in, as it were, even into the supreme source of what later purports to be a static and closed system.

Much has been written on the early history of the Halakhah before it became crystalized in the Tannaitic period.[3] The most striking phenomenon in this connection is the one attested to in the statement: "In former times there were no controversies in Israel,"[4] i.e., in the very early period the law was so clear, straightforward, and unambiguous that it was never debated and there was no need for any prolonged discussion in order to determine what the law was in particular cases. The statement continues that the *mahaloket*, the debate among the sages, began with the disciples of Hillel and Shammai (approximately at the beginning of the present era). From the time of these two Houses—the House of Hillel and the House

23

of Shammai—and onwards down through the Tannaitic and Amoraic periods until the close of the Talmud at the end of the fifth
century, fierce debates become the standard feature of the
Halakhah. From the historical point of view it is a major problem
why the change from apparent certainty to the kind of uncertainty
that demands debate and controversy for its resolution should have
come about. It is plausible to suggest that what occurred was a total
shift from the development of the Halakhah out of the life of the
people to academic consideration in the more rarefied atmosphere
of the schools. Schoolmen are notoriously fond of debate and discussion. Beyond this generalization—and it is no more than a
generalization regarding an extremely complex problem when the
historians of the Hakakhah try to be more specific, it is now usually
acknowledged that a strong element of sheer guesswork enters into
the investigation. Baer,[5] for instance, may well have a point when
he suggests that much of the early Halakhah proceeded by rule of
thumb; the farmers and landowners, for instance, working out for
their own use and guidance regulations to which they were prepared to submit in order to survive. It would otherwise be difficult
to account for an early legal formulation, recorded in the Mishnah[6]
in the first person: "Whenever I am responsible for looking after
something (e.g., an animal) I have prepared any damage it may do
(and must therefore pay for the damage)." Nevertheless, the evidence is far too scanty to permit any convincing reconstruction of
Halakhic origins in historical terms. The period from the return
under Ezra and Nehemiah down to the earliest formulations of the
Halakhah that are now extant, i.e., the formative period of the
Halakhah, remains shrouded in darkness. The same observation
applies to the attempt of Ginzberg,[7] followed by Finkelstein,[8] at
explaining the debates between the two Houses on sociological
grounds—the House of Shammai representing and legislating for
the "patrician" party, the House of Hillel for the "plebeians." The
proposed solution is not only too neat,[9] but critical studies of the
Tannaitic literature tend to cast serious doubts as to whether, in the
ancient records of the debates between the two Houses, we have
anything like verbatim reports rather than a reading back of later
opinions into the "sayings" of the original protagonists.[10] It would
be an extraordinarily rash scholar, today, who would be ready to
pronounce with confidence on, say, the actual nature and workings
of the Sanhedrin in Temple times.

Offsetting the fluidity of the early Halakhah are the Tannaitic
formulations in Mishnah, Tosefta, Baraita, and Halakhic Midrash.

These texts were treated as sacred and as well-nigh infallible by the Amoraim. It is taken for granted in the Talmud that an Amora does not take issue with a Tanna in matters of Halakhah unless he can find support for his opinion in a statement by another Tanna.

An acute problem is raised for the student of Halakhah who appreciates that the major portion of the Babylonian Talmud, the supreme authority for the Halakhists, is academic and is not largely a work of practical guidance and prescription. Material that is in the main theoretical, with its chief purpose the discussion of the Torah for its own sake, that is, at least partly, for the sheer intellectual delight of exploring the ramifications of God's word, has to serve as the authority for the practical application of the law. Farfetched though this analogy undoubtedly is, it is not entirely unlike an attempt to extract English law in practice from references to legal topics in English literature. This factor served to arrest the dynamism of the Halakhah since pure theory can afford to divorce itself from the actual demands of Jewish life. It is all the more remarkable that the Halakhists managed to overcome, to some extent, this obstacle provided by the very nature of the source material.

It is important for our inquiry to examine further the factors in the Babylonian Talmud that do tend to freeze the flow of the practical law. First, the Amoraim were chiefly concerned with the task of interpretation by means of legal abstraction. The genius of the Amoraim consisted in trying to discover general legal principles to embrace the detailed and particular formulations of the Tannaim. By noting, for example, specific instances in the Tannaitic literature in which the principle of retrospective specification seemed to operate, the Amoraim developed the abstract concept and coined the term *bererah* for this concept. Similarly, by noting examples of a prohibition taking effect even when a different prohibition had already done so, the Amoraim tried to work out the complicated formulas regarding this topic, stating that in some circumstances the second prohibition does take effect—e.g., where it is more comprehensive in scope than the first—whereas in other circumstances it does not. Of the utmost significance for pure legal theory, this type of brilliant, subtle analysis is far removed from the concrete situations for which guidance is sought in the Halakhah.[11]

Second, there is the much-discussed question of forced and artificial interpretations of the Mishnah by the Amoraim in the Talmud. Maimonides and other teachers have permitted themselves, in their role of commentators, to explain the Mishnah in accordance with what they consider to be the *peshat* ("plain meaning") even where this differs from the Amoraic *derash*, the quasi-homiletical interpretation that frequently emerges in Talmudic passages and which, in some instances, was possibly never intended to be a real explanation of the Mishnah but is simply part of the Talmudic casuistry.[12] To the chagrin of a Halakhic historian like I. H. Weiss, the commentator Yom Tov Lippmann Heller is at pains to remark that to explain the Mishnah, as he does, in accordance with its plain meaning and at variance with the explanation given in the Talmud, is only permitted as an exercise in commentary, but never so as to influence the actual law in practice. The rationale for Heller's distinction is evidently that the Halakhah—the rule for practice—does not depend on the original meaning of a statement or formulation but on the later understanding of that statement or formulation by the Talmud, even if the latter is based on error. Or, to state it more accurately, the final Talmudic understanding cannot be in error so far as the practical law is concerned since the Halakhah is based not on whether or not a given interpretation is historically correct but on the final formulation itself as found in the Talmud, a work which, as Maimonides states,[13] "has been accepted as the authority by the whole house of Israel." The final decision is, then, far more a matter of procedure than of absolute truth.

Third, the principle that the formulation of the actual law is procedural and therefore beyond criticism on grounds of accuracy or inaccuracy finds a measure of support in the Talmud itself. Some evidence shows that the term *Halakhah* in the sense of a practical ruling does not denote, in the Talmud, which opinion among many is "true" or "correct," but rather which opinion is actually to be followed in practice irrespective of the theoretical validity upon which it is said to be based. (The term *Halakhah* is from a root meaning "to go" or "to walk." It is the procedure to be followed in Jewish life; the way in which the Jew is expected to go). Thus, in the famous story[14] in which R. Eliezer appeals to heaven and a heavenly voice *(bat kol)* declares that he is right, the Halakhah follows the majority opinion against that of R. Eliezer because of the principle "it is not in Heaven" (Deut. 30:12). The Torah has been given to humans in the person of the sages to interpret according to the usual procedural rules. These rules, among which is that the majority opinion is decisive, have been ordained by the Torah itself so that any appeal against them to "Heaven" is inadmissible. The point of the tale is surely not that the voice from Heaven spoke falsely or in order to tempt the sages. The meaning would seem to be that from God's absolute standpoint, R. Eliezer's opinion was correct, but the Halakhah is to be determined not by any absolute standards of truth but from the relative point of view of the sages who, as human beings, can have no guarantee that whichever opinion they decide to follow must be the right one. This is surely the significance of the "punch line" of the story. Elijah reported to R. Nathan many years later that when the incident took place God laughed and declared, "My sons have conquered Me." Elijah's sons got the better of God because it is their relative truth that determines the law not His absolute truth. Similarly, in the other story of the heavenly voice deciding in favor of the House of Hillel against the House of Shammai,[15] the voice from on high is made to declare "Both these and these are the words of the living God but the Halakhah is in accordance with the House of Hillel," upon which the Talmud asks, if both are the words of the living God why does the Halakhah follow the opinions of the House of Hillel? The reply, highly significant for our purpose, is that the Halakhah is in accordance with the House of Hillel because the members of this House were more modest and self-effacing than the members of the rival House. This is an odd reason, on the face if it, reminiscent of those who opposed Bertrand Russell's criticism of Kant because, they protested, Kant was kind to his mother. Russell replied that one does not have to be a great philosopher in order to be kind to one's mother. But if the Halakhah is a procedural matter it does make sense to say that the House of Hillel was "rewarded" for its humility by having the Halakhah decided in its favor. A similar idea, that the Halakhah is purely a matter of procedure, appears to be the basis of the Talmudic statement, "Whenever the Halakhah is uncertain (*rofefet*) so far as the Court is concerned and you do not know what is to be done (literally, "you do not know the state of the law") go out and see how the community conducts itself and do likewise."[16]

Fourth, and most important of all, the Babylonian Talmud, far from being a code of law (although it does contain many thousands of rules and regulations), is a literary work with much evidence of the use of contrivance and literary device in its formation.[17] Exactly the same type of argumentation is employed, for instance, where the discussion centers around laws of contemporary relevance as where the concern is with the laws of the sacrificial system, which had long been in abeyance during the Amoraic period.[18] The same kind of argument and counterargument is also employed too in matters of Aggadah that is employed in matters of Halakhah.[19]

One or two examples illustrate how the post-Talmudic codifiers used such theoretical, literary, and contrived passages as their sources for practical law. The significant point here is that the very process of codification frequently involves placing on the source material a weight it was never intended to bear, or, to vary the metaphor, treating a poem or a novel about lawyers and their discussions as if it were intended solely or primarily to convey advice and guidance for judges.

Thousands of purely academic problems are found in the Babylonian Talmud, many of them farfetched and all of them clearly intended as academic exercises. This kind of problem—the *baya*—has rightly been compared by Guttmann[20] to the type of problem set, say, by the pure mathematician, such as how long it would take for three men, working at different speeds, to paper a room, or to Zeno's problem of how Achilles ever manages to overtake the tortoise. This kind of problem is not intended to be practical but to serve the interests of mathematics or physics by establishing the principles involved in the science of number or motion. One example, taken more or less at random, is the problem set by the fourth century Babylonian Amora, Rava.[21] Before the advent of Passover it is necessary to search the house thoroughly to see whether it contains any leaven and, if it does, to remove the leaven from the house. Supposing, asks Rava, a mouse is seen entering a house that has been searched and found to be clean of leaven. The mouse has a morsel of bread in its mouth, and is later seen coming out of the house with a morsel of bread in its mouth. Are we to conclude that it is the same mouse and the same morsel (i.e., and, consequently, the house does not require to be searched again) or are we to be apprehensive that it might be a different mouse and morsel (so that the house must be searched again)? Supposing, continues Rava, we say that it is the same mouse, then what would be the law where a white mouse having leaven in its mouth is seen entering the house and then a black mouse with leaven in its mouth is seen coming out of the house? Here, since it is a different mouse, it must be assumed that it is a different piece of leaven, or, possibly, it can be argued, it is the same piece of leaven which the black mouse has taken from the white mouse (and the house requires no further search). If we argue that mice do not snatch food from one another, what is the law if a mouse is seen to enter the house with leaven in its mouth and then a weasel comes out of the house with leaven in its mouth? Weasels certainly take food from mice and it can therefore be assumed that it is the same piece of leaven, or it may be assumed to be a different piece of leaven, otherwise it would have been the mouse, not the leaven, that was in the weasel's mouth. And, further, what is the law where the weasel comes out with both the mouse and the leaven in its mouth? The Talmud concludes, as it invariably does when faced with an insoluble problem of this type, *teyku*, "it remains standing" i.e., the problem remains. It is hard to believe that this series of problems ever had anything to do with practical law. In practice it is unlikely in the extreme that any of these questions would ever come before a rabbi for a practical decision, still less that there would ever be a series of questions calling for a decision. Rava's series belongs to the quite different *genre* of purely theoretical problems that are found in abundance throughout the Babylonian Talmud. Yet Maimonides,[22] as a codifier, records these cases in his statement of the Passover laws and in exactly the same form and with the same serious intent he gives to all the severely practical rules regarding the proper observance of Passover.

The contrived nature of many Talmudic passages can readily be determined from the way the arguments are presented so as to lead to a climax;[23] from the arrangement of the arguments in a neat series;[24] from the setting of the arguments by "sacred" numbers, especially three and seven;[25] and from the use of fictitious or legendary material for the purpose of the argument.[26] And yet the codifiers are bound to base their practical rulings on this material, originally intended as a purely intellectual exercise—albeit one of the highest order, as the religious obligation to study the Torah for its own sake. The result of all this is that the Halakhah tends to operate apart from the actual life of the people, acquiring its own norms and methodology independently of the demands of the law in practice. Instead of life influencing the development of the law, the theoretical Halakhah tends to mold life in its own image.

All these factors must be taken into account and they do militate against the flexibility of the Halakhah. Yet for all that, the complete rigidity which might have resulted was avoided. There are tensions among the Halakhists between the law and the need for its adjustment to life,[27] but those very factors in the Talmudic literature that make the rigidity are themselves capable of promoting a degree of flexibility. The contrived argument, for example, is often presented in the Talmud in such a manner as to leave open to the codifiers a number of options so that the Halakhist is able to choose those he wishes if these can be fitted more readily into his general outlook on Judaism. Although, in many instances, the Talmud states that the Halakhah is such-and-such or in accordance with this or that

teacher, and this became the unchanging law, there are still
sufficient instances in which the Talmud offers no decision for
practice. Here the codifiers can debate the issue and there is room
for maneuvering even on the grounds of extra-Halakhic considerations. In addition, there are the numerous instances in which the
later Halakhists consider new questions for which the solution of
the Talmudic sources can be approached through the use of analogy, leaving open possibilities for greater flexibility by either
affirming or denying, when these are demanded, the exactness of
the analogy. Means were thus at hand for the post-Talmudic
Halakhists, for all their complete and utter deference to the Talmud, to be creative and to introduce, whenever they saw fit, extra-
Halakhic considerations into the Halakhah itself.

This chapter cannot end without a word or two on the way in
which some of the great post-Talmudic Halakhists came to enjoy
the same or similar authority to the Talmud itself.[28] The Gaonim,
for example, enjoy great authority as does the *Rif*. In some places
the authority of Maimonides was accepted in toto and all his rulings
were followed. The *Shulhan Arukh*, together with Isserles' glosses,
came to be accepted as the most authoritative Code.[29] The general
principle here is that of acceptance by the community, i.e., these
rulings are to be followed not so much because of their inherent
correctness but because of the communal consensus, the ultimate
authority residing in this consensus. Nevertheless, none of the
post-Talmudic authorities ever came to enjoy exactly the same degree of authority as the Talmud, that of an infallible guide from
which it is forbidden ever to depart.

NOTES

1. On the Talmud as the ultimate authority in Jewish law see Boaz Cohen, *Kunteros ha-
Teshuvot*, pp. 18–25. Jacob Reisher; *Solet le-Minhah*, 76:2, 8, quoted by Perla, *Otzar*, no. 655,
p. 49, makes the interesting observation that if anyone wishes to be strict on matters that the
Amoraim have unanimously declared to be permitted, e.g., that forbidden food is neutral-
ized in a mixture of one to sixty *(battel be-shishim)*, such a person is to be suspected of heresy.
This statement is also quoted in PT to YD end of 116 (not 115 as in Perla).

2. R. Isaac Alfasi, the *Rif, Eruvin* end, lays down the rule, later accepted generally
among the Halakhists, that the Babylonian Talmud, being a later work than the Yerushalmi,
is to be followed on matters where the two Talmuds are in conflict. See the sources quoted in
Malachi ha-Kohen's *Yad Malakhi, Kelaley Sheney Ha-Talmudim*, no. 2, p. 177a; and in Medini,
Sedey Hemed, Kelaley Ha-Posekim, no. 2, vol. 9, pp. 127–30.

3. Z. Frankel, *Darkhey ha-Mishnah*; S. J. Rapoport, *Erekh Millin*; N. Krochmal; *Moreh
Nevukhey ha-Zeman*; I. H. Weiss; *Dor Dor ve-Doreshav*; I. Halevy, *Dorot ha-Rishonim*; J. N.

Epstein, *Mevuot le-Sifrut ha-Tannaim;* Hanoch Albeck, *Mavo le-Mishnah;* De-Friess, *Mehkarim be-Sifrut ha-Talmud;* Tchernowitz, *Toledot ha-Halakhah;* Baer, *Yesodot;* Louis Ginzberg, *Mekomah shel ha-Halakhah;* Louis Finkelstein; *The Pharisees;* G. Allon, *Mehkarim;* G. F. Moore, *Judaism;* J. Z. Lauterbach, *Rabbinic Essays,* pp. 163–256; J. Neusner, *The Rabbinic Traditions About the Pharisees;* Zevi Karl, *Mishnayot: Pesahim,* Appendices, pp. 93–110.

4. *Tosefta, Hagigah* 2:9 and *Sanhedrin* 7:1, quoted in JT, *Sanhedrin* 1:4 (19c) and in BT, *Sanhedrin* 88b with variants. See Tchernowitz, *Toledot ha-Halakhah,* part IV, pp. 283f. and De Friess, *Mehkarim,* pp. 172–78.

5. Baer, *Yesodot,*

6. *Bava Kama* 1:2.

7. Ginzberg, *Mekomah.*

8. Finkelstein, *The Pharisees.*

9. Allon, *Mehkarim,* vol. 2, pp. 181–222.

10. See the devastating but wholly justifiable critique of earlier scholars in Neusner, *Rabbinic Traditions* vol. III, pp. 320–68 and the same author's massive *A History of the Mishnaic Law of Purities.*

11. It is fruitful in this connection to study the work of Baruch Benedict Goitein (d. 1842) entitled *Kesef Nivhar.* Goitein gives a very comprehensive account of these abstract formulations in the Talmud each of which is followed by statements and ruling on them in the Codes. From this it can be seen very clearly how many difficulties the codifiers encounter in using abstract debates and discussions for the purposes of practical law.

12. See *Rif* to *Berakhot* chapter 5, Vilna ed. p. 24a; Maimonides, *Commentary to the Mishnah, Peah* 1:5 and *Nedarim* I:1; Heller, *Tosefot Yom Tov* to *Berakhot* 3:2; *Peah* 1:5; *Kilaim* 5:5; *Sheviit* 4:10; and especially to *Nazir* 5:5; Lipshutz, *Tiferet Yisrael* to *Bava Metzia* 1:1. On the whole question see Rapoport, *Erekh Millin,* introduction; Pineles: *Darkah shel Torah;* I. H. Weiss, *Dor,* vol. 3, pp. 218–27. Weiss, p. 219, quotes in the name of the gaon of Vilna that just as there is *peshat* and *derash* in biblical exegesis there are both of these in Mishnaic exegesis and the Amoraim sometimes follow the method of *derash.*

13. *Yad,* introduction; cf. *Yad, Manrim* 2:1 and *Kesef Mishneh* ad loc.

14. *Bava Metzia* 59b.

15. *Eruvin* 13b.

16. JT *Peah* 7:5 (20c); *Maaser Sheni* 5:2 (56b); *Yevamot* 7:3 (8a); and in shorter form BT *Berakhot* 45a; *Eruvin* 14b; *Pesahim* 56a; *Menahot* 35b. Cf. *Berakhot* 23a, "People now follow the opinions of three venerable teachers," i.e., in three matters the lenient opinions of three ancient teachers, although these are minority opinions, are followed in practice and hence this is the Halakhah. Cf. *Pesahim* 66a, "Leave it to Israel; if they are not themselves prophets they are the sons of prophets" and *Tosafists* to *Shabbat* 48a s.v. *mai shena* where the fact that everyone does something *(maasim be-khol yom)* is sufficient evidence that it is permitted according to the Halakhah. Shalom Mordecai Schwadron (Responsa, *Maharsham,* vol. 6, no. 5) quotes these two latter sources to show that if everyone does something it must be right in practice. Further examples of the appeal to *maasim be-khol yom* are *Sukkah* 44a; *Ketubot* 68b; 95b; *Bava Kama* 95b; *Bava Metzia* 15b; 110b; *Bava Batra* 173b and *Tosafists* to *Berakhot* 46a s.v. *ad heikhan* and to *Shabbat* 27b s.v. *kol ha-yotze* and see Medini, *Sedey Hemed, Kelalim, mem,* 209, vol. 4, pp. 299–300. But on reflection the appeal to *massim be-khol yom* is not strictly relevant to our theme since there the meaning is, in all probability, any understanding of the law that is contrary to daily practice must be in error because it is highly unlikely that an illegal practice would have been tolerated for so long without protest. Thus the appeal is really a reductio ad absurdum and does not mean that the practice itself determines the Halakhah.

17. On the literary character of the BT see my *Studies in Talmudic Logic and Methodology.*

18. Cf. the objection to a statement of Halakhah on matters that have no application until the Messianic Age, see *Sanhedrin* 51b and *Zevahim* 45a and *Tosafists* to *Yoma* 13a s.v. *halakhah*.

19. See, e.g., the lengthy *sugya* on sufferings in *Berakhot* 5a–b where the main concern is not with the theological problem raised by the fact that men suffer but with carefully worked out "ploys" in a sustained piece of argumentation.

20. M. Guttmann, *Sheelot Akademiot*.

21. *Pesahim* 10b.

22. *Yad, Hametz u-Matzah* 2:13.

23. See, e.g., *Berakhot* 3a–b on demons and for further examples see my *Studies in Talmudic Logic and Methodology*, pp. 60f.

24. See, e.g., the *sugya* of *rubba* ("probability") in *Hullin* 11a–12a.

25. See especially S. J. Friedman's splendid article, *Mivneh Sifruti*, on the number sequence in the Talmudic *sugya* and the same author's *Perek ha-Ishah Rabbah*. Friedman refers, together with further examples of his own, to the observation of the Hasidic master Jacob of Izbica that in the opening passage of *Pesahim* there are fourteen attempted proofs of whether the term *or* means "day" or "night." The first seven of these proofs are from biblical texts, the second seven are from Tannaitic sources. Six of the first set of attempted proofs are that *or* is "day" but the fourth, the middle one, is that *or* is night. Six of the second set of attempted proofs are that *or* is "night"but the middle one, the fourth, is that *or* is "day." Such a carefully worked out, numbered sequence is quite obviously contrived. It is a literary form totally different from a real discussion or argument on the meaning of a term in a legal source or document. It is worth noting that the expression is found frequently in the BT (see, e.g., *Berakhot* 27a; *Pesahim* 5b; *Yevamot* 46b; *Avodah Zarah* 43a) "prove from this three things." never "two" or "four" or any other number. It is impossible that every source should yield three and only three implications unless the whole is a purely literary device. Cf. in this connection *Shabbat* 40a and the sets of three sayings in *Avot*. Another good example of a numbered sequence is the *sugya* in *Niddah* 13a–b where *seven* possible solutions are given in order to defend R. Judah against the suggestion that he acted unlawfully.

26. See my articles, "Are There Fictitious Baraitot in the Babylonian Talmud?" and "How Much of the Babylonian Talmud is Pseudepigraphic?".

27. Cf. the pioneering work on the theme of this book by S. Zucrow, *Adjustment of Law to Life in Rabbinic Literature*. Although Zucrow's work suffers greatly from a lack of proper historical perspective, from too much special pleading, and from a certain superficiality in parts, he deserves much credit for amassing a considerable body of material a good deal of which I have used. Cf. the interesting observation of M. Friedmann in his edition of the *Sifre* (to Deut. 345) that the Torah is compared by the rabbis to a bride because the Torah is made to give birth to the Oral Torah through her marriage to Israel's sages who cause her to conceive!

28. See ET, vol. 9, s.v. *halakhah*, no. 32, pp. 333–39.

29. For the authorities who take issue with the *Shulhan Arukh* see Dembitzer, *Kelilat Yofi*, introduction, pp. 11b–17b and for the final vindication of the SA.

[2]

The Spirit of the Halakhah

Although, as we have noted in the previous chapter, the Halakhah tends to operate within its own categories, with the overt motivation in Halakhic discussions being a purely legal one, the alleged or possible extralegal reasons for a particular law only finding its way into the Halakhic process with difficulty, there are many examples of laws being interpreted so as to give expression to general Jewish ideas and values. No Pauline antithesis exists between the letter of the law and its spirit, in the sense that the spirit is more significant than the letter or that the law should be governed by external considerations of a supposedly higher order which have the power of anulling or overriding the actual law. If such were the case, if the law were so fluid as to be capable of total manipulation in obedience to other factors than those inherent in the Halakhic process, there could be no effective law at all. Jewish law does permit a degree of flexibility. What it does not do is provide the machinery for its own dissolution. But all this is a far cry from the contention that the Halakhah never serves any other values. This chapter gives some illustrations of how the law is made to give expression to ideas and ideals other than that of mere obedience; of how, in other words, Aggadic interpretations are given to Halakhic details in the Halakhah itself.

The question, which was often discussed in the Middle Ages, of "reasons for the precepts" *(taamey ha-mitzvot)* is not strictly germane to our theme. Some teachers frowned on any attempt at explaining why the Torah commands this or that but even those thinkers, like Maimonides in his *Guide for the Perplexed*, who did

33

suggest possible reasons for the precepts, only allowed the reasons they advanced to be plausible or even probable conjectures. They never allowed the reason suggested to have any voice in the actual Halakhic process. Our investigation is concerned with "reasons" given in a Halakhic context, where the law comes first, at it were, and is then given a wider interpretation in extra-Halakhic terms. Nevertheless, as Heinemann' study of the question has shown,[1] there were three motives for the search by the medieval thinkers for "reasons" and these motives did make themselves felt with regard to attitudes toward the law, though not on the law itself. The thinkers who accepted the idea that "reasons" be suggested for the precepts had a threefold motivation. First, there was the theological motive. God must not be seen as a tyrant issuing arbitrary rules merely as a test of obedience. None of the precepts is to be understood as having no reason at all other than submission to God's will rather as if He commanded people to stand on their heads to show their complete deference to His will. To understand the *mitzvot* in this way was, for these medieval teachers, to have an inferior concept of Deity. Second, if the reason for a particular rule is known, these thinkers argued, the rule will be followed with all the more enthusiasm because of its appeal to the intellect. Thirdly, there is the apologetic motive. Jews, taunted by their Gentile neighbors for obeying irrational rules, felt bound to defend their religion by pointing out the sublime worth of the *mitzvot*. All this really belongs to the Aggadah and is basically independent of the Halakah; yet in a work like the *Sefer ha-Hinnukh*, attributed to R. Aaron of Barcelona, the suggested "reasons" are listed together with the Halakhaic details and an attempt is made throughout the work to show how the "reasons" fit in with the Halakhic details. Even here, however, no attempt is made to adjust the law to what the "reason" might appear to demand. The reservation is always implicit that "reasons" for the law are one thing but the actual law is another, and it is the law alone in all its details which enjoys authority. Our investigation in this chapter is concerned with the very different question of how the rules and regulations of the Halakhah became vehicles for the expression of general Jewish values by the reading of such values into the law and the details of the law.

The Mishnah[2] rules that a dry, withered palm branch (*lulav*) must not be used on the festival of Sukkot when one is commanded to take the *lulav* in the hand. The Palestinian Talmud[3] gives as the reason for this law, "The dead praise not the Lord" (Ps. 115:17), i.e., it is inappropriate to sing God's praises by means of that which is lifeless and stale. Another rule is that the *lulav* must be held in the manner in which it grows on the tree—it must not be held upside down.[4] The implication is that the Torah assists in the natural growth of all things and, so far as human beings are concerned, was never intended to thwart their nature or frustrate their development. A similar idea is behind the statement of the third-century Babylonian Amora, Rav,[5] that when one genuflects in prayer one should bow at the words "Blessed art Thou" but straighten the head and body at "O Lord." Samuel, Rav's colleague, quotes in support the verse, "The Lord raiseth them that are bowed down" (Ps. 146:8). On the question of genuflexions during prayer, there is the further interesting statement[6] that an ordinary person bows only at the beginning and end of his prayers, the high priest at the beginning and end of each benediction, whereas the king must remain in a bowed position during the whole of his prayers. Rashi offers the explanation, "The greater the person the more need there is for him to humble himself and be submissive." A simple detail of the law is thus made to serve as a homily against the abuse of power.

As early as the biblical period the symbol of the right as denoting justice is given expression in the law that the right shoulder of a peace offering be given to the priest (Lev. 7:32), and well as in the law that the sacrificial blood be placed on the tip of the right ear, the thumb of the right hand, and the big toe of the right foot (Lev. 8:24; 14:14). This symbolism is applied to the *mezuzah*, which is to be placed on the right doorpost.[7] Even with regard to dress the rule is that the right shoe and sock should be placed on the foot before the left,[8] the law desiring to invest a trivial action with significance by making it serve as a reminder that justice should predominate. With regard to *teffilin*, on the other hand, the rule is that they are to be placed on the left, the "weaker," hand,[9] possibly, though this is not stated explicitly, to express symbolically the idea that is it the weaker side of man's nature that must be fortified. Maimonides[10] adds that when the *tefillin* are placed on the arm they will be opposite the heart, a symbol that the heart is to be directed to God's service.

Many of the Halakhic details are based on the idea that there is a scale of values, priority being accorded to the higher. In Rabbinic thought the study of the Torah is the supreme religious value. A scholar who is a *mamzer* takes precedence over the high priest if the latter is an ignoramus.[11] In the same vein, Abraham Gumbiner[12] rules that it is right and proper to run from a synagogue, the house of prayer, to attend the Bet ha-Midrash, the house of study, because the study of the Torah is of a higher order even than prayer. If a man's father and his teacher (of the Torah) are held to ransom he must give priority to ransoming his teacher "since his father brings him into this world whereas his teacher, who teaches him the Torah, brings him into the life of the World to Come."[13] A book of the prophets must not be placed on top of a scroll of the Torah because the Torah possesses a higher degree of sanctity than the prophets.[14] A man takes precedence over a woman[15] when it comes to returning a lost article as well as with regard to "keeping them alive" because a man has more religious duties to perform than a woman, if, in fact, this is really the meaning of "keeping them alive." Many commentators[16] understand the term to mean not that the life of a man must be saved before that of a woman but that a man must first be provided with a livelihood by the community, if he is poor, because the man is normally the breadwinner of the family. A woman takes precedence over a man with regard to the provision of clothes from the charity chest. She must also be redeemed first from captivity. But where the captors are likely to indulge in the sexual abuse of their victims a man must be redeemed first since for him it is unnatural.[17] That which occurs with regularity takes precedence over that which is less regular.[18] For example, the perpetual offering must be offered up in the Temple before the additional offerings of the sabbaths and festivals. That which is more sacred takes precedence over that which is less sacred,[19] e.g., the blood of a sin offering, which is for the purpose of atonement, must be sprinkled before the blood of a burnt offering. The latter, as a free will offering, possesses a lesser degree of sanctity since, unlike the sin offering, it is optional.

That the feelings of others must be taken into account is expressed in the rabbinic interpretation of the verse: "This is the law of the sin offering: In the place where the burnt offering is killed shall the sin offering be killed" (Lev. 6:25). If the sin offering were to be killed in a special place of its own, everyone present at the time in the Temple courtyard would know the identity of the sinners, who would be put to shame.[20] On the same basis is the rule that prayers, which include confession of sins, must be recited softly so that a man's sins are exposed only to his Maker not to other human beings.[21]

Some rules of prayer also give expression to other Jewish values. Prayers should be recited in Western lands with the worshiper facing east toward the Holy Land and Jerusalem.[22] The *havdalah* prayer, which refers to the distinction between the sacred and the profane, the Sabbath and weekdays, is inserted in the prayer for knowledge since the ignorant are incapable of appreciating life's necessary distinctions.[23] The Hallel, the Psalms of praise, are not recited in full on the last days of Passover, as they are on the other festivals, out of sympathy for the Egyptians who lost their lives when Israel was delivered from bondage at the Exodus, the event celebrated on Passover.[24] The eyes should be covered when the first verse of the Shema, Israel's declaration of faith, is recited in order for the worshiper to close his mind to distractions so that he might give all the powers of his concentration to the mighty words.[25] When grace before meals is recited it should be over a whole loaf rather than over a piece of bread even if the latter is of better quality. Wholeness is to be preferred over other kinds of excellence.[26]

The correct Jewish response to suffering seems to be expressed in the rule that when a mourner rends his garment in grief at the death of a near relative he should do so while standing, not while sitting.[27] As Dr. Hertz puts it: "According to ancient Jewish custom, the ceremony of rending our garments when our nearest and dearest on earth is lying dead before us, is to be performed *standing up*. This teaches: Meet all sorrow standing upright. The future may be dark, veiled through the eyes of mortals—but not the manner in which we are to meet the future. We cannot lay down terms to life. Life must be accepted on its own terms. But hard as life's terms may be, life never dictates unrighteousness, unholiness, dishonour."[28] If this interpretation is considered too homiletical, the rule about standing upright might have been intended to denote a rising to the tragic occasion, that the rite should not be performed perfunctorily as it would be if it were performed while sitting.

The principle that "counsel for the prosecution cannot act at the same time as counsel for the defense" *(eyn kategor naaseh sanegor),*[29] i.e., that it is improper to use that which recalls sin and evil for the service of atonement and the good, is given expression in a number of rules. The high priest, when he enters the holy of holies on the Day of Atonement, must wear only his garments of fine linen, not his "golden" garments, because gold recalls the sin of the golden calf.[30] According to the sages, who debate the matter with R. Meir, the shofar on Rosh ha-Shanah must not be that of a cow for the same reason.[31] Because of the same principle, a stolen *lulav* cannot be used on Sukkot.[32] A priest who has been guilty of homicide must not recite the priestly blessing.[33] Hands that have shed blood cannot be raised in blessing. According to one opinion it is wrong to write prayers and supplications on paper that have been previously used for idolatrous writings, even if the original writing has been erased.[34] Even though a strong case is made out in the Talmud for the view that a wife can be divorced by the delivery into her hand of a sum of money or its value, the Talmud rejects this in obedience to the same principle.[35] Since the delivery of money or its value into the hand of a woman constitutes a valid marriage, if given and accepted for that purpose, it is unseemly to use the same means which effect a valid marriage for the purpose of severing the marriage bond. On the other hand, the superficially similar but basically quite different principle—only that which can become corrupt is a suitable instrument for overcoming corruption—appears to be expressed in the law that unleavened bread (*matzah*) is only valid to be eaten on the first night of Passover if made from grain that is capable of fermentation.[36]

The verse, which is understood by the rabbis as referring to the Torah, "Her ways are ways of pleasantness" (Prov. 3:17) finds its expression in the Halakhah.[37] Although an argument is advanced for the view that certain prickly plants could have been intended by the Torah for use on Sukkot, the argument is rejected in favor of the *lulav* and myrtle since the Torah would not have enjoined that which is "unpleasant" and so offend against this principle.[38] Again, although an argument can be advanced that when a man dies leaving a son and then the son dies levirate marriage should apply, this argument is rejected since it is "unpleasant" for the widow, who is free at the time of her husband's death to marry another, should later become bound to the levir.[39] A renowned sixteenth-century authority[40] goes so far as to rely on this principle to argue that if a tyrant threatens to kill a Jew unless another Jew will allow his hand to be amputated, the latter is by no means obliged to yield to the horrible request in order to save his neighbor's life. "Furthermore," this authority writes, "it is written: "Her ways are ways of pleasantness" so that it is necessary that the laws of our Torah should be in full accord with reasonableness and common sense. How, then, can we possibly imagine that a man should allow his eyes to be put out or his hand or foot amputated in order to save his neighbor's life. Consequently, I can see no reason for such a law unless it is done as a special act of saintliness. Then happy is the portion of one able to bring himself to do this but where there is danger to life itself he is a stupid saint since his own doubtful risk takes precedence over the certain death of his neighbor."

Another principle invoked in the Halakhah is: "The Torah is concerned that the people of Israel suffer little financial loss," literally: "The Torah has pity on Israel's money,"[41] i.e., whereas Judaism, at times, does demand heavy financial sacrifices, it also seeks, whenever possible, to avoid placing its adherents under severe financial burdens, This principle, it is suggested, is behind the rule that the mouths of the horns blown in the Temple during fast days were covered with silver rather than with the more precious gold.[42] So, too, it is suggested, the box into which the two lots for the service of the Day of Atonement were placed was made of wood rather than of silver or gold.[43] In the same spirit, Menahem Meiri writes:

> Whenever a sage is called upon to render a decision and he is able to find adequate reasons for permissiveness without having his decision attacked by a reliable authority, it is improper for that sage to be excessively pious, seeking overmuch to be stringent and discovering reasons for it. He should rather take into consideration the financial loss (involved if he declared forbidden that which the law permits). For the Torah itself took this factor into consideration.[44]

We should note here how the Halakhah invokes another principle found in the same verse in Proverbs: "and all her paths are peace." This is the principle of *darkhey shalom*, "ways of peace," i.e. the Torah has, as one of its main aims, the promotion of peace and harmony in human relationships and the avoidance of strife and contention.[45] This is the reason given for the rule that a priest read the first portion of the Torah in the synagogue. If this high honor were to be available to all, the congregants might quarrel among themselves for the privilege.[46] Because it might lead to contention, it is forbidden for people who have long worshiped in a particular house to transfer their place of worship to the house of another.[47] Although, according to the strict law, a minor has no power of acquisition, because it will otherwise lead to quarrels, the sages ordained that if a minor finds an article abandoned by its owner he may keep it.[48] Because of "ways of peace" even heathen should be greeted with Shalom ("Peace to you").[49] For the same reason the heathen poor must be helped from the charity funds just as the Jewish poor are helped; they should be visited when they are sick and comforted when they mourn.[50]

Although the *Shulhan Arukh*[51] rules that a *kohen* who is a bachelor should recite the priestly blessing, Isserles quotes the opinion of the *Mordekhai* that he should not do so since the blessing must be recited in a joyful spirit and an unmarried man is joyless. On the same principle, Isserles remarks further that in "these lands," where even on the Sabbath we are worried about our livelihood, the priestly blessing is only recited on festivals when we are in a joyous frame of mind. The basic idea is that blessing involves giving and communion with others of which the joyless person is incapable. This is in line with modern psychological theories about the neurotic person as self-centered and incapable of love because he has no love of self!

The verse: "Offer it now to thy governor" (Mal. 1:8) is relied on to express the idea that something unsuitable as a gift to a human potentate is thereby rendered unfit as a gift to God. Thus, wine with a bad smell cannot be offered as a libation on the altar[52] and wheat kernels found in cows' dung cannot be used in the preparation of a meal offering.[53] This principle is not only made to apply to offerings in the Temple, it applies also to anything used for purposes of divine worship so that, for example, wine having a bad smell must not be used for kiddush.[54] Sachets of spices, placed in the wine of Gentiles to impart an aroma are permitted. (i.e., it is allowed to enjoy their fragrance even though they have absorbed the flavor of the forbidden wine) but should not be used for the Havdalah because of our principle.[55]

Another principle at work in the Halakhah is that of not allowing one festive occasion to encroach on another—*eyn mearvin simhah be-simhah*—i.e., because then one takes away some of the joy reserved for the other. For this reason it is forbidden to have a wedding on the intermediate days of the festivals.[56] A similar principle is that it is wrong to perform two or more *mitzvot* at the same time—*eyn osin mitzvot havilot havilot*.[57]

NOTES

1. *Taamey ha-Mitzvot*. Many scholars hold that the attribution of the *Sefer ha-Hinnukh* to R. Aaron ha-Levi of Barcelona is inaccurate. On the work see EJ, vol. 7, pp. 1126–27; Tchernowitz, *Toledot ha-Posekim*, vol. 2, pp. 95–105; Gersion Appel, *A Philosophy of Mizvot*.

2. *Sukkah* 3:1.

3. JT *Sukkah* 3:1 (53c).

4. *Sukkah* 45b; SA, OH 651:2.

5. *Berakhot* 12a.

6. Ibid. 34a–b.

7. *Menahot* 34a; SA, YD 289:2.

8. *Shabbat* 61a; SA, OH 2:4.

9. *Menahot* 36b–37a; SA, OH 27:1.

10. *Yad, Tefillin* 4:2.

11. Mishnah, *Horayot* 3:8.

12. Magen Avraham to SA, OH 90, note 26. Cf. for the primacy of Torah study over prayer *Shabbat* 10a.

13. Mishnah, *Bava Metzia* 2:13. On this question see the chapter on "Father and Teacher" in Gerald Blidstein, *Honor Thy Father and Mother*, pp. 137–57.

14. *Megillah* 27a; SA, YD 282:5.

15. Mishnah, *Horayot* 3:7. See S. Dichowsky's article, "Rescue and Treatment."

16. See Meiri, *Bet Ha-Behirah, Horayot* p. 284.

17. Mishnah, *Horayot* 3:17.

18. Mishnah, *Zevahim* 10:1.

19. Mishnah, *Zevahim* 10:2. Cf. for the similar principle that a positive precept overrides a negative precept, *Yevamot* 3b–8a and very frequent.

20. JT *Yevamot* 8:3 (9c).

21. *Sotah* 32b. Further examples of rules introduced in order to prevent the shaming of others are the borrowing of garments by the young maidens so as not to embarrass those who have no fine clothes of their own (Mishnah, *Taanit* 4:8); that presents of food for mourners should be taken to them in simple baskets (*Moed Katan* 27a); and that the dead should be buried in simple shrouds (*Ketubot* 8b).

22. *Berakhot* 30a; SA, OH 94:1.

23. *Berakhot* 23a.

24. *Arakhin* 10a–b; SA, OH 490:4, see *Taz* ad loc.

25. SA, OH 61:5.

26. *Berakhot* 39b; SA, OH 168:1.

27. *Moed Katan* 20b–21a; SA, YD 340:1.

28. J. H. Hertz, *Authorised Daily Prayer Book*, p. 1104.

29. See ET, vol. 1, pp. 327–28.

30. *Rosh ha-Shanah* 26a.

31. Ibid. 26a.

32. JT *Sukkah* 3:1 (53c).

33. *Tosafists* to *Yevamot* 7a s.v. *sheneemar*.

34. SA, YD 139:14.

35. *Kiddushin* 5a.

36. *Pesahim* 35a, see Sevin, *ha-Moadim ba-Halakhah*, p. 241.

37. See ET, vol. 7, pp. 712–15.

38. *Sukkah* 32a and 32b.

39. *Yevamot* 87b.

40. David Ibn Abi Zimra, Responsa *Radbaz*, no. 1052 (627). For a very comprehensive discussion of this question see Kirschenbaum, "The 'Good Samaritan' in Jewish Law."

41. See ET, vol. 11, pp. 240–45.

42. *Rosh ha-Shanah* 27a.

43. *Yoma* 39a. But frequently in connection with the Temple the opposite principle operates "There is no poverty in the place of riches," e.g., Temple vessels requiring repair are not repaired but discarded and new vessels purchased, *Zevahim* 88a. For the contradiction and the attempts at its resolution see ET, vol. 1, pp. 326–27.

44. *Bet ha-Behirah, Hullin* p. 164.

45. See ET, vol. 7, pp. 717–24.

46. *Gittin* 59b.

47. SA, OH 153:17.

48. Mishnah, *Gittin* 5:8; *Bava Metzia* 8a.

49. Mishnah, *Gittin* 5:9.
50. *Gittin* 61a.
51. SA, OH 128:44.
52. *Bava Metzia* 97b.
53. *Menahot* 69a.
54. *Bava Batra* 97b; SA, OH 272:1.
55. SA, OH 297:3.
56. *Moed Katan* 8b.
57. *Sotah* 8a.

Exemptions and Extensions

The element of flexibility in the Halakhah can be observed, for example, in the allowances made for exemptions to the law and for exceptional circumstances. As in every legal system, there is tension in the Halakhah between the demand for clear, hard and fast, unqualified rules—"hard cases make bad laws"—and humanitarian and other considerations that demand a degree of flexibility.

There are many examples in the Halakhah of the tendency to allow no exceptions to the rule. We are told,[1] for example, that one Boethus b. Zonin asked the sages why Syrian cakes shaped in figures must not be made on Passover. The Sages replied that because the woman who makes these intricate cakes might easily tarry over them they can become leaven and thus forbidden on Passover. But, objected Boethus, it is possible to make the cakes in a mold and so form them without any delay. To this the sages replied, "Then people will say, All Syrian cakes are forbidden but the Syrian cakes of Boethus are permitted," that is, since the majority of bakers do not have these molds there is sufficient reason for banning the making of the cakes and it would be misleading to make exceptions to the rule by permitting bakers like Boethus, who did have the molds, to make the cakes. This statement, "People will say . . ." became a legal maxim to be applied whenever an attempt is made to argue for exemptions to a rule, even where the grounds for the exception are reasonable, when so to argue will lead to abuses. For example, the Mishnah[2] rules that it is forbidden to cut the hair and beard on the intermediate days of the festivals, the reason being in order to encourage people not to wait until then but to have their hair cut and beard trimmed before the festival so that they do not "enter into the Festival in an unkempt state." The question is then raised, what of a man who, through no fault of his own, was unable to attend to his hair and beard before the festival? May such a man have his hair and beard attended to during the intermediate days, since the reason for the prohibition does not apply in his case? To this Abbaye replies by quoting the maxim, "People will say, All Syrian cakes are forbidden but the Syrian cakes of Boethus are permitted."[3] Similarly, when an attempt was made to permit one of two brothers and who never shared their meals with another to eat meat dishes and the other to eat dairy dishes at the same time (forbidden by the law to members of the same family because they might share their food and so inadvertently come to eat meat and milk together) on the grounds that the reason for the prohibition does not apply to them the maxim, "People will say . ." is quoted to show that the rule brooks no exceptions.[4]

A similar principle aimed against exceptions to the law is, "The Rabbis make no distinctions,"[5] although this frequently operates in favor of leniency,[6] i.e., once permission has been granted by the rabbis it is a blanket permission. There is, however, considerable ambiguity about when this principle is to be applied and there are exceptions to this rule that there are no exceptions.[7] In any event, it has been argued that the rule does not apply to communal regulations instituted for a particular reason. The regulation only has binding force in circumstances to which the reason applies, it being assumed that those who drew up the communal regulations did so with the necessary reservations and this is implied in the wording of the regulations by the fact that the reasons for them are stated.[8]

All this does not mean that the Halakhah never allows for exceptional circumstances. In this chapter a number of exceptions and a number of exemptions from rules otherwise binding are noted.[9]

The principle of granting exemptions to the law was discovered by the rabbis in the Torah itself, which allows (Deut. 21:10–14) a heathen woman, captured in war, to be taken to wife. The Torah, it is said, "speaks with reference to the evil inclination," that is, it is better to permit the marriage since even if it were forbidden, the soldier, in the heat of his passions inflamed by the battle, will take the woman in any event.[10] Other general principles of this order found in the Rabbinic literature are, "The Torah was not given to the ministering angels,"[11] i.e., excessive scrupulousness cannot be expected of mere mortals; "The Holy One, blessed be He, does not behave like a tyrant in relations to His creatures";[12] and "No decree is imposed on the community unless a majority of the community is able to abide by it."[13] In deference to this latter principle, it is said that the attempt to prohibit the oil of heathens was frustrated.[14] In obedience to the same principle, it is said, the attempt was rejected to ban all marriage after the destruction of the Temple.[15]

By rabbinic tradition and exegesis women are exempt from carrying out those positive precepts that depend on a given time for their performance.[16] According to some post-Talmudic authorities, the reason for this exemption is that it would have been unfair to impose such burdens on married women (and so all women are exempted) whose first duty is to their husbands and families.[17] It is doubtful, however, whether this is really the reason. No reason is given in the Talmudic sources so that this is a doubtful illustration of exemption because of circumstance.

From the Book of 1 Maccabees (2:29–41) we learn that the soldiers allowed the enemy to slay them rather than take up arms on the Sabbath but, eventually, this course was seen to be utterly wrong so that defense of life was permitted even on the Sabbath. In the rabbinic tradition it is universally accepted that the Sabbath not only may but must be profaned in order to save life.[18] All the precepts, except the prohibition of idolatry, murder, adultery, and incest, must be set aside in order to save life.[19] Some of the Sabbath laws were relaxed in favor of a sick person confined to his bed even where his life is not in danger.[20] A sick person is permitted to eat before the morning prayers[21] and a sick or aged person is exempt from bowing at the appropriate times during the prayers.[22] R. Judah exempts a blind man from the performance of the precepts but the Sages disagree and hold the blind man to be obligated.[23]

Scholars who spend all their time studying the Torah were, in former times, exempt from reciting the daily prayers.[24] Ben Azzai held himself to be exempt from the obligation to marry and have children because, he said: "My soul is in love with the Torah."[25] This found its way into the Codes in modified form[26]; although there is opposition to permanent bacherlorhood for the scholar, the scholar is permitted to postpone the date of his marriage until he has amassed a considerable degree of learning.

Examples of exemption are found even to laws having biblical sanction. The Torah itself releases the man on a distant journey from being obliged to come to the Temple to participate in the Passover sacrifice (Num. 9:14). The rabbis interpreted the verses

enjoining dwelling in the *sukkah* on the Festival of Sukkot (Lev.
23:42–43) so as to obviate the need to dwell there where discomfort
will result,[27] and where the weather is inclement, for example.
Relaxations of the laws of evidence were made in order to permit an
agunah, a woman whose husband is missing and presumed dead, to
remarry.[28]

With an appreciation of economic needs and the value of money,
the Halakhists follow the Talmudic principle that no man should
give away more than a fifth of his wealth to charity, because to do
so might lead to his eventual impoverishment.[29] On the basis of this
principle, the Halakhists rule that no more than this amount should
be spent on religious requirements such as a *tallit, etrog,* or *tefillin.*[30]
A man carrying a money bag when at the onset of the Sabbath is
not obliged to abandon it but may carry it home with him. A
proselyte, unaware of this exemption to the law, is reported to have
said that before his conversion he was convinced that the Jews were
lax in their Sabbath observance since no money bags had ever been
found in his native town.[31] R. Moses Isserles, the *Rama,* the renowned author of the glosses to the *Shulhan Arukh,* which enjoy the
greatest authority among Ashkenazi Jews, developed in a highly
original way the concept of "heavy loss," *hefsed merubbah.*[32] The
principle adopted by *Rama* is that, especially with regard to the
question of forbidden food, wherever heavy financial loss would be
incurred if the rabbi were to decide that something is forbidden, he
can rely on lenient authorities of weight who permit it, even though
these authorities are not followed where there is no such loss.[33]

The rabbis had much respect for man's dignity and this, as well
as the appreciation of man's aesthetic needs, finds its expression in
some of the laws. An elder or scholar is not obliged to carry out the
mitzvah of restoring a lost article to its rightful owner if by so doing
he would lower his dignity; if, for example, it would involve leading an animal or carrying a heavy load in a public place.[34] A man
reciting the Shema may interrupt his devotions in order to pay
respect to one to whom respect should be shown extending a greet-
ing.[35] With fine sensibility, it is said, the House of Hillel, dis-
agreeing with the more literalistic House of Shammai, argued that a
bride should be praised as "beautiful and charming" even if to
praise her in this way is to depart from the strict truth.[36] The
Mishnah exempts from the prohibition of having the hair cut on the
intermediate days of the festival those whose hair is long because
they were in prison or in mourning or under the ban and so were
unable to have this done before the festival.[37] A fastidious person is

exempt from the law which prohibits bathing during the period of mourning for a near relative.[38]

Exemptions from the law were made in order to promote peace and harmony in the home. The Torah itself, remark the rabbis, allows God's sacred name to be erased in order to make peace between husband and wife (the reference is to Numbers, chapter 5).[39] The Torah also exempts a bridegroom from conscription to the armed forces during the first year of his marriage (Deut. 24:5, and there is a similar rule in Deut. 20:7). Acting on the same principle, the rabbis permit a bride, during the first thirty days of her marriage, to bathe even on the Day of Atonement or during the period of her mourning for a near relative.[40] In certain circumstances a marriage may take place even if a parent of the bride or groom has just died.[41]

There are also exemptions to certain rules for those otherwise preoccupied. A man who has to attend to the burial of a near relative is exempt from reciting his prayers.[42] Shorter versions of the prayers were introduced for the benefit of workmen and travelers.[43]

In all the instances referred to in this chapter considerations other than those of pure legal theory were invoked not in order to introduce something foreign into the Halakhah but as part of the Halakhic process. Some of these are examples of rabbinic extension of the law known as *takkanah*. It is generally accepted that where the older rules are inadequate in coping with new circumstances, it is perfectly legitimate for the sages or a particular community to introduce new legislation. Generally speaking, where the new legislation is introduced in order to safeguard religious law, e.g., by prohibiting hitherto permitted acts in order to make "a fence around the Torah" (for instance, the prohibition of handling a saw on the Sabbath lest it be used to saw wood) it is termed a *gezerah*, "decree." Where the new legislation is intended to promote social well-being it is known as a *takkanah*, "ordinance" (literally "a putting right"). There is a definite tendency to limit religious ordinances (*gezerot*) to the Talmudic sages but the right to issue social ordinances (*takkanot*) is given without qualification to communities throughout the ages.[44]

The key text for the right to introduce new legislation of this nature is, "Thou shalt not decline from the sentence which they shall show thee, to the right hand, nor to the left" (Deut. 17:11), understood as scriptural warrant for the sages of Israel to introduce new laws in order to safeguard the values taught by the Torah.[45]

As for the verse, "Thou shalt not add thereto, nor diminish from it" (Deut. 13:1), this was understood to mean only that there must be neither addition to nor subtraction from a particular *mitzvah* e.g., by having three or five sections in the *tefillin* instead of the required four.[46] Maimonides,[47] however holds that the prohibition of adding to the Torah is involved if a rabbinic ordinance is followed not as a rabbinic rule but as a law having the force of biblical authority.[47] Communities in the Middle Ages were responsible for enactments and ordinances at first binding upon these communities themselves but later extended, in some instances, to be accepted as the law by all Jews. Prominent among communal ordinances are the *Takkanot Shum* (of the three communities Speyer, Worms, and Mainz) in the eleventh century; the ordinances of the Council of the Four Lands in Poland; and the new legislation in the State of Israel.

A strange and much discussed statement regarding an apparent exemption from the law is that of R. Illai: "If a man sees that his *yetzer* is getting the better of him, let him put on black and cover himself in black and do what his heart desires but let him not profane the name of Heaven in public."[48] None of the *Posekim* understood this literally. Rabbenu Hananiel, in fact, declares, "God forbid that he is permitted to sin but R. Illai means that the weariness resulting from his journey, the need to find lodgings and the wearing of black, will shatter his *yetzer* and keep him from sin."[49] Others,[50] however, do tend to take it more literally if the impulse is really uncontrollable. In any event, this is treated by the *Posekim* as hyperbole and, as we have noted, none of them dreamt of recording it as a rule in their Codes.

An exception should be noted in connection with telling lies. It is permitted to tell a lie if the motive is the promotion of peace.[51] Another type of exemption from the severest standards of truth is that of a judge who cannot be expected, it is said, to have superhuman insights. All that is demanded of a judge is that he decide on the basis of that which "his eyes see."[52]

NOTES

1. *Persahim* 37a.
2. Mishnah, *Moed Katan* 3:1.
3. *Moed Katan* 14a.
4. *Hullin* 107b.
5. *Yevomot* 66a and 107a; *Ketubot* 52b; *Bava Metzia* 53b.
6. See *Tosafists* to *Eruvin* 65b s.v. *hatam*.

7. See the discussion in Malachi ha-Kohen, *Yad Malakhi*, nos. 357–59. and in Medini, *Sedey Hemed, Kelalim*, no. 93, vol. 3, pp. 302–3.

8. See ha-Kohen, *Yad Malakhi*, no. 358.

9. See Nahmanides' Commentary to *kedoshim*, beg., ed. Chavel, pp. 115–16, on going beyond the letter of the law as itself part of the law but as varying, unlike the actual law, according to individual circumstances.

10. *Kiddushin* 21b. Cf. *Hullin* 17a that during the years of the conquest of the land in the days of Joshua a dispensation was granted for the soldiers to eat food otherwise forbidden, see Maimonides, *Yad, Melakhim* 8:1 and Herzog: *Hekhal Yitzhak, OH, no. 42.*

11. *Berakhot* 25b; *Yoma* 30a; *Kiddushin* 54a; *Meilah* 14b.

12. *Avodah Zarah* 3a.

13. *Bava Kama* 79b; *Horayot* 3b.

14. *Avodah Zarah* 36a.

15. *Bava Batra* 60b.

16. Mishnah *Berakhot* 3:3 and *Kiddushin* 1:7.

17. See ET, vol. 2, p. 244, column 2, from Abudraham (14 century), *Seder Tefillot shel Hol, Shaar* III, p. 25.

18. *Yoma* 84b–85b, *of.* Kahana, *Mehkarim*, pp. 117–25.

19. *Pesahim* 25a–b.

20. See SA, OH 328 for details. For another example of the relaxation of Sabbath law for a good purpose see *Gittin* 8a that it is permitted to instruct a non-Jew to draw up the bill of sale for a house acquired from a non-Jew in the land of Israel even on the Sabbath because of the *mitzvah* to settle the Holy Land. This is recorded in SA, OH 306:11.

21. SA, OH 89: 2–4.

22. SA, OH 113–5.

23. *Bava Kama* 87a.

24. *Shabbat* 11a; SA, OH 106:3.

25. *Yevamot* 63b.

26. SA, EH 1:3–4. A similar exemption to the law is, according to some authorities, that *kohanim* may contaminate themselves by coming into contact with the corpse or grave of a distinguished scholar at his funeral, see *Ketubot* 103b, *Tosafists* s.v. *oto ha-yom*, where R. Hayyim Kohen is quoted as saying that had he been present at the funeral of Rabbenu Tam he would have contaminated himself, but the *Tosafists* disagree with this ruling. Cf. Bezalel Ashkenazi, *Shita Mekubbetzet* to *Ketubot* ad loc: and Michaelson, *Tirosh ve-Yitzhar*, no. 70, who quotes an impressive array of works, including Kabbalistic and Hasidic, which discuss the question.

27. *Sukkah* 25b–26a.

28. *Yevamot* 88a; 116b.

29. *Ketubot* 50a.

30. See *Tosafists* to *Bava Kama* 9b s.v. *ileyma* and SA, OH 656.

31. *Avodah Zarah* 70a.

32. For some examples see *Rama* to SA, YD 31:1; 32:5; 35:5.

33. See ET, vol. 10, pp. 32–41 and for *Rama's* originality in this matter Tchernowitz, *Toledot ha-Posekim*, vol. 3, pp. 62f.; A. Siev:"*ha-Rama ke-Fosek u-Makhria,*" pp. 331–33. A further example of relaxation in the face of economic difficulty and where food is scarce is that of legumes on Passover otherwise forbidden by custom to the Adhkenazim, see Seymour Siegel, "The War of the *Kitniyot* (Legumes)."

34. *Bava Metzia* 30a.

35. Mishnah *Berakhot* 2:1.

36. *Ketubot* 17a. The *locus classicus* for the question of setting aside a law because of human

dignity is *Berakhot* 19b–20a where there are qualifications to the principle. Although the Mishnah (*Betzah* 5:2) rules that marriages may not be solemnized on the Sabbath, Isserles once permitted this and even officiated himself when the festivities prevented the actual betrothal to take place before the Sabbath on the grounds that the bride was a poor orphan who would suffer great embarrassment if the wedding were to be postponed, see *Teshuvot Rama*, No. 125.

37. Mishnah *Moed Katan* 3:1. This is not contradiction to the source quoted in note 3 supra since these are *categories* of persons whereas there the exception is rejected on behalf of an individual who does not belong to any of these categories.

38. Mishnah *Berakhot* 2:6. For further examples of exemptions on grounds of fastidiousness and human dignity see SA, OH 97:2 and 103:2.

39. *Shabbat* 116a; *Nedarim* 66b; *Makkot* 11a; *Hullin* 141a.

40. Mishnah *Yoma* 8:1.

41. *Ketubot* 3b–4a.

42. Mishnah *Berakhot* 3:1.

43. SA, OH 110:1; 191:1. An example of exceptions made on behalf of guests is that although it is forbidden to clear out a storehouse on a Sabbath or festival it is permitted if the place is required for guests, Mishnah *Shabbat* 18:1. Cf. *Rama* SA,YD 69:6 for a relaxation of the law of salting meat for the sake of guests.

44. On *Takkanot* see Elon's article in EJ and his *Mishpat ha-Ivri*, pp. 391ff. Hillel's *prosbol*, by virtue of which debts could be collected without the sabbatical year releasing them is the best known of the early *takkanot*, see Mishnah *Sheviit* 10:3–4 and the discussion on this in *Gittin* 36a–b. For further *Takkanot* in the Tannaitic period see Mishnah *Gittin* 4:2–7; 5:3; and 8:9. On the power of the sages to set aside a Torah law see the discussion in *Yevamot* 89a–90b, and for the whole question of a temporary suspension of the law, *horaat shaah*, see Et, vol. 8, pp. 512–27. For the *Takkanot* of Usha see *Ketubot* 49b–50a. For medieval *Takkanot* see Finkelstein; *Jewish Self-Government in the Middle Ages* and Shohet; *The Jewish Court in the Middle Ages;* the comprehensive article "Takkanot Ha-Kahal" by Isaac Levitats in EJ and the bibliography listed there. The distinction between *gezerah* and *takkanah* mentioned in the text is that of Maimonides' Introduction to his Commentary to the Mishnah, but the two terms are rarely used interchangingly.

45. See, e.g., *Shabbat* 21b and 23a for the rabbinic institution of the kindling of the Hanukkah lights on the basis of this text, and see Maimonides; *Sefer ha-Mitzvot*, beg., and Commentaries for the wider question of whether the text is interpreted to mean that rabbinic ordinances come to enjoy, on the basis of this text, full biblical authority, albeit of a general nature.

46. *Sifre, reah*, 82 and see the discussion in *Rosh ha-Shanah* 28b.

47. *Yad, Mamrim* 2:9 but see *Rabad*'s stricture ad loc. On the whole questions see the booklet *Bal Tosif* by Judah Copperman.

48. *Hagigah* 16a; *Kiddushin* 40a.

49. *Tosafists* to *Kiddushin* 40a s.v. *ve-yaaseh*.

50. *Tosafists* to *Hagigah* 16a s.v. *ve-yaaseh* and see Rashi to *Kiddushin* ad loc. and Trani; *Hiddushey Maharit* to Kiddushin ad loc. For this passage as the source of anti-Talmudic attacks and for the replies see Bloch; *Israel and the Nations*, pp. 316–23.

51. *Yevamot* 65b.

52. *Sanhedrin* 6b.

[4]

The Influence of Philosophy

We find among the Karaite authors the accusation that the Talmudic rabbis, especially in their hermeneutical principles, so prominent a feature of Talmudic exegesis and argumentation, were unduly influenced by Greek philosophical thought and were thus guilty of importing foreign notions into their Halakhah.[1] The Karaites had an axe to grind. Nevertheless, the question is still open, in Saul Lieberman's formulation: "How much Greek in Jewish Palestine?".[2] The problem defies any neat solution since even if Greek influences were at work they can only be detected by comparing ideas in the rabbinic literature with similar ideas among the Greek literature, and such an exercise is fraught with difficulty as a result of the silence on the part of the rabbis about the whole question. As Lieberman notes, for example, none of the Greek thinkers, neither Socrates nor Plato, nor Aristotle, is ever mentioned in the vast rabbinic sources. Even Philo does not appear by name in the Jewish literature until he was resurrected, as late as the sixteenth century, by Azariah de Rossi. What is certain is that a number of medieval Halakhists approached their subject with suppositions derived from their studies of Greek philosophy in its Arabic garb. We are not concerned here with the wider question, the core of medieval Jewish philosophy, of how Judaism can be reconciled with Aristotelianism, how revelation can be squared with reason, but with the extent of philosophical methods and reasoning as influences on Halakhic study and practice.

The greatest and most influential Halakhic work, Maimonides' *Mishneh Torah* or *Yad ha-Hazakah*, bears throughout the mark of its

51

author's philosophical stance. The systematic form of the work, the presentation of the laws in logical sequence and according to a beautifully arranged scheme, the orderly shaping of material scattered through the vast Talmudic literature in a properly coherent pattern, all this in itself owes much to Maimonides' philosophical approach. More directly, Maimonides formulates his philosophical, theological, and ethical views as part of the Halakha, giving to them the same authority and stating them with the same precision as the topics traditionally associated with the law. For the first time in Jewish legal codification we are presented, in Maimonides' Code, with sections of a law code bearing such highly revealing titles as *Hilkhot Yesodey ha-Torah*, "The *Laws* of the Foundations of the Torah;" *Hilkhot Deot* "The *Laws* of Ethical Conduct." In the former section Maimonides presents Aristotelian physics and metaphysics and in the latter section his advocacy of the golden mean, the middle way, in exactly the same manner as that in which he presents all the details of the law in other sections of his Code. Each detailed statement is a Halakhah, a rule for the regulation of thought and belief as well as of practice. Believing, as Maimonides did, that his philosophical views were true and that truth has the sanctity of Torah, he has no hesitation in taking the further step of incorporating into the Halakhah the truths of which he had become convinced.[3]

We consider first Maimonides' *Hilkhot Yesodey ha-Torah* in which he elaborates on the cosmological ideas of his day, holding that contemplation on the marvels of the universe leads to the love and worship of the Creator. The doctrine of the spheres and their music is described. The spheres are disembodied intelligences; their motion in their revolution around the earth being evidence of the power of the prime mover. Furthermore, to the consternation of traditional Talmudists, Maimonides identifies Aristotelian physics and metaphysics with, respectively, the Talmudic *Maaseh Bereshit* ("The Work of Creation") and *Maaseh Merkavah* ("The Work of the Chariot") and, applying a Talmudic statement to his own purpose, he gives these a far higher priority over the "debates of Abbaye and Rava." It is only when we realize that the term "the debates of Abbaye and Rava" stood in Maimonides' day for the whole range of traditional Talmudic-Halakhic studies, that his radicalism becomes fully apparent. Paradoxically, the supremacy of philosophy and theology over Halakhah has here become itself part of the Halakha since Maimonides gives this supremacy Halakhic status by incorporating it into his Code.[4]

Maimonides' *Hilkhot Deot* treats of character formation, the conduct of daily life and even the promotion of bodily health, in Halakhic terms. In this section all the demarcation lines, which might have been drawn in earlier Jewish sources between the Halakha and ethical advocacy in the Aggadah, have been virtually eliminated. Whether a man should wear expensive, ostentatious clothes or whether he should dress modestly, for example, is treated as a legal question of exactly the same order and in the same manner of utter seriousness as, say, whether a certain food is forbidden or permitted or whether A is obliged to compensate B for a certain type of injury. Undoubtedly under the influence of Maimonides, this kind of Halakhic extension is to be observed in such much later works as the *Orah Mesharim* of Menahem b. Abraham Treves (Dreifuss),[5] rabbi in Salzburg (d. 1857), and the *Hafetz Hayyim*[6] of Israel Meir Kagan (1838–1933). Treves' work is subtitled: *Shulhan Arukh le-Middot*, "Arranged Table of Character Traits," i.e., a Halakhic statement of the type of ethical conduct and disposition demanded of the Jew and presented in the form of a *Shulhan Arukh*. It is certainly no accident that this author adopts the term used by Karo for his famous Code or that Maimonides' *Hilkhot Deot* is a primary source of the work, quoted repeatedly. To refer to a few of Treves' chapter headings: "The Laws (*halakhot*) of the Love and Fear of God"; "The Laws Governing Respect for Human Dignity"; "The Laws Governing Shyness" (i.e., when one should be modest and unassuming): "The Laws Governing Pride"; "The Laws Governing Bad Temper"; "The Laws Governing Envy"; "The Laws Governing the Pursuit of Peace." The work *Hafetz Hayyim* (after which the author is known universally as "*the* Hafetz Hayyim") treats, in a Halakhic manner, the evils of malicious gossip and slander and tale bearing. These topics are given much prominence in the rabbinic literature but there they belong, in the main, to the Aggadah, or, at least, they are on the borderlines between Halakha and Aggadah. For the first time they are given a detailed Halakhic foundation and are presented with constant references to debates among the authorities, with Halakhic-type argumentation and with the actual rule *(pesak halakha)* being given, all entirely typical of the traditional Halakhic works.

Maimonides' philosophical views also made themselves felt in many of his detailed Halakhic formulations in other sections of his Code. When describing, for instance, the procedures to be adopted for a conversion to Judaism, Maimonides adds to the Talmudic regulations that the prospective convert must be prepared to accept

the basic beliefs of Judaism.[7] For Maimonides, it is not alone Jewish observances that the prospective convert must be ready to follow but it is essential for him to be thoroughly conversant with the
true beliefs by which Maimonides sets such great store in his other
works as well. Similarly, when Maimonides formulates the laws
governing the seven laws of the sons of Noah,[8] he adds that these
must be accepted by a Gentile (if he is to qualify as one of "the
saints of the nations of the world") because he believes that these
laws were divinely revealed to Moses. If he keeps them solely
because his reason tells him to do so he is a "sage" of the nations of
the world but not a "saint." Here, too. Maimonides introduces into
the Halakhah a question of correct belief that belongs to
Maimonides' general theological outlook on the need for divine
revelation in the scheme of proper Jewish faith.

In obedience to his philosophy, according to which belief in
magic is nonsensical, Maimonides studiously omits from his Code
all Talmudic references to magic, superstition, astrology, and demons.[9] Even when he does record laws found in the Talmud based
on a belief in the efficacy of magical practices, Maimonides either
omits the Talmudic reason entirely or else interprets this so as to be
in accord with his own refined faith. For instance, the Talmud[10]
states that one may utter incantations for snakes and scorpions on
the Sabbath. Maimonides[11] understands this to mean incantations
for the purpose of curing snakebite and he formulates the law: "It is
permitted to whisper an incantation for a snakebite even on the
Sabbath in order to set the victim's mind at rest and strengthen his
heart (i.e., it has only a psychological effect). Even though this is
totally ineffective, the Sages permitted it because the victim believes in it and it is therefore permitted in order to prevent him
going out of his mind." The *Shulhan Arukh*[12] records Maimonides'
statement *verbatim*, thus admitting into the most authoritative Code
of Jewish practice a formal protest against magical and superstitious
beliefs, even those held by the spiritual giants of the past. This led
the gaon of Vilna[13] in the eighteenth century to object vehemently
both to Maimonides' original formulation and to the *Shulhan Arukh*
for recording it. The gaon roundly declares that all the sages of
Israel take issue with Maimonides on this subject. Maimonides,
continues the gaon, was "led astray by his study of the accursed
philosophy." The gaon has no difficulty in recording numerous
Talmudic references from which it emerges clearly that the Talmudic rabbis did believe in the existence of demons, in amulets and
incantations, and in the general efficacy of magic. The significant

feature in all this for our purpose is that even the gaon records his view in his Halakhic commentary to the *Shulhan Arukh*, invoking the other sages so as to render Maimonides' opinion a minority one, which can then be rejected *on Halakhic grounds*.

Further examples can be multiplied of Maimonides' pervasive philosophical attitudes even in his Halakhic formulations.[14] Questions of belief based on Maimonides' general outlook are given the status of Halakhah in spite of the frequently noted contradictions, apparent or real, between Maimonides' *Guide for the Perplexed* and his *Mishneh Torah*.[15] Thus, Maimonides has detailed rules on types of unbelief;[16] on the nature of the Hereafter;[17] on the Messiah;[18] on the incorporeality of God;[19] all formulated as "laws" *(halakhot)*. To these should be added the many instances throughout his Code where Maimonides provides a theological explanation for given laws or introduces a new philosophical note of his own, usually at the end of each section.

Another Halakhist of note who allows his philosophical attitudes to have a voice in his Halakhic works is Menahem Meiri of Perpignan (1249–1316). In Meiri, as in Maimonides, the very systematic and logical presentation of the material is itself indicative of the philosophical stance. In all his gigantic commentaries to the Talmud that come under the title *Bet ha-Behirah*, Meiri writes as a philosopher as well as a Halakhist.[20] Like Maimonides, too, Meiri either omits entirely or else reinterprets the Talmudic passages in which there is expressed or is implicit a belief in the efficacy of magic, even when these passages are Halakhic in nature. A good example is Meiri's treatment of the Talmudic law[21] that the Shema should be recited again before one retires to sleep in order to ward off the demons, with the qualification that this is not necessary for a scholar who need have no fear of the demons since he is protected by the Torah he studies. According to Meiri the malevolent demons *(mazikim)* referred to in the passage are false and harmful beliefs (in the context Meiri seems to mean Christian beliefs, which, for him and for all Jews, compromise pure monotheistic beliefs).[22] These false beliefs tend to invade the mind during the dark hours when the mind is dormant and uncritical but are laid to rest when the Shema, the affirmation of God's complete unity, is recited. A scholar does not require this antidote because his regular Torah studies have rendered him immune from any invasion of heretical ideas. Consistently, through all his works, Meriri adds always the reasonable view, rejecting either explicitly or implicitly, any superstitious notions. In a later chapter we see how Meiri

develops his ideas about the relationship of Judaism to other faiths
and how he allows these ideas to have their say in his Halakhic
formulations.

It is not sufficiently appreciated that the methods of Halakhic
study have themselves been greatly influenced, at least among some
of the most outstanding Halakhists, by philosophical thought.
Many of the medieval Halakhists were also philosophers and theologians of note.[23] Their Halakhic works, though not always their
philosophical works, were widely studied by later Halakhists. The
result has been that a large number of later Halakhists, even those
who were either indifferent or even hostile to philosophy, are found
to be using, in their Halakhic works, the philosophical and analytical methods they had learned from their Halakhic mentors,
often without being aware of it. Talmudic reasoning itself follows
logical patterns of the utmost rigor. Nevertheless, the Halakhist
analytical thinkers, down to the present day, have approached the
Talmudic Halakhah with tools fashioned originally in the Greek
schools. That this is so can be seen, among other things, when
philosophical terms, from the vocabulary of the Hebraic translators
of the philosophical works written originally in Arabic, are substituted for the older Talmudic terminology, new concepts being
frequently expressed by these terms. It is more than a question of
semantics. As in every science, the terms used affect the whole
reasoning process.

Here, too, examples abound. A whole book can easily be compiled on this question of how analytical methods, originating, in
part, at least, from outside Judaism, were used extensively by distinguished Halakhists. In the following paragraphs we can only
sketch briefly the manner in which such methods operate among
some of the best-known Halakhists.

Nahmanides (1194–1270), in his Commentary to the
Pentateuch,[24] blends his philosophical, theological, and kabbalistic
views with his discussions of Halakhah. A major portion of his
Novellae to the Talmud consists of the acute analysis of Halakhic
concepts.[25] Many examples come to mind. One is in Nahmanides'
comment to the first Mishnah of *Berakhot*, a comment found at the
beginning of his collection of Novellae. It would appear from the
sources, Nahmanides notes here, that whereas a drunken man may
not say his prayers he may recite the Shema and various benedictions. According to Nahmanides' analysis, an obvious distinction
has to be made. The Shema and the benedictions are in the nature
of declarations. Although these, too, must be recited with proper

intention, *kavvanah*, even a drunken man is capable of having the somewhat perfunctory type of intention required for a simple declaration. In prayer, on the other hand, man is engaged in a dialogue with his Maker and for dialogue a much more penetrating type of intention is demanded than that of which a drunken man is capable. Nahmanides' analytical methods were followed by his disciple, R. Solomon Ibn Adret, the *Rashba* (ca. 1235–ca. 1310)[26] and by the latter's disciple, R. Yom Tov Ishbili (d. 1330), [27] the *Ritba*, both of whom were students of philosophy who also belong in the ranks of the foremost Halakhists.

Another famed fourteenth-century Halakhist who had great influence on later Halakhic studies was Vidal Yom Tov of Tolosa, author of *Maggid Mishneh* to Maimonides' *Mishneh Torah*, an indispensable work for all students of the Code. This author appears to have been the first actually to use philosophical and logical terms to describe Halakhic concepts, terms such as "quantity," "cause," "transfer," and "identity."[28]

R. Nissim of Gerona (ca. 1310–ca. 1375), the *Ran*, is probably the most acute and penetrating of the medieval Halakhic analysts. Despite the *Ran*'s lukewarm attitude toward philosophy, he was familiar with the discipline. Even in his sermons *(Derashot)* and even when taking issue with the philosophers, the *Ran* uses philosophical terminology.[29] One of the *Ran*'s disciples was the renowned philosopher Hasdai Crescas. In his commentary to Alfasi's digest, in his Novellae to the Talmud[30] and, especially, in his commentary to tractate *Nedarim*—the standard commentary to this tractate—the *Ran* engages in the subtle analysis of Halakhic concepts. Among the lengthy pieces of such analysis, mention might be made of his treatment of the annulment of leaven before Passover and its relationship to abandoned property, *hefker*,[31] the legal nature of a woman's consent to her marriage,[32] the principle of the neutralization of forbidden food *(bittul)*,[33] and the principle of retrospective specification *(bererah)* in its various forms.[34]

The works of these *rishonim* had the greatest influence on all subsequent Halakhic theory. Prominent among the *aharonim* who embraced the analytical method was Aryeh Laib Heller (d. 1813), of Stry in Galicia, author of *Ketzot ha-Hoshen*,[35] *Avney Milluim*,[36] and *Shev Shematata*.[37] In his remarkable theological introduction to the latter work, Heller states his views on Judaism generally, drawing on the writings of the more rationalistic Jewish theologians but with more than a touch of Halakhic-type casuistry. In his Halakhic work Heller is a pioneer of the application in detail of the analytical

method to Halakhic concepts. Among the concepts he examines are
agency,[38] simultaneous acquisition,[39] admission of monetary in-
debtedness and the basis on which this operates,[40] and the treatment of doubt in Jewish law.[41] Heller's contemporary, Jacob
Lorbeerbaum (ca. 1760–1822), in his *Netivot ha-Mishpat*,[42] takes up
many of the issues raised by Heller, subjecting Heller's arguments,
in turn, to analysis. Typical of Lorbeerbaum's analytical approach
is his observation that all rabbinic laws are binding because of the
biblical injunction to obey the sages of Israel.[43] The rabbinic prohibitions and injunctions are not intrinsic, i.e., a thing forbidden by
the rabbis is not forbidden in itself but only because the dictates of
the sages must be obeyed. It follows, according to Lorbeerbaum,
that one cannot offend unwittingly against rabbinic law as one can
against biblical law. Since the offense is one of disobedience alone
and is not intrinsic, there is no offense at all where the act is done
unwittingly. Lacking conscious intent, the act is no act of disobedience and is hence not a wrongful act at all. The debates and discussions between Heller and Lorbeerbaum, the *Ketzot* and the *Netivot*,
became the staple diet of later students of the Halakhah.[44] In the
Lithuanian yeshivot these names were always on the lips of both
teachers and students.

These Lithuanian yeshivot, from the early nineteenth century
down to the present day, were certainly no friends of either philosophy or of secular learning of any kind. Yet in these yeshivot, in
particular, the analytical methods of earlier Halakhists were
adopted and developed into a fine art. It must also be appreciated
that in these yeshivot the main thrust of Halakhic studies was not at
all in the direction of practical Halakhah but entirely toward
theoretical and purely academic investigation. Indeed, in many of
the yeshivot, any ultimate career in the practical rabbinate was
frowned upon by the best students, who tended to remain in the
yeshivah until they were quite advanced in years—some of them
into their forties and fifties—studying the theoretical concepts over
and again. The central aim of the students was *zu kenen lernen*, "to
be able to study," i.e., to acquire the analytical concepts and
to hone these in an ever more refined manner. In the majority
of yeshivot of this type only the eight tractates—*Bava Kama*,
Bava Metzia, *Bava Batra*, *Yevamot*, *Ketubot*, *Nedarim*, *Gittin*, and
Kiddushin—were studied in depth because it is in these that the most
fruitful opportunities are afforded for the keen analysis of legal
concepts. A major reason for this one-sidedness was probably
sociological—there were too few rabbinic posts for the large num-

bers of students to fill, a virtue being made of necessity. But another factor was undoubtedly the history of Halakhic studies to which the yeshivot were heirs. The earlier Halakhists, as we have noted, and this includes particularly the *Tosafists* to the Talmud, tended to give priority to theory over practice, at least in the sense that study was supreme not only because it led to practice but because study was itself the highest form of religious practice. It is worth noting in this connection that the analytical methods pursued in the Lithuanian Yeshivot were attacked by more traditional Halakhists as a foreign importation.

The fiery, traditionalist scholar, R. Jacob David Willowsky (1838–1913), known as *Ridbaz*, notes in this connection:

A certain Rabbi invented the "chemical" method of study. Those in the know refer to it as "chemistry" but many speak of it as "logic." This proved to be of great harm to us for it is a foreign spirit from without that they have brought into the Oral Torah. Not this is the Torah delivered to us by Moses from the mouth of the Omnipresent. This method of study has spread among the Yeshivah students who still hold a Gemara in their hands. In no way does this type of Torah study bring men to purity. From the day this method has spread abroad this kind of Torah has had no power to protect its students. The few discerning scholars weep in secret over this. For our sins, from the day the Yeshivah of Volozhyn was closed and nine other Yeshivot proliferated, nothing whatsoever has been achieved. For such is not really a Yeshivah at all but a mere gathering since the majority of them do not even have a Principal . . .[45]

Aryeh Karlin, in a work published as late as 1938, can still write:

The Way of Thinking and Method of Study. In former times such a question would have seemed perverse and have had no place. What can "The way of thinking and method of study" possibly mean? We have a received chain of tradition from the Gaonim, Rishonim and Aharonim on the way in which the Torah should be studied. To our good fortune this chain has never been severed through the many generations united and bound together by a thread of scarlet. Together with their different ways of study there was a common principle, namely, the knowledge and understanding of the Torah in all its comprehensiveness. Each one introduced new theories and expositions through the way the spirit moved them and by their own intellectual powers. This one approached his studies in a comprehensive manner, the other delved more deeply into the profundities of the subject. This one analyzed concepts logically, the other placed greater emphasis on the general principles

and definitions of the Talmud. But anyone familiar with the work of
the Gaonim knows only too well that, despite the many different approaches, a common spirit prevails among them. All was governed by
the great equalizer—the way and spirit of the Torah. They never allowed this or that method to obtrude in their works for only the truth of
the Torah was before their eyes, each bringing to bear his own ideas
according to the gifts God had given him. None of them ever made
claim to have invented a new way. Consequently, each took into account the opinions of his predecessors and of the other great geniuses of
the spirit. It was all a matter of seeing the same coin—the coin of the
Torah—from different angles. Now, however, new times have come,
numerous "methods" proliferating in the world of the Torah students.
The Halakhah does not, however, follow a "method." They lay claim
to being pioneers, the creators of the world of logical method in the
study of the Torah. They are real revolutionaries about whom it is
essential to protest. These methods have altered the whole face of
Halakhic studies, uncovering new facets. The "Telzer" method and
"the method of R. Hayyim" (Soloveitchik), which now proliferate in
the Yeshivah world, have done far more harm than good. I beg the
great scholars to pardon my sharp expressions but they are spoken from
the depths of my heart and I am ready to accept full responsibility for
them. Let the great scholars ignore this playing with concepts, peculiar
to these methods. Let them ignore the style used and its hypnotic effect
on the minds of immature students, and they will see the emptiness,
not to say the ignorance, of Torah learning among these students, the
direct result of these methods which are a retreat from those methods of
study received by tradition from generation to generation among the
righteous of the world.[46]

Thus Karlin attacks the new methods as untraditional. He continues in the same vein, accusing the exponents of the new methods
of having a negative religious effect on the students for whom it has
all become a pastime rather than study of the Torah sacred in itself.
Karlin's critique is extreme and unfair but it contains, nonetheless,
more than a germ of truth. Something new and untraditional has
been introduced into the heart of Halakhic study, although, as we
have tried to show, this kind of interpretation by methods that
come from without the Jewish camp is itself part of a good deal of
the Halakhic tradition.

   The most outstanding of the Lithuanian pioneers, referred to by
Karlin, was R. Hayyim Soloveitchik (1853–1918), Rabbi of Brisk
(Brest–Litovsk) and originator of the "Brisker *derekh*," "the method
of Brisk," consisting of a breaking up of Halakhic concepts into
their component parts.[47] Typical of R. Hayyim's approach is his

attitude to the gravely sick on the Day of Atonement. Such persons may eat on the Day of Atonement if to fast would place their lives in danger. R. Hayyim was notoriously lenient in deciding such matters and, when challenged, he resorted to his Halakhic methodology. There are, he said, two distinct laws—*sheney dinim*, a favorite expression of the Brisker school. The first of these is the obligation to save life; the second is the obligation to fast on Yom Kippur. For a sick person whose life will be in danger if he fasts, the two laws are in conflict and the Halakhah comes down on the side of saving life. What is the position where there is a degree of doubt as whether or not the sick person should eat? R. Hayyim argues that the usual rule—that where there is doubt about a biblical law the stricter view is to be adopted—cannot apply here since both obligations are biblical. R. Hayyim used to say, "It is not that I am lenient with regard to Yom Kippur. I am strict with regard to saving life."[48] Because of his strong theoretical bent, R. Hayyim, though the official rabbi of Brisk, was reluctant to render decisions on practical matters of Jewish law unless there was a pressing need. He left other cases to be decided by his Bet Din. Revealing in this connection is the story of R. Hayyim submitting a difficult case to his contemporary, R. Isaac Elhanan Spektor of Kovno. R. Hayyim sent a telegram to Rabbi Spektor but insisted that the reply should consist solely of the actual ruling not the reasoning behind it. Had Rabbi Spektor presented his reasoning in his reply. R. Hayyim's integrity would not have allowed him to rely on the decision if his reasoning could fault the arguments for it.[49] As it was R. Hayyim felt able to rely on the actual decision of a renowned Halakhic authority. There could hardly be a more telling example of how Halakhic theory became divorced from practical Halakhah.

The Telzer method, also referred to by Karlin, was that developed in the yeshiva of Telz in Lithuania, especially by the heads of the yeshivah, R. Simeon Shkop (1860–1940)[50] and R. Joseph Laib Bloch (1860–1930).[51] The method was known as that of *biggayon*, logic. In his *Shaarey Yosher*[52] R. Simeon discusses if, as Nahmanides[53] holds, rabbinic law is only binding by rabbinic law, not, as Maimonides holds,[54] by biblical law, why should it be binding at all? What is the authority of the rabbis for demanding that we should obey the laws they have ordained. Logically, it would seem, it is begging the question to hold that rabbinic law is binding because the rabbis so say.[55] Discussing the reliance on probability in Jewish law, R. Simeon embarks on a philosophical investigation into the whole notion of probability with special reference to mathematical or statistical probability.[56] To illustrate the problem, he asks how can the man who buys ten tickets for a lottery have greater odds in his favor than a man who buys only one ticket, since whichever ticket is drawn as the winning ticket is only a single ticket with all the odds against it. Rabbi Bloch was influenced to some extent by his colleague. R. Simeon. Bloch is particularly interested in the examination of states of mind in the performance of given acts. He tries to show that the Halakhah takes into consideration all the possible varieties and vagaries of human thought and intention, drawing fine distinctions between acts carried out with proper awareness and those performed in a more perfunctory way.[57] Rabbi Bloch was also the author of theological lectures, later published as essays, which are given the title *Shiurey Daat* ("Lectures on Knowledge"). His son and successor quotes a remark by a student at Telz Yeshivah that in Rabbi Bloch's theological lectures there is found the precision and intellectual rigor typical of the Halakhah whereas in his Halakhic lectures there is a strong poetical element, typical of the Aggadah.[58]

Three Eastern European Halakhists of genius applied logical analysis of Halakhic concepts independently of the yeshivot. These were R. Joseph Engel (1859–1920) of Poland and R. Joseph Rosin (1858–1936), known, after his birthplace, as the Ragadshover gaon, and R. Meir Simhah Kohen (1843–1926), the latter two serving as rabbis in Dvinsk, Latvia. R. Joseph Engel is the author of voluminous Halakhic treatises in which he applies the analytical method with great acumen. To refer to but one example, the Talmud rules that a post which serves technically as a "wall" for the purpose of the Sabbath boundaries serves as a "wall" of a *sukkah*, even though in other circumstances, e.g., on a weekday, it does not qualify as a "wall" for the *sukkah*.[59] The principle stated in the Talmud is, seeing that the post does qualify as a "wall" for the Sabbath law this in itself renders it a "wall" for the *sukkah* law so that on the Sabbath of the festival it would be valid. Engel asks why not reverse the argument and say that just as it does not qualify as a "wall" for the *sukkah* it does not qualify as a "wall" for the Sabbath. His reply is based on a distinction between positive and negative.[60] (Incidentally, for "positive" and "negative" Engel uses the medieval philosophical terms *hiyyuv* and *shelilah*). It is logically feasible to postulate that once the concept "wall" has been applied to an object for certain purposes that object can serve as a "wall" for other purposes as well; it has become a "wall." The opposite argument is logically unsound since logically there is no such concept as a "not-wall." There is no such entity as a "not-wall"; it is simply a case of the absence of a wall. To negate a concept from a given object confers no actual status on that object, not even a negative status. The Ragadshover gaon, with a phenomenal mastery of the whole of the rabbinic literature, saw Maimonides as his true master. It is rumored that he would walk about holding a book written by Maimonides exclaiming in delight: "My teacher, my teacher." He studied in depth Maimonides' *Guide for the Perplexed* and utilizes the philosophical concepts he found there for the purpose of Halakhic analysis.[61] R. Meir Simhah was a religious thinker of note, as is evident from his Commentary to the Torah, *Meshekh Hokhmah.*[62] He was a Halakhic luminary of world renown as well. Typical of the blend of philosophy and Halakhah in R. Meir Simhah's *Or Sameah*[63], a running Commentary to Maimonides' *Mishneh Torah*, is his lengthy essay on the old theological problem, with which Maimonides grapples *in his Code*,[64] the problem of how human free will can be reconciled with God's foreknowledge. It is obvious from this essay that R. Meir Simhah believes that theological questions derserve to be treated with the same seriousness and with the same reliance on well thought-out arguments as do purely legal problems. The methods that R. Meir Simhah uses in this essay are exactly the same as those he employs when he is discussing the more formal legal decisions in Maimonides' Code.[65]

Reference must also be made to the Polish Halakhists, R. Abraham Bornstein of Sochachov (1839–1920),[66] Hasidic master and son-in-law of the Kotzker Rebbe, and Bornstein's disciple, R. Joab Joshua Weingarten (1847–1922),[67] both of whom employ the method of logical analysis in their works, as well as to R. Jacob Reines (1839–1915) who published his program for a comprehensive work on logical analysis as applied to Talmudic studies both Halakhic and Aggadic. The work was never completed but the two small volumes of the program, entitled *Hotam Tokhnit*,[68] show to good effect how Reines' methods operate. Reines was also the author of a philosophical lexicon *Sefer ha-Arakhin.*[69]

Finally, we refer to R. Moshe Avigdor Amiel (1883–1946), a preacher of note, who quoted in his sermons the famous non-Jewish as well as Jewish Philosophers.[70] In his *ha-Middot le-Heker ha-Halakhah*, Amiel gives a masterly survey of the work of the Halakhic analysts throughout the ages and attempts a systematic presentation of Halakhic concepts[71] in a philosophical vein.

It has not been our intention in this chapter to suggest that the Halakhah has been in any way subservient to philosophy and to philosophical reasoning. It must be repeated that the Halakhic process has its own rules and categories. For all that, evidence has been adduced to show that many of the foremost and influential Halakhists were at least as interested in the Halakhah as a philosophical discipline as they were in the Halakhah for practice, and that they were by no means averse to using creatively a terminology and especially a methodology both of which go back ultimately to the philosophical rather than to the legal tradition.

NOTES

1. See Saul Lieberman, *Hellenism in Jewish Palestine*, pp. 47–82.

2. See Baer, *Yisrael ba-Amim* and Lieberman's critique of Baer, "How Much Greek in Jewish Palestine?."

3. See especially S. Rawidowicz's edition of Maimonides' *Sefer ha-Madda* and the Symposium, "Mishneh Torah Studies" in JLA, vol. 1, part 1, pp. 3–176.

4. *Yad, Yesodey ha-Torah* 6:13. The Talmudic passage in which the distinction is made between *Maaseh Bereshit* and *Maaseh Merkavah* as the "great thing" and the debates of Abbaye and Rava as the "small thing" is *Sukkah* 28a. See *Kesef Mishneh* to *Yad* ad loc. for the strong opposition this statement aroused. For the use of the term "the debates of Abbaye and Rava" to denote the whole of the Talmudic Halakhah see the sources quoted in *Kesef Mishneh* and in Frank E. Talmage, *David Kimhi*, p. 36. Talmage refers to the letter of Judah Alfakkar (Letter III, 2c, in *Kovetz Teshuvot ha-Rambam*) where the term is used in this sense by both Alfakkar and Kimhi. Centuries later, it might be noted, Y. M. Epstein begins his Code, the *Arukh ha-Shulhan*, with *Diney Yesodey ha-Torah*. "The *Laws* of the Principles of the Jewish Faith" (*Arukh ha-Shulhan* I, 1:1–4). Isserles at the beginning of his glosses to SA, OH 1:1 quotes a passage from Maimonides' *Guide*. Cf. the remark of Jacob Emden, *Sheilot Yaavetz*, I. no. 10, that he used to read works in Hebrew on physics and metaphysics in the privy because these are secular and it is sheer delusion to give them the status of *Maaseh Bereshit* and *Maaseh Merkavah*.

5. See the introduction to the *Orah Mesharim* where the author observes that he had never seen any work on these topics in which they are treated Halakhically (*li-fesak halakhah*), i.e., in the form of legal decisions. For a similar statement of ethical maxims as Halakhah see the list provided by Abraham Gumbiner in his *Magen Avraham* to SA, OH 156. Cf. the recording of ethical conduct as "law" in SA, OH 156 (business ethics) and 240 (sex ethics).

6. The *Sefer Hafetz Hayyim* was first published in Vilna in 1873 anonymously, and it was not until much later that the author's identity became known. See, especially, the note in the introduction (New York edition p. 5) in which the author defends his work against the accusation that many of his statements are based on the moralistic work by Jonah Gerondi (*Shaarey Teshuvah*) and, therefore, the claim of the book to be a Halakhic work is unfounded. (On R. Jonah Gerondi and his moralistic work see A. T. Shrock, *Rabbi Jonah ben Abraham of Gerona*).

7. *Yad, Issurey Viah* 14:2. Maimonides' wording follows exactly that of the passage of *Yevamot* 47a except for the additions regarding belief in the basic principles of the Jewish faith, see *Kesef Mishneh* ad loc.

8. *Yad, Melakhim* 8:11. The standard texts have the reading "neither a sage nor a saint" but the correct reading, attested to by ms., is "only a sage not a saint." See the edition of

S. T. Rubinstein, *Rambam la-Am*, vol. 17, p. 398 note 69. On this subject see Atlas, *Netivot*, pp. 21–40.

9. See I. H. Weiss, *Dor*, vol. 3, pp. 223–24 and note 7.

10. *Sanhedrin* 101a.

11. *Yad, Akum* 11:11.

12. YD 179:6.

13. *Biur ha-Gra* to YD 179, note 13. The gaon further observes that all the Talmudic references he quotes must not be understood in a metaphorical sense (as Maimonides understands them) but literally except that they have an "inner meaning." This, he says, is not the "inner meaning" of the philosophers but of "the masters of truth," i.e., the Kabbalists.

14. See Twersky, "Some Non-Halakic Aspects of the *Mishneh Torah*."

15. See Strauss, "The Literary Character of the Guide for the Perplexed" and David Hartman, *Maimonides*.

16. *Yad Teshuvah* 3:6–9.

17. Ibid. 8.

18. *Yad, Melakhim* 11 and 12.

19. *Yad, Teshuvah* 3:7, cf. *Rabad*'s stricture ad loc.

20. See especially his arrangement of the material in Halakhic form in his *Hibbur ha-Teshuvah*, although this deals with the theme of repentance. Cf. Meiri on evil as negative in his comment on a Halakhic passage, *Bet ha-Behirah*, to *Shavuot* 27a, pp. 78–79.

21. *Berakhot* 4b–5a and JT *Berakhot* 1:1 (2d).

22. *Bet ha-Behirah*, *Berakhot*, p. 17. Cf. Meiri's comment (p. 11) to *Berakhot* 3a–b where he omits the reason given in the Talmud why one should not enter a ruin, "because of the demons," substituting for it "where there is danger to life." Other examples are his comment on *Pesahim* 109b about the baneful effect of "pairs," *zuggot*, *Bet ha-Behirah*, *Pesahim*, pp. 234–35; and his comment on the reference to Elijah and Joseph the Demon in *Eruvin* 43a, *Bet ha-Behirah*, *Eruvin*, p. 162.

23. See M. A. Amiel, *ha-Middot le-Heker ha-Halakhah*. Amiel, vol. I, p. 138 writes: "It is also no accident that many of the greatest masters of the Halakhah were also Israel's greatest philosophers." Amiel goes on to advance the interesting theory that Aristotelian philosophy is more in accord with Halakhic type argumentation than is Neoplatonism, even though it is the latter that is closer to "Israel's spirit." Thus, the great Talmudists and Halakhists like Maimonides were Aristotelians, whereas thinkers like Gabirol and Abraham Ibn Ezra, who were not particularly noteworthy as Talmudists, were NeoPlatonists. For the use of philosophical terms in the Halakhic discussions see Amiel, vol. I, pp. 92f. Saul Berlin, in his notorious forgery, *Besamim Rosh*, no. 251, puts into the mouth of the *Rosh* (Asher b. Yehiel): "Everyone acknowledges that no one can possibly grasp the main principles of the Torah and the *mitzvot* as a result of the reasoning he acquires from the plain meaning of Scripture and the words of the Rabbis but only as a result of reasoning cultivated by the study of the books compiled by the thinkers among the nations." This is one of the reasons why the rabbis detected that the book is a forgery since the *Rosh* himself, *Teshuvot ha-Rosh*, no. 55, explicitly rejects the idea that we have anything to learn, so far as the Torah is concerned, from non-Jewish works and he boasts of his ignorance of these works. Cf. Baneth, *Parashat Mordekhai*, *Orah Hayyim*, no. 5.

24. Cf. his introduction where he puts forward the view that the Torah, from one point of view, is a series of combinations of divine names and yet in the body of the Commentary he usually refers in detail to the Halakhah.

25. Nahmanides' Novellae have been published in various editions; the edition of his Responsa is by B. Chavel.

26. Both the Responsa and the Novellae of *Rashba* are found in various editions.

27. *Ritba's* Novellae have been published in various editions; his Responsa have been edited by Kapah.

28. See Amiel, *ha-Middot le Heker*, vol. I, p. 92. Cf. the *Maggid Mishneh's* analysis of Maimonides' ruling (*Yad, Shabbat* 17:12) that a post *(lehi)* can be made from an *asherah*, a tree dedicated to idolatry which has to be destroyed in fire. Here *Maggid Mishneh* makes the observation that the point, line, and plane of a geometrical figure are "imaginary" *(dimyon)*.

29. See Leon Feldman "Nissim ben Reuben Gerondi."

30. The Commentary of *Ran* to *Nedarim* is printed together with the text in most editions and takes the place of Rushi to the extent that one refers to the study of "*Nedarim* with the Ran."

31. Commentary to Alfasi, *Pesahim*, beg.

32. Commentary to *Nedarim* 30a.

33. Commentary to Ibid. 52b.

34. Commentary to Ibid. 45b–46a.

35. Although the *Ketzot* is printed together with SA, HM in many editions and is in the form of a Commentary to SA, HM, hence the name, the work is basically not a practical law manual but a series of profound discussions of abstract legal theory.

36. The work was published posthumously, Lemberg, 1816, with an index compiled by Heller's son-in-law, S. J. Rapoport, one of the pioneers of the new Jewish learning, *Jüdische Wissenschaft*.

37. Although, as Heller remarks in his introduction, this work was originally compiled by him in his youth, he evidently added some later material before publication and the introduction itself was compiled much later.

38. *Ketzot* to HM 182, note 1.

39. *Ketzot* to HM 200, note 5.

40. *Ketzot* to HM 34, note 4.

41. This is the theme of the whole *Shev Shematata* but especially in I, beg.

42. The *Netivot* is usually printed together with SA, HM.

43. *Netivot* to HM 234, note 3.

44. Among the many examples of debates between the two see the discussion in HM 51 on whether witnesses who become disqualified because they have offended against a communal regulation not to testify in certain cases of marriage become disqualified only after the act of testifying (so that their testimony to the act is valid) or even for the act itself.

45. Responsa, introduction (no pagination). Cf. H. H. Agush, *Marheshet*, (quoted by Sevin, *ha-Moadim ba-Halakhah*, p. 91) who apologizes for his lack of familiarity with these new methods of study: "I am afraid that I am bare of the cloaks of light provided by the logical study of the Talmud which have recently appeared on the scene. . . . I have never tried my hand at these. My approach in my Halakhic studies is that of the broad and clear highway provided by our teachers ancient and modern."

46. Aryeh Karlin, *Lev Aryeh*, introduction. On the Lithuanian analytical school see the arricles in English by Norman Solomon in *Diné Israel*.

47. R. Hayyim's Novellae to Maimonides' Code are published under the title *Hiddushey Rabbenu Hayyim ha-Levi*. The best treatment of R. Hayyim's methods is that of S. Sevin, *Ishim ve-Shittot*, pp. 43–70.

48. See S. Sevin, *ha-Moadim be-Halakhah*, p. 82 and *Ishim ve-Shittot*, pp. 59–60.

49. Sevin, *Ishim ve-Shittot*, pp. 58–59. Cf. Sevin's preface to this story:

"Why did R. Hayyim refuse to write Responsa? Some think that his remoteness from the area of practical decisions stemmed from the fact that he belonged to the ranks of 'those who fear to render decisions,' being afraid of the responsibility it entails. But this is not so. The real reason was a different one. R. Hayyim was aware that he was incapable of simply following convention and that he would be obliged, consequently, to render decisions contrary to the norm and the traditionally accepted whenever his clear intellect and fine mind would show him that the law was really otherwise than as formulated by the great Codifiers. The pure conscience of a truthful man would not allow him to ignore his own opinions and submit but he would have felt himself bound to override their decisions and this he could not bring himself to do."

50. See *Sefer ha-Yovel*, the Jubilee Volume in honor of R. Simeon, for important biographical details, and S. Sorski, *Rabbi Shimeon ve-Torato*.

51. See D. Katz, *Tenuat ha-Musar*, vol. 5, pp. 17–109; Sorski, *Marbitzey Torah u-Musar*, vol. 2, pp. 29–57; and Rabbi Bloch's *Shiurey Halakhah* and *Shiurey Daat*.

52. See R. Simeon's introduction to his *Shaarey Yosher* where he insists that a teacher must not state his opinions dogmatically but must seek to establish them by means of reasonable argument. Applying a Talmudic saying, R. Simeon declares that only if one has an angel for his teacher can he learn from the teacher's "mouth." If the teacher is a human being the learning must be from the teacher's "head," i.e., the teacher must win over his pupils by proving his case.

53. Commentary to Maimonides' *Sefer ha-Mitzvot, Shoresh* I.

54. *Sefer ha-Mitzvot, Shoresh* 1.

55. *Shaarey Yosher*, vol. I, *Shaar* I, chapter 7, pp. 17–20.

56. Ibid., vol. I, *Shaar* 3, chapters 1–4, pp. 149–60.

57. See, e.g., his treatment of the potential acquisition of property in *Shiurey Halakhah*, no. 12, pp. 62–66.

58. A. Bloch in the essay "Halakhah and Aggadah."

59. *Sukkah* 7a–b.

60. *Tziyonim la-Torah*, no. 1, part 1. Cf., for his method, his analysis (*Lekah Tov*, I, beg.) Whether the principle of agency operates because the agent is treated as if he were the principal or because the act is not required to be performed by the principal himself in order to be valid.

61. On the Ragadshover see Sevin, *Ishim ve-Shittot*, pp. 75–121 and M. M. Kasher *Mefaneah Tzefunot*.

62. On R. Meir Simhah see Sevin, *Ishim ve-Shittot*, pp. 137–65.

63. R. Meir Simhah is reported to have said that whereas he could have written his *Or Sameah* even when he was young his *Meshekh Hokhmah* could only have been written when he was of mature years.

64. *Yad, Teshuvah* 8:5.

65. *Or Sameah* vol. 1, pp. 25–29.

66. Author of *Egley Tal* on the Sabbath laws and Responsa *Avney Nezer*.

67. Author of *Helkat Yova*.

68. Reines also refers to his method as that of *higgayon*, "logic."

69. See p. 1 of this book, under the heading "Aggadah and Halakhah," where Reines remarks:

"Among the many differences between the Halakhah and the Aggadah is also the following. The Halakhah is intended for the purpose of imparting knowledge whereas the Aggadah is also intended to make an impression and have an effect (on the character). Whenever anyone gives expression to an Halakhic theme, his sole aim and intention is to convey some information to his audience, to make them appreciate the law in all its clarity. It is otherwise with regard to the Aggaddah. Here, quite apart from the information that is conveyed, there is another aim, that of producing an effect. For the majority of the Aggadot are intended for the purpose of straightening the character and opinions. Consequently, these demand that, apart from conveying information, there be an effect and an impression on the hearts of the audience. Arising out of this distinction many others follow with regard to the style and relationship of the two disciplines."

70. See, e.g., his *Derashot El Ammi*, vol. I, in many of the sermons.

71. See sup. note 23. On the subject of this chapter it is worth noting that the famous nineteenth-century Halakhist R. Isaac Schmelkes of Lemberg discusses at length in his introduction to his Responsa collection, *Bet Yitzhak*, *Orah Hayyim* (i), Kant's categorical imperative and the Jewish attitude toward Kantian ethics. Cf. in the same introduction (xviii) the author's very interesting remark that a judge must see to it not only that his decision is in accord with the letter of the law but must also take note of possible exceptions so that his decision will be both legally and ethically sound.

[5]

The Influence of Mysticism and Kabbalah

Although it is usually taken for granted by the Halakhists that only decisions arrived at by normal reasoning processes are binding, and that those communicated by supernatural means of one kind or another, are not, the matter is not quite so simple. Thus, in the Talmud[1] there is the famous story, referred to in a previous chapter,[2] about R. Eliezer's appeal to a heavenly voice, where R. Joshua refuses to pay heed to that voice in order to decide against the majority opinion of the sages because "It *is* not in Heaven" (Deut. 30:12)—the Torah has laid down rules for the investigation of the Halakha, including the rule that the majority opinion be followed, and, therefore, no appeal to heaven to countermand such rules is admissible. Yet in another Talmudic passage[3] the opinions of the House of Hillel are said to be binding against those of the House of Shammai because a heavenly voice had so declared. Various attempts were made by the Commentators[4] to reconcile our reliance on the heavenly voice in the one case and our refusal to be guided by it in the other, and why the Halakha rejects the opinion of R. Eliezer and yet accepts the opinions of the House of Hillel. The fact remains that in at least one passage far-reaching legal decisions are said to have been arrived at by divine communication.[5]

Among the medieval Halakhists there is considerable ambiguity on the question. According to a rabbinic comment on the verse 'These are the commandments which the Lord commanded Moses' (Lev. 27:34) the word *these* is stressed to yield the thought that no prophet has the authority to introduce any new laws.[6] In the context this refers to the doctrine of the immutability of the Torah,

69

that once God had given the Torah to Moses He will not introduce any new *mitzvot*. It by no means follows from this rabbinic statement that when matters of law are debated the ruling—the actual Halakhah—cannot be communicated through a prophetic vision or by other supernatural means. Maimonides, on the other hand, is totally uncompromising in the matter. In his Commentary to the Mishnah Maimonides writes:

> If a prophet advances a legal theory and another man advances a rival theory, the prophet then declaring: "The Holy One, blessed be He, has told me that my theory is the right one," do not listen to that prophet. If a thousand prophets, all of the rank of Joshua and Elijah, advance a certain theory and a thousand and one sages hold the opposite opinion, the majority opinion must be followed. The Halakhah is in accordance with the view of the thousand and one sages and not in accordance with the view of the thousand prophets. And so do our Sages remark (Hullin 124a): "By God! Even if Joshua b. Nun declared it with his own mouth I would not accept it or listen to him." And they said further (*Yevamot* 102a): "If Elijah comes and declares that *halitzah* is to be performed with a shoe we listen to him but if with a sandal we do not listen to him." They mean to say one must neither add to nor diminish from a *mitzvah* through a prophetic communication in any way whatsoever. And so, too, if a prophet testifies that the Holy One, blessed be He, said to him that the law in connection with a *mitzvah* is such-and-such and that the theory of so-and-so is correct, that prophet must be put to death as a false prophet, as we have established it. For no Torah is ever given after the first prophet (Moses) and nothing must be added to it nor taken away from it, as it is said: "It is not in Heaven" (Deut. 30:12). The Holy one, blessed be He, gave us no permission to learn from the prophets, only from the sages, those who advance (natural) theories and opinions. He did not say: "And thou shalt go to the *prophet* who will be in that time" but "And thou shalt go to the priests, the Levites, and to the judge who will be in those days" (Deut. 17:9). The Sages have dwelt on this topic at length and it is true.[7]

It is fairly obvious that Maimonides has gone far beyond his sources. There is no necessary conclusion from the fact that a sage, who believes that his opinion is in full accord with the Torah of Moses, will refuse to depart from that opinion because Joshua disagrees with it, or because the people, who, as the Talmud states in the passage quoted by Maimonides, become accustomed never to perform *halitzah* with a sandal, will keep fast to their custom even if Elijah tells them it is wrong, that the prophetic vision has no voice in Halakhic debate. It is possible that Maimonides' refusal to countenance any interference by a prophet with the normal Halakhic process has been influenced by the stress on the role of Mohammed by Islam. Consciously or otherwise, Maimonides felt obliged to play down the importance of subsequent claims to prophetic inspiration of a kind that might affect the Halakhah in reaction to his Islamic background.

Maimonides, consistent in his view, sees fit to record it categorically in his Code:

> So, too, if he uprooted any matter we have by tradition or if he declared, regarding some law of the Torah, that the Lord has communicated to him that the law is such and that the Halakhah follows the opinion of So-and-so, he is a false prophet and incurs the penalty of strangulation, even if he performs a miracle (to substantiate his claim) since he seeks to deny the Torah in which it is stated: "It is not in Heaven."[8]

R. Meir Simhah of Dvinsk[9] suggests that Maimonides draws a distinction between a supernatural communication in a particular instance—i.e., that such-and-such is the law in this particular case—which is inadmissible, and a communication regarding the fitness of a person or persons to enjoy Halakhic authority. In the latter case no law is communicated, only a simple piece of information, say, that the House of Hillel is more reliable than the House of Shammai, so that the law in each particular instance is, in fact, decided by the normal reasoning processes of the House of Hillel. All that the Heavenly voice does is to impart this important piece of information that the reasoning processes of the House of Hillel are more reliable (or, if our suggestion is correct),[10] the House of Hillel deserves to be "rewarded" by having the Halakhah decided in its favor). Something of the kind is no doubt the reasoning behind Maimonides' statement since he does follow in his Code the Talmudic ruling that the Halakhah is in accordance with the views of the House of Hillel and in the Talmud this is said to be in obedience to the Heavenly voice.[11]

Thus far the matter is academic. There are no known instances in post-Talmudic history of a man claiming to decide Halakhic questions on the basis of a prophetic vision or a voice from Heaven. But in an astonishing medieval work a scholar does make an appeal to Heaven of a rather different kind in order to arrive at the Halakhic ruling and this work itself came to enjoy a degree of Halakhic respectability. The work in question is *Sheelot u-Teshuvot min ha-Shamayyim* ("Responsa from Heaven") by Jacob of Marvège (twelfth–thirteenth centuries). Using such techniques as fasting and prayer, Jacob put questions of practical Halakhah to his Heavenly mentors, the replies being given to him in dreams, which he then recorded.[12] Among the questions that were hotly debated in the Middle Ages on which Jacob sought direct divine guidance are whether women, when they carry out those precepts from which the law exempts them, may recite the benediction: "Who has commanded us . . ."; and on the correct order, debated by Rashi and Rabbenu Tam, of the sections in the *tefillin*. Despite the elaborate discussions around the legitimacy of Jacob's appeal, some of his decisions did manage to find their way into the official Codes. The rationale for this is said to be similar to that suggested to explain Maimonides. Jacob's mentors on high were not deciding a law that was in doubt but were simply informing him which authorities were to be relied upon.[13] There is a strong element of artificiality about this rationale and it is *post factum*. The more likely explanation is that the French authorities did not apply the principle of "It is not in Heaven" except where the Heavenly communication, as in the case of R. Eliezer and R. Joshua, was opposed to the majority ruling.

Among the group of German mystics known as the *Hasidey Ashkenaz* ("the German Saints"),[14] in the twelfth and thirteenth centuries, two moralistic works were produced in which there is a blend of mysticism and law. These works came to acquire a quasi-Halakhic standing so that opinions found in them are not infrequently quoted as authoritative by the Codes. The works are the *Sefer Hasidim*, largely by R. Judah the Saint of Regensburg (d. 1217), and the *Rokeah* by Juda's disciple, R. Eleazar of Worms (ca. 1165–ca. 1230). The *Rokeah* has an elaborate scheme of penances,[15] unknown in the earlier literature, which, nonetheless, found their way into the Codes, albeit with reservations. The Ethical Will of R. Judah the Saint, generally printed together with the Sefer Hasidim,[16] has a number of rules contrary to those in the Talmud, e.g., that a man must not marry his niece[17] or a woman with the same name as his mother[18] and yet these rules, too, became the subject of much Halakhic discussion, becoming part of the authoritative Codes.[19]

With the rise of the Kabbalah new problems came to the fore regarding the relationship of this theosophical system to the Halakhah. From one point of view the ideas contained in the Kabbalah tended to reinforce Halakhic demands. Since, according to Kabbalistic doctrine, every one of man's deeds has a cosmic effect, influencing the "upper worlds" for good or for ill, promoting or frustrating the flow of the divine grace, the whole of the Halakhic discipline, its dos and its don'ts, become a mighty instrument of cosmic significance. As Scholem[20] puts it: "The religious Jew became a protagonist in the drama of the world; he manipulated the strings behind the scene. Or, to use a less extravagant simile, if the whole universe is an enormous complicated machine, then man is the machinist who keeps the whole going by applying a few drops of oil here and there, and at the right time. The moral substance of man's action supplies the "oil," and his existence therefore becomes of exteme significance, since it unfolds on a background of cosmic infinitude." In the Kabbalah, man's worship is, in a sense, not for man himself but for God,[21] in that it is God's will that His benevolence should depend on human deeds. Whereas the rationalists like Maimonides[22] can find no real reasons for the details of the Halakhah, why, for instance, there should be four sections in the *tefillin* rather than three or five, or why only a garment having four corners requires *tzitzit*, the Kabbalah endows every detail with its own cosmic meaning. In this way the Kabbalah strengthened the Jew's allegiance to the Halakhah.[23] Yet the very fact that there now existed a parallel syatem to the Halakhah created its own tensions.

The early Halakhists operated without any recourse to the Kabbalah. The Talmud, the source of all later Halakhah, was compiled long before the emergence of the Kabbalah as a complete system. Once the Kabbalistic doctrines had become accepted in wide circles as revealed truth, the inevitable result was a degree of conflict, even of flagrant contradiction, between the rulings of the classical Halakhah and those that stemmed from the Kabbalistic scheme. This or that action, required by the Kabbalah for the "improvement" or "rectification" *(tikkun)* of the worlds on high, might have been relegated to a secondary place or totally ignored by the traditional Halakhah. Conversely, a practice established as innocent and permissible by Halakhic reflection on the Talmudic sources, might, according to the Kabbalah, be baneful in the extreme because of its effect "up there" and was to be avoided categorically. How to decide in matters where there is conflict between the Talmud and the Codes on the one hand and the Kabbalah on the other, became itself a matter of Halakhah, part of the Halakhic process, with precise rules being laid down by the codifiers on the procedures to be adopted.[24] The general rule is that the Kabbalah is allowed to determine the rule in practice but only where the Talmud and Codes offer no guidance either because they are altogether silent on a particular question or because their view is ambiguous.[25] Furthermore, many new rules and customs based on the Kabbalah were incorporated in the Codes.

One can trace how the Kabbalah came increasingly to find its way into the Codes. One of the earliest scholars to grapple with the problem in an Halakhic manner was R. Solomon Luria (d. 1574).[26] The question put to Luria was whether the *tefillin* should be put on while sitting down, as the Kabbalah suggests, or while standing, as the traditional Halakhah seems to demand in accordance with the established custom. Luria replies that all the renowned teachers followed in their decisions only the Talmud and the Codes. He adds the novel observation that even from the Halakhic point of view the law is not in accordance with the opinions of R. Simeon b. Yohai, the author of the Zohar as the Kabbalists hold. R. David Ibn Zimra (1479–1573), on the other hand, is forthright in his partial acceptance of the Kabbalistic rules for practice:

"Wherever you find that the words of the Kabbalists disagree with the decision of the Talmud you must follow the Talmud and the Codes. But whenever, as in this instance, there is no actual disagreement, since the matter is referred to neither in the Talmud nor in the Codes, it is proper to rely on the Kabbalah."[27]

Haham Zevi Ashkenazi (1660–1718)[28] follows R. David Ibn Abi Zimra that where the Kabbalah is in conflict with the Codes we must follow the latter. Against the background of the Shabbetean movement, which relied on the Zohar for its doctrines regarding the Messiah and of which movement the Haham was a fierce opponent, this scholar remarks that the Zohar is an extremely difficult book to decipher correctly so that in any event we can never be sure that we have grasped the correct meaning of those passages which appear to be in conflict with the established Halakhah. The very influential Halakhist, Abraham Gumbiner (d. 1683) records, nonetheless, with approval the rule that where the Kabbalistic rule is stricter than the rule as found in the Codes it is advisable to follow the Kabbalah.[29]

There are numerous other examples of the influence of the Kabbalah on the practical Halakhah. R. Joseph Karo, author of the *Shulhan Arukh*, gives Halakhic status to the Zohar and other Kabbalistic works on the question of reading the Torah together with the official reader;[30] of the wearing of *tefillin* on the intermediate days festivals;[31] on not reciting the prayers behind another person;[32] that a synagogue should have twelve windows;[33] and that

248 words must make up the total of the Shema.[34] Isserles, in his glosses to the *Shulhan Arukh*, follows the Tikkuney Zohar in demanding that a wedding ring be used in the marriage ceremony[35] though the Talmud speaks of any object of value and knows nothing of a wedding ring. Obedient to his rule, mentioned previously, Abraham Gumbiner[36] quotes the practice of the great Kabbalist Isaac Luria, the Ari never to sleep during the daytime. To wear a beard and never to remove it by means permitted according to Talmudic law (i.e., by means other than with a razor) is advocated by many Halakhists on the basis of passages in the Zohar.[37] Among more recent Halakhists who rely heavily on the Zohar and the Kabbalah are Yosef Hayyim of Baghdad (1835–1909);[38] Hayyim Eleazar Shapira of Munkacs (1872–1937);[39] Malkiel Tenenbaum of Lomza (d. 1910); and Obadiah Hadayah of Jerusalem (1890–1964). On the question of wearing a beard Tenenbaum writes, after stating that according to the strict law it is permitted to remove the beard by means other than with a razor:

> However, it is stated in the Zohar that they were strict in this matter. Now the Zohar is also the work of our sages, of blessed memory, just like the whole of the Talmud, except that where the Zohar is in conflict with the Talmud we follow the Talmud, as the Codifiers rule. But where there is no explicit dissent in the Talmud we are obliged to follow the explicit statements in the Zohar. Consequently, it is a definite law *(din gamur)* that the beard must not be removed with scissors.[40]

Tenenbaum[41] although permitting artificial insemination when the donor is the husband (AIH) states, on the basic of a Zoharic passage, that it should not be done when the wife has her period. Hadayah[42] defends the Sephardi, as contrasted to the Ashkenazi, custom of wearing the *tallit katan* underneath the garmets on the basis of the Lurianic Kabbalah, and he uses Kabbalistic ideas[43] in connection with the Halakhic status of women. In the school of the Vilna gaon the view is put forward that there is never any real conflict between the Zohar and the Talmud. Thus Asher ha-Kohen[44] reports that his teacher R. Hayyim of Volozhyn, disciple of the gaon, stated, in the name of his master, that where there appears to be a conflict between the Zohar and the Talmud it is only because either one or the other has been misinterpreted. The goan therefore always follows the Talmud (i.e., because the Zohar really concurs) except for one rule where he follows the Zohar and even here it is because the Zohar is not actually in conflict with the

Talmud but simply adopts a stricter view. This attitude appears to have been consistently adopted in circles close to the gaon and continued as an established tradition. Because of this R. Y. M. Epstein of Novaradok (1828–1909) refers when he writes in his great compendium of Jewish law, *Arukh ha-Shulhan:*

> Know that in connection with *tefillin* and also with regard to other *mitzvot* there are practices based on the Kabbalah. The *Posekim* lay down this rule: Where the Gemara and the Codes are in conflict with the Zohar we follow the Talmud and the Codes. But if the Zohar adopts the stricter view anyone who so desires may follow the stricter view of the Zohar. On a matter not mentioned at all in the Gemara it is certainly right and proper to follow the Zohar, though we exercise no compulsion in this matter. So writes the *Magen Avraham* (Gumbiner) in the name of *Radbaz* (David Ibn Abi Zimra). However, I have a tradition that it is impossible for the Zohar really to be in conflict with the Gemara, except for where the matter is debated in the Gemara itself. But wherever the law is decided in the Gemara the Zohar really holds the same view and if there are passages where they did not explain the Zohar in this way they failed to hit on the true meaning so that it is necessary to adopt an interpretation of the Zohar that would bring it into line with the Gemara.[45]

From all the foregoing it can be seen how uncertain the Halakhists were on whether to allow the Kabbalah to have a voice in determining the Halakhah. With hardly any exception[46] the Halakhists adopted the attitude that the Zohar and, to a large extent, the later Kabbalah as well, were sacred. Yet they were so conscious of the conflicts between the Kabbalah and the Halakhah that they were presented with the constant dilemma of how to be loyal to the one without denigrating or diminishing the power of the other. It would be unreasonable to expect consistency in dealing with a basically insoluble problem. Wherever possible the Kabbalistic rules were acknowledged and, as we have noted, the Kabbalah eventually became one of the authoritative sources of the Halakhah. Indeed, for the Kabbalists themselves there emerged a number of Kabbalistic Codes or rules of conduct for those who wished their lives to be directed and governed by Kabbalistic doctrines. Prominent among the Codes that follow the Lurianic Kabbalah are *Peri Etz Hayyim* by Luria's chief disciple, R. Hayyim Vital; *Nagid u-Metzavveh* by the seventeeth century Kabbalist Jacob b. Zemah and the same author's *Shulhan Arukh ha-Ari;* and the nineteenth century Kabbalistic and Hasidic work *Taamey ha-Minhagim* by A. I. Sperling.[47]

Before leaving the subject of the influence of mysticism on the practical Halakhah, a phenomenon should be noted that only emerged fully in this century, namely the appeal to charismatic personalities among the Halakhists. These individuals, according to the theory current in many Orthodox circles, have the right to declare the *daat Torah*, "the opinion of the Torah,' even on political questions, without being required to substantiate their opinions by quoting for them chapter and verse in the sources. On this view the *Gadol be-Yisrael*, the great Halakhic authority, through his constant Torah studies, acquires a built-in Torah response to every situation. He is endowed with mystical power and his rulings enjoy guidance from on high as well as a guarantee that they are free from error. It is difficult to find support for any such view in the traditional Halakhic sources.[48]

In addition to its influence on the practical Halakhah, the Kabbalah brought about a remarkable transformation in the area of Torah study. For the Kabbalist the highest form of study was that of the Kabbalah, the "soul of the Torah." To be sure the traditional importance of Halakhic studies was never allowed to yield entirely to Kabbalistic studies but the Kabbalist was faced with two contending subjects with claims on his time and energy. While giving the traditional form of Halakhic studies its due, the Kabbalists still gave priority to the study of the Kabbalah. The two greatest of the sixteenth century Kabbalists in Safed, Luria and Cordovero, were themselves Halakhists of renown but it is obvious that a major portion of their comparatively short lives (Luria died at the age of thirty-eight, Cordovero at the age of forty-seven) must have been devoted to the Kabbalah. Cordovero, probably the most prolific author in the whole of Jewish history, wrote hardly anything on the Halakhah.

In this connection Hayyim Vital's remarks about his teacher, Luria, deserve to be quoted in full:

Also in connection with the study of the Halakhah in depth, together with his companions, I witnessed my master, of blessed memory, engaging in his Halakhic studies until he became weary and covered in perspiration. I asked him why he went to such trouble. He replied that profound application is essential in order to shatter the shells (*kelipot*, the demonic forces), the difficulties which inhere in every Halakhah and which prevent one from understanding that Halakhah. Consequently, it is essential at that time to go to great trouble, becoming weak in the effort. That is why the Torah is called *Tushiyah* (Isa. 28:29) because it weakens (*matteshet*) the strength of whoever engages in its study.[49] Hence it is proper to go to much trouble and to become weak through the exertions of Halakhic studies. Also with regard to dialectics *(pilpul)* and deep study of the Halakhah my master, of blessed memory, used to say that these are a preparation to the shattering of the shells, the Halakhic problems, the solutions to which cannot be attained except by means of severe application and with great intensity, as is well-known. For all that, the actual engagement in Torah study does not consist in deep study but rather by reading the Torah in the four approaches called, as is well-known, *Pardes*.[50] Just as when one desires to eat a nut he must first break the shell, so, too, one must first engage in deep study. And my master, of blessed memory, used to say that one whose mind is sufficiently clear, subtle and keen to reflect on the Halakhah for one hour or, in the majority of cases, two hours, it is certainly good that he bothers himself at first with this deep study for one or two hours, for the reason stated. But one who knows himself to be hampered in his efforts at deep study, so that for him to grasp the meaning of the Halakhah he is obliged to expend much time and effort, he does not behave correctly. He is like the man who spends all his time cracking nuts without ever eating the kernels. Far better for such a one to engage in the study of the Torah itself, namely, the laws, the Midrashim and the mysteries. My master, of blessed memory, was, however, blessed with a swift perception. In the majority of instances he would reflect on the Halakhah by means of six methods of *pilpul*, corresponding to the six days of the week, and would then reflect on the seventh way, the way of the mystery, corresponding to the Sabbath on which day there are no *kelipot*.[51]

This kind of relegation to second place of deep Halakhic study in favor of the "mysteries," the Kabbalistic doctrines, is based on the oft-quoted passage in the Zohar[52] in which the rabbinic term *gufey Torah*,[53] "bodies of the Torah," meaning the main parts of the Torah, is reinterpreted; *gufey* being taken literally as "bodies." For the Zohar the laws of the Torah, the Halakhic rules and regulations, are "bodies of the Torah." They have the same relationship to their inner, mystical meaning as body to soul. In a lengthy essay[54] Hayyim Vital went to great pains to point out that priority must be given to Kabbalistic studies over every other form of Torah study, including that of the Halakhah. Although, for the Kabbalist, Halakhic studies still belong to the study of the Torah and, in this sense, are an end in themselves, as they are in the traditional scheme, yet in another and more important sense they are, for him, only a means to an end. They are an essential preparation, but only a preparation, for the Kabbalists's supreme task in life—the study, contemplation, and practice of the Kabbalah.

NOTES

1. *Bava Metzia* 59b.
2. See supra, p. 27.
3. *Eruvin* 13b.
4. See *Tosafists, Hullin* 44a, top, and ET, vol. 5, pp. 1–4. On this question see Elon, *ha-Mishpat ha-Ivri*, chapter 7, pp. 223–51. Cf. *Bava Batra* 12a–b, where from the context it would seem that the reason why "a sage is superior to a prophet" is because the sage, too, is the recipient of a kind of inspiration, and the application to sages of the verse: "The secret of the Lord is with them that fear Him" (Ps. 22:14) in *Hagigah* 3b; *Sotah* 4b; 10a; *Sanhedrin* 48b; 106b; *Niddah* 20b.
5. On dreams and the Halakhah see infra, p. 132 and *Sanhedrin* 30a where it is explicitly ruled out that a dream can be relied on to establish the facts in a case. On this subject see J. Newman, *mi-Diney ha-Halom ba-Halakhah*. The thirteenth century Halakhist Isaiah b. Mali Di Trani, the *Rid*, after first stating that dreams are irrelevant to the Halakhah, nevertheless goes on to record that Elijah appeared to him in a dream to support a legal ruling he had given, *Teshuvot ha-Rid*, no. 112, pp. 507–12, and see the editor's remarks in his introduction, pp. 37–39.
6. *Sifra* to Lev. 27:34, *be-hukkotai*; BT, *Temurah* 16a.
7. In *Rambam la-Am* ed., vol. 18, pp. 27–28.
8. *Yad, Yesodey ha-Torah* 9:4.
9. *Or Sameah* to Maimonides in *Yad, Yesodey ha-Torah* 9:6.
10. Supra, p. 27.
11. For a very subtle, although not too convincing, analysis of the whole question see Rabbi A. I. Kook, *Etz Hadar*, no. 34 and his collection of Letters, *Iggerot ha-Rayah*, Letter 103; quoted and discussed by Zevi Kaplan, *me-Olamah shel Torah*, pp. 80–83.
12. See my translation of part of this work in *Jewish Mystical Testimonies*, pp. 73–79.
13. See Hayyim Joseph David Azulai *Shem ha-Gedolim*, s.v. *Rabbenu Yaakov he-Hasid*, pp. 62–64; H. H. Medini, *Sedey Hemed, mem*, no. 136, vol. 4, p. 252; and Reuben Margaliot's introduction to his edition of *Sheelot u-Teshuvot min ha-Shamayyim*. Medini, *Sedey Hemed, lammed*, no. 30, vol. 3, p. 282 refers to the question of whether a decision by a scholar on the point of dying is held to belong to the realm of the supernatural and therefore inadmissible. On decisions rendered by Elijah on his visits to the sages, e.g., in *Berakhot* 3a; *Eruvin* 42b; see the observations of Moses Trani, *Bet Elohim*, chapter 60; Zevi Hirsch Chajes in his note to BT, *Berakhot* beg., and in his *Torat Neviim*, chapter 3, in *Kol Kitvey*, vol. 1, pp. 17–22. Cf. Federbusch, *Hikrey Yahadut*, pp. 75–82. R. Abraham Ibn David *(Rabad)* supports his Halakhic opinions (strictures to *Yad, Lulav* 8:5) with the remark that the holy spirit has long been present in his school and *(Tumat Mishkav u-Moshav* 7:7) that God has revealed His secret to them that fear Him but these expressions may not have been intended to be taken too literally, see the discussion in Twersky, *Rabad*, pp. 291–99.
14. On the *Hasidey Ashkenaz* see Scholem, *Major Trends*, pp. 80–118.
15. *Rokeah, Hilkhot Teshuvah*, pp. 28–36. For references to this in the Halakhic literature, see, e.g., Isserles to *Shulhan Arukh, Orah Hayyim* 334:26 and *Yoreh Deah* 184:4; Landau, *Noda bi-Yhudah*, First Series, OH, no. 35; Sevin, *ha-Moadim ba-Halakha*, pp. 65–66; Scholem, *Major Trends*, pp. 104–6, who notes the aftereffects of Christian influence here; and my *Theology in the Responsa*, Index, s.v. "penance."
16. See *Sefer Hasidim*, ed. Margaliot, pp. 10–50 where the copious notes have numerous references to the Halakhic discussions around the provisions of Judah's Ethical Will.
17. No. 22.

18. No. 23.

19. See the notes of Margaliot to these two items and OP, vol. 1, pp. 100–107 and see inf. p. 233 on the hen that crows like a cock. Examples of statements in the Will of the Saint which found their way into the *Shulhan Arukh* are no. 1 that two men who were enemies during their lifetime must not be buried in adjacent graves, YD 362:6; no. 2, that a grave must be left open overnight, YD 339:1, *Rama*; no. 35, that the same person should not be honored with Sandek duty for more than one son of the same man, *Rama*, YD 265:11; no. 41, that geese should not be killed in the months of Tevet and Shevat unless the *shohet* eats the heart or liver, *Rama*, YD 11:4. On this latter see Shapira, *Darkhey Teshuvah*, ad loc., note 46, that according to some authorities this smacks of "the ways of the Amorites" but where it is the custom it should nonetheless be followed.

20. Scholem, *Major Trends*, pp. 29–30.

21. See Isaiah Horowitz, *Shelah, Asarah Maamarot, Maamar* 4, p. 38b.

22. *Guide*, III, 26.

23. See Scholem, *Major Trends*

24. See Medini, *Sedey Hemed, Kelaley ha-Posekim*, no. 2:12–13, vol. 9, pp. 130–31 and ET, vol. 9, pp. 244–45.

25. See ET, the examples given *inf.* and the remarks of *Hatam Sofer* and *Minhat Eleazar* quoted supra, pp. 13–14.

26. *Teshuvot Rashal*, no. 98.

27. *Teshuvot Radbaz*, no. 1,111.

28. *Haham Tzevi*, no. 36.

29. To SA, OH 25:1, note 20.

30. *Bet Yosef* to OH 141.

31. *Bet Yosef* to OH 31 and SA, OH 31:2, from which *Rama* dissents. Cf. Zimmels, *Ashkenazim and Sephardim*, pp. 30–31 and 113 and Hayyim Eleazar Shapira, *Ot Hayyim ve-Shalom* to OH 31.

32. SA, OH 90:22.

33. SA, OH 90:4.

34. SA, OH 61:3.

35. *Tikkuney Zohar* IV, *Rama* to SA, EH 27:1. The gaonim refer to the practice of using a wedding ring by the Jews of Palestine, i.e., under Roman influence: see Lewin, *Otzar ha-Geonim, Kiddushin.* p. 9 and Lewin's notes.

36. OH 4, note 15.

37. Removing the beard by means other than with a razor is permitted in the Talmud, *Makkot* 21a and SA, YD 181:10, but the Zohar III, 130b frowns on this, see BH to YD181 note 5 and PT note 6 that Luria, the Ari, never trimmed his beard. Cf. Menaham Mendel of Lubavitch, *Tzemah Tzedek*, YD, no. 93 and Shapira, *Darkhey Teshuvah* 181 note 17. For a full but one-sided treatment of the question see the massive work of Moshe Weiner, *Hadrat Panim—Zakan*, pp. 518–613.

38. In his Responsa collection *Rav Pealim*, which also contains sections on purely Kabbalistic topics. See my article "The Responsa of Rabbi Joseph Hayyim of Baghdad" and my *Theology in the Responsa*, pp. 261–74.

39. In many of the Responsa in his *Minhat Eleazar*, see e.g., vol. II, no. 48 and sup. p. 27.

40. *Divrey Malkiel*, part 5, no. 81.

41. Ibid., part 4, no. 107.

42. *Yaskil Avdi*, vol. 5, OH, no. 3.

43. Ibid., vol. 5, HM, no. 1.

44. *Orhot Hayyim, maamarim*, no. 15. R. Zevi Hirsch of Zhydachow, *Sur me-Ra*, pp. 51b–53a, similarly argues that it is impossible for the Zohar and the Talmud really to be in

conflict and that "the true recipients of an appearance of Elijah such as the authors of the Zohar, Nahmanides, his colleagues, the Ari and the Baal Shem Tov, never tolerated even the slightest degree of departure from the Gemara." R. Yitzhak Eisik of Komarno, *Shulhan ha-Tahor* 61:1, p. 75, similarly remarks, "There is never found any matter, great or small, in the Gemara that is in contradiction with the Zohar." R. Zevi Hirsch refers, in passing, to this idea as found, for the first time, in Delmedigo's *Matzref le-Hokhmah* but does not supply the reference. It is in chapter 18 of the work, pp. 84–85.

45. OH 25:29.

46. E.g., Eleazar Fleckeles, *Teshuvah me-Ahavah*, no. 26, where the authority of the Zohar is totally rejected in Fleckeles' opposition to Shabbeteanism.

47. On these works see the remarks of Scholem, *Kabbalah*, p. 194.

48. See, e.g., Moses Feinstein, *Iggerot Mosheh*, YD, vol. 2, no. 5; I. Domb, *The Transformation*, pp. 73–74; Alan J. Yuter, "Mehitzah, Midrash and Modernity."

49. *Sanhedrin* 26b.

50. *Pardes* = *peshat* ("plain meaning"); *remez* ("allegorical meaning"); *derush* ("homiletical meaning"); *sod* ("secret meaning," here the Kabbalah).

51. *Shaar ha-Mitzvot, va-ethanan*, p. 79. On this theme in the writings of Hayyim Vital see the analysis by J. M. Hillel, *Ahavat Shalom*, pp. 173–94.

52. Zohar III, 152a. For further Kabbalistic sources with the same import see Delmedigo, *Matzref le-Hokhmah*, chapter 3, pp. 17a–19a.

53. See *Avot* 3:18.

54. Introduction to *Shaar ha-Hakdamot*, printed in editions of the *Etz Hayyim* of Vital as an Introduction to the work, see, e.g., the edition of Tel-Aviv, 1960, vol. 1, pp. 5–24.

[6]

Hasidism and Halakhah

Insofar as Hasidism is strongly influenced by the Kabbalah, the relationship of this movement to the Halakhah resembles very closely that of the Lurianic Kabbalists. But Hasidism also developed its own Halakhic way. Certain aspects of Hasidic life came to have at least a quasi-Halakhic status for the Hasidism. In spite of the fact that there is a strong element of quietism in early Hasidism and that the pioneers of the movement stressed the need for spontaneity in religious observance and were somewhat suspicious of excessive scrupulousness, there developed rules and regulations as to how the Hasid is expected to conduct his life.[1] The truth of the matter is that considerable tensions are present in Hasidism between the need for an ever fresh response and the demands of the law, which the Hasidism, as loyal and faithful Jews, were bound to obey. It is also true that Hasidism, like other movements of revolt against the established order, eventually fostered its own orthodoxies.

Aaron Wertheim, in his pioneering work on the subject, *Halakhot ve-Halikhot ba-Hasidut* ("Laws and Ways in Hasidism"), has culled an impressive number of practices that are peculiar to Hasidism, which, for the Hasidim, have the binding force of law. Wertheim has been severely criticized by A. Rubenstein[2] for his generalizations and for his failure adequately to trace the history of the practices he examines. Some of the practices Wertheim records as peculiar to Hasidism really antedate the rise of the movement and some of them, confession to the Zaddik, for instance, are followed only by small groups among the Hasidim.[3] For all the substance in

Rubinstein's critique, Wertheim deserves much credit for calling attention to the existence of a real Hasidic Halakhah.

Certain practices, known long before the rise of Hasidism, were adopted by all Hasidim as their own, both by investing these with special Hasidic meaning and by placing much emphasis on them as an integral part of the religious life of the Hasid. Regular immersion in the ritual bath *(mikveh)* was a sine qua non for all Hasidim. Especially after marital relations, it was held to be incumbent upon the Hasid to immerse himself in the *mikveh* before he could recite his prayers or study the Torah. The Talmud speaks of this immersion as *tevilat Ezra*, attributing it to the Court of Ezra after the return from the Babylonian exile.[4] But the Talmud eventually rules[5] that the obligation has been canceled because the view is followed that "words of Torah cannot suffer contamination."[6] Although the *Shulhan Arukh*[7] records this as the final ruling, there are opinions among the Halakhists that it is still advisable to keep the law of immersion, which, it is said, is a powerful aid to the correct mood for prayer.[8] The Kabbalists[9] were particularly insistent on the value of *tevilat Ezra*. For the Hasidim *tevilat Ezra* is not an optional act of special piety but a definite obligation.[10] Furthermore the Hasidim held that immersion is not only a means of removing contamination but is an act whereby purity is positively cultivated and increased with the result that frequent immersions were held to be of high religious significance, a form of worship and an end in itself.[11] Attributed to the Baal Shem Tov, the founder of the Hasidic movement, are the special "intentions" *(kavvanot)* that should be in the mind at the time of immersion.[12] Similarly, although the Halakhists debate whether or not *tefillin* are to be worn on the intermediate days of festivals, the Hasidim adopt the view that *tefillin* must in no circumstances be worn on these days because there is support for this view in the Zohar.[13] The question of whether or not the two pairs of *tefillin*, those of Rashi and Rabbenu Tam, should be worn is debated in the Halakhic sources but here, again, the Hasidim follow the view that they should be worn because to wear both pairs is described as "an act of special piety" *(hasidut)*[14] and because the wearing of the two pairs of *tefillin* is referred to in the Zohar. Although the obligation to wear a girdle during prayer is referred to in the Talmud,[15] the Tosafists[16] argue that this is no longer necessary since in Western lands trousers are worn and these serve the same purpose. But the Hasidim see in the wearing of the girdle, which separates the higher from the lower part of the body, an essential prerequisite for prayer.[17] The recital of *le-shem yihud* ("For the sake of the unification of the Holy One, blessed be He, and His Shekhinah") before carrying out a *mitzvah* was introduced by the Kabbalists but was eagerly adopted by the Hasidim with their special emphasis on devotion and religious awareness. This Hasidic adoption of the practice led to the famous attack on the Hasidim by R. Ezekiel Landau of Prague.[18]

In addition to adopting older practices to suit their own purposes, the Hasidim developed some entirely new regulations, those governing the relationship between the Zaddik, the charismatic leader, and his followers, the Hasidim. Naturally, the Hasidim claim to find support for the doctrine of the Zaddik in the classical sources of Judaism but, historically considered, the whole doctrine is a Hasidic innovation.[19] There are certainly no rules governing this relationship found anywhere outside the Hasidic movement; the Hasidim find support for their rules in this matter only by reinterpreting rules about the respect due to scholars so as to apply to the Zaddik and his followers.[20] According to these new rules the Hasid is obliged to journey periodically to his master even if this involves defiance of his parents; the fifth commandment, it is held, being inoperative in such circumstances.[21] The Hasid presents his petition to the Zaddik who will then pray on his behalf. The petition is presented in writing in the form of a *kvittel*, "slip of paper," on which the name of the petitioner and that of his mother are recorded together with his particular request; which may be, for example, for recovery from illness, for sustenance, for children, or for assiduity in the study of the Torah. A sum of money (*pidyon neffesh*, "soul redemption") is given to the administrators of the Zaddik's Court on behalf of the Zaddik and there are precise rules as to how all this should be carried out.[22] At the communal meal the Zaddik first tastes a little of each dish and the remainder (*shirayyim*) is distributed among the Hasidim in the belief that the food, first tasted by the Zaddik, is beneficial to both body and soul.[23] There are even procedures on how the telling of Hasidic tales about the great masters should be conducted, to retell the mighty deeds of the saints being held to be of great religious value.[24] The *mofet*, the miracle performed by the Zaddik, also finds it echoes in the Halakhic literature. In the last century, R. Solomon Kluger of Brody attacked bitterly another rabbi who permitted a *kvittel* to be written on the Sabbath on behalf of a person who was dangerously ill. This rabbi had so much confidence in the Zaddik's healing powers that he ruled that the writing of the *kvittel* came under the heading of saving life, which takes precedence over Sabbath observance.[25]

In connection with Halakhic studies the older conflicts found among the Kabbalists existed for Hasidim as a movement that accepted the Kabbalah as revealed truth. The Hasidim, also considered the questions of how much time to devote to the Kabbalah and how much to the Halakhah, and which studies were the most significant. Not all Hasidic masters encouraged their followers to study the Kabbalah but even for those Hasidim who did not study the Kabbalah there were the classical Hasidic works to be studied—the Hasidic "Torah," as this was called. Furthermore, in Hasidism, there was severe tension between the need in Halakhic studies for total application and concentration on the extremely difficult topics of study and the Hasidic ideal of *devekut*, "attachment,"[26] according to which God was to be in the mind at all times. How could the devout Zaddik or Hasid possibly have God in mind while he was delving deeply into the complicated debates and discussions that Halakhic study demands? Again, Hasidism stressed the idea of *Torah lishmah*,[27] "Torah for its own sake," which rabbinic term Hasidism understood as Torah study for the sake of God, i.e., as a devotional exercise. This interpretation of the rabbinic ideal and its adoption by the Hasidim tended to relegate to second place the role of the intellect and to the denigration by the Hasidim of the non-Hasidic scholars as careerists, at the worst, or, even at the best, with being in love with the workings of their own minds, the Torah they studied possessing no power to heal the soul and promote holy living. The Mitnaggedim, the opponents of Hasidism, were quick to retaliate by dubbing the Hasidim ignoramuses.[28] But caution must be exercised here. Although from the little we know of the historical Baal Shem Tov he does not seem to have been anything like a distinguished Halakhist,[29] the Hasidic movement did produce an astonishingly large number of Halakhists, some of them of the very first rank, who evidently found no difficulty in combining the most rigorous application to the Halakhah with the Hasidic ideals. The famed Hasidic master and distinguished Halakhist, referred to in a previous chapter, Abraham Bornstein of Sochachov, could write in the introduction to his *Egley Tal:*

I have heard it said by some folk who stray far from the reasonable method of Torah study, that one who, when he studies and introduces novel theories, rejoices and takes pleasure in his studies, does not study

the Torah for its own sake. Such a one, they say, is not to be compared
to one who simply studies without any pleasure in his studies, engaging
in these only because they constitute a *mitzvah*. One who takes delight
in his studies, on the other hand, introduces an element of self-interest
in his learning. Verily this is a notorious error. On the contrary, it
belongs to the main *mitzvah* of Torah study that one should enjoy it and
take delight in it. For then the Torah becomes absorbed in the blood
and by taking delight in the Torah such a scholar becomes attached
(davuk) to the Torah.

This author's use of the word *davuk* here is intentional. Whatever
the attitude of the early masters was on the alleged incompatibility
of the *devekut* ideal with the profound scholarly application that is
attended by the joy of discovery and intellectual comprehension,[30]
by the late nineteenth century, among some Hasidic teachers at
least,[31] the wheel had come round full circle. The traditional ideal
of Halakhic study has been reintroduced, albeit with the mystical
rider that *devekut* is still the ultimate aim but is to be achieved
through mystical unification with the Torah.

The existence of Hasidic Codes of law is a feature to be noted
when discussing the relationship between Hasidism and Halakhah.
The early Hasidic master R. Shneor Zalman of Liady (1747–1813)
compiled, at the behest of his master, R. Dov Baer, the maggid of
Meseritch (d. 1773), the great organizing genius of the movement
and chief disciple of the Baal Shem Tov, a special *Shulhan Arukh*,
now known as *Shulhan Arukh ha-Rav*.[32] This work is distinguished
for its lucid style and skillful arrangement of the material. It has
become an authoritative Halakhic work even for those with no
connection with the Hasidic movement. On the whole, the rulings
in the *Shulhan Arukh ha-Rav* follow the traditional Halakhic approach, giving weight to Kabbalistic and Hasidic views only where
this is allowed by the kind of development in the Halakhah itself
that we have noted in the previous chapter.[33] But in his *Siddur*,
R. Shneor Zalman does give preference to the Kabbalah and to
Hasidic practices and he is reported as advising his immediate followers to prefer the rulings given in the *Siddur* where these are in
conflict with the *Shulhan Arukh*.[34] The Hasidim belonging to the
school of *Habad* (Lubavitch), of which R. Shneor Zalman was the
founder, always follow, the rulings given in the *Siddur*. A collection
of *Habad* rules and regulations, in Halakhic form, has been published with the title *Sefer ha-Minhagim*.[35]

A less well-known *Shulhan Arukh* by a Hasidic master is the
Shulhan ha-Tahor of R. Yitzhak Eisik of Komarno (1806–1874). Here

the Kabbalistic and Hasidic rules and customs are given total preference, occasionally in a quite striking, not to say provocative, manner. At the same time, this master stressed the importance of Halakhic studies in the traditional manner, sternly rebuking those who are lax in their Halakhic studies out of fear that their application to these might interfere with the ideal of Torah for its own sake.[36]

The Hasidic masters of the Munkacs dynasty combined in their writings and in their practical rabbinic careers the two disciplines of Halakhah and Kabbalah. R. Zevi Hirsh Shapira (1850–1913), the second leader of Munkscs, was the author of *Beer Lahai Roe* on the *Tikkuney Zohar* as well as of the Halakhic compendum *Darkhey Teshuvah* on *Shulhan Arukh Yoreh Deah*. The latter work has won wide acceptance as the standard textbook on the subjects treated in this section of the *Shulhan Arukh* for non-Hasidic as well as for Hasidic rabbis. The *Darkhey Teshuvah* not infrequently invokes the opinions of the Kabbalah and Hasidism.[37] R. Zevi Hirsch's son and successor, R. Hayyim Eleazar Shapira (1872–1937), wrote a number of Kabbalistic-Hasidic works as well as works of Halakhah. In his Halakhic works, *Nimmukey Orah Hayyim* and *Ot Hayyim ve-Shalom*, as well as in his Responsa collection, *Minhat Eleazar*, R. Hayyim Eleazar consistently refers to the Kabbalah and to Hasidic thought and practice.[38]

Finally, it should be noted that with the proliferation of Hasidic dynasties in the nineteenth century, each group developed its own particular customs and practices, that were followed strictly by the Hasidim belonging to that group. For this purpose detailed accounts of the pattern of life adopted by the masters were drawn up, among which are Y. M. Gold's *Darkhey Hayyim ve-Shalom* on the regimen of R. Hayyim Eleazar Shapira of Munkacs; J. D. Weissberg, *Otzar ha-Hayyim* on R. Hayyim Halberstam of Zans (1793–1876);[39] and Zevi Hirsch Rosenbaum, *Raza de-Uvda* on R. Eliezer Zeev of Chryzanow (d. 1944).

NOTES

1. See Rivka Schatz Uffenheimer, *ha-Hasidut ke-Mistika*, pp. 163f. This tension existed particularly in the matter of prayer at the correct times as laid down in the Talmud and the Codes. Although otherwise obedient to the *Shulhan Arukh* and the traditional Halakhah, many Hasidim could not allow themselves to be tied down to the fixed times of prayer, see my *Hasidic Prayer*, chapter 4, pp. 46–53. An oft-quoted Hasidic *bon mot* is that whereas the Hasidim fear God the Mitnaggedim fear the *Shulhan Arukh*.

2. See Rubinstein's lengthy review of Wertheim in *Kiryat Sefer*.

3. See Wertheim, sup., p. 22. As Rubinstein (p. 284) rightly notes, the practice of confession to the Zaddik is peculiar to R. Nahman of Bratzlav. Cf. A. Rapaport Albert, "Confession in the Circle of R. Nahman of Bratzlav." In fairness to Wertheim, he himself (p. 63) admits that some of the Hasidic practices he lists, such as immersion, are pre-Hasidic.

4. *Bava Kama* 82a.

5. *Berakhot* 22a.

6. *Berakhot ibid.*

7. OH 88.

8. See ET, vol. 4, pp. 141–48.

9. See e.g., Elijah de Vidas, *Reshit Hokhmah*, *Shaar ha-Ahavah*, Chapter 11.

10. See R. Yitzhak Eisik of Komarno, *Shulhan ha-Tahor*, 88, p. 110; Wertheim, in kiryat sefer, pp. 66–68; and R. Kalonymos Kalman Epstein, *Maor va-Shemesh*, *emor*, beg., who states that the reason why the Shabbateans pursued their evil way was because they studied the Kabbalah without observing *tevilat Ezra* and so were led into error and distortion.

11. Immersion on the eve of Sabbaths and festivals was first advocated by the Lurian Kabbalists, see Hayyim Vital's *Peri Etz Hayyim*, *Shaar ha-Shabbat*, chapters 3 and 4, and this was followed by the Hasidim, see Wertheim, pp. 144–46. The purpose of this immersion, according to Luria, is to distinquish the Sabbath from the week days and Luria urges another immersion on Sabbath morning because the day of the Sabbath possesses a higher degree of holiness than the preceding night. R. Yitzhak Eisik of Komarno (*Shulhan ha-Tahor* 260:7) writes, "It is a *mitzvah* and an obligation, arising out of the words of our master, the *Ari*, and of the words of the holy Zohar, to have immersion in a river or a *mikveh* every Sabbath eve. And a man is obliged, according to our master, the *Ari*,to have immersion on the Sabbath day before the prayers. One who goes against his words, unless he cannot help it, may be dubbed a sinner for all his (Luria's) words, even the least of them, are that which he had neither from an angel nor from a Seraph but from the mouth of the Holy One, blessed be He, Himself." Cf. Sperling, *Taamey ha Minhagim*, no. 249, p. 120.

12. For these intentions see R. Shneor Zalman's *Seder Tefillot*, ed. New York, 1965, pp. 629–30. They are found for the first time in Menaham Mendel of Vitebsk's *Peri ha-Aretz*, *lekh lekha*. This work was first published in Kopust in the year 1811 so there is room for doubt as to whether the attribution to the Baal Shem Tov is correct.

13. On the wearing of *teffilin* on *Hol ha-Moed* see *Menahot* 36b and *Tosafists* ad loc s.v. *yatzeu shabbatot*. The *Tur* (OH 31) states that they should be worn but without the benediction being recited, but he adds that his father, the *Rosh*, did recite the benediction. Karo (*Bet Yoesef* to *Tur* 31) cites the Zohar that they should not be worn and rules accordingly in SA, OH 31:2 but Isserles notes that the Ashkenazi custom is to wear them. Cf. Zimmels, *Ashkenazim and Sephardim*, pp. 30–31 and p. 113. On the Hasidic decision not to wear teffilin, on the basis of the Kabbalah, see Wertheim, *Halakhah*, pp. 79–81 and Hayyim Eleazar Shapira, *Ot Hayyim ve-Shalom* to OH 31.

14. Wertheim, *Halakhah*, pp. 77–79.

15. *Shabbat* 10a.

16. *Tosafists* to *Shabbat* ad loc., s.v. terihuta.

17. Wertheim, op. cit., p. 73.

18. Wertheim, pp. 71–72; cf. my *Hasidic Prayer*, chapter 12, pp. 140–53.

19. See Dressner, *The Zaddik* and my lecture, "The Doctrine of the Zaddik."

20. See Perl: *Megalle Temirin*, p. 2b.

21. See the letter on this theme by R. Shneor Zalman of Liady in Hillmann, *Iggerot Baal ha-Tanya*, Letter 32, pp. 48–49. Cf. the Responsum of Simhah Bunen Sofer, *Teshuvot Shevet Sofer*, OH, no. 17 on the Hasid leaving his home to be with his rebbe on the festivals and thus

neglecting his family obligations. Sofer quotes the rabbinic saying (*Rosh ha-Shanah* 16b) that a man is obliged to visit his teacher on a festival. Although Sofer did not belong to the Hasidic movement, he concludes, in defense of the Hasidic practice, that a man with a great reputation for sanctity (i.e., the Hasidic Zaddik) qualifies as a teacher for this purpose.

22. Werthheim, *in Kiryat Sefer*, pp. 161–64.

23. Ibid., pp. 167–69.

24. Ibid., pp. 169–70.

25. See Kahana, *Mehkarim*, pp. 410–11.

26. See Scholem's article *"Devekut"* and Uffenheimer, *ha-Hasidut ke-Mistika*, chapter 12, pp. 157–67.

27. The main aim of R. Hayyim of Volozhyn's *Nefesh ha-Hayyim* is to demonstrate that the Rabbinic doctrine of *Torah lishmah* does not refer to *devekut* but means "for the sake of the Torah." See especially Norman Lamm, *Torah Lishmah* for an analysis of R. Hayyim's view.

28. This contemporary dismissal of Hasidic claims to be learned in the Torah is repeated often in the anti-Hasidic polemics collected by Wilensky in his *Hasidim u-Mitnaggedim*. In this connection reference should be made to the famous letter of Ezekiel Paneth (1783–1845) defending his teacher, the Hasidic Zaddik, R. Menahem Mendel of Rymanov (d. 1815). Paneth was not himself a Hasidic rabbi but was a strong admirer of Hasidism and his son became the founder of the Hasidic dynasty of Dej. (The letter has been reprinted many times, e.g., in Alfasi, *Toledot ha-Hasidut*, pp. 148–54). After protesting that his teacher was a great Halakhist, Paneth continues, "Apart from all this, where do we find in the whole of the Torah that it is a *mitzvah* to be a great (Halakhic) sage and keen-witted (in Halakhic debate)? The only obligation is to fulfill the verse: "Thou shalt meditate therein day and night" (Jos. 1:8), not to be idle from words of Torah even for a moment. . . . Nevertheless, it is necessary for one to be numbered among the sages of his generation for an ignorant man cannot be a Hasid. But the main thing is for the fear of God to have priority over learning. I write this only to remove the misconception from your heart. With regard to our master, may his light shine, both (i.e., the fear of God and profound learning) are found in him."

29. See Scholem, *"Demuto ha-Historit shel Rabbi Yisrael Baal Shem Tov."*

30. See Schatz Uffenheimer, *ha-Hasidut ke Mistika*, chapter 12, pp. 157–67.

31. But see Rosenbaum's Introduction to his *Raza de-Uvda*, where he complains that the Hasidim today (the work was published in 1976) are too enamored of the Halakhic learning of the non-Hasidic Halakhists, failing to appreciate that only the kind of Torah study and the fear of God belonging to the way of the Baal Shem Tov will bring the redemption nigh: "Not as those in error who are envious of ordinary scholars with the result that in the Yeshivot of the Hasidim there has been a daily influx of lecturers and teachers of those who do not conduct themselves in the tried Hasidic way."

32. The latest edition of this work in four volumes, New York, 1976, contains many additional notes and comments by the leaders of the *Habad*-Lubavitch movement.

33. See Tchernowitz, *Toledot ha-Posekim*, vol. 3, pp. 261–73.

34. See the prefatory note to *Shulhan Arukh ha-Rav* in the New York edition, vol. 1, pp. iii, where it is stated that in this edition the rules (*pesakim*) as given in the *Siddur* are also recorded at the end of each section "for in many instances he decided otherwise than in the *Shulhan Arukh* and one should follow the *Siddur* because the *Siddur* was compiled at a later date." Cf. Tchernowitz, op. cit. who calls attention to the fact that in R. Shneor Zalman's projected second edition (*Mahadura Tinyana*) of his *Shulhan Arukh* (part of which is printed in the New York and other editions) he does rely very heavily on the Kabbalah and Hasidic practice.

35. Typical of the booklet is the section (pp. 90–93) on the rules for the celebration of the nineteenth of Kislev (*yat Kislev*), the anniversary of R. Shneor Zalman's release from prison where he had been imprisoned by the Russian authorities on a charge of treason instigated by

the *Mitnaggedim*. Also to be noted are the rules for celebrating a birthday and a housewarming (p. 81) both of which find only the scantiest support in the traditional Halakhic sources.

36. See his remarks in his Commentary to *Avot:Notzer Hesed*, to *Avot* 1:12.

37. See, e.g., his remarks on table rapping, 179 note 6, and see sup., p. 80.

38. See sup., p. 75.

39. See, e.g., pp. 157–58 on the Hasidic observance of Yahrzeit; pp. 193–94 on the Kabbalistic prohibition of studying Scripture at night; pp. 295–97 on staying in the *sukkah* even when it is raining hard; pp. 177–78 on the *kvittel*; pp. 245–48 on *shirayyim*.

7

Responses to the Gentile World

The Talmudic rules on Jewish–Gentile relationships were formulated and developed against a pagan background. Tractate *Avodah Zarah* is largely concerned with the attempt at keeping Jews as
far apart as possible from idolators and idolatrous worship. But
even in such an environment and with such motivation, the Talmudic Halakhah was bound to see a measure of compromise. Total
seclusion of Jews from the surrounding culture in Palestine and
Babylon was simply not possible even if it might have been considered desirable. Rabban Gamaliel, for instance, is said to have
defended his habit of bathing in a bathhouse in which there was a
statue of Aphrodite.[1] Strong efforts were made by the Jewish
teachers to avoid undue strife and conflict with their pagan neighbors[2] and there were numerous references in the Talmud to positive friendships between the rabbis and the pagan kings, noblemen,
sages, and ordinary folk. Even if some of this material is legendary,
the fact that it is recorded in the Talmud is itself indicative of the
actual situation. In Babylon, the Amora Samuel was responsible
for the dictum: "The law of the government is law" (*dina de-
malkhuta dina*), a dictum that was to have a lasting effect in later
generations on the adjustment of Jewish communities to their non-
Jewish surroundings.[3] Marcus Jastrow has rightly noted how the
researches of a host of modern scholars into the Talmudic literature
"is enough to prove the marvellous familiarity of the Rabbis with
the events, institutions, and views of life of the world outside and
around their own peculiar civilisation."[4] "What is more," Jastrow
continues, "we have been familiarized with the philosophical im-

91

partiality and sober superiority with which they appreciated what
was laudable and reprehended what was objectionable in the intellectual and moral condition of the 'nations of the world,' as they
called the gentile world around them; kings and empires, nations
and governments, public entertainments and social habits, they
reviewed through the spy-glass of pure monotheism and stern morality." All this certainly suggests that the Halakhic problem, even
in the Talmudic age, was rather more complicated than one that
could be solved by any neat declaration in terms of "us" and
"them."

The post-Talmudic Halakhah on Jewish-Gentile relationships
was developed against either an Islamic or a Christian background.
On both theoretical and practical grounds a reappraisal of the Talmudic attitudes and rules was required in order to cope with the
new situation. First, there was the question of whether Christianity
and Islam were to be considered idolatrous faiths, both being obviously closer to Judaism than any of the pagan religions. The question was bound to be asked, did a devout Christian or Muslim
offend against one of "the seven precepts of the sons of Noah,"
namely, the prohibition of idolatry? Furthermore, the problem
arose and became very acute of the legal status of a Jewish convert
to one of these two faiths. In Talmudic times there was no such
thing as conversion to a rival religion. The Jew who indulged in the
worship of the pagan gods did not become "converted" to paganism. He was treated very severely in Talmudic law as a *mumar*
("apostate") to idolatry and, according to some opinions, he was
given the status of a non-Jew for certain purposes, e.g., any act of
shehitah carried out by him would be invalid even if the act were
carried out in the prescribed manner.[5] But he was still a Jew for
other purposes of the law so that a marriage he contracted with a
Jewish woman was held to be valid.[6] A bill of divorce—the *get*—
would be required before the woman could marry another man. In
the post-Talmudic period, when conversion to another religion—
Christianity or Islam—became a distinct possibility the question
arose whether such a conversion did sever all the apostate's connection with Judaism so that he now had the status of a non-Jew for all
purposes.

With regard to Islam, Maimonides rules that this is not an idolatrous religion, the Muslims being pure monotheists.[7] This idea is
carried to the extent that if a Jew is compelled to embrace Islam
under the threat of death he is not obliged to suffer martyrdom.[8]
Later authorities, notably R. Yom Tov Ishbili, the *Ritba*, and

R. David Ibn Abi Zimra, the *Radbaz*, disagreed.[9] These authorities argued that whereas, as Maimonides states, Islam is not to be construed as an idolatrous faith so far as non-Jews are concerned (the Gentile Muslim is an observer of the seven Noahide laws and so qualifies as one of "the righteous among the nations of the world"), yet, when a Jew is compelled to embrace Islam this involves his rejection of the Torah of Moses and he must be ready to lay down his life rather than be guilty of such an act of disloyalty. This is as cogent an illustration as any of how theological considerations influenced the Halakhah. As early as the Gaonic period some of the laws regarding the use of Gentile wine were relaxed on the grounds that these laws were only to be applied in all their severity to the wine of idolators not to the wine of Muslims.[10] Some of the geonim did hold that a conversion to Islam severed all the apostate's connection with Judaism. He was no longer to be treated as a Jew for any purposes of the law. For instance, if a man who died without issue had a brother who had been converted to Islam, the widow could marry another without having to undergo *halitzah* in order to release her from the levirate bond. It was as if the dead man had no surviving brother. Other gaonim disagreed with this ruling, holding that the Talmudic rules still applied. The convert to Islam was to be treated no differently from the Talmudic *mumar* who, for the purposes of divorce and release from the levirate bond, does not lose his Jewish status.[11]

With regard to Christianity the matter was rather more complicated because of the Christian doctrine of the Trinity but more especially because of the doctrine of the Incarnation.[12] All the early Halakhists who lived in Christian lands held Christianity to be a form of idolatry. On grounds of expediency, however, some of the more burdensome of the Talmudic rules governing the relationship between Jews and idolators were relaxed, the change in the law being casuistically defended in such a way as to suggest that no abolition of the Talmudic rules was being proposed only that these laws did not apply to the new situation.[13] It was in the thirteenth century that Menahem Meiri developed the idea, and he was the first great Halakhist so to do, that Christians were not to be treated as idolators, with the consequence that many of the Talmudic rules and regulations were not to be applied to those whom Meiri calls "nations governed by religion."[14] Meiri created a third Halakhic category—unknown in any of the earlier sources available to us—between Jews and idolators. Meiri, embarrassed by the Talmudic ruling[15] that it is forbidden to have any business dealings with

Gentiles on Sunday ("the first day of the week") because of the Notzerim, is obliged to make the fanciful suggestion that the term does not denote Christians (the Nazarenes, of Nazareth) but the Babylonians (the successors of Nebuchadnezzar) and that the "first day" is not prohibited because of the Christian Sunday but because sun worship is alleged to have taken place on the first day of the new week.[16] Yet, even for Meiri, there was no total abolition of all the Talmudic rules. The gaonic principle, applied originally to Islam, of relaxation in the matter of Gentile wine was accepted so far as the use of wine manufactured by Christians was concerned (i.e., the wine could be sold)[17] but the drinking of the wine was forbidden. No Halakhist ever thought of applying Maimonides' ruling about Islam to Christianity and, of course, Jews throughout the ages were ready to suffer martyrdom rather than embrace Christianity.[18]

Among all the Halakhists the Talmudic teachings regarding *hukkot ha-goy*, "copying Gentile practices," are applied to the practices of both Muslims and Christians, though there is considerable debate on how they are to be applied or, rather, as to which practices fall into this category and which do not.

The expression *hukkot ha-goy* occurs in Leviticus 20:23: 'You shall not follow the practices of the nations *(be-hukkot ha-goy)* that I am driving out before you. For it is because they did all these things that I abhorred them.' A second verse (Lev. 18:3) with the same import is "You shall not copy the practices of the land of Egypt where you dwelt,' or of the land of Canaan to which I am leading you; nor shall you follow their laws *(u-ve-hukkotehem lo telekhu)*." In the context "the practices of the nations" *(hukkot ha-goy)* refer to the sexual offenses, listed in the chapter, of which the Canaanites were guilty, and the other verse refers to these same offenses of which both the Canaanites and the Egyptians were guilty. The "nation" *(ha-goy)*, in the singular, in the one verse is the Canaanite nation and "their laws," in the plural, and in the other verse it means the "laws" (i.e., the norms, the mores) followed by the Canaanites and the Egyptians. Thus the original meaning of *hukkot ha-goy* is sexual immorality practiced by the heathen nations.

In the rabbinic view, however, *hukkot ha-goy* is extended to practices over and above the specific offenses listed in the Leviticus chapter, the term now being made to cover either practices that have idolatrous or immoral associations (for which the term generally used is *hukkot ha-goy*) or superstitious and magical practices (for which the term generally used is *darkhey ha-emori*, "the ways of the Amorites"). This is stated in the following rabbinic passages.

The *Sifra* [19] to Leviticus remarks, "'You shall not copy the practices of the land of Egypt or of the land of Canaan.' One might have supposed this to mean that you should not erect buildings (like theirs) or plant trees (like theirs); therefore Scripture goes on to say: "nor shall you follow their laws.' I refer only to laws laid down by them and their fathers and grandfathers. What did they do? A man married a man and a woman a woman. A man married a woman and her daughter and a woman was married to two men. Therefore the verse concludes: 'nor shall you follow their laws'." In this passage the verse is understood according to its plain meaning, as referring to sexual offenses, but with the elaborations stated. However, in another passage in the *Sifra*[20] it is stated, "'Nor shall you follow their laws.' What has Scripture left out without stating it (explicitly)? It has already been said, "Let no one be found among you who consigns his son and daughter to the fire, or who is an augur . . ." (Deut. 18:10). Why, then, does it say: "nor shall you follow their laws"? The meaning is you must not follow their practices, the things laid down for them, for example, theaters, circuses, and arenas. R. Meir says, These are the ways of the Amorites listed by the Sages. R. Judah b. Beterah says, It means that you must not stab (an animal to death?); that you must not grow a lock of hair; and you must not trim the front of the hair. You might perhaps say, they have their laws *(hukkim)* but we do not, therefore Scripture says: "My laws (alone) shall you observe" (Lev. 18:4). But the evil inclination may still hope to have (unworthy) thoughts, saying that their laws are superior to ours. Consequently, Scripture says: "Observe them faithfully, for that will be proof of your wisdom and discernment" (Deut. 4:6)." Clearly, here the *Sifra* is determined to apply the law to practices not mentioned in Scripture but which were prevalent in Roman Palestine in the first two centuries of the present era and which were held to be "un-Jewish" in spirit. The Tannaitic Halakhah is obliged to take note of the contemporary situation and to legislate accordingly. The reference to theaters, circuses, and arenas is especially noteworthy as well as the remarks about their laws being superior. The problem of the Jew in an environment different from his own is generally posed by the subconscious feeling that he is perhaps confronted with a culture that is superior to his own. The new Halakhic rules must deal with this tempting by the "evil inclination."

The Mishnah rules, "Men may go out (into the public domain on the Sabbath) with a locust's egg or a jackal's tooth or with a nail (from the gallows of) a person who has been crucified."[21] So says R. Meir. But the Sages say, "This is forbidden even on week-days because it is of the ways of the Amorites." In another Mishnah it is stated that the afterbirth of an animal should not be buried at the crossroads or hung upon a tree because of the ways of the Amorites.[22] The seventh and eighth chapters of *Tosefta Shabbat* list the practices forbidden because of the ways of the Amorites.

The Mishnah records a debate between R. Judah and the Sages.[23] According to the Sages, a person condemned to be executed by the sword has to be decapitated with a sword while he stands upright "as the Roman government does." R. Judah objects that this is a degrading mode of execution. R. Judah therefore holds that the condemned man's head is placed on a block and chopped off with an ax. To this the sages retort, "No death is more degrading than this." The Babylonian Talmud[24] to this Mishnah quotes a Baraita in which it is stated that R. Judah admits that the method he advocates is more degrading but he holds that it is still preferable to the method adopted by the Roman government since Scriptures says, "nor shall you follow their laws." Defending the opinion of the sages, the Talmud remarks that since execution by the sword is mentioned in the Torah "we do not learn it from them," i.e., the prohibition of *hukkot ha-goy* only applies to practices *derived* from pagans and not to practices that Jews know from their own sources but which were incidentally also adopted by pagans. On this view Jews were not obliged to give up any of their own practices merely because pagans have also adopted these practices. In proof for this distinction another Baraita is quoted in which it is stated that funeral pyres may be kindled in honor of departed kings and it is not forbidden because of the ways of the Amorites. This can only be because the practice of kindling funeral pyres for kings is mentioned in Scripture (Jer. 34:5) and is not derived from the pagans, even though the pagans, too, follow this custom. (It might be noted that in this passage the terms *hukkot ha-goy* and *darkhey ha-emori* are used interchangeably).

In tractate *Avodah Zarah*[25] a different reason is given for why the kindling of funeral pyres does not offend against the rule of *hukkot ha-goy*. The reason given here is that the kindling is done in order to pay homage to the dead king and is not a *hukkah*, i.e., a pagan practice. The first passage, in tractate *Sanhedrin*, would, then, appear to be in conflict with the passage in *Avodah Zarah* (a conflict much discussed by the medieval Halakhists). According to the *Sanhedrin* passage that funeral pyres are a *hukkah*, even a *hukkah* is permitted if it is not derived from "them" but found in Scripture. But according to the *Avodah Zarah* passage, only those practices are permitted that are not peculiar to the pagans, that do not fall under the heading of *hukkah*. The implication is that *hukkah* is forbidden even if it is also found in Scripture and is not derived from "them." On the other hand, in one respect, the passage in *Avodah Zarah* is more lenient in that if a practice is a matter of honor and the like (i.e., if it is a reasonable practice and not a *hukkah*) it is not forbidden at all.[26] A further ground for leniency in the matter is the statement of Abbaye and Rava that any practice which has a remedial purpose is not forbidden because of the ways of the Amorites.[27]

From all the foregoing it is clear that the Talmudic sources are open to a strict as well as a lenient interpretation. When we find, among the post-Talmudic Halakhists, some favoring the more lenient interpretation, and others the stricter, it is fairly safe to conclude that they have arrived at their actual decisions, based on their interpretations of the sources, on sociological as well as on purely Halakhic grounds. Where the surrounding culture presented little danger to Judaism or where practices adopted from the non-Jewish environment had become too deeply rooted among the people to be easily eradicated, a lenient interpretation of the Halakhah becomes evident. Where the danger was real or where practices could more easily be eradicated, the stricter interpretation tends to prevail. It is surely no accident that the whole question of *hukkot ha-goy* looms very large among the Halakhists and tends to be interpreted in terms of the utmost strictness in the nineteenth century, the century that witnessed the Emancipation of the Jews in Europe and the rise of the Reform movement.[28]

R. Eliezer of Metz (ca. 1115–1198)[29] lays down a firm rule that the concept *hukkot ha-goy* only applies to the *religious* practices of Gentiles and that one should not add to those practices mentioned as forbidden by the sages merely because such additions might seem plausible. R. Isaac b. Sheshet Perfet (1326–1408)[30] of Algiers (the *Ribash*) holds that the concept *hukkot ha-goy* only applies to practices for which there is no reason (i.e., taboos and the like). If we are to ban certain practices, *Ribash* argues, simply because they are carried out by Gentiles we ought to ban such things as funeral orations. R. Joseph Colon (d. 1480), the *Maharik*, was asked whether a Jewish doctor in Islamic lands may wear the special cloak worn as a distinguishing mark of apparel by doctors in these lands.[31] *Maharik* permits it on the grounds that the cloak is simply a mark of distinction and of office. He is followed by Isserles, who writes, in his gloss to the *Shulhan Arukh* where the prohibition is recorded of wearing Gentile garments:

> All these things are only forbidden when the idolators do them for the sake of loose conduct, for example, when it is their intention to wear red garments, the garments of noblemen, and the same applies to immodest dress. The rule also applies to any practice which has become a custom of theirs without any reason so that one must fear that the practice belongs to the ways of the Amorites and that there inheres in it a trace of idolatry inherited from their ancestors. But it does not apply to a practice the advantage of which is evident. For example, if it is their habit for every skilled physician to wear a special cloak to denote that he is proficient in his craft, a Jewish physician is permitted to wear such a cloak.[32]

For the reasons mentioned earlier, some of the nineteenth-century Halakhists extended the scope of *hukkot ha-goy* in the most extreme way. The principle was invoked against the use of an organ in the synagogue;[33] against having the head uncovered;[34] against adopting Gentile names;[35] against hunting animals for sport;[36] having weddings in the synagogue;[37] the wearing of canonicals by the rabbi and cantor;[38] not growing a beard;[39] and even against the wearing of a tie.[40]

The opposite tendency—to allow the law to be consciously influenced by the practices of the Gentile world—is also to be observed among the Halakhists. It is held to be wrong to perform certain acts, innocent in themselves, if the result will be to bring Judaism into disrepute by appearing to suggest that the moral and religious standards that Judaism sets for its adherents are inferior to those set by other religions. The principle is found in the Talmud. A convert to Judaism is treated by the law as one who is newly-born. Strictly speaking, then, the convert should be allowed to marry his mother or his sister if they, too, have been converted. But such marriages are forbidden by rabbinic law. If they were permitted it would be said that the converts have come from a higher degree of sanctity to a lower degree, i.e., higher standards of morality were demanded of them before their conversion.[41] The same principle is behind the comment of the *Sefer Hasidim:*[42] "If there is something the Gentiles hold to be forbidden but which is not forbidden to Jews, it is wrong for Jews to eat that thing lest the name of Heaven be profaned. If, for example, A Gentile witnessed an act of bestiality committed by another Gentile and he informed his fellow Gentiles that they must not eat the meat of that animal and the meat was then sold to Jews, no Jew must eat thereof." The post-Talmudic tractate *Kutim*[43] derives this principle from the verse: "For thou *art* an holy people" (Deut. 7:6), which is interpreted to mean: "Allow no other people to be holier than you."

The ban against polygamy, attributed to R. Gershom of Mayyence around the year 1000, but which is probably of a slightly later date, was accepted in Ashkenazi but not in Sephardi or Oriental communities. The ban can be said to have developed naturally out of Jewish law.[44] There is evidence in support of the view that whereas polygamy was legitimate in Talmudic law it was not at all widely practiced in Talmudic times.[45] But the influence of the Christian background was almost certainly the cause of the official ban against polygamy in, and for the Jews of, Christian Europe. In an extreme statement of opposition to the ban, the fiery, independent Halakhist, R. Jacob Emden (1695–1776) can write:[46] "Actually it is correct to refuse to forbid a Jew from marrying two wives (at the same time) for to do so would be an offense against "you shall not follow their laws," except that the offense is only by omission (i.e., the offense involves no positive act of copying Gentile practices). Also because of the danger to Jews who reside among Gentiles (for whom polygamy is a grave sin) if they marry two wives, Rabbenu Gershom was obliged to promulgate the ban, although such a ban is, in reality, illegal." Emden refers specifically to the "danger" but it may well be that the Christian influence made itself felt because of the "higher standards" principle to which we have referred, especially since the tendency of the Talmud is, in any event, to uphold monogamy as the Jewish ideal.[47]

Finally, an example may be quoted from Talmudic times in which an ancient law relating to the acceptance of converts from certain nations was set aside. According to the rabbinic interpretation of "An Ammonite or a Moabite shall not enter into the assembly of the Lord" (Deut. 23:4) a member of one of these groups may not marry a Jewess even after his conversion to Judaism. The law does not apply to female converts from these nations. Ruth was a Moabite woman.[48] The Mishnah[49] tells of one Judah, a convert from Ammon who came before Rabban Gamaliel and R. Joshua. R. Joshua permitted him to marry a Jewess on the grounds that Sennacharib "confused all the nations" i.e., by moving them around as part of his political strategy so that the original nations no longer reside in their land and it can be assumed that anyone who claims to belong to a particular nation does not really belong. As the Talmud elaborates it, the majority principle is invoked and the probability is that any particular person does not belong to the forbidden nations. This rule is recorded in the *Shulhan Arukh*[50] which adds an Edomite, forbidden otherwise (Deut. 23:8–9) in the first three generations. An Egyptian is also forbidden until the third generation (Deut. 23:8–9) but here the *Shulhan Arukh*[51] records a debate between Maimonides and Asher b. Yehiel, the *Rosh*, the latter holding that the Egyptians remained unaffected by Sennacherib's policies. R. Jacob Emden[52] argues that a convert from Rome or from Italy generally should be forbidden since the Talmud identifies Rome with Edom and they are also not subject to the changes in the law. Emden advises an Italian convert to marry a female convert to Judaism to whom the males of the forbidden nations are permitted. The identification of Rome with Edom is, in reality, a late Rabbinic polemic.[53]

NOTES

1. *Mishnah Avodah Zarah* 3:4.

2. See *Mishnah Gittin* 5:9 and *Gittin* 61a; *Bava Metzia* 32b; *Avodah Zarah* 26a.

3. *Nedarim* 28a; *Gittin* 10b; *Bava Kama* 113a; *Bava Batra* 54b; 55a, see Shiloh, *Dina de-Malkhuta Dina*.

4. M. Jastrow, *Dictionary*, preface, p. XIII.

5. *Hullin* 5a.

6. *Yevamot* 47b.

7. *Teshuvot ha-Rambam*, ed. Blau, no. 448, vol. 2, pp. 725–28; *Yad, Maakhalot Asurot* 11:7.

8. *Iggeret ha-Shemad*, in *Iggerot ha-Rambam, Rambam la-Am*, vol. 20, pp. 29–86.

9. Responsa, *Radbaz*, 1163 (92).

10. See Maimonides, *Yad, Maakhalot Asurot* 11:7.

11. See B. M. Lewin, *Otzar ha-Geonim*, vol. 7, *Yevanot*, pp. 34–37.

12. On the attitudes of the Jewish authorities to Christianity see Katz, *Exclusiveness and Tolerance*; Federbusch, "The Attitude of Judaism to Christianity" in his *Hikrey Yahadut*, pp. 217–36; Jacob Schachter, *Sefer Mishli*, p. 231 note 3; Lampronti, *Pahad Yitzhak*, s.v. *goy*, vol. II, p. 7a; Rivkes, *Beer ha-Golah* to HM 525 note 9; Lerner, *Hadar ha-Karmel*, vol. II, nos. 44 and 45, pp. 33f. Maimonides, *Yad, Akum* 9:5, states that Christians (correct reading *edomim*, not, as current editions, *kenaaanim*) are idolators; cf. his Commentary to *Mishnah Avodah Zarah* 1:3 in uncensored editions. The oft-quoted statement that according to the Halakhah a Christian is not an idolator because a Noahide is not prohibited from *shittuf* ("association"), see ET, vol. 3, s.v. *ben noah*, p. 350 note 72, is based on a misunderstanding, see Katz, *Exclusiveness and Tolerance*, p. 163. The Talmud (*Sanhedrin* 63b; *Berkhorot* 2b) states that it is forbidden to be in a business partnership with an idolator because in a dispute an oath may be required and the idolator will take the oath by his gods. It is forbidden for a Jew to bring this about even indirectly. But the *Tosafists* ad loc note that the Middle Ages Jews have

disregarded this prohibition because when Christians take the oath they take it in the name of God. Even though, at the same time they associate the name of God with the name of Jesus, Gentiles are not forbidden *shittuf*. The meaning here is that a Gentile, a Noahide, is not forbidden from associating *(shittuf)*, *when taking an oath*, the name of another being together with that of God. The *Tosafists* do not mean that Christianity is not idolatry. (Cf. Reuben Margaliot, *Margaliot ha-Yam*, vol. 2, p. 22a note 8 for further sources on *shittuf*). But later commentators took the term *shittuf* in its connotation in medieval Jewish philosophy, i.e., in the sense of *belief* in God and an *associate* or *associates*, hence they concluded that according to the *Tosafists* Christianity is not idolatry. Thus there was born the notion that a Noahide is not forbidden to associate *(shittuf)* belief in God with belief in another. See R. Nissim of Gerona, the *Ran*, to Alfasi, end of first chapter of *Avodah Zarah*, that the *Tosafists* refer only to *shittuf* when a Gentile takes on oath, i.e., he is forbidden, as a Noahide, to be a Christian but there is no special prohibition, over and above this, in his taking a Christian oath. Isserles to SA, OH 156; states, "Some authorities are lenient in the matter of a Jew becoming a business partner with a Gentile nowadays, for their intention (when they take the oath) is to the Creator of heaven and earth." Cf. Isserles to SA, YD 147:3. R. Ezekiel Landau (*Noda Biyhudah*, Second Series, YD, end of no. 148) points out the error in the conventional understanding of *Tosafists* and claims that Isserles, too, only refers to the prohibition of a Gentile taking an oath. But Eisenstadt, *Pithey Teshuvah*, YD 147 note 2, while agreeing with Landau's basic analysis, cannot agree that this is Isserles' intention since Isserles in his *Darkhey Moshe* to *Tur* YD 151 applies the maxim regarding *shittuf* to laws other than those about taking an oath and hence clearly understands the term *shittuf* in its theological sense. Zevi Hirsch Shapira (*Darkhey Teshuvah* 147 note 12) quotes an authority who holds that even if the principle of *shittuf* is accepted in the theological sense, it only applies when a Gentile believes in One Supreme Being, not where the belief is in all three persons of the Trinity as equals. Cf. ET loc. cit. where this opinion is quoted in the name of Jacob Emden. Shapira, *Darkhey Teshuvah* 150 note 2 remarks that even according to the lenient authorities it is not permitted for a Jew to enter a church building but he states this in a somewhat uncategorical way. On the question of selling a building to be used for Christian worship see the discussion in Braun, *Shearin ha-Meztuyyanim ba-Halakhah*, 167 note 7, vol. 4, pp. 159–60. The Vilna gaon (*Biur ha-Gra* to YD 147 note 3) rules that althought it is not permitted to use the term *Christ*, it is permitted to speak of Jesus and that in the Talmud Jesus is referred to by name.

13. See Tosafists to *Avodah Zarah* 2a s.v. *asur*.

14. E.g., *Bet ha-Behirah* to *Bava Kama*, 37b, p. 122 and to 1113v, p. 530. See Katz *Exclusiveness and Tolerance*, chapter V, pp. 114–28 and for further passages see Meiri quoted there. Cf. Meiri's remarks in his introduction to his *Hibbur ha-Teshuvah* (p. 2) that he was moved to compose the work because of the taunts of Christians that Jews do not attach much significance to the concept of repentance.

15. *Taanit* 21b.

16. *Bet ha-Behirah* to *Avodah Zarah* beg.

17. See Isserles to SA, YD 123:1. For the sale of crosses by Jews see Isserles to YD 141:1 who permits it on the grounds that these are not objects that are themselves worshiped but are decorative (in name of *Mordekhai* but not found in current editions of the *Mordekhai*). On the basis of this R. Joseph Saul Nathansohn (*Shoel u-Meshiv*, I, 3, no. 71) permits a Jew to wear a medal in the form of a cross. Cf. JE, vol. IV, s.v. "Cross," pp. 368–69.

18. Katz, "Though He Sinned, He remains an Israelite" gives a very interesting account of how an Aggadic saying came to assume Halakhic status in the school of Rashi. The saying "Though he sinned, he remains an Israelite" (*Sanhedrin* 44a) is Aggadic and simply means that even when an Israelite commits a sin he does not thereby forfeit his high rank of "Israelite." There is no reference at all to apostasy in this passage. Rashi and his school,

however,used this saying to deny that a Jew can ever be converted to another faith. He remains a Jew and is obliged to keep all the *mitzvot*. As Katz says, "The emphasis on an apostate remaining a Jew constituted a weapon employed by the Jewish community to counter Christian propaganda which insinuated that the Jew achieves, through baptism, a superior religious status, releasing him from any obligation to the law." For Rashi's view see Elfenbein, *Teshuvot Rashi*, nos. 171, 173, and 175. For the question of whether an apostate can help form a *minyan* for prayer see Medini, *Sedey Hemed*, vol. IV, no. 156, pp. 267–71, who decides in the negative as he does on whether a donation by him to the synagogue should be accepted, quoting Isserles and *Baer Hetev* to SA, OH 154:11.

19. *Sifra*, ed. Weiss, p. 85b.

20. Ibid., p. 86a, see Weiss's note on p. 85b that this is an addition to the *Sifra*.

21. *Shabbat* 6:10.

22. *Hullin* 4:7.

23. *Sanhedrin* 7:3.

24. Ibid., 52b.

25. *Avodah Zarah* 11a.

26. See *Tosafists* to *Sanhedrin* 52b s.v. *ela* and to *Avodah Zarah* 11a s.v. *ve-i* and *Ran* to *Avodah Zarah* 11a.

27. *Shabbat* 67a and *Hullin* 77b. Cf. Maimonides, *Guide*, 3, 37.

28. See, e.g., the famous counterblast to Reform; *Eleh Divrey ha-Berit* and H. J. Zimmels, "*Inyaney Hukkot ha-Goyyim.*"

29. *Sefer Yereim*, no. 313. See Kahana's article, "*Ha-Yahadut ve-ha-Sevivah ha-lo-Yehudit*" in his *Mehkarim*, pp. 306–316.

30. *Teshuvot Ribash*, no. 158.

31. *Teshuvot Maharik*, *Shoresh* 88. On the basis of this Obadiah Yosef (*Yabia Omer*, 4, YD, No. 27) permits mourners to wear black.

32. Isserles to YD 178:1.

33. *Eleh Divrey ha-Berit*, cf. Berliner, *Ketavim Nivharim*, vol. I, pp. 171–87. Cf. Walkin, *Zekan Aharon*, I, no. 6, addressed to London in 1927, forbidding on grounds of *hukkot ha-goy*: (a) a mixed choir in the synagogue; (b) the use of the organ in the synagogue, even on weekdays; and (c) the *bat mitzvah* service. Walkin adds the further *motif* that it is aping the Reformers!

34. Following *Turey Zahaz* to CH 8 note 8, and 61 note 1. But see Hoffmann, *Melammed le-Hoil*, II, no. 56, that in Germany for the head to be uncovered was not held to be *hukkot ha-goy*. Cf. Responsa *Hatam Sofer*, HM, *Hashmatot*, No. 191. See *Hiddushey Hatam Sofer* to *Nedarim* 30b that this is why single girls do not wear head covering in the synagogue, because women do cover their heads in church! See Waldinberg: *Tzitz Eliezer*, vol. 12, no. 13.

35. *Teshuvot Maharam Shik*, YD, No. 169.

36. Lampronti, *Pshad Yitzhak*, s.v. *tzedah*.

37. R. Meir Arik (1855–1926) of Tarnow, Responsa, *Imrey Yosher*, part II, no. 178. Cf. Medini, *Sedey Hemed*, vol. 7, pp. 5–13 and Herzog, *Hekhal Yitzhak*, EH, II, p. 103.

38. See Shapira, *Darkhey Teshuvah* 178:18 but see the interesting Responsum of Hodayya, *Yaskil Addi*, vol. 5, no. 15, that it is only forbidden if the canonicals are the same as those of the Christian priests, otherwise how can the rabbis in Turkey and other countries wear the headgear of the sheiks?

39. See Weiner, *Hadrat Panim*, pp. 438–61.

40. See Y. M. Gold, *Darkhey Hayyim vee-Shalom*, no. 878, p. 322.

41. *Yevamot* 22a. Cf. Maimonides, *Yad*, *Mamrim* 5:11 that for the same reason it is forbidden for a proselyte to insult his non-Jewish father. Cf. Walkin, *Zakan Aharon*, II, No. 87, that

possibly for the same reason a proselyte must recite the *kaddish* for his Gentile father, though he concludes that there is no actual obligation.

42. *Sefer Hasidim* ed. Margaliot, 829, and see Margaliot's note referring to tractate *Kutim*.

43. *Kutim*, chapter 1. For a further example see Gumbiner, *Magen Avraham* 244 note 7 that although it is permitted to allow a Gentile contractor to build a synagogue on the Sabbath it should not be done because of *hillul ha-shem* since Gentiles do not allow work of this kind to be done on Sunday.

44. See the sources quoted in OP, vol. I, pp. 14–87 and for the historical background Falk, *Jewish Matrimonial Law*, pp. 13–34.

45. See S. Lowy in JJS, IX, pp. 115–38 and the other sources quoted by Falk, *Jewish Matrimonial Law*, p. 1, note 1.

46. *Sheilot Yaavetz*, vol. II, no. 15.

47. See Falk's study.

48. JT *Yevamot* 8:3 (9c).

49. *Yadaim* 4:4; *Berakhot* 28a. A similar development in the law is the following. The Talmud (*Sukkah* 51b) quotes, "You shall henceforth return no more this way" (Deut. 17:16) to show that the Alexandrian Jews sinned by returning to live in Egypt. Maimonides, *Yad, Melakhim* 5:7–8, records as a definite rule that it is forbidden for Jews to reside permanently in Egypt, and yet Maimonides himself lived there and, of course, there were many important Jewish communities and famous rabbis in Egypt. R. David Ibn Abi Zimra, who was the head of Egyptian Jewry for many years, defends his practice (*Radbaz* to *Yad*, ad loc.) on the grounds that it is only forbidden to go there initially for the purpose of settling there permanently, but once people have gone there for a temporary stay they may later change their minds and settle there. For a survey of the Halakhah on this matter see J. David Bleich, "Settlement in Egypt."

50. EH 4:10.

51. EH 4:10.

52. *Sheilat Yaavetz*, Part I, no. 46, see OP. vol. I, p. 63, note 24:2.

53. See Gerson D. Cohen: "Esau as a Symbol in Early Medieval Thought."

8

Halakhah and Sectarianism

Our concern in this chapter is not so much with the differences in matters of Halakhah between the rabbis and their followers on the one hand and the various sectarians on the other, as it is with the responses to the sectarians' challenges that are given Halakhic expression, i.e., with new rules and regulations introduced for the purpose of combating sectarian ideas and practices.

The three groups toward which there is an explicit Halakhic reaction in the Talmudic period are the Samaritans,[1] the Sadducees,[2] and the Minim.[3] There is a vast literature on the origins and identity of these three groups but our concern here is with the Halakhic reaction to these groups as stated in the Talmudic literature; in other words, not with what actually happened in the pre-Talmudic era but with how the rabbis of the Talmud considered the problem, giving it explicit expression in new laws. The extent to which Talmudic statements about the origins and identity of these groups reflect historical reality is, therefore, irrelevant to our discussion, although it does make the inquiry extremely difficult. Adding to the difficulty is the notorious exercise of censorship, external and internal, on the Talmudic sources so that terms like *Kutim* ("Samaritans"), *Tzaddukim* ("Sadducees"), and *Minim* ("Sectarians") are not infrequently substitutions in our texts for earlier, more correct readings. In addition to the examination of Halakhic attitudes to these groups in Talmudic times, something must be said also with regard to the similar question of Halakhic attitudes toward the Temple of Onias.[4]

From the complete absence of any reference in the Talmudic

sources to any attempt by a follower of the rabbis to become a Samaritan or vice versa, it would seem to follow that the terms Israelites and *Kutim* are ethnic groupings. Consequently, the rabbis were chiefly concerned with establishing the Halakhic status of the Samaritans vis-à-vis the Jews. The account, accepted naturally by the rabbis as historical, in chapter 17 of the second book of Kings, tells how the Assyrian king, after his conquest of Samaria, settled there peoples from Kutah (hence the name *Kutim*) and from other places. These people at first, did not "fear the Lord" but when He sent lions to plague them they eventually served the Lord but they also served other gods, their native ones. The question of Samaritan status in the Talmudic Halakhah is thus made to depend on whether the *Kutim* were "true converts" *(gerey emet)* to Judaism or "lion converts" *(gerey arayot)*. The question is debated by the Rabbis and there is considerable ambiguity in the matter.[5] The Mishnah[6] makes a clear distinction between a *Kuti* and a *nokhri* ("heathen"). The former is treated as a Jew and can help make up the quorum of three for grace after meals *(zimmun)*. Similarly, another Mishnah[7] states that if one gives wheat that has been tithed to a *Kuti* to grind, one need have no fear that he has substituted for it untithed wheat, whereas the doubt that he has substituted it for untithed wheat remains if the untithed wheat is given to a *nokhri* to grind. On the other hand, a Mishnah states that R. Eliezer says, "Whoever eats bread of a Samaritan it is as if he had eaten swine's flesh."[8] A Baraita[9] states that eating the meat of an animal killed by a *Kuti* is permitted since the *Kuti* has the status of a Jew. There is a discussion in the Talmud[10] as to whether the Samaritans are to be trusted in such matters, one opinion holding that those *mitzvot* accepted as binding by the Samaritans are observed by them with greater care and scrupulousness than Jews exhibit in carrying out the same *mitzvot*. Nevertheless, the Talmud[11] concludes that in the days of R. Ammi and R. Assi (third century in Palestine) they decreed that the Samaritans are to be treated as heathens in every respect *(goyyim gemurim)*.

The post-Talmudic minor tractate *Kutim* records tha various Talmudic statements and debates regarding the Samaritans. The problem in post-Talmudic times was largely academic. Maimonides[12] ruled that the *Kutim* "were kept afar" *(nitrahaku)* and that any animal killed by them is forbidden. The *Shulhan Arukh*[13] also rules, "A *Kuti*, nowadays *(ha-iddanah)*,[14] has the status of an idolator." The question arises, however, whether this refers only to reliance on the *Kuti* in connection with *shehitah* and so forth. From

the Talmud[15] it would appear that for purposes of betrothal the
Samaritans are to be treated as Jews, so that if a Samaritan betrothed a Jewish woman she would require a *get* from him before
she could marry another; this is the ruling of the *Shulhan Arukh*.[16]
The Samaritan is held here to have the status of an apostate Jew.
Other authorities hold, however, that when the Talmud eventually
rules that the Samaritans are to be treated as heathens *in every
respect*, this applies even where it would result in leniency; for
example, if a Samaritan killed an animal it would be treated as if the
animal had not had *shehitah* so that it would be permitted to kill the
animal's young on the same day without offending against the law
which prohibits the *shehitah* of an animal and its young on the same
day (Lev. 22:28). On this view the ruling of the *Shulhan Arukh* that a
get is required is only by rabbinic law and was introduced as a
special measure because of the severity of the sin of adultery.[17]
Although this problem is now a practical one, since there are
Samaritans in the State of Israel, the rabbis are opposed to marriages between Jews and Samaritans. However, the Samaritans
themselves recognize the validity of a marriage between a Samaritan and a Jewess provided she agrees to follow the Samaritan traditions. The certificate of marriage issued for this purpose by the
Samaritan high priest is recognized by the Israeli minister of the
interior.[18]

According to the Tannaitic accounts, the Pharisees debated with
the Sadducees on various Halakhic matters.[19] A number of Phar-
isaic laws are said to have been intended for the express purpose of
refuting the Sadducees. Thus it is said[20] that in the Temple, at the
close of each benediction, they used to say, "For everlasting" (*min
ha-olam*, literally used here as "for all the time of the world") but
when the Sadducees[21] had corruptly taught that there is only one
world (i.e., they rejected the doctrine of the World to Come) it was
ordained that they should say, "From everlasting to everlasting"
(i.e., "for this world and for the World to Come"). The Sadducees
also ordained that when a man greets his fellow he should use God's
name, even though this is normally forbidden. The meaning of this
may be because the Sadducees also denied God's providence as
extending to each individual so that it was necessary to say, "God
be with thee" in order to refute them.[22]

In a Mishnah[23] it is said that the elders of the court, before the
high priest began his service on Yom Kippur, would make him take
a solemn oath that he would carry out the service (since no one else
was there to observe it) in the manner as understood by the

Pharisees and he would change nothing. This was because the Sadducees interpreted the verses regarding the order of the day (Lev. 16) to mean that the incense was to be placed on the fire-pan before the high priest entered the Holy of Holies whereas the Pharisees held that the incense was to be placed on the fire-pan in the Holy of Holies. Suspecting the high priest of having Sadducean leanings, the elders of the court were obliged to administer the solemn oath.

According to the Sadducees, the red heifer (Num. 19) could not be prepared by one who had become contaminated, even if he had subsequently undergone immersion, until the man had first waited until the sun had gone down—a *tevul yom*, "one who had immersed himself that same day" (see Lev. 22:6–7). The Mishnah[24] states that the elders would intentionally cause the priest who burned the heifer to become contaminated and he would then immerse himself, proceeding then to burn the heifer. This was done "because of the Sadducees so that they should not say, "It is to be carried out by those for whom the sun has set." On the other hand, precisely because of the need to demonstrate the error of the Sadducees, which was done by contaminating the priest,[25] compensation was found in the rules according to which excessive care against contamination had otherwise to be taken in the preparations of the red heifer.[26]

According to further report,[27] Rabban Johanan b. Zakkai defeated the Sadducees in his debate with them over the laws of inheritance. The Sadducees held that if a man dies leaving a daughter and the daughter of his son, both have equal status in the sharing of the estate, whereas according to the Pharisees the granddaughter alone inherits the estate, taking the place of her father, the son of the deceased. To mark the victory over the Sadducees a special festival was introduced on the twenty-fourth of Tevet, the day of the victory.

However influential the Sadducees may have been in Temple times, their party vanished from Jewish life so that even the Talmudic reports about the Sadducees and a similar group, the Boethusians, were only of academic interest since no actual Sadducees were in existence to present a challenge to the Rabbis. (The ideas of the Sadducess did enjoy a subterranean life for centuries, some of them emerging later among the Kaarites). It is thus at first glance curious to find Maimonides[28] stating that the Sadducees "nowadays" have the status of the Samaritans before the latter were declared to be as heathens so that if a *get* is signed by two witnesses, one of whom is a Sadducee, the *get* is valid. The *Shulḥan Arukh*[29] also records that if it is seen that the *sheḥitah* has been carried out properly, it is valid if performed by a Sadducee. The difficulty is resolved when it is appreciated that, as we shall see, Maimonides identifies the Sadducees with the Karaites. The *Shulḥan Arukh*, in all probability, is simply quoting Maimonides but it is also possible that the *Shulḥan Arukh* uses the term *Tzadduki* not in its original meaning of "Sadducee" but of heretics *like the Sadducees* who deny the Oral Torah. Maimonides, when speaking of the *epikorsin* ("heretics") states explicitly "those who, like Tzaddok and Boethus, deny the teachings of the expounders of the Oral Torah."[30] The "Sadducee" is no longer the member of a particular group but is a "type." He is a heretic who denies the Oral tradition.

The term *Min* (plural *Minim*) is of uncertain etymology possibly from the word *min*, "species." In any event, the references to *Minim* in the Talmudic literature are to various sectarians who hold heretical views. Frequently, the reference is to Jews who entertain dualistic theories or to Gnostics or Christians. Here, too, a number of rules have been introduced with the explicit aim of refuting the doctrines and practices of the sectarians. The best-known of these laws is the introduction of a special benediction into the *Amidah* in which the *Minim* were cursed, obviously with the intention of preventing the *Minim* from participating in Jewish worship.[31]

The Mishnah[32] states that in the Temple the priests would recite the Ten Commandments together with the Shema. The Talmud[33] reports that attempts were made at various times, both in Palestine and Babylon, to introduce the Temple practice into the daily recital, i.e., to make it a rule that together with the Shema the Ten Commandments should be recited daily by all. The sages, however, refused to allow this "because of the complaints of the *Minim*" (*taarumot ha-minim*). The Jerusalem Talmud[34] uses the expression "the claims of the *Minim*" (*taanot ha-minim*) and explains this as "that they (the *Minim*) should not say, these (the Ten Commandments) alone were given to Moses at Sinai." Although the Talmud only states that "they wished to introduce it," the strong term "they canceled it" or "abolished it" might suggest that in the much earlier period it was the practice of Jews to recite the Decalogue daily outside the Temple when they recited the Shema. The Nash Papyrus, dating from the second century *b.c.e.*, contains both the Shema and the Decalogue. In any event, the practice, which otherwise would have been considered admirable, was objected to because, it is said, the practice might have given encouragement to those sectarians who held that only a part of the Torah was given by God to Moses and not the whole of the Torah.

As a result of the Talmudic statement, the Decalogue was never subsequently recited together with the Shema. It is, however, the universal custom for the congregation to rise and to remain on their feet when the Ten Commandments are read from the Scroll in the synagogue service. We learn from the Responsa of Maimonides[35] that in the twelfth century, opinions were divided on whether this practice of standing is correct. Those who opposed the practice, and Maimonides sides with them, argued, on the basis of the Talmudic passage, that it is forbidden to give any such special prominence to the Decalogue. As late as the eighteenth century, voices were still raised against this practice of standing during the reading of the Decalogue but it was argued, and eventually accepted, that the rabbinic opposition did not apply in this instance since the Decalogue is read as part of the whole Torah and not in isolation. This is quite different from a recital of the Decalogue on its own accompanied only by the Shema.[26] On this matter the *Shulhan Arukh*[37] further states that is is a good practice to recite the Decalogue daily in private but it is forbidden to recite it as an act of public worship. Abraham Gumbiner[38] adds the comment "especially, nowadays, and, therefore, it is not to be written out on a special tablet for congregational reading." The custom of having a replica of the two tablets of stone containing the Decalogue on the walls of the synagogue or over the Ark has become very widespread. Nevertheless, R. Hayyim Eleazar Shapira of Munkacs[39] states that his father, R. Zevi Hirsch, author of *Darkhey Teshuvah*, expressed strong disapproval of this custom, persuading many synagogues which had such a replica to remove it. Shapira adds, "It is proper to take care in this matter and great is the stumbling it brings about, whether it is in the synagogues of the innovators (*hamithadeshim*, i.e., the Reformers, the Neologs, as they were called in Hungary), in the synagogues of those who incline slightly in the direction of the innovators (probably referring to the status-quo congregations), or in the Batey Midrash of the Hasidim in many places. We are obliged to protest and to prevent it being done." A disciple of Shapira,[40] after quoting him with approval, adds that the practice of having the Decalogue over the Ark can be defended on the grounds that the Ark contains the Scrolls of the Torah so that the arguments of the *Minim* are automatically refuted. It is wrong, however, he says, to have the Decalogue on any other part of the synagogue and *a fortiori* to have it as an engraving on a watch chain and the like.

A number of rules with the aim of opposing *darkhey ha-minim*, "the ways of the sectarians," are stated in the Mishnah. Thus it is stated[41] that one who refuses to wear colored garments while he acts as a prayer leader may not officiate in this capacity even in white garments, and one who declares that he will not officiate while wearing sandals may not officiate even when he is barefoot. Although the term *darkhey ha-minim* is not used in this section of the Mishnah, it is used in the next, so that it is highly probable, as the Talmud observes, that this is also on the same grounds.[42] As the Talmud puts it, "We suspect such a person of having had *minut* injected into him." It is far from clear what type of heresy is referred to here. What is the significance of the insistence that only white should be worn and that the feet should not be shod during prayer? Various suggestions have been put forward, such as that these are pagan customs (Rashi), that white garments were worn by the Essenes (although there is no explicit reference to the Essenes anywhere in the Talmudic literature), or that these are magical practices or the practices of the Judaeo-Christians.[43] The same Mishnah states that one who placed his *tefillin* on his forehead or upon the palm of his hand follows *derekh ha-minut*, "the way of heresy," obviously because the *Minim* interpreted literally the verse "And thou shalt bind them for a sign upon thine hand, and they shall be for frontlets between thine eyes" (Deut. 6:8), whereas in the rabbinic tradition the *tefillin* of the head are worn on the head itself, not the forehead, and the hand *tefillin* are worn on the upper arm, not on the actual hand. The Mishnah continues that one who wears the *tefillin* covered with gold or upon his sleeve "it is the way of the outsiders" *(ha-hitzonim)*. Here, too, the meaning is probably that some sectarians would cover their *tefillin* with gold, whereas the Rabbis forbade this as they did the wearing of the hand *tefillin* on the sleeve instead of on the bare arm. The suggestion that "the way of the outsiders" does not refer to sectarians but to ignorant folk displaying their zeal in a way disapproved of by the more staid teachers of Judaism is extremely unlikely.[44]

Another Mishnah states that it is *derekh ha-minut* to say, "The good shall bless thee."[45] Rashi understands the heresy is the result of the implication that only the good need bless God, whereas the wicked must also be included. But the Jerusalem Talmud[46] simply remarks, "It involves a belief in two powers" *(shetey reshuyyot)*, the usual rabbinic term for the dualistic heresy, i.e., the good bless the god of light and the wicked bless the god of darkness.[47] The same Mishnah states that we silence one who says in his prayers, "Over the nest of the bird do Thy mercies extend," "For the good be Thy name remembered," or "We give thanks, we give thanks." The Babylonian Talmud[48] sees the objection to the prayer about the bird's nest (referring to the law in Deut. 22:6–7) either because it suggests that God only has mercy on birds and not on other creatures, or because it suggests that the laws of the Torah are based solely on the idea of mercy whereas they are, in reality, divine decrees. The Jerusalem Talmud[49] advances two other reasons for this objection. It seems as if the worshiper is complaining that God only has mercy upon dumb creatures and not on him, or because it sets limits on God's powers and mercies, reading *ad*, "up to," instead of *al*, "over." God's mercies are made to extend only up to the bird's nest and not beyond. The objection to the second expression is explained in the Babylonian Talmud in that it suggests that God is only to be praised for the good, whereas Jewish teaching demands that man praises God for whatever may befall man.[50] The objection to repeating "We give thanks" is that it appears to be dualistic, thanks being rendered to both the god of light and the god of darkness. The Talmud in the same passage adds that the same applies to one who repeats the first verse of the Shema.

Maimonides records the rule that one who refuses to lead the prayers because his garments are colored must not lead them even if his garments are white, but he qualifies this as referring only to the same service.[51] Abraham Ibn David, the *Rabad*, objects that if the man is suspected of heresy he cannot be allowed to lead any further services. Evidently, Maimonides holds that since there is only a suspicion of heresy, the man is not banned forever merely on the strength of a general suspicion.[52] The *Shulhan Arukh* records the rule in Maimonides' understanding of it.[53] Whatever the original heresy may have been against which the Mishnah warns, it is extremely unlikely that any people in the Middle Ages insisted on leading the prayers in white garments, and even if such people were found it would hardly have been because they embraced the ancient heresies, which had long been forgotten. What we have here, is the codification of a law found in the Talmudic literature as a kind of abstract, purely academic rule recorded for no other reason than that it is found in the Talmud. Both Maimonides[54] and the *Shulhan Arukh*[55] record the law against repeating, "We give thanks," but here the law has practical application as a law for daily practice mentioned in the Talmud, not necessarily because of the fear of the dualistic heresy. It is also possible that the codifiers were still minded to combat dualism in their day. Maimonides[56] records the rule about placing the *tefillin* on the forehead or on the palm of the hand and refers to it as "the ways of the Sadducees" but does so in the section in which he describes the correct manner of wearing the *tefillin*.

The Talmud[57] states that a Sefer Torah written by a *Min* must be burned but that one found in the possession of a *Min*, though it may not be used because he may have written it, should not be burned but stored out of sight. Maimonides[58] records this also with regard to *tefillin* and *mezuzot*, but instead of the term *Min* he uses the term *epikoros* as does the *Shulhan Arukh*.[59] Maimonides, by using this term, evidently means *a fortiori* a *Min*, since in his classification of the *Min* and the *epikoros*, neither of whom, in his view, have a share in the World to Come, he considers a *Min* to have a greater degree of unbelief than the *epikoros*.[60] For Maimonides these terms refer to types of unbelievers. Five are called *Min*, he observes: one who denies that there is a God; the believer in dualism; the believer in God's corporeality; one who denies God's eternity; and one who worships an intermediary. Three are called *epikoros*: one who denies prophecy; one who denies the prophecy of Moses; and one who denies God's knowledge of human affairs. Maimonides[61] gives further Halakhic status to all this by ruling that there are to be no mourning rites on the part of a near relative when the *epikoros* or *Min* dies.

The Temple of Onias was built at Leontopolis in Egypt in the middle of the second century B.C.E. The Mishnah rules:

> The priests who ministered in the Temple of Onias may not minister in the Temple in Jerusalem; and needless to say another matter (i.e., priests who had served idols); for it is written: "Nevertheless the priests of the high places came not up to the altar of the Lord in Jerusalem, but they did eat unleavened bread among their brethren" (2 Kings 23:9). Thus they are like those that have a blemish: they are entitled to share and eat of the holy things but they are not permitted to offer sacrifices.[62]

This was seen by the post-Talmudic authorities as stating a general principle with regard to those who had behaved heretically but had later repented. Maimonides formulates the Mishnah in its original meaning except that instead of the Temple of Onias, obviously a matter of past history, he refers to one who has served in any

Temple outside Jerusalem.[63] Rabbenu Gershom of Mayyence (960–1028) relies on the Mishnah in reply to a question put to him whether a *kohen* who had been an apostate but who had later returned to the Jewish fold may enjoy the privileges of the priesthood, i.e., to be called first to the Torah and to recite the priestly blessing.[64] Gershom understands the Mishnah to mean that even a priest who had worshiped idols but has repented is only disqualified from offering sacrifices in the Temple but he may enjoy the other priestly privileges like the priest with a blemish to whom he is compared. But centuries later, in the battle against Reform, Rabbi Amram Grünwald (1853–1910) of Hungary quotes the same Mishnah to prove the exact opposite. The question addressed to Rabbi Grünwald[65] by the Bet Din of Munkacs was whether a Reader who had served as such in a neolog or a status-quo congregation may serve in this capacity in an Orthodox congregation. Grünwald rules unreservedly that he cannot serve as Reader and remarks that all Orthodox rabbis concur that such a man is banned from officiating. It is, he says, like the priests who had served in the Temple of Onias who, even if they have repented, may never again serve in the Temple in Jerusalem.

The sect that is particularly featured in the post-Talmudic Halakhic discussions is the Karaites, who were acknowledged to be Jews by all the Halakhists but as Jews who denied the Oral Torah.[66] Maimonides identifies the Karaites with the Sadducees and states that they are not *Minim*.[67] The attitude to be adopted toward the Karaites appears to have been an important and severely practical question in Maimonides' day judging by the references to them in Maimonides' Responsa. Maimonides was asked whether the Karaites can help to form a *minyan*, the quorum for prayer. His reply is that they cannot, for although they are Jews they themselves do not accept the whole idea of the *minyan*.[68] Since the Karaites are Jews their marriages, if performed in the correct manner, are valid, but since their divorce procedures are incorrect their divorces are invalid.[69] The Karaites were very strict with regard to the laws of Niddah, the menstruant. Maimonides holds it to be wrong to place a taboo on food and drink that has been touched by a Niddah for this is to follow the Karaite practice.[70] Maimonides discusses further the attitude to be adopted toward the Karaites.[71] He remarks that the Karaites who reside in Islamic lands and elsewhere deserve to be treated with respect. They should be looked upon as friends, treated humbly and compassionately, provided that they, too, do not insult the rabbis, not even their contemporaries and *a fortiori* they must not ridicule the teachings of the Talmudic sages whom we follow. In this spirit it is right and proper for us to pay them friendly visits, to inquire of their welfare, to circumcise their children even on the Sabbath, and to bury their dead and comfort their mourners. The rabbis urge us to maintain friendly relations even with the heathen, all the more than to those who reject paganism and believe in God. But if they profane openly days that are sacred to us (the Karaites having a different calendar) it is forbidden to visit them on any of the festivals. Rabbi Tarfon said[72] he would never enter the house of a *Min*, not even in order to save his life, but Rabbi Tarfon would not have said this of the Karaites who are not *Minim* and believe in God. Their sons should be circumcised, and it may well be that they will follow the true path when they grow up. Hai Gaon, says Maimonides, teaches to the same effect. Maimonides gives the same ruling in his Code.[73] After recording the severe attitude of condemnation to be adopted toward heretics who deny the Oral Torah, Maimonides continues:

> All this only applies to one who denies the Oral Torah in thought and deed following the opinions of his own frivolous mind and the waywardness of his own heart, denying in the first instance the Oral Torah, as did Zadok and Boethus and all their successors in error. But as for the children of these mistaken ones and their children's children, whose fathers misled them, who have been born into the Karaite fold and brought up to follow their opinions, these are like an infant captured by heathen and brought up by them not to follow the ways of the precepts. Such a person can be compared to one who is forced to sin against his will. Even if he later became aware that he is a Jew and he witnessed the Jews and their religion, he is still as one forced since he has been brought up in his error. So, too, are the children of those of whom we have spoken, who hold fast to the ways of their ancestors, the Karaites who committed the error in the first instance. Consequently, it is proper to cause them to return and to draw them with friendly words until they revert to the strength of the Torah.

There was a widely held view, shared by Maimonides, that the Karaites were the descendants of the ancient Sadducees. The tendency in modern scholarship is not actually to identify the two sects but to acknowledge that many of the Sadducean ideas and practices did eventually find their way into Karaite life.

In the sixteenth century, R. David Ibn Abi Zimra, who, incidentally, also follows the view that the Karaites are the descendants of the Sadducees, quotes these opinions of Maimonides at length to prove that intermarriage with the Karaites is permitted.[74] If inter-marriage with the Karaites were forbidden Maimonides would have said so when he discussed the question of our relationship to them. Moreover, one of Maimonides' Responsa does deal with the question of intermarriage. This is the Responsum in which Maimonides accepts Karaite marriages as valid but not Karaite divorces. The possible objection to intermarriage with the Karaites, since they are Jews, can only be that since their divorces are invalid when a Karaite divorcee remarries and has children from her second husband, the children are *mamzerim*. But the truth is that the children are not *mamzerim*, continues Ibn Abi Zimra. Apart from the doubts about particular Karaites, that they might not be the descendants of divorcees who have remarried since Karaite marriages are conducted in the presence of Karaite witnesses and these, as sinners, are disqualified from acting as witnesses, it must follow that these marriages are invalid and no *get* is required. Maimonides holds that the Karaites' marriages as well as their divorces are invalid so that when, in the afore-mentioned Responsum, he states that their marriages are valid he must be referring to those marriages that were performed correctly in the presence of witnesses belonging to the rabbinic camp. Ibn Abi Zimra refers to a report of a large group of Karaites, who, shortly after the days of Maimonides, returned to the fold. Their descendants, he says, are well known in the Egyptian community and no one has ever dared to challenge their legitimacy. He concludes that if two other rabbis of renown would concur he would declare intermarriage with the Karaites (after their return to the fold) to be permitted.

Not all Halakhists agree with R. David Ibn Abi Zimra's ruling. R. Joseph Karo in his *Bet Yosef*[75] quotes a Responsum of Rabbenu Shimshon to the effect that intermarriage with the Karaites is forbidden because of the fear of *mamzerut*. Karo does not quote this opinion in his *Shulhan Arukh* but Isserles states, "It is forbidden to intermarry with the Karaites and they are doubtful *mamzerim* and we do not accept them if they wish to return."[76] This latter statement does not necessarily mean that friendly relations with the Karaites are not to be encouraged. Isserles may have meant only that Karaites are not to be welcomed back into the fold because of the fear of *mamzerut*. His statement has been understood as not forbidding Karaites from worshiping together with Jews who follow the rabbis in Rabbinite synagogues.[77] Others, again, argue that since, at the most, there is only a doubt regarding the question of *mamzerut*, it is better to overlook this in order "not to close the door in the face of the Karaites."[78] In the State of Israel today the Rabbis are opposed to intermarriage with the Karaites.[79] R. Ezekiel Landau makes an interesting distinction between a Karaite among Karaites (to which the ruling of Isserles would apply) and a man or woman of Karaite ancestry but not living among Karaites.[80] In the latter instance we apply the principle "whatever comes away comes away from the majority," that is, even on the strictest view the majority of Karaites are certainly not *mamzerim*. It is fairly obvious from all these references that Halakhic attitudes toward the Karaites were not determined solely on purely Halakhic grounds but also depended on such things as the attitudes of the Karaites themselves and on the strength or weakness of the challenge they presented.

There are also references in the Halakhic literature to the Shabbeteans, the followers of the seventeenth-century false Messiah, Shabbetai Zevi.[81] But these are very few in number, naturally so since the Shabbeteans posed little threat to traditional Judaism after Shabbetai's conversion to Islam and the later crypto-Shabbeteans kept their views and practices secret. Nevertheless, we do find echoes of the Shabbetean heresy and the rabbinic reaction to it in the Responsa literature. Haham Zevi Ashkenazi, for instance,[82] holds that the Codes are to be followed when these are in conflict with the Zohar and the Kabbalah.[83] Very conscious of Shabbetean antinomianism, Ashkenazi remarks that the Zohar is an extremely difficult book to decipher. If it is to be allowed to depart from the Codes in obedience to what is imagined to be the meaning of the Zohar, then "the foundations of the Torah are destroyed." We have seen how many (of the Shabbeteans) have set the Torah at naught because of their claim to follow the Zohar.

More than any other Halakhist, Rabbi Eleazar Fleckeles (1754–1826) of Prague is very conscious of the need to combat the Shabbetean heresy. Prague was a center of the Shabbetean movement at the end of the eighteenth and the early nineteenth century. A Responsum of Fleckeles,[84] dated 1791, is addressed to his pupil, Mordecai of Kojetein, who wished to know whether it is permitted to intermarry with the Shabbeteans and the Frankists, the followers of Jacob Frank, Shabbetai Zevi's successor in Poland. In the particular case that Fleckeles mentions, Mordecai is inclined to allow the marriage on the grounds that the girl in question is very young and has not therefore become at all accustomed to sectarian ways. Fleckeles is indignant that Mordecai could ever have entertained such an idea. He declares that to allow even children to marry the children of these heretics is to be guilty of giving one's children to Moloch, for all their desire is only to convert others to their perverse faith. They are far worse than the Samaritans and the Karaites and *a fortiori* than the Gentiles. For the Gentiles among whom we reside are not idolators and commit no wrong. They belong among "the righteous of the nations of the world." Not so the Shabbeteans and the Frankists who are idolators and notorious sinners. Fleckeles reminds Mordecai of the attitude adopted by Ezra. We, too, must be exclusive with regard to these sectarians. From Fleckeles' remarks it appears that it was Mordecai himself who wished to marry the girl. The only way he can see, says Fleckeles, for Mordecai to marry the girl is if he is sure beyond doubt that her family's attachment to Shabbeteanism is only a rumor and entirely without foundation.

In a Responsum,[85] dated 1794, addressed to another pupil of his, Hayyim Hirsch, Dayan in Kojetein, Fleckeles discusses whether one should answer "Amen" after hearing a benediction recited by a Shabbetean. Fleckeles refers to the ruling of Maimonides that one must not answer "Amen" to a benediction of an *epikoros*.[86] The Shabbeteans do not have God in mind when they recite a benediction but Shabbetai Zevi, whom they worship as a god. In each generation they have a different god (referring to the Shabbetean and Frankist doctrine of God's incarnation in the successive Messiahs of the sect) and they are the worst of all heretics who have arisen among our people. Another Responsum records the reply of Fleckeles' teacher, R. Ezekiel Landau, addressed to Fleckeles in 1780 when Landau was rabbi of Prague.[87] Fleckeles had asked Landau whether a Sefer Torah written by a scribe suspected of being a crypto-Shabbetean may be used. Landau remarks that a mere rumor is not sufficient reason for invalidating the Sefer Torah but if subsequently the scribe revealed that he is a Shabbetean or it became otherwise known, this makes the suspicion justifiable and the Sefer may not be used.

In the struggle of the Orthodox with the Reformers, the Orthodox rabbis repeatedly used the Halakhic sources we have quoted in this chapter regarding attitudes to earlier heresies and they applied these with regard to relations with the Reformers. We have already noted how R. Amram Grünwald uses in this connection the Mishnaic rule regarding the priests who had once officiated in the Temple of Onias. Again and again in the polemics against Reform Judaism we find the Orthodox rabbis referring to the Reformers as Sadducees or *Minim*, or as being comparable to the

Karaites. There are instances of this in practically all the Responsa of the nineteenth century. We need only give here a single instance. Rabbi Moses Schick (1807–1879) of Huszt in Hungary (the town in which Grünwald later served as rabbi) was a determined opponent, like his master, R. Moses Sofer, of Reform Judaism. Schick was by no means the most extreme among the Orthodox Halakhists, yet in a Responsum[88] he asks his colleagues to declare openly that if the imposition of the *herem*, the ban, were permitted in Hungarian law, it would be essential to impose the ban on the Reformers. In any event, Schick continues, let us make it quite clear that the Reformers are not Jews; that it is forbidden to intermarry with them and that it is forbidden to pray in their Temples. This was the attitude, he remarks, adopted throughout the ages by the teachers of Israel toward heretical Jewish sects. Ezra refuse to recognize the Samaritans even though they posed as friends and offered to cooperate with him in rebuilding the Temple. Rabban Gamaliel composed the benediction against the *Minim* when the Judaeo-Christians began to grow in sufficient numbers to threaten Judaism from within. And, Schiek adds, only recently the foremost rabbis had adopted the same attitude toward the Shabbeteans.

From our survey of Halakhic attitudes to sectarians, the theory this book seeks to suggest acquires a degree of support. Ostensibly operating with pure legal theory, the Halakhists had a theological, even a political, ax to grind. Their concern was to ward off every threat to the integrity of the Torah as they saw it. In their battles they used every weapon at hand, and what more powerful a weapon than the Halakhah in which they enjoyed their expertise.

NOTES

1. On the Samaritans see the survey in EJ, vol. 14, pp. 725–58.

2. See Finkelstein, *The Pharisees;* Neusner, *The Rabbinic Traditions About the Pharisees;* and the articles "Pharises" in EJ, vol. 13, pp. 363–66 and "Sadducees" in EJ, vol. 14, pp. 620–22.

3. On the *Minim* see JE, vol. VIII, pp. 584–95 and EJ, vol. 12, pp. 1–3.

4. See EJ, vol. 12, pp. 1404–5.

5. For the question of *gerey emet* versus *gerey arayot* see *Kiddushin* 75b; *Bava Kama* 38b; *Sanhedrin* 85b; *Hullin* 3b (cf. Tosafists ad loc. s.v. ka-savar); *Niddah* 56b. Although the Talmudic literature contains no references to someone "becoming" a Samaritan there are references to people "becoming" a Sadducee or a *Min.* See, e.g., *Berakhot.* 29a.

6. *Berakhot* 7:1.

7. *Demai* 3:4.

8. *Sheviit* 8:10.

9. *Hullin* 3b.

10. *Hullin* 4a.

11. *Hullin* 6a.

12. *Yad, Avot ha-Tumah* 2:10. It must be noted, however, that Maimonides identifies the Samaritans not with the *Kutim* but with the Boethusians. See his Responsa, ed. Freimann, no. 46, pp. 46–47 and Freimann's note 4 that there were Samaritans in Cairo in Maimonides' day.

13. *Yoreh Deah* 2:8.

14. See infra p. 139.

15. *Kiddushin* 76a.

16. EH 44:10, see *Biur ha-Gra* ad loc. note 19.

17. See OP, vol. 14, p. 123 note 31.

18. See EJ, vol. 14, pp. 746–47.

19. Mishnah, *Yadaim* 4:6–8.

20. Mishnah, *Berakhot* 9:5.

21. So in the Mishnah text in the *Gemara, Berakhot* 54a. This is probably the result of the censor. In all the older Mishnaic texts the reading is *ha-minim*. See DS. Nevertheless, the meaning here is undoubtedly the Sadducees.

22. See Albeck's Commentary *ad loc.*

23. *Yoma* 1:5.

24. *Parah* 3:7.

25. See *Zevahim* 113a.

26. *Parah* 3:2.

27. *Bava Batra* 115b–16a.

28. *Yad, Avadim* 6:6.

29. YD 2:9.

30. *Yad, Teshuvah* 3:8.

31. *Berakhot* 28b, and see the discussion in *Berakhot* 29a; for the generally accepted view that this was aimed at the Judeo-Christians see Elbogen, *ha-Tefillah be-Yisrael*, pp. 27–29 and notes.

32. *Tamid* 5:1.

33. *Berakhot* 12a.

34. *Berakhot* 1:5 (3c).

35. Ed. Freimann, No. 46, pp. 46–47 and the lengthier version, pp. 359–61.

36. See Sevin, *ha-Moadim ba-Halakhah*, p. 326 and Gold, *Measef le-Khol ha-Mahanot*, p. 14 note 61 and Hadaya, *Yaskil Avdi*, vol. II, Nos. 1 and 2, vol. VII, no. 1.

37. OH 1:5.

38. *Magen Avraham* note 9.

39. *Nimmukey Orah Hayyim*, pp. 4–5. Gumbiner's source for his remarks about the special tablet for congregational reading is Yom Tov Lippmann Heller, *Divrey Hamudot, Berakhot* 1:9.

40. Gold *Measef-le-Khol*, p. 14 note 62. Cf. the sources objecting to and defending the practice in Kahana, *Mehkarim*, pp. 368–69.

41. Mishnah, *Megillah* 4:8.

42. *Megillah* 24b.

43. See Rabbinowitz, *Mishnah Megillah*, p. 128.

44. Ibid., pp. 129–30.

45. *Megillah* 4:9.

46. Ibid. 4:9 (75c).

47. This is the explanation given by *Korban ha-Edah* to JT ad loc. But Albeck (*Commentary to the Mishnah, Moed*, p. 367) and Rabbinowitz, *Mishneh Megillah*, pp. 130–31, understand, for

no good reason, that the JT interprets the Mishnah as meaning that a man should not say to his fellow, "The Good shall bless thee," implying that it is the god of light and not the god of darkness. This is unwarranted since, Rabbinowitz objects, the Mishnah in the context is obviously speaking of a man addressing God.

48. *Megillah* 25a, and the parallel passage, *Berakhot* 33b.

49. *Megillah* 4:10 (75c).

50. Mishnah, *Berakhot* 9:5.

51. *Yad, Tefillah* 10:5.

52. See *Kesef Mishneh* in name of *Ribash*.

53. OH 53:15.

54. *Yad, Tefillah* 9:4.

55. OH 121:2 and 61:9 in connection with Shema repeated twice. See Ettlinger, *Binyan Tzion*, no. 31 on the custom of reciting three times the thirteen attributes of mercy on the festivals when the Torah is taken out of the Ark.

56. *Yad, Tefillah* 4:3.

57. *Gittin* 45b.

58. *Yad, Tefillin* 1:13.

59. OH 39:4; YD 281:1.

60. *Yad, Teshuvah* 3:7–8.

61. *Yad, Evel* 1:10.

62. *Menahot* 13:10 and see *Menahot* 109a–110a.

63. *Yad, Biat ha-Mikdash* 9:14.

64. Responsa, ed. Eidelberg, no. 4, pp. 57–60.

65. *Arugot ha-Bosem*, no. 15.

66. See EJ, vol. 10, pp. 761–85; OY, vol. IX, p. 215.

67. Responsa, ed. Freimann, no. 46, pp. 46–47, where Maimonides also identifies the Samaritans with the Boethusians, see sup. p.   .

68. Responsa, ed. Freimann, no. 14, pp. 14–15.

69. Ibid., no. 163, p. 159.

70. Ibid., no. 99, pp. 95–96.

71. Ibid., no. 371, pp. 339–42.

72. *Shabbat* 116a.

73. *Yad, Mamrim* 3:3.

74. Responsa, *Radbaz*, no. 73.

75. *Tur* EH 4. Rosenthal, "Karaites," pp. 431–32 identifies the Rabbenu Shimshon referred to by Karo as Samsan of Sens.

76. EH 4:37.

77. See OP, vol. I, p. 208 note 176.

78. See the sources quoted in OP, vol. I, pp. 206–7 note 175.

79. See especially Waldinberg, *Tzitz Eliezer*, vol. 12, no. 66, pp. 176–78 who quotes an extraordinary letter of Rabbi Pesah Zevi Frank who not only forbids intermarriage with the Karaites but refuses to treat them as Jews for the purpose of the Law of Return in Israel.

80. *Noda Bhiyudah*, EH, No. 5.

81. See Scholem, *Shabbetai Sevi;* Carmilly-Weinberger, *Censorship*, chapter 5, pp. 59–105; and my *Theology in the Responsa*, Index: "Shabbetai Zevi." Cf. the astonishing statement of Hayyim Palaggi (*Kol ha-Hayyim*, p. 18a column 2) that he has a tradition from his teachers and ancestors to the effect that one should speak neither good nor evil about the Shabbetai Zevi affair. This statement aroused the ire of R. Hayyim Eleazar Shapira of Munkacs (*Hamishah Maamarot*, pp. 157–58) who is horrified at the thought that one should not attack the Shabbetean heresy and accuses the Sephardim of being naive and overly-credulous in

these matters. Scholem (Hebrew ed. *Shabbetai Tzevi*, vol. II, pp. 590–91) points out that originally this saying was simply intended to let the controversy die down but was later suspected of favoring the Shabbeteans; see also Tamar, "Hints," p. 149 note 3.

82. Responsa, *Haham Tzevi*, no. 36.

83. See sup., pp. 73–74.

84. *Teshuvah me-Ahavah*, no. 8.

85. Ibid., no. 69.

86. *Yad, Berakhot* 1:13.

87. *Teshuvah me-Ahavah*, no. 112, par. 3. Mordecai Baneth, *Parashat Mordekha YD*, no. 6, discusses the same question. (It is possible that this is, in fact, the same case.) Baneth permits the use of the *Sefer Torah*. Among his reasons is the interesting one that the Shabbeteans are not *Minim* because they do not really believe in the truth of their doctrines but espouse these doctrines in order to avail themselves of the sexual permissiveness that follows from these doctrines.

88. *Teshuvot Maharam Shik*, OH, No. 305.

9

Responses to Changed Conditions and Social Needs: 1

The Halakhic literature contains many instances of a resort to legal theory not for the purpose of determining the law but to provide justification for existing practice where this is in conflict with the older law as laid down in the Talmud. Legal casuistry then seeks to demonstrate that the practice in question, despite what appears on the surface to be the case, is not, in fact, in opposition to the law. The usual procedure in these instances is either to demonstrate that the practice is in accord with a minority opinion, which, though rejected, can still be relied on in exceptional circumstances, or to point to the safeguarding of other values which justifies a departure from the standard rule. The device that is most frequently resorted to is to note that the older rule is based on conditions which no longer obtain. Examples of such changes in the law as a result of changing conditions and new social needs are given in this and in the next chapter.

In medieval French and German communities, for example, the people evidently could not be persuaded to attend separate synagogue services for the afternoon and night prayers, probably, among other reasons, because nightfall in summer in these Western lands was at a much later hour than in the East, especially in the summer, so that it was asking too much to expect people to leave their homes again late at night to attend another, separate service. It was the practice in these communities for the night prayers to follow immediately the afternoon prayers, with the result that the

Shema (part of the night service) was recited while it was still day. This is in flat contradiction to the Talmudic rules, according to which the Shema must be recited at night.[1] Nontheless, the contemporary practice was defended by the Halakhists, the defense taking various forms. The main defense was to try to show that other authorities than the Mishnah were to be relied on, but another line of defense was to suggest that the early recital of the Shema did not suffice for the fulfillment of the obligation and that this obligation was carried out at the correct time because people were accustomed to reciting the Shema again before retiring to rest and they did this when it was night.[2] Israel Isserlein (1390–1460), the foremost Halakhic authority of the day in Germany, was faced with the situation where a community recited the night prayers so early in the afternoon that it was not only the recital of the Shema that was in question but the validity of the night prayers themselves. There is Talmudic precedent for reciting these prayers in the late afternoon but certainly not, as in this community, while there were many hours to go until nightfall. Nevertheless, Isserlein tries hard to find some legal justification for the current practice and, though unsuccessful in his quest, still condones what he is forced to admit is an unlawful practice. Isserlein's Responsa are different from the normal run in that they are not replies to actual questions submitted to him but to hypothetical questions of his own invention. Some of the problems he considers are, however, obviously practical ones, of concern for the practical life of his people. The Responsum we are examining is the very first in his collection. This is how Isserlein formulates the problem: "In the majority of the communities it is the practice, in the long summer days, to recite the night Shema and the night prayers three or four hours before the stars appear. Is there any defence or reasonable justification for this practice since many scholars are at one with the masses in this practice?"

Despite his efforts, Isserlein is unable to find any Talmudic warrant for the departure from the law. His conclusion is, as we have noted, to condone the departure notwithstanding the lack of legal support. This conclusion must be quoted in full:

> Consequently, it seems, there is no defence for the practice according to the theory and reasoning of the Talmud. But one must surmise that the habit was adopted as a result of the weakness that has descended into the world so that the majority of the folk are hungry and wish to have their meal while it is still full daylight in the long days. If they were to have their meal before the afternoon prayers they would spend so much

time over it that they would not come to the synagogue at all . . .
Because of this the scholars were unable to prevent the people from
saying their prayers and reciting the Shema while it is still full daylight.
. . . I have also heard in the Yeshiva from one of the great scholars that
he had heard of a tradition according to which in Cremieu they used to
recite the night prayers and the Shema on the eve of the Sabbath so
early in the day that the Rabbi of the town, a renowned scholar of
former times, together with all the communal leaders, used to go for a
post-prandial stroll by the banks of the river Donjon and yet would
return home before nightfall. It has also been found in a manuscript, in
the name of a famous scholar, that he gave a ruling to say the night
prayers and recite the Shema while it was still full day in order to be
present at a wedding banquet. From all this, it appears that in former
times it was held to be a light matter to render a lenient decision in this
connection. . . . So it seems that even a scholar, in a community where
they say the prayers and recite the Shema very early during the long
days and is unable to prevent them from so doing, has no obligation to
separate himself from them but should say the prayers and recite the
Shema together with them and he has thereby fulfilled his obligation.
But if he is separate in any event from the rest of the people in his
stricter religious observances, he should say his prayers and recite the
Shema at the times the Sages ordained according to all the authorities.

Thus, Isserlein not only condones the departure from the law but
advises scholars, who know that the contemporary practice is unlawful, against separating themselves from the community, unless
they have a reputation for extraordinary piety. Evidently nothing
was to be done to make the people feel guilty, the alternative being
that during the summer months there would have been no congregational prayer at all.

The Talmud is very strict regarding washing the hands not only
before meals but also after meals.[4] Yet the *Tosafists*[5] point to the
total neglect in France of *mayyim aharonim*, the washing after the
meal. The justification is given that, unlike the washing before
meals, which is ritualistic and hence permanently binding, the
washing after meals is stated in the Talmud to be for the purpose of
removing from the hands every trace of a certain type of salt—*melah
sedomit*—used in food which could cause blindness if it came into
contact with the eyes. "Nowadays," the *Tosafists* observe, we no
longer use this kind of salt and since the original law was only laid
down to prevent danger to the eyes the ancient law is no longer
operative. It is interesting to note in this connection that the Zohar
is very strict that the law of *mayyim aharonim* be observed.[6] Accord-

ing to the mystical interpretation given in the Zohar, the law *is* ritualistic and is not only because of danger to the eyes. Once the Zohar began to be relied on in matters of practice, as we saw in the chapter on the influence of the Kabbalah, a reversal of the *Tosafists'* argument took place, it being postulated that had the Zohar been known to the *Tosafists* they would not have defended the abolition of this law.[7]

Another instance of the same kind of reasoning to justify a current practice that is in conflict with the law is found in the *Tosafists* to the passage in the Mishnah where the rule is laid down that dancing or even clapping the hands for joy is forbidden on a festival, a ruling that was ignored by the French Jews.[8] The defense offered by the *Tosafists* is that the reason given in the Talmud for the Mishnaic law is that if it were permitted to dance or to clap the hands on a festival, this might lead to the fashioning of a musical instrument to assist the jollifications. To repair or fashion a musical instrument on the festival is forbidden by biblical law so that the Mishnaic rule is in the nature of a safeguard, to avoid the infringement of a biblical law. "Nowadays," argue the *Tosafists*, we lack the skills to fashion or repair musical instruments.[9] Since the reasoning behind the law is no longer cogent, the law can be ignored.

The Talmud is opposed to child marriages, i.e., to a father exercising the right, given to him in biblical law, of marrying off his minor daughter before she is old enough to choose for herself the man she wishes to marry.[10] This, too, was ignored by French Jewry. Here the defense by the *Tosafists* is to admit that child marriages are unlawful, though valid if carried out. Yet in the harsh conditions of the time, the *Tosafists* postulate, it is essential that such marriages be allowed. If child marriages were outlawed, the opportunities for marriage may not later arise and the poor girls would remain unmarried all their lives.[11]

Still another instance provided by the *Tosafists* is in the very significant area of Torah study. According to the Talmud, a man must divide his study periods into three, devoting an equal time to the study of the Bible, the Mishnah, and the Talmud.[12] Although the Bible was assiduously studied by the French Jews, as witnessed by the activities of the great commentators, Rashi, Rashbam, and the *Tosafists* themselves, their studies were concentrated on the difficult Babylonian Talmud, often to the exclusion of all else. The defense by the *Tosafists*[13] of the contemporary practice, in the name of Rabbenu Tam, is on the grounds that the Babylonian Talmud contains in itself all three topics to be studied since this Talmud is a Commentary to the Mishnah and also quotes Scripture with the greatest frequency.

These are but a few examples of change in the law, other examples are given in this and in the next chapter. But this whole question of changes in the law because of changed conditions is complicated by the existence of a Mishnaic rule that seems to militate against any possibility of change.[14] This is the rule that no court is empowered to set aside a law promulgated by another court unless the second court is superior to the first "in wisdom and number." I. H. Weiss has argued that this rule referred originally only to two contemporary courts but that it was later extended even to courts in different periods in order to preserve the unity and stability of the law, rigidity being the price that had to be paid if anarchy was to be avoided.[15] Be that as it may, eventually the rule found its way into the Talmud in its extended form, applying even to two courts one later than the other. Moreover, the idea evolved that no post-Talmudic court could ever be the equal, let alone the superior of a court composed of the Talmudic sages.[16] The combination of these two ideas—that a later court can only set aside the rulings of an earlier court if it is possessed of greater wisdom, and that the later court can never, in fact, be possessed of greater wisdom—might effectively have prevented any progress at all in the development of the law were it not that various qualifications to the rule were introduced by the Halakhists in order to promote at least a degree of flexibility, without which the Halakhah would have become petrified. Maimonides,[17] applies the rule against change even where the original reason for the earlier court's ruling no longer obtained, but Abraham Ibn David, the *Rabad*,[18] holds that a later court is empowered to set aside laws laid down by an earlier court, even where the later court is inferior, when the original reason behind the promulgation of these laws no longer obtained. For all that, the virtual dogma of the infallibility of the Talmudic sages or, at least, the ideas that all the Talmudic laws were permanently binding because they had been accepted as such by the consensus of the whole House of Israel, undoubtedly came to operate in favor of an extreme conservatism. If changes in the law did, nonetheless, take place, it was because, as in the illustrations given from the *Tosafists*, the original law was seen not as categorical but as having application only in the circumstances where the reasoning behind it still had meaning. In the nineteenth century, with the rise of the Reform movement and the resultant clamor for radical changes in the law, the Halakhists found themselves bound to consider anew the question of which changes were legitimate and which unlawful.[19] For all their valiant attempts at a consistent theory of change, no acceptable theory emerged from their deliberations. How could they have done otherwise, as we have noted, the changes came first and the theory was no more than an attempt to legitimize a change, whether or not unlawful, that had already taken place under the pressure of events over which the Halakhic theorists had no control. The Halakhah did manage to retain its viability by yielding to the demands of contemporary life. In the simile the rabbis use for the ideal character, the Halakhah was not like the unyielding cedar tree, which a really powerful wind can break, but like the pliant reed, which allows itself to be moved by the winds and is thus never uprooted by them.

A rather different method adopted by some of the Halakhists, when confronted with the need for change, was to argue that the Mishnaic rule which bans any change by an inferior court only applies where there is clear evidence that a law was actually promulgated by the earlier, superior court. If the earlier court had stated that its members had taken a vote to declare that such-and-such is the law, then, indeed, that law can never be repealed, even if the reasons behind the decision are known and no longer obtain. But if, say, the Talmud states that such-and-such is the law because of this or that reason, without stating that there was an actual meeting of the court and a formal ruling by the court, then whether that Talmudic law continues to be binding does depend on whether or not the reason is still operative. A contingent rule only becomes categorical when it has been declared so to be; otherwise it remains contingent and subject to alteration. For instance, the Talmudic law[20] prohibits drinking the milk obtained from Gentiles unless a Jew has been present at the milking on the grounds that the Gentile might have introduced into the milk a quantity of forbidden milk such as the milk of asses or camels. Some, but by no means all,[21] Halakhists like Hezekiah da Silva (1659–1695), in his *Peri Hadash*, hold that the prohibition has fallen into abeyance "nowadays" when unclean milk is hardly available or where the government authorities have very strict regulations against the adulteration of milk. The argument followed is that the Talmudic sages did not issue a "court order," a blanket prohibition by a court voting on the matter, so that the question of repeating a ruling of an earlier court does not arise. All they did was to warn against the use of Gentile milk because it might contain forbidden milk. There was never any

prohibition against Gentile milk, because of the fear of adulteration, only a stern warning against the possibility of adulteration. It
follows that in a situation where no fear of adulteration need be
entertained, there is no prohibition. That this analysis is correct
can be seen not only from the absence of any reference to a formal
court prohibition but also from the qualification in the original
statement that Gentile milk is permitted where a Jew is present at
the milking. Where a Jew is present there is no fear that the milk
has been adulterated, and the same aim is achieved whenever adulteration is known not to have taken place. In countries where the
adulteration of milk is illegal, Jews know that there has been no
adulteration with the result that, in such countries, a Jew is, as it
were, always "present at the milking."

Nowhere is the principle of change in response to changed social
conditions more pronounced and far-reaching than in the area of
women's rights and status. From the earliest period in the history of
the Halakhah, efforts have been made to introduce new legislation
in order to prevent injustices to women that could result from any
direct application of the earlier law. The Ketubah, the marriage
settlement, was introduced in order to curb the husband's powers
given to him in biblical law.[22] The laws regarding the provisions of
the Ketubah effectively prevented hasty divorce without the wife's
consent and made ample provision for her if she became a widow or
was divorced by her husband. Although only the husband could
divorce his wife, legal machinery was introduced by means of
which the wife, in certain circumstances, one of which was when
the husband took up an unpleasant occupation such as that of a
tanner, could petition the court for a divorce.[23] In these circumstances, the husband could be compelled, by the exercise of physical force, if necessary, to issue the *get*. Assent under duress, not
normally considered valid, was treated as valid assent for this purpose, it being argued that the husband essentially wishes to behave
correctly so that eventually, albeit as a result of the physical coercion exercised by the court, he does give his unqualified assent to
the divorce.[24] The conservative attitude continued to prevail, however, among many of the post-Talmudic Halakhists, who were
extremely reluctant to engage in this kind of coercion except in
those cases where the Talmud explicitly demands it.[25]

It is plausible to suggest, judging by their different Halakhic
approaches, that the French and German Halakhists in the Middle
Ages were more concerned to uphold the position and social standing of women than were their counterparts in Islamic lands. Thus

Maimonides[26] denies the community the right to appoint a woman to any communal office, whereas the French authorities only debate whether she could be appointed as a judge, some of them permitting even this.[27] Maimonides, rules that a married woman who fails to carry out her wifely duties may be physically chastised by her husband,[28] whereas the authorities who flourished in a Christian environment were horrified at the very thought.[29] The Talmud rules that a married woman need not recline at the Passover Seder, out of respect for her husband, unless she is "a woman of high rank" *(ishah hashuvah).*[30] A famous German authority roundly declares: "All our women are of high rank."[31] Although the Talmud[32] exempts women from the performance of precepts depending on a given time, such as hearing the *shofar* on *Rosh ha-Shanah* and taking the *lulav* on *Sukkot,* it would seem that this means that if women do voluntarily carry out these precepts they should not recite beforehand the benediction "Who has *commanded us* to. . . ." Yet the practice in France was for women not only to carry out these precepts but to recite the benediction, their practice being defended by the French Halakhists.[33]

A very far-reaching change, in favor of greater leniency, among the post-Talmudic authorities is in connection with the Sabbath laws. According to the Talmud, the prohibition of carrying objects on the Sabbath into and in the public domain is derived from the prohibition of carrying on the Sabbath by the Israelites in the wilderness where they encamped during their journeyings to the Promised Land.[34] Without anything remotely approaching an explicit statement in the Talmud to this effect, the post-Talmudic Halakhists limited the scope of the prohibition by arguing that since there were 600,000 males in the wilderness camp, no domain qualifies as a "public" one unless it is regularly transversed by at least 600,000 persons. There is thus no "public domain" according to biblical law (though there is a rabbinic prohibition) "nowadays" and this principle is accepted by the later codifiers with various leniencies that stem from it.[35] We can only guess at the reason for this limitation on the full application of the law, but it may well have been social, based on the need to make Sabbath observance easier and more attractive than would have been the case if every act of carrying into the public domain involved a Sabbath desecration by biblical law and hence of the most severe kind.

The history of the Jewish criminal law is one of constant adjustment to social needs. Theoretically, after the destruction of the Temple, no court is legally empowered to inflict capital punishment. Indeed, according to the reports, such powers ceased in practice long before the actual destruction of the Temple.[36] Fines could only be imposed by ordained scholars in the Holy Land.[37] To have insisted, however, on these limitations would have meant that all powers of coercion, indeed, of proper administration of the law, would have become impossible in the Diaspora communities, an obviously unacceptable situation if Jewish law were to continue to be operative. A number of countermeasures were, therefore, introduced. The Babylonian authorities were allowed to exercise essential juridical functions on the basis of the legal fiction that they were acting on behalf of the ordained Palestinian authorities, empowered to delegate their authority.[38] Another astonishing principle is that where the times demand it a court was authorized to act against the Torah law, i.e., to inflict otherwise illegal punishments.[39] This latter maxim means that what the law has taken away with one hand it has given back with the other. In practice, since when the "times demand it" the court is, in any event, acting with an authority that is basically outside the law, any court, when it senses that social needs require it, could inflict fines and other punishments without regard to the due processes of law. This paradox, of the law itself giving its practitioners extralegal powers, resulted, in theory at least, in the courts possessing virtually unlimited powers to do as they pleased if they felt it to be for the furtherance of justice and, moreover, there were now no checks on abuse by the courts. It is notorious that in medieval Spain, the Jewish communities, acting through their courts, not only flogged offenders with the utmost severity but occasionally even went so far as to execute criminals whose activities were held to threaten the safety of the Jewish community.[40]

Particularly in laws based on the ancient rabbinic knowledge of the physical nature of humans and animals and of scientific matters generally, difficulties arose when increased and more accurate knowledge tended to cast doubts on the continuing application of these laws. Thus, the statement in the Talmud[41] that a woman who marries after the age of twenty is only capable of conceiving until she reaches the age of forty and not afterwards, and the law based this statement, had to be qualified by the later Halakhists.[42] Some of the Halakhists, faced with the obvious facts and yet reluctant to admit that the Talmudic sages could have been in error, even with regard to science, went so far as to postulate that changes had taken place in nature since Talmudic times.[43]

In all the instances noted in this chapter the principle of change in the law, where social needs and changing conditions warrant it, is fully accepted, although the matter is far from simple and tensions abound.[44] The instances to which we referred demonstrate how the necessary changes were introduced. There are very many further examples of these adaptions to change, some of which we examine in the next chapter.

NOTES

1. Mishnah, *Berakhot* 1:1 and *Berakhot* 2a–3a.

2. Rashi, *Tosafists*, and the other standard medieval commentators to *Berakhot* ad loc.

3. *Terumat ha-Deshen*, no. 1, p. 5. Isserles refers to this opinion in his gloss to SA, OH 235:1. Thus a decision on extralegal grounds by Isserlein, because of the latter's renown, came to enjoy a degree of Halakhic authority. Cf. sup., p. 15.

4. *Berakhot* 53b; *Hullin* 105a.

5. *Tosafists* to *Berakhot* 53b s.v. *viyhitem* and to *Hullin* 105a s.v. *mayyim rishonim*. For another illustration of the attitude of *Tosafists* to a law based on changed eating habits see *Tosafists* to *Pesahim* 115b. s.v. *lamah okerin*.

6. *Zohar* II, 265a.

7. See SA, OH 181:10 and note of *Magen Avraham*, note 10.

8. Mishnah, *Betzah* 5:2, *Betzah* 36b.

9. *Tosafists* to *Betzah* 30a s.v. *tenan*.

10. *Kiddushin* 41a.

11. *Tosafists* to *Kiddushin* 41a s.v. *asur*.

12. *Kiddushin* 30a.

13. *Tosafists* to *Kiddushin* 30a s.v. *lo tzerikha*. In connection with the whole question of changes in the law because of changed conditions, the following Talmudic passages should be noted, in which the term *ha-iddana* ("nowadays") occurs: *Berakhot* 21a (see DS and parallel in *Hullin* 136b); *Shabbat* 95a; *Taanit* 17a; *Ketubot* 3a; *Kiddushin* 71b; *Bava Metzia* 42a; *Avodah Zarah* 69b. These passages are no doubt the source for the principle enunciated by *Tosafists*. Cf. the brief but important article by Immanuel Löw: "Ha-'Iddànā" in HUCA.

14. *Eduyyot* 1:5.

15. Weiss, *Dor Dor ve-Doreshav*, vol. II, pp. 61–66.

16. See the oft-quoted, "If the early ones were like angels then we are like human beings but if the early ones were like human beings then we are like donkeys" (*Shabbat* 112b). Cf. *Yad, Mamrim* 2:1 and *Kesef Mishneh* ad loc. on the Talmud as the final authority.

17. *Yad, Mamrim* 2:2.

18. *Rabad* on *Yad, Mamrim* 2:2.

19. See the summary by Israel Lipshutz (1782–1860) in his *Tiferet Yisrael, Eduyyot* 1:5, pp. 171a–b; and the series of articles by Ettlinger and others in the journal *Shomer Tzion ha-Neeman*, vol. I, pp. of issues 1846–1847.

20. *Avodah Zarah* 35b.

21. See SA, YD 115:1; *Peri Hadash* ad loc.; ET, vol. 15, pp. 178–79 for all these opinions.

22. See Louis M. Epstein, *The Jewish Marriage Contract*.

23. Mishnah, *Ketubot* 7:10, *Ketubot* 77a.

24. *Kiddushin* 50a.

25. See SA, EH 154:21.

26. *Yad, Melakhim* 1:5.

27. See *Tosafists* to *Bava Kama* 16a s.v. *asher tasim* and Uziel, *Piskey Uziel*, pp. 228–34.

28. *Yad, Ishut* 21:3 and 10.

29. See *Rabad* to *Yad* ad loc. and Isserles to SA, EH 154:3.

30. *Pesahim* 108a.

31. See Isserles to SA, OH 472:4.

32. *Kiddushin* 33b–35b.

33. See Maimonides, *Yad, Tzitzit* 3:9 that they must not recite the benediction, whereas *Rabad*, ad loc., holds that they may recite it. Cf. *Tosafists* to *Eruvin* 96a s.v. *dilma;* Jacob of Marvège, *Sheelot u-Teshuvot Min ha-Shamayyim*, no. 1; and sup. p. 72. The SA OH 589:6 rules that they may not recite the benediction, following Maimonides, whereas Isserles follows the Ashkenazi authorities that they may. Another instance of German "liberalism" on the question of women is the ruling of the *Sefer Hasidim* (ed. Margaliot, no. 578; ed. Wistinetzki, No. 965) that the obligation to rise before the aged applies also to rising before an aged woman. On whether a woman may perform *shehitah* see Duchinsky, "May a Woman act as Shohetah?" from which is appears that the Sephardi authorities tended to permit a woman to be a *Shohetet;* whereas the Ashkenazim tend to forbid it, but this is only a generalization and is no contradiction to our contention. For women as rabbis see Azulai, *Shem ha-Gedolim*, s.v. *rabbanit*, p. 112.

34. *Shabbat* 96b; 98a; *Eruvin* 22b.

35. See *Tosafists* to *Shabbat* 6b s.v. *kan;* to *Shabbat* 64b end. But see SA, OH 345:7 and Commentaries for dissenting voices and the article on the subject by S. H. Kook, *Iyyunim u-Mehkarim*, pp. 87–90 and see Shapira, *Minhat Eleazar*, vol. 3, no. 4 and that in large cities such as London, Paris, Vienna, and Berlin this leniency does not apply in any event because 600,000 persons do pass through the main streets daily.

36. *Sanhedrin* 41a; cf. Mishnah, *Makkot* 1:10.

37. Bava Kama 27b.

38. Bava Kama 84b.

39. *Yevamot* 90b; *Sanhedrin* 46a; cf. Karo *Bet Yosef* to *Tur* HM 2.

40. See S. W. Baron: *The Jewish Community*, pp. 70f. and D. M. Shohet, *The Jewish Court in the Middle Ages*, pp. 133–50. Especially the Spanish authorities allowed the execution of informers who were a real danger to the community; see R. Nissim of Geronae, *Hiddushey ha-Ran* to *Sanhedrin* 46a and see Margaliot, *Margaliot ha-Yam*, vol. I, p. 91b note 6 that his father told him of an actual case where an informer was drowned on Yom Kippur as late as the nineteenth century, and see the further sources he quotes in note 9, e.g., Maimonides, *Yad, Hovel u-Mazik* 8:11 and Responsa, *Rashba* 5, No. 238 and the oft-quoted passage in *Teshuvot ha-Rosh, Kelal* 17:8 and *Kelal* 18:13 and the astonishing Responsum (*Eitan ha-Ezrahi*, no. 45) of Abraham ha-Kohen Rapoport (1584–1651) where he advises mutilation but not execution for an informer who laid false accusations against the Jews of Poland.

41. *Bava Batra* 119b.

42. See Herzog, *Hekhal Yitzhak*, EH, vol. I, no. 6, p. 54.

43. See *Tosafists* to *Moed Katan* 11a s.v. *kavvara* to *Avodah Zarah* 24b s.v. *parah;* and to *Hullin* 47a s.v. *kol;* and the sources quoted by Medini, *Sedey Hemed, maarekhet tet*, 5, vol. 3, pp. 7f. Gumbiner, *Magen Avraham*, OH 576:3 applies this principle to not fasting "nowadays" during an epidemic despite the injunction of the Talmud.

44. On the right of contemporary authorities to hold views different from the earlier *Posekim* se Feinstein, *Iggerot Moshe*, YD, No. 101 end, p. 186. The author was criticized for advancing his own theories when these are in contradiction to the views of the *aharonim*. It is not only permitted to do this, he maintains, but it is the duty of a contemporary authority to work out rulings on matters not found in the earlier sources, and even if the *aharonim* deal

with the matter we are not obliged to follow them if our reason tells us that they are in error. We are even allowed occasionally to take issue with some of the *rishonim* if their reasoning is less than convincing. He quotes *Bava Batra* 131a: "A judge can only decide in accordance with what his own eyes see," which *Rashbam* ad loc. applies also to a judge's reasoning powers. But Feinstein qualifies this that he must not decide against the SA and *Rama* because these have been accepted as the final authorities in all our lands. To be sure, he continues, one must be very cautious in rendering a decision in practice against that of earlier *Posekim* but where the need is great independence is in order. Schwarz, *Maaneh le-Iggerot*, no. 123, pp. 273–76 takes issue with this, arguing that whereas the *rishonim* do rely on their own reasoning, it is the practice of the *aharonim* to support their case by quoting many proofs from the Talmud and the *rishonim*. Schwarz points to a Responsum of R. Akiba Eger (no. 105 end) where this authority remarks that because of a difficulty we have no right to depart from views found in the *rishonim*. But all this is highly subjective, a good deal depending on general attitudes.

10

Responses to Changed Conditions and Social Needs: 2

The previous chapter noted some of the general principles that operate when the Halakhists perceive a need to legislate for change in conditions and circumstances. This chapter continues with an examination of the same theme, referring to many detailed examples of how the process actually functions.

First to be noted are the examples of changes in the laws concerned with the status of certain classes of persons.

There is much discussion in the Talmudic sources regarding the status in Jewish law of habitual sinners. A person who commits a sin for which the penalty is flogging is disqualified from acting as a witness in a court of law, if there are witnesses to his offense.[1] The case came before the renowned German Halakhist R. Akiba Eger (1761–1837),[2] a strong opponent of the Reform movement, of a man who had formally betrothed a girl in the presence of two witnesses. An attempt was made later to invalidate the marriage on the grounds that one of the witnesses was known to be guilty of shaving with a razor, a biblical prohibition, the commission of which disqualifies a witness according to this Talmudic law. R. Akiba Eger could not see his way to disqualify the witness and so invalidate the marriage. One of his arguments is that some Jews, who are otherwise observant, do shave with a razor because they are unaware that it is sinful so to do, and according to the *Shulhan Arukh*[3] if it can be assumed that the sin is not committed intentionally the witness is not disqualified. "One can say," remarks

R. Akiba Eger, "that the witness who has shaved with a razor, an offence which, for our sins, has proliferated among so many, does not consider this to be forbidden. Indeed, according to the evidence that has been recorded, when he was rebuked for his offence he replied that many respectable people do this, and since it is true that this plague has spread nowadays even among those who are scrupulous in other religious matters, it appears to them to be no grave sin."

According to the Talmudic rule, one who profanes the Sabbath in public is treated as a non-Jew to the extent, according to some authorities, that his wine is treated as Gentile wine which a Jew is forbidden to drink.[4] R. Jacob Ettlinger (1798–1871) of Altona was asked to rule on this matter (the Responsum is dated 5,621 = 1861).[5] Ettlinger suggests that Jews who profane the Sabbath "nowadays" do not do so as an act of unbelief or defiance but because they are unaware of the seriousness of the offense and are not, therefore, to be treated as if they were non-Jews. Ettlinger, after stating his opinion that the wine of one who profanes the Sabbath is, indeed, forbidden according to the ancient law, continues:

> So far I have spoken about the law itself of how to treat the wine of one who profanes the Sabbath in public. But I confess that I am unable to decide what the law is regarding Jewish sinners in our time since, for our sins, the plague has spread all around to the extent that for the majority of them the profanation of the Sabbath is regarded as something permitted so that, possibly, they have the status of one who holds that a sin is really permitted, such a person being treated in law only as one near to the stage of presumptuous sin. Some of them recite the Sabbath prayers and the *Kiddush* and then profane the Sabbath by carrying out work forbidden by Biblical law and work forbidden by Rabbinic law. The reason why one who profanes the Sabbath is treated as an apostate is none other than that such a one denies the creation and its Creator but this person acknowledges them by his prayers and his *Kiddush*. All the more with regard to their children who come after them, who have never even heard of the Sabbath laws.

Not all Halakhists agree with Ettlinger. R. Samuel Ehrenfeld (1835–1883) of Mattersdorf[6] and R. Solomon Kluger (1785–1896) of Brody[7] are both very strict, refusing to make exceptions on the kind of grounds suggested by Ettlinger but these two authorities flourished in Hungary and Galicia, respectively, where the profanation of the Sabbath was less rife than in Ettlinger's day in Germany.

The Responsum of David Hoffmann (1843–1921), rector of the Orthodox Rabbinical Seminary in Berlin is very interesting in this connection. Hoffmann was asked whether those who profane the Sabbath in public can be counted in the *minyan*, the quorum for prayer.[8] Hoffmann refers to Ettlinger. The part of his Responsum in which Hoffmann deals with the contemporary situation in Germany, Hungary, and America is worth quoting:

> Nowadays, however, it is customary to be lenient even in Hungary, *a fortiori* in Germany. I recall a man whose shop was open on the Sabbath. He was a member of our congregation, *Adat Yisrael*. When he was in mourning he led the services in the synagogue belonging to our community but the Warden knew how to persuade him to desist from so doing because, he said, the members would object. The man then went to the synagogue *Hevra Shas* where, even though the Warden there was Orthodox and God-fearing, the man was allowed to take the services without let or hindrance. When I asked this Warden why he did not prevent him, the Warden replied, it is the established practice in this *Bet ha-Midrash* from times past that they do not prevent from taking the services a man whose shop is open on the Sabbath. Since the Rabbis there were renowned scholars it can be assumed that they had their reasons. Possibly they relied on that which is stated in Responsa, *Binyan Tzion ha-Hadashot*, No. 23 (by Ettlinger) that those who profane the Sabbath in our day are to be treated, to some extent, like children brought up by Gentiles since, for our sins, the majority of Jews in our country profane the Sabbath but it is not their intention to deny the principles of our faith. See what is there recorded. And so, too, did Rabbi Meshullam Zalman ha-Kohen, of blessed memory, tell me in the name of the Gaon, author of *Shoel u-Meshiv* (R. Joseph Saul Nathansohn of Lemberg) who has written that people in America do not become disqualified as a result of them having profaned the Sabbath because they are considered to be children brought up among Gentiles. Be that as it may, whoever is lenient in allowing these persons to make up the *minyan* can find support among the authorities. On the other hand, whoever is able to go to another synagogue without putting others to shame, this is obviously better than to rely on the dispensation, and he should prefer to offer his prayers together with observant Jews. There is another reason which can be added for the purpose of leniency. In our day it is not considered to be a *public* desecration of the Sabbath since most people are guilty of the offence. Where the majority is guiltless and a minority sin brazenly, every member of that minority denies the Torah by committing the abomination high-handedly and thereby separates himself from the Community of Israel. But since, for our sins, the majority breaks down the fence, their very offence affords the remedy. The individual imagines that it is not such a grave sin and

it is, therefore, not necessary to keep it private, so that the public offence is really a private one. On the contrary, it is the observant, nowadays, who are dubbed separatists and abnormal, while the sinners declare that they simply behave in the normal way.

Whereas Hoffmann quotes Ettlinger as saying that the majority of Jews in Germany profane the Sabbath, what Ettlinger actually says is that the majority of German Jews who profane the Sabbath are unaware that what they do is a grave sin. In any event, for some Halakhists, the conditions of life in Western lands resulted in the virtual erasement of the laws regarding the status of the Sabbath-breaker.

Another type of sinner considered by the Halakhah is the *epikoros*, obviously a term derived from the Greek philosopher Epicurus but in the rabbinic literature denoting the unbeliever, the heretic.[9] In theory, though there is no evidence that theory was ever translated into practice, the *epikoros* had no legal claim to live; he was to be "lowered into a pit and not brought out again,"[10] i.e., where possible he was to be murdered indirectly. Maimonides, when recording the law, states "this *was* the law" as does the *Shulhan Arukh*, "they used to kill them in the period of the Temple." Thus this law was, in any event, never of any practical consequence. But with regard to other matters of the law it is clear that the *epikoros* is to be treated as the worst of sinners. According to Maimonides it goes without saying that the *epikoros* is disqualified from acting as a witness in a court of law.[11] Even here it is difficult to determine how far the law was actually followed since the evidence is scanty in the extreme and it is, moreover, hard to define what exactly is meant by the *epikoros*. In the twentieth century, R. Abraham Isaiah Karelitz, the *Hazon Ish*, states that, nowadays, when there are no open miracles (so faith is harder), to treat the *epikoros* with all the severity of the law does nothing to repair the breach and that, on the contrary, we must try to the best of our ability to encourage unbelievers to see the light by loving them and making them welcome.[12] Rabbi A. I. Kook, chief Rabbi of Palestine, known for his friendliness even toward the unbelievers among the pioneers who were rebuilding the land, argues in similar vein. Kook declares that unbelievers, nowadays, do not fall at all under the heading of *epikoros*, a term which only applied to the atheists of former ages who defiantly attacked Judaism.[13]

The majority of the Talmudic instances in which disparagement of the *am ha-aretz*, the man ignorant of the Torah, is expressed, are in the realm of Aggadah. One of these, however, has a quasi-Halakhic status—that an *am ha-aretz* must not marry the daughter of a *kohen* ("a priest").[14] The rule was totally ignored by the people and their view was defended by the Halakhic authority and Hasidic master R. Yekutial Judah Teitelbaum (1808–1882) on the grounds that "nowadays" everyone has a little learning so that no one qualifies as an *am ha-aretz*.[15] At a much earlier period, the German authority R. Jair Hayyim Bacharach (1638–1702)[16] states that the Talmudic references to the *am ha-aretz* are not to be applied to contemporary ignoramuses so that whereas the Talmudic rabbis frown on the marriage of the daughter of an *am ha-aretz* to a scholar[17] this is ignored by contemporaries.

Scholars—*talmidey hahamim*—are afforded many privileges in the Halakhah. They are exempt from communal taxation, for example.[18] Based on a passage in the Jerusalem Talmud[19], the Halakhah states that one who insults a *talmid haham* is fined a pound (in weight) of gold *(litra de-dahava)*.[20] This latter rule was not merely academic. Maimonides records:

> The law has been laid down that whoever puts a scholar to shame, even if only by means of verbal abuse, is fined, the Court extracting from him 35 denars of gold, which corresponds to the weight of nine selas less a quarter. We have a tradition that this fine is collected everywhere, in the Holy Land and in the Diaspora. Many instances of this are known to us from Spain. There were scholars who waived their rights and it is a noble thing so to do. Other scholars summoned the offender to Court and the judges brought about a compromise settlement. But the judges used to say to the perpetrator: "You are liable to pay him a pound of gold".[21]

Scholars would have been more than human if they had never abused their privileges. There are recorded instances of scholars provoking the masses to insult them so as to enrich themselves with the fines to which the law gives them title, as is stated in the Responsa collection of R. Joseph Colon (d. 1480), the *Maharik*.[22] Something had to be done to check these abuses. Both in Colon and in the collection of R. Jacob Weil (d.ca. 1450,)[23] the idea is put forward that "nowadays" no one is sufficiently learned to qualify as a *talmid haham* for the purpose of this fine. Isserles[24] quotes as the accepted ruling the opinions of Colon and Weil that nowadays the law of the pound of gold no longer applies because there are no longer to be found scholars of the high caliber to whom the law originally applied. Isserles[25] rules that for the purpose of the exemption from communal taxation contemporary scholars are treated as *talmidey hahamim*, thus compromising between the need to show respect to scholars and assist them to study, and the need to prevent abuses.[26] Obviously, in this whole area much depended on the status and character of the scholars in particular communities. Weil flourished in Germany and Isserles flourished in Poland. Joseph Trani (1568–1639), the *Maharit*, head of the Yeshiva in Constantinople and eventually chief rabbi of Turkey, takes strong issue with the Colon ruling, holding that the fine still applies and that it is absurd to refuse to impose it on such artificial grounds as that scholars nowadays are not really scholars.[27]

Still another possible change of status in the Halakhah is in connection with a deaf mute, *heresh*, who, according to the law, is treated for most purposes as an imbecile and is consequently exempt from the performance of all the precepts.[28] R. Simhah Bunem Sofer of Pressburg (1842–1906) discusses whether a deaf mute who had been trained in a school for the deaf to communicate adequately is still treated as an imbecile.[29] He remarks that he had often heard his father and predecessor in the Rabbinate of Pressburg, R. Abraham Wolf Sofer (1815–1871), say that he was in doubt about this and that once on a visit to Vienna he was invited to inspect the Institute for the Deaf and Dumb in that city. He was so impressed with the remarkable advances he saw there that he was inclined to the view that the pupils of such a school were to be treated as normal persons and he urged the principal of the school to buy *tefillin* for them.

We turn now to examples of change apart from questions of personal status. The law that one must not drink liquids that had been left exposed, because a snake may have injected its venom into the liquid, is found in the Mishnah.[30] Maimonides records it categorically, holding that one who offends against this law is to be flogged.[31] In France, however, it was the practice to ignore this law and the *Tosafists* again defend the local custom, this time on the grounds that no poisonous snakes are found in France so that the law has become inoperative since the original reason for it no longer applies.[32] The *Shulhan Arukh*[33] follows this ruling, stating: "Liquids that had been left exposed were forbidden by the Sages because we are afraid lest a snake had injected its venom into them when it drank of them. But now that snakes are not found among us it is permitted."[34] We noted in the previous chapter how all questions of change in the law have to cope with the rule that one court cannot override the decision of an earlier court of superior wisdom.[35] The *Tosafists* are aware of the problem but argue that the prohibition in the first instance was limited to places where there is danger from snake venom. There was no blanket prohibition that cannot be abrogated. The *Tosafists* add a further illustration of the principle that where the original law was only conditional it falls into abeyance in circumstances to which the condition does not apply.[36]. The Talmud permits the burial of a corpse by Jews on the second days of festivals.[37] But Ravina states that "nowadays" it is forbidden because of the Guebers, the Persian fire worshipers (who used to compel Jews to do forced labor but exempted them from it on the festivals. If the Guebers witnessed Jews burying their dead on these days they will conclude that they are not really sacred days and will compel the Jews to work on them). Here we have first a change in the law, from permissiveness in favor of strictness, because of the changed conditions (the rise of the Guebers) and, then, argue the *Tosafists*, the French Jews do bury their dead on the second days of festivals and are justified in so doing because the reason for the change no longer applies. The change in the law by which burials were forbidden was only because of the Guebers, and since such folk are not to be found in France it is right to revert to the original law. Here we have clear reference to a process of double change in the law, all because conditions change.

According to the law as laid down in the Talmud there is an obligation to marry and have children and this can be enforced by the court.[38] But in a Responsum, addressed to the judges and communal leaders of Tunis, R. Isaac b. Sheshet Perfet (1326–1408), the *Ribash*, rabbi of Algiers, after having stated the details regarding coercion in these matters, makes the following observation:

> However, all this is from the point of view of the strict law according to the Talmud. But what shall we do when we have never witnessed in our generation, nor have we heard of it in many generations, that the Court ever concerns itself to use coercion where a woman has been together with her husband for ten years without bearing him children or where she is too old to bear him children, and this even if he has no children. . . . Nor have we ever witnessed a Court being concerned to prevent the marriage of a minor girl . . . or the marriage of the daughter of a *kohen*[39] or of a scholar to an *am ha-aretz* or of the daughter of an *am ha-aretz* to a scholar. If the Courts were to be concerned with the strict law in such matters so as to exercise coercion they would have to be consistent and then the majority of older women (i.e., who married late) would have to be divorced from their husbands and receive their

ketubah, as well as their dowry. Now since "there is no *ketubah* settlement unattended by quarrels," conflict and strife would have increased. Consequently, the Sages of generations past looked the other way in matters of marriages, never preventing them taking place and *a fortiori* never enforcing a separation, provided that the partners are willing and there is no question of any impediment on the grounds of Biblical law and no impediment because the Rabbis have forbidden such a marriage on grounds of holiness (i.e., where the Rabbis have extended the laws of affinity and consanguinity).[40]

Thus Perfet admits that the older law has been abandoned and seeks to justify this on the grounds that to be too strict in the matter will be self-defeating and lead to constant strife. Because such a statement appears in the Responsa of such a great authority as Perfet, the departure from the law, justified by him, became itself law and is so codified by Isserles[44] who quotes Perfet verbatim.

Changes in the law, where social conditions demanded these, were sometimes effected through legal fictions, by means of which the original law was not abolished but circumvented. An illustration of this is the sale of *hametz*, "leaven," before Passover.[42] According to the rabbinic understanding of "and there shall be no leavened bread be seen *with thee*" (Exod. 12:20), it is permitted to have in the house during Passover leaven belonging to a non-Jew.[43] The normal procedure in Talmudic times, in the event leaven could not be disposed of before Passover, was to sell the leaven to a non-Jew.[44] The sale of the leaven in such circumstances was a real sale, the leaven being removed from the Jewish home by the non-Jew before Passover. There is, however, an instance, mentioned in the *Tosefta*, where a Jew and a non-Jew are traveling by ship and the Jew needs his leaven for use after Passover.[45] Here, the procedure, as stated, is for the Jew to sell his leaven to the non-Jew before Passover but with a tacit understanding that he will buy it back after Passover. The sale is a proper sale but the Jew trusts his non-Jewish companion to sell the leaven back to him after Passover. The *Tosefta* insists that the sale must be quite unconditional, the non-Jew having the full right to retain the leaven if he so desires. This form of sale was adopted in the Middle Ages even where there was no urgency, mentioned in the *Tosefta*, such as where the Jew was on a sea journey and the like.[46] At this stage, though the leaven will be returned after Passover, it is actually removed for the duration of the festival from the possession of the Jew into the possession of the non-Jew. But in seventeenth-century Poland many Jews earned their living as innkeepers, with large quantities of alcohol manufactured from grain and so qualifying as "leaven." It was simply not possible for them to remove the leaven into the possession of a non-Jew. R. Joel Sirkes (1561–1640) provides the remedy of a formal sale.[47] The procedure suggested, and widely adopted, was for the Jew to sell the leaven and the space it occupied to the non-Jew on the understanding (but with no actual condition to this effect) that he will sell it back after Passover. It was obviously not possible for the non-Jew to pay for all the leaven. Instead he acquired the leaven formally, leaving a deposit with the Jewish vendor. The sale, though formal, was carried out with all the legal requirements for it to be valid. At a still later stage, a special bill of sale was drawn up to make the sale more concrete and less suggestive of evasion. Later still, instead of each Jewish householder selling his own leaven in this way, the town rabbi acted on behalf of all the Jewish townsfolk, selling their leaven in this formal way by power of attorney. Although voices were raised periodically against the formal sale of *hametz*, it won the support of the great Halakhists and continues to be the standard procedure among the majority of Orthodox Jews down to the present.

The sale of *hametz* served partly as the basis of a very revolutionary *hetter* ("permission," "dispensation") on the same principle of permitting something otherwise forbidden through a formal sale effecting a transfer of property. This is the *hetter* by means of which soil cultivation is possible in the Holy Land during the Sabbatical year (Exod. 23:10–11; Lev. 25: 1–7; 20–22).[48] At the time of the early settlements in the nineteenth century it was widely felt that to allow the land to remain uncultivated during the Sabbatical year would result in economic ruin for the Yishuv. In 1888, a number of famous rabbis issued the *hetter* for 1889, which was a Sabbatical year. This resulted in one of the fiercest Halakhic debates of all time, some Halakhists siding with those who issued the *hetter*, others rejecting it as totally unfounded. In 1910 Rabbi A. I. Kook, then rabbi of Jaffa and subsequently chief rabbi of Palestine, repeated the *hetter*, despite considerable opposition led by R. Jacob David Willowsky, known as *Ridbaz*.[49] The *hetter* is still in operation in the State of Israel and is recognized by the Israeli chief rabbis, Sephardi and Ashkebnazi, although some religious Kibbutzim do not avail themselves of it. The *hetter* involves the formal sale of all Jewish land to a non-Jew on the same lines as the formal sale of *hametz*. The land then cultivated is non-Jewish land, which, according to many authorities, may be cultivated during the Sabbatical year. Rabbi Kook, in an acute analysis of the use of legal fiction

in matters of this kind, defends the *better* but also bases his decision
on the opinion of the majority of the Halakhists that, in any event,
the laws of the Sabbatical year are binding, nowadays, when the
majority of Jews do not reside in the Holy Land, only by rabbinic,
not by biblical, law. The opponents of the *better* advance a number
of arguments to support their view that the sale of the whole of
Eretz Yisrael to an Arab Sheikh is quite different from the formal
sale of *hametz*. First, the resort to legal fiction is here so blatant that
it borders on sheer evasion. Secondly, it is by no means certain that
non-Jewish land may be cultivated on the Sabbatical year. Third,
there is the question of whether it is, in fact, permitted to sell land
in Eretz Yisrael to non-Jews in view of the Talmudic statement
forbidding this.[50] In this latter case the argument is that one cannot
have it both ways. If the sale is real there is the prohibition of
selling land to a non-Jew. If this is permitted on the grounds that it
is only a formal, not a real, sale then how can the sale be effective
for the purpose of the Sabbatical year? The matter is complicated
by the fact that many authorities hold that the Talmudic injunction
against selling land to non-Jews in Eretz Yisrael only applies to a
sale of land to idolators and Muslims are not idolators. The whole
problem has been aired extensively with considerable Helakhic in-
genuity employed by both sides in the debate. But no great feat of
the imagination is required to see that for both sides other considerations than those of pure legal theory are involved. The lenient
authorities wished to give encouragement to the new settlers and
prevent economic disaster and this led them to discover Halakhic
means to circumvent the law. The stricter authorities, too, ap-
pealed to such theological motivation as the need to give a powerful
religious dimension to Israel's return to its land and, above all, the
need to demonstrate that the land is God's who is capable of providing for those who trust in Him by obeying His laws.

Adjustment of the law in response to changed economic conditions is also and particularly evident in the development of the laws
against usury. In the kind of agricultural community envisaged in
the biblical laws against usury, loans were made normally for the
sole purpose of buying farm equipment and the like. The granting
of a loan in such a society was an act of benevolence from which it
was forbidden for the lender to gain by cashing in on his neighbor's
need. There was hardly any lending as a business investment. To a
large extent the same conditions still obtained in Roman Palestine
during the period of the Tannaim and Amoraim. But in Babylon,
during the Amoraic period, commercial life was far more highly

organized and largely in Jewish and Armenian hands, the Sassanian rulers of the Persian Empire holding commerce to be an inferior occupation and beneath their dignity to engage in personally, although they evidently had no objection to benefiting from it indirectly. The need was thus keenly felt in Sassanian Babylon for business loans to be permitted in Jewish law. The result of this was the evolution of a complex of laws in which lending on interest for investment purposes was allowed provided certain conditions were satisfied. Chapter 5 of the Mishnah to Bava Metzia deals with the laws of interest. It is significant to note how little elaboration on these laws is provided in the Palestinian Talmud and how much is provided in the Babylonian Talmud. One of the institutions developed by the Babylonian Amoraim became the basis for permitting loans on interest in the post-Talmudic period. An investment of money in business by a "sleeping partner" was known as *iska* ("trading"), the usual arrangement being two shares of the profits for the trader and one for the investor. To avoid any infringement of the usury laws the rabbis enacted that half the sum involved in an *iska* arrangement should be in the nature of a loan and hence at the risk of the trader, the other half a trust and hence at the risk of the investor. The profits then received are not in the nature of "payment for waiting" (the Talmudic definition of usury) but rather of a speculation, the trader acting as the investor's agent for the sale of his share.[51] In the late Middle Ages an elaboration of this was worked out—the *hetter iska*—according to which the trader guaranteed the lender against loss and promised him a fixed profit; loans for investment purposes thus came outside the laws of usury. R. Samuel b. David Moses ha-Levi (d. 1681) in his *Nahalat Shivah* gives the text of the document (the *shetar*) for this purpose.[52]

In connection with changed economic conditions, the medieval codifiers such as Maimonides totally ignore the statements in the Mishnah disapproving of certain occupations such as physician, ass driver, camel driver, shopkeeper, and shepherd.[53] Maimonides and Nahmanides, as well as other medieval Halakhists, were themselves physicians. Evidently they understood the Mishnah not as a categorical ruling but simply as good advice because in the time of the Mishnah those who followed these occupations were unscrupulous or dishonest. The influence of the social background in these matters made itself felt even in the Talmudic period in Babylon, where, for example, the Amora, Samuel, was a physician.

Important changes of the most far-reaching kind took place in the area of study. The rabbinic interpretation of "For after these words" (Exod. 34:27) is that only *these* words, that is, words of Scripture, may be recorded in writing but the "Oral Torah" must not be written down." The verse says, "Write these words" and then says, "For after these words," to teach you that words of the Oral Torah you are not permitted to express in writing and words of the Written Torah you are not permitted to recite by heart."[54] But in exceptional circumstances, i.e., where the law is new and would otherwise be forgotten, it is permitted to write down something of the Oral Torah, on the basis of the verse: "It is time for the Lord to work, they have made void Thy Law" (Ps. 119:126). This verse is interpreted as, "It is better that one letter of the Torah (the verse forbidding the writing donw of the Oral Torah) should be uprooted than that the whole of the Torah be forgotten."[55] The question of how much of the Oral Torah was written down in Talmudic times is a very complicated one. Rashi, and the French school generally, hold that very little was actually recorded in writing (only in the exceptional circumstances referred to previously) so that, according to this school, the Mishnah and the Gemara were not recorded in writing until the post-Talmudic period. Maimonides, and the Spanish school generally, hold that both the Mishnah and the Gemara were recorded in writing by their editors because this, too, belonged to the exceptional circumstances for which permission was granted in that otherwise these works would have been forgotten. There are two versions of the famous Letter of Sherira Gaon, a French and a Spanish, according to which the gaon, in his description of how the Mishnah and the Gemara came to be, states either that these were recorded in writing or were handed down verbally.[56] In any event, the Talmud was eventually recorded in writing in obedience to the principle of *et laasot*, "it is a time to do things for the Lord," i.e., in order to prevent the Oral Torah from being forgotten. The result has been that writings on the Oral Torah became so much the norm that the original interdict on writing it down was completely overlooked. Since the Talmud permits the writing down of the Oral Torah in exceptional circumstances, the *Tosafists* argue, a blind person may recite Torah passages by heart and need have no fear of any infringement of the other prohibition, that of reciting the Written Torah by heart, since the blind man's circumstances are obviously "exceptional."[57]

Were it not for the removal of the ban on writing down the Oral Torah there could never have been an Halakhic literature at all. The Halakhah itself owes its continued existence to the principle of *et laasot*. The only instance recorded of a rabbinic scholar refusing

to write down his Halakhic novellae in obedience to the original law
is that of R. Nathan Adler of Frankfurt (1741–1800), of whom it is
said that he knew the whole Talmud by heart. He would only write
down very brief notes in the belief that to do more than this was to
infringe the law since for him, with his remarkable memory, the
special dispensation was not required. Such an attitude seems to
have been peculiar to this famous Kabbalist and mystic.[58]

When Halakhic manuscripts came to enjoy a wide circulation a
further change, or, better, an elaboration of another old law took
place. The Babylonian teacher Rabbah states that it is a religious
duty for every Jew to write a Sefer Torah.[59] Maimonides has this as
a definite ruling in his Code.[60] But Asher b. Yehiel (d. 1327), the
Rosh, observes that, "nowadays," the Scroll is kept in the synagogue
and the original law now embraces the writing of other books on
the Torah since the reason for the original law was clearly for the
purpose of study.[61] His son, Jacob, records this in his *Tur*:

> My father, the *Rosh*, of blessed memory, writes that this was only stated
> in former generations, when they used to write the Sefer Torah and
> study therein. But nowadays, when they write a Sefer Torah and place
> it in the synagogue to read therefrom in public, it is a positive precept
> for everyone who can afford it to write the books of the Pentateuch, the
> Mishnah, the Gemara and the Commentators on these in order that he
> and his sons might meditate therein. The duty of writing a Sefer Torah
> is for the purpose of studying therein, as it is written: "And teach it to
> the children of Israel, put it in their mouths" (Deut. 31:19) and by
> means of the Gemara and its commentary he will come to know the
> meaning of the precepts and the laws. Consequently these are the very
> books a man is obliged to write and which he may not sell except for the
> purpose of studying the Torah or marrying.[62]

This ruling is also given in the *Shulhan Arukh*.[63]

An example of a law which by its very nature is interpreted as
depending on social conditions is, "A woman shall not wear that
which pertains unto a man, neither shall a man put on a woman's
garment, for whosoever doeth these things is an abomination to the
Lord thy God" (Deut. 22:5). The rabbis extend this to any acts
peculiar to one sex; e.g., it is forbidden for a man to remove the hair
of his armpits or his pubic hair[64] or to use a mirror.[65] But R. Nissim Gerondi's understanding of the relevant Talmudic passages is
that these acts are only forbidden where they are peculiar to
women.[66] In places where men, too, shave their pubic hair or use a
mirror there is no prohibition. In other words, since men do these

things in these places they fall under the heading of men's "garments" as well as of "women's" and the law does not apply, except, as R. Nissim suggests, for exceptionally pious people. The *Shulḥan Arukh*[67] rules that it is forbidden for a man to look into a mirror or to remove the hair of his armpits or his pubic hair[68] but Isserles quotes R. Nissim and permits these practices when they are not peculiar to women.[69] Isserles,[70] indeed, goes so far as to permit, on Purim, the practice of donning fancy dress, men dressing as women and women as men, on the grounds that since it is done solely for the purpose of Purim jollification there is no infringement of the law. Possibly, the argument here is that since this has become the norm on Purim and there is no sinful intention, then on Purim garments of men are worn by women and of women by men so that on this day the garments are not peculiar to either sex. David ha-Levi, the *Taz*, quotes, however, in the name of his father-in-law, Joel Sirkes, the *Baḥ*, that it is better to forbid it.[71] A further interesting example of an interpretation of this law so that it does not come into conflict with local custom, is the defense by R. Zevi Hirsch Shapira of the custom of pious married women in parts of Eastern Europe to shave their heads and cover them with a kerchief so that no hair can be seen.[72] The *Shulḥan Arukh*[73] rules explicitly that it is forbidden for women to shave the hair of their heads because of the law which forbids a woman to wear a man's "garment," but Shapira defends the Eastern European custom on the grounds that it is done as a mark of extreme modesty so that it is clear to everyone that these pious women have not the slightest intention of copying the practices of men and it is not only permitted but is an admirable custom.

An example of how the sexual mores of the surrounding culture influenced the Halakhah is provided in connection with the laws regarding homosexual practices.[74] There is a debate[75] between R. Judah and the sages, the former holding that two bachelors must not sleep together under the same sheet because it may lead to them committing sodomy, whereas the sages hold that it is permitted because "Israelites are not suspected of committing such a sin."[76] Maimonides records the view of the sages as law.[77] Karo, however, first records the same ruling but adds: "But in these generations when profligates are numerous it is proper for males never to be alone together."[78] R. Josel Sirkes, writing in seventeenth-century Poland, comments on this, "He (Karo) wrote this with regard to his country and his times and it would appear that he holds it is forbidden according to the law for males to be alone together. But in our land, where it is unheard of for anyone to be lax in this matter there is no need for separation. Nevertheless, whoever does keep separate, it is praiseworthy of him."[79] It is clear from all the commentators that, the actual practice in this matter tended to follow the norm in each particular time and place. Thus, Rabbi A. I. Kook understands the difference between Karo and Sirkes to be that the former lived in a hot climate, where the blood becomes overheated, whereas the latter lived in a cold climate.[80] Rabbi Kook draws the conclusion that even now in Eastern lands it is as well for males not to be alone together. It is more probable, however, the the differing attitudes of Karo and Sirkes are the result of the relative abhorrence of homosexuality and the degree to which it was practiced among Jews and this, in turn, appears to have depended on the attitudes and practices which prevailed in the non-Jewish environment.

The institution of a professional, salaried rabbinate is itself an example of extension, change, and elaboration of the Halakhah in response to social and economic change. In Talmudic times the prohibition of receiving any remuneration for acting as a judge or for teaching the Torah was in force.[81] The judges and Torah teachers had their own occupations by means of which they earned their living.[82] In medieval Europe this situation no longer obtained. Scholars were usually unable to devote themselves to the service of the community without receiving a salary, except for the fortunate few who had private means. The *Tosafists* know of the contemporary practice of receiving a salary for teaching the Torah and they defend this departure from the Talmudic rule on the grounds that without this the scholars would be unable to exist so that the salary is not, in fact, for teaching but for them having to give up any alternative methods of earning a living.[83] The *Tur* similarly remarks:

> My father and master, the *Rosh*, of blessed memory, writes that it is the practice, nowadays, to teach all subjects for payment and this is permitted if the teacher has no other means of earning a living. And even if he has other means it is permitted if the remuneration is clearly for the purpose of compensating him from having to engage in other employment since he turns aside from all his occupation and business affairs.[84]

The *Shulhan Arukh* quotes this *verbatim*.[85] Eventually, the position of professional rabbi became established in all the great communities and there developed around it a special law of its own. Isserles, for example, writes:

If a Rabbi resides in a town and teaches the Torah there, another Rabbi is permitted to settle there and teach, even though the latter decreases thereby, to some extent, the income of the former. If, for instance, the community had appointed the first one to be their Rabbi and receive a salary, the second one may, nevertheless, reside in the town and serve as a Rabbi in connection with all matters, just like the first one, provided he is a great scholar and possesses the ability to serve in this capacity. But if a sage is a visitor to the town, he must not cause any loss to the resident Rabbi by officiating at weddings and pocketing the remuneration since it is the Rabbi's means of sustenance. He may, however, officiate at a wedding provided he hands over the fee to the Rabbi. He may also act as a judge in a case between two litigants residing in the town if these present themselves to him because they find the town Rabbi unacceptable to them. But he must not render decisions in matters of religious law nor must he preach and by so doing hold office in the place of his colleague. Whoever has an established position as a town Rabbi, even if he took this office for himself, must not be deposed even if a greater scholar than he came to reside in that town. And even the Rabbi's son or grandson takes precedence over all others provided he follows in his father's footsteps in the fear of God and has some degree of learning. But in a place where it is the custom to appoint a Rabbi for a fixed period or where the custom is to elect anyone they choose, this may be done. However, when a man has been elected by the community, *a fortiori* if the election has won the consent of the (non-Jewish) governing body, not even the greatest of scholars may usurp the resident Rabbi's position.[86]

It can be seen from this passage in Isserles and from the sources he quotes in support how gradually an entirely new category has been introduced into Jewish law.[87] In the course of time, even the limitations recorded by Isserles were set aside, the rabbi of a town having a contract and proper financial arrangements just like any other communal official and with adequate safeguards against unfair competition.[88] Rabbi Moses Sofer, for example, states that the rule recorded by Isserles only applied in his day when it was not the custom actually to elect a town rabbi, every scholar controlling the affairs of his community.

But, nowadays, where a Rabbi is appointed and he moves residence to settle in the town and they fix his salary, just like any other employee, and included in his stipend are the fees for officiating at weddings and divorces and so forth, he does not act in any way unlawfully by receiving his salary. It may be that the community acts unfairly by making the Rabbi's remuneration depend on fees paid by its individual members but there is no shame attached to the Rabbi receiving these fees if it is done in a dignified manner. The Rabbi is fully entitled to all fees paid within the borders of his jurisdiction. It is, consequently, forbidden for anyone to encroach on his livelihood and to do so is a matter of downright robbery.[89]

R. Moses Sofer, in particular, in a number of his Responsa, aims at establishing proper legal procedures with regard to the status and emoluments of the town rabbi[90] but it is not without significance that this was not done until as late as the nineteenth century.

There are instances of Talmudic permissiveness, too, being overruled by contemporary custom and this is defended Halakhically. According to the ruling in the Talmud there is no obligation to recite the night prayer but it is entirely optional *(reshut)*.[91] Nevertheless it appears that Jewish communities did have regular night services and this very fact served to make these services obligatory. Maimonides rules: "The night prayer is not obligatory as are the morning and afternoon prayers. Nevertheless, all Israel in all their habitations have had the custom of reciting the night prayer and have taken it upon themselves as an obligation."[92] The ruling in the Mishnah[93] that a Sefer Torah need not be written in Hebrew but may be written in Greek was ignored in the Middle Ages, it being argued that the Rabbis are no longer in possession of the original Greek language and it became the universal practice for the scrolls to be written only in Hebrew.[94]

A very striking example of change in the law is in connection with a husband who has been lost at sea. The Talmudic law is strict in this matter. If the water is limitless *(mayyim she-eyn la-hem sof)*, i.e., has no visible boundaries, the wife is not allowed to remarry because her husband may have survived.[95] At the beginning of the thirteenth century a ship went down and R. Eliezer of Verona permitted the wife to remarry after a number of years had elapsed on the grounds that the Talmud does not say that the wife may *never* remarry, only that "she is forbidden," which means, according to this authority, that it is left to the court to determine whether it is likely that, after a lengthy period of time has elapsed and if the particular circumstances warrant it, the husband is still alive. This is known in the Halakhic literature as "the permission advanced by R. Eliezer of Verona on the grounds of circumstantial evidence." (In reality, because of a confusion of name, this is usually given us "by R. Eliezer of Verdun," instead of "of Verona"). This dispensation was not accepted in itself by the later Halakhists but was relied on, nevertheless, when it could be added to other reasons leading to a lenient decision.[96] In the nineteenth century R. Moses Sofer adds the further consideration that, nowadays, when communications have improved beyond all recognition from those of former times (he cites the postal service, the telegraph, and newspapers), it is all the more convincing to suppose that if the husband were still alive he would have found means of notifying his family.[97] R. Moses Sofer, too, only uses the argument together with other reasons for leniency but he does attach significance to it. In this he is followed by R. Isaac Elhanan Spektor, the foremost nineteenth-century authority of the problem of the missing husband.[98] This argument, together with others, was used to permit the wives of the crew to remarry when the Israeli submarine Dakkar went down at sea.

An example of change in the law in favor both of strictness and leniency is provided by R. Asher b. Yehiel, the *Rosh*. The biblical law forbids the wearing of a garment with a mixture of wool and linen: "You shall not wear cloth combining wool and linen" (Deut. 22:11). According to the Mishnah, the biblical law does not apply to canvas or to silk, yet whereas canvas is permitted together with wool even according to rabbinic law, silk is forbidden by rabbinic law because of appearances *(marit ha-ayyin)*, i.e., silk looks like linen and there is the appearance of something forbidden.[99] Canvas, which does not have the appearance of ordinary linen, is permitted to be worn in a garment of wool even by rabbinic law because the appearance is not deceptive. The *Rosh* was obliged to leave his native Germany for Spain and in 1305 he was appointed rabbi of Toledo. The *Rosh* writes:

> When I was in Germany I forbade the stitching of a garment of canvas underneath a garment of wool because garments of canvas are not often found in Germany and people will imagine it to be a garment of linen. Nowadays, too, silken garments are often found among us so that everyone recognises these for what they are. Consequently, it is now permitted to stitch a garment of silk underneath a garment of wool and strands of silk are also permitted in a garment of wool.[100]

Thus the *Rosh* reverses the rule of the Mishnah. In Mishnaic times, he argues, canvas was clearly recognized as such but silk could be confused with linen. "Nowadays" the opposite is true; silk is never confused with linen but canvas, being rare, is. Consequently, the law is reversed. A garment of wool with a silk lining may be worn but not one with a canvas lining. The *Tur* records the ruling of his father, the *Rosh*.[101] The *Shulhan Arukh* records the ruling of the *Rosh* permitting silk together with wool but fails to record the other rule of the *Rosh*, that canvas is forbidden.[102] Isserles, however, notes: "And it is forbidden to stitch a garment of canvas underneath a garment of wool in a place where canvas is not usually found because of *marit ha-ayyim*. But in a place where it is found it is permitted."[103] Thus, in a place where canvas is found the law reverts to the original ruling of the Mishnah. Shabbetai ha-Kohen, the *Shakh*, quotes Polish authorities who state that "in our lands" canvas is permitted because there is an abundance of canvas.[104]

Another change in the law in Russia and Poland is based on different conditions of climate. Although it is normally forbidden for a Jew to instruct a non-Jew to heat the home on the Sabbath it is permitted in very cold climes on the grounds that if there is no heating, people will fall sick and it is therefore permitted, just as a Jew may instruct a non-Jew to do work on behalf of a sick person.[105] It appears, too, that, on similar grounds, it was not the normal practice of the Polish Jews to sleep in the *sukkah* but only to eat there, even though sleeping in the *sukkah* is strictly enjoined in the Talmud.[106] The Talmud does exempt, however, from observing the *mitzvah* of the *sukkah* where this causes him distress.[107] Thus Isserles writes:

> The reason why it is now the custom to be lenient with regard to sleeping in the *sukkah*, for only the excessively scrupulous sleep now in the *sukkah*, is, some say, because there is distress to sleep there in cold climes (*Mordekhai*). But it seems to me that the *mitzvah* of *sukkah* is for a man and his wife to sleep there together, just as they sleep together during the rest of the year. It follows that where it is not possible for husband and wife to sleep together, because they have no separate *sukkah* for the purpose, he is exempt. But it is good to be strict in this matter and be there together with his wife just as he is during the rest of the year if he can possibly arrange to have a separate *sukkah* for the purpose.[108]

It is undoubtedly true that many Polish and Russian Jews did sleep in the *sukkah*, but various attempts were made by later authorities to defend the widespread custom not to sleep there. This is in addition to the defense mentioned by Isserles.[109]

According to the law as stated in the Mishnah, it is not only forbidden to put out a fire on the Sabbath but, with the exception of sacred books and a minimum amount of food and clothing, it is even forbidden to save anything from the flames.[110] If this were permitted, people might be led to putting out the fire in their haste to save whatever they can. The Jerusalem Talmud understands the

Mishnah as following the opinion of R. Simeon who holds that even if the fire were put out on the Sabbath it would be a rabbinic, not a biblical offense.[111] This is because, R. Simeon holds, the act of putting out the fire is only biblically forbidden where the act is performed for that express purpose not where the purpose is only to save things from the flames *(melakhah she-eyno tzarikh le-gufo)*. Mordecai b. Hillel (d. 1298), the German Halakhist, records that in his day people disregarded the prohibition of putting out the fire on the Sabbath since, as stated in the Jerusalem Talmud, the prohibition is only rabbinic.[112] Mordecai's actual formulation is worth recording because it affords an excellent illustration of how a current practice demanded to be defended, albeit reluctantly, even though it found no support in the Talmudic sources:

> Nowadays, it is the practice in the majority of lands to put out a fire on the Sabbath but they have nothing in the sources on which to rely (to permit this). They say, however, that they are afraid, if the fire be allowed to spread, that it might bring about the death of infants who are unable to run away. Furthermore, there is the fear that it may lead to loss of life because of the dread of the government and of the Gentiles who might kill the Jews for allowing the fire to spread. This is why they put out fires and since we follow R. Simeon they rely on this. There is no clear permission to do this but this falls under the heading of those matters regarding which the Sages say: "Leave Israel alone. It is better that they should sin unintentionally than that they should sin presumptuously.[113]

Thus, we learn that in the second half of the thirteenth century the Talmudic law was ignored "in many lands," Mordecai defending it only because people will do it in any event so that it is better to leave them in ignorance of the fact that they are committing a sin. But not all Mordecai's contemporaries were so hesitant in defending the current practice. In a Responsum on the subject, Israel Isserlein[114] (1390–1460) quotes the far more categorical statement of Isaac b. Moses of Vienna (d. 1250), author of *Or Zarua*, who rules that it is *permitted* to put out a fire on the Sabbath, giving as an additional reason that if Jews refrain from putting out fires the Gentiles will hear of the spoils to be had for the taking and in their eagerness to plunder the Jews might even kill them. In fact, as in every case where there is a possible danger to life, the putting out of the fire should be done by the great scholars of the community in order to demonstrate to the people that it is permitted beyond doubt, the exact opposite of Mordecai's reluctant dispensation. Isserlein thoroughly approves. Karo quotes these permissive views in his *Bet Yosef* but in his *Shulḥan Arukh* simply states all the laws about putting out a fire on the Sabbath, implying that they still are to be followed.[115]

Isserles, writing in sixteenth-century Poland, adds this note to Karo's ruling in the *Shulḥan Arukh:*

> All these laws regarding a fire breaking out on the Sabbath only applied in their days but, nowadays, when there is the fear that life might be endangered, both the earlier and the later authorities, of blessed memory, write that it is permitted to put out a fire on the Sabbath because not to do so can be dangerous and the more energetic one is in putting the fire out the better it is. Nevertheless, it all depends on the circumstances and if they are confident that no danger will result it is forbidden to put out the fire. But where there is the slightest fear that otherwise danger may result it is permitted to put out the fire, even if it breaks out in the house of a Gentile, and this is the practice.[116]

Thus, the older Talmudic law, which forbids even the saving of things from the fire let alone putting the fire out, became a dead letter.

Another instance where Isserles follows Insserlein in declaring that an ancient law is "nowadays" ignored is in connection with sessions of the court. The Jerusalem Talmud states that it is forbidden for the court to sit on the eve of Sabbaths and festivals.[117] The reason for this ruling appears to be because the judges will be unable to concentrate adequately on the cases before them in their preoccupation with the Sabbath and festival preparations. The *Shulḥan Arukh* [118] gives this as the ruling but Isserles in his gloss quotes Isserlein that, "nowadays," the courts do sit on these days in order to avoid having scholars spend too much time in the courts.[119] The meaning of this is that on the eve of Sabbaths and festivals scholars are on vacation in any event, their presence not being required in the schools, so it is better that they should sit as judges on these days rather than have them sit for longer periods on days when their presence is needed in the school.

In this connection of the functioning of the courts a revolutionary change eventually came about. The Talmudic sources are insistent that Jews must never take their disputes to non-Jewish courts even if the laws of the latter do not differ essentially from Jewish law.[120] The principle "the law of the kingdom is law" *dina de-malkhuta dina)* only applied to Jewish courts, i.e, these, when administering Jewish law, had to obey the law of the country.[121] It certainly did not mean that the Jewish courts were to will themselves out of existence. It could not have been put more forcibly than by Maimonides:

> Whoever takes his suit to be decided by the laws of the Gentiles and in their Courts, even when their laws are the same as ours, is a wicked man and it is as if he had blasphemed and insulted, raising his hands against the Torah of Moses our teacher, as it is said: "Now these are the ordinances which thou shalt set before them" (Exod. 21:1)—"before *them*" and not before Gentiles; "before *them*" and not before those lacking in expertise. If the Gentile power prevails and the man with whom he has a suit is powerful so that he cannot be forced to submit to the decision of the Jewish judges, he should first be summoned to the Jewish Court and if he refuses permission should then be obtained from the Jewish judges to obtain redress through the Gentile Courts.[122]

This is the unqualified ruling of all the authorities and is recorded in the *Shulhan Arukh*.[123] But, as Elon has noted, in the nineteenth century, in Western Europe, even Orthodox Jews tended increasingly to resort to the Gentile courts.[124] Even in Eastern Europe, where the Jewish courts still flourished, these tended more and more to rely on arbitration rather than engage in creative jurisprudence until some Halakhists even there justified resort to Gentile courts on the grounds—never countenanced by the earlier Halakhists—of *dina de-malkhuta dina*. Elon tellingly quotes from two distinguished Eastern European Halakhists—R. Meir Dan Plotzki and R. Isaac Elhanan Spektor. Rabbi Plotzki, after discussing at length the prohibition of resorting to Gentile Courts, writes:

> Although there are no practical applications, since the whole of this law does not apply to the (Gentile) judges in our day, who are not idolators, God forbid, and are not included in the Talmudic term "Courts" (of heathens) and it is obvious that it is necessary to be judged only by them because of the law of the land. Yet I wrote what I did for the sake of pure theory with application to lands like China and Japan where they worship idols and do have the status of "Courts."[125]

Rabbi Spektor writes:

> If here and there arguments are put forward (in the book) in matters of civil law, they all apply only to former times. But, nowadays, these matters must be decided solely by the laws of the Courts and we must never call into question any of their aims and principles, God forbid. Nevertheless, the source of these laws still have their place in a theoret-

ical sense and for the sake of theoretical discussion just as there is reward for studying all those laws which no longer have application in our day.[126]

This is by no means the whole story. Elon acknowledges that these two Halakhists are undoubtedly writing with an eye on the censor and with tongue in cheek and Jews did, and still do, resort to the Jewish Courts.[127] But, as Elon continues and rightly so, this fear of the censor and the remarks it occasioned are themselves evidence that, to some extent, at least, the Halakhists were compelled to acquiesce in the abrogation of Jewish autonomy.

A startling example of a law being virtually abrogated for a time and later brought into operation again is the law of *tefillin*. The Talmudic rule everywhere is that *tefillin* must be worn all day and that one who does not wear them is 'a sinner in Israel with his body."[128] Yet the *Tosafists*[129] refer to the neglect of this *mitzvah* in their day and virtually defend the neglect by noting that even in Talmudic times people tended to neglect *tefillin*[130] and that the "sinner in Israel" reference is not to one who never wears *tefillin* but to one who disparages the *tefillin*. There is sufficient evidence of widespread indifference to *tefillin* in France and Germany during the eleventh and twelfth centuries, this being defended, or, at least condoned, by the Halakhists either on the grounds suggested by the *Tosafists* or because, "nowadays," people are insufficiently clean in mind and body to wear the *tefillin*.[131] R. Moses of Coucy relates how he traveled through Spain in the year 1236 to urge the people to wear *tefillin* and to inform them that the fear of physical and spiritual impurity was only a cogent reason for not having to wear the *tefillin* for the whole of the day; they must be worn for the morning prayers.[132] Eventually, people did take once again to wearing *tefillin* but the older Talmudic practice of wearing them for the whole of the day was abandoned, except for the exceptionally pious. The *Tur*[133] expresses the compromise that was adopted in his day and he is followed by the *Shulhan Arukh*:

> The *mitzvah* of *tefillin* involves the wearing of these during the whole of the day. But because they require a clean body, no one wearing them must break wind or have the mind on other matters, and it is not given to everyone to take such care, it is the custom for them not to be worn for the whole of the day. Nevertheless, every man must be careful to wear them when he recites the Shema and says his prayers.[134]

This has remained the practice down to the present day.

Behind the defense offered for not wearing the *tefillin* for the whole of the day—that we are unable to be as scrupulous as the men of former generations—there is implied the virtual dogma of the progressive degeneration of men through the ages. "We" are as pygmies in relation to "them," the giants of the past. This notion served as a justification for other changes in the law. For example, it is argued that "we" are unable to concentrate adequately in our prayers. The Talmud insists that prayers must not be recited when the mind is likely to be disturbed, when, for instance, one has just returned from a long journey or when one is in a bad temper.[135] But the *Shulhan Arukh* states: "No one should say his prayers in a place where there are distractions or at a time when his mind is disturbed. But, nowadays, we take no notice of all this since in any event we do not have too much concentration in our prayers."[136] According to the Talmud it is necessary to concentrate while reciting all the benedictions of the Amidah.[137] The prayers need not be recited again where there had been a failure in concentration unless the first benediction had been recited without concentration. The *Shulhan Arukh*[138] records this but Isserles, following the *Tur*, adds, "Nowadays, we do not repeat the prayers when these have been recited without *kavvanah* ('concentration') since it is likely that we will fail to concentrate the second time round as well so what point is there in reciting the prayers again." The Talmudic law makes a distinction between different kinds of locusts of danger to the crops.[139] If some species appear in the land the alarm must be sounded and there is to be a public fast, whereas for less dangerous species there is prayer only. The *Shulhan Arukh* states, however, that since, nowadays, we are no longer expert in determining these different species we sound the alarm and fast whenever any species of locust appears.[140] The Talmud permits a roast goose to be eaten in certain circumstances, even when it has been roasted with a doughy paste around it, where it can be assumed that the blood has been drained off and indications are given for this such as the type of flour used and the degree of redness in the dough.[141] But the *Shulhan Arukh* rules that since we no longer have the expertise to make these fine distinctions, it is forbidden in all circumstances.[142] Again, in certain circumstances, where there is doubt as to whether an animal is *terefa*, certain tests can be applied and these are given in the Talmud. But Isserles quotes with approval the opinion that in these later generations we are no longer sufficiently expert to apply the tests and the animal is always to be treated as *terefa* where these doubts arise.[143]

Even with regard to physical matters it was generally accepted that there has been a deterioration from earlier ages and this notion, too, had its influence on the law. Already in Talmudic times it was held that "nowadays" people are physically much weaker.[144] Despite the rule of the Mishnah[145] and the *Shulḥan Arukh*[146] that boys must fast the whole day on *Yom Kippur* from the age of twelve, Abraham Gumbinar[147] quotes Joel Sirkes, the *Baḥ*, to the effect that "nowadays" boys do not fast until they are of age (13) because they all are engaged in the study of the Torah which makes them weak and it can in any event be assumed that "nowadays" they are too weak to fast.

Laws affecting residence in the Holy Land were, at times, subject to change. The Talmud waxes eloquent on the virtue of residence in Eretz Yisrael, ruling, for example, that a husband can compel his wife to come with him to live in Eretz Yisrael and she can so compel him.[148] It was obviously not practical to follow this rule in the Middle Ages. The *Tosafists* state explicitly that this rule is no longer binding because of the dangers of the journey.[149] Rabbenu Hayyim is quoted by the *Tosafists* as going so far as to declare that "nowadays" there is no obligation at all to settle in the Holy Land since there are so many precepts binding upon those who live there that we do not have the means adequately to carry out. The *Shulḥan Arukh*[150] simply records the Talmudic law, making no reference to the reservations suggested by the *Tosafists*. Indeed, many authorities take issue with the statement of Rabbenu Hayyim in this matter.[151] The Talmudic sources are very strict that it is categorically forbidden to breed "small cattle" (sheep and goats) in Eretz Yisrael because these cause damage to the fields.[152] But the *Shulḥan Arukh* rules that "nowadays," when it is very unusual for Jews to own field in Eretz Yisrael, it is permitted.[153] In the same section, the *Shulḥan Arukh*[154] records the view stated in the Talmud[155] that it is forbidden to keep a vicious dog unless it is kept chained up with an iron chain, but that in border towns in Eretz Yisrael it is permitted, i.e., so that it serves as a guard dog against infiltration by a possible enemy or invader. Isserles, however, adds the gloss: "But some say that, nowadays, when we reside among the Gentiles and the nations, it is permitted in all circumstances and go out and see how people behave (i.e., and they do keep vicious dogs as watch-dogs). Nevertheless, if it so vicious that it might harm people it is forbidden to keep it unless it is chained up with an iron chain."

Some further, more or less random, examples of changes in the

law conclude this chapter. Certain foodstuffs are forbidden in Talmudic law because these may contain Gentile wine or other forbidden material but nowhere in the Talmud is saffron bought from
Gentiles forbidden. R. Solomon Ibn Adret, the *Rashba*, was asked
whether it is true that he does not eat saffron bought from Gentiles
to which he replies that the report is correct.[156] The reason he gives
is because "in our country" (Spain) they sprinkle a considerable
amount of wine over the saffron. The *Shulhan Arukh*[157] simply
records this new ruling of *Rashba* as authoritative but Shabbetai ha-
Kohen, the *Skakh*, observes that everyone now eats saffron bought
from non-Jews, those who refrain from eating it being in a very
small minority, and this is evidently because *Rashba* knew that in
Spain it did contain wine whereas this is no longer the case.[158]

It appears from the Talmud that it is forbidden to allow the
fringes of the garment—the *tzitzit*—to drag on graves because this
is to mock at the dead who can no longer carry out the precepts.[159]
The implication of the Talmudic passage is that it is permitted if
the *tzitzit* do not actually touch the graves. The *Shulhan Arukh* rules
that this distinction only obtained in Talmudic times when people
wore *tzitzit* in their ordinary, four-cornered robes.[160] "Nowadays"
our ordinary garments are not four-cornered and so do not have
tzitzit attached to them. We only wear *tzitzit* in the special four-
cornered garment worn for that purpose. This garment has been
adopted and is worn for the sole purpose of carrying out the precept. Since this is so it is now forbidden to have the *tzitzit* uncovered in a cemetery, even if they do not actually touch the
graves, for the very appearance of the special garment is a mocking
of the dead who can no longer wear this special garment.

The Talmud states that when one sees a *merkulis* (Mercurius, a
statue or image of Hermes, Mercury) one must recite the benediction "Blessed art Thou, who shows long-suffering to those who
transgress His will."[161] The *Tosafists*[162] note that the *Tosefta* has the
reading "an idol," instead of a *merkulis*, so that the benediction must
be recited on seeing any idol. The reason we do not recite this
benediction is because it was only ordained that it be recited when
one sees the idol periodically, not when it is seen all the time, as
"we" do. It is highly probable that behind this is the obvious need,
in medieval France and Germany, for Jews not to provoke their
non-Jewish neighbors. In this connection the formulation by the
Shulhan Arukh[163] and Isserles is noteworthy. The *Shulhan Arukh*
rules that the benediction must be recited when one sees a *merkulis*
or any other idol but only if it is seen periodically i.e., at intervals

of not less than thirty days. Isserles simply states, "We do not recite this benediction nowadays."

Although, according to the Talmud, the Hanukkah lights were to be placed outside the house in the street, so that all can see them,[164] Isserles[165] records the universal practice in his day, where Jews resided among non-Jews, to place the Hanukkah lights in the privacy of the home.

The Talmud states that a scholar's robe should be so long that it reaches to the ground, or, at least, so that only one handbreadth of his bare legs can be seen.[166] Abraham Gumbiner says that no one takes any notice of this "nowadays" and suggest as the reason because the bare legs are not visible in any event since stockings are worn.[167] Abraham Gumbiner again, on the ruling of Isserles that it is permitted to bathe an infant in hot water on a festival, states that it appears to him, since "we" do not normally bathe an infant daily, it is forbidden on the festival.[168]

The Talmud[169] rules that workmen are to recite only a shorter form of grace after meals, since the time is their employer's but the *Shulhan Arukh*[170] rules, in the name of an earlier authority, that "nowadays" they should recite the full grace. Since nowadays it is unusual for employers to be so particular about it, then it is as if, when the workmen are hired, there is an explicit arrangement in their contract to allow them to recite the full grace.

Finally, we must note two examples of a change of a biblical law recorded in the Mishnah.[171] The Mishnah states, "When murderers increased, the rite of beheading the heifer's neck (Deut. 21:1–9) ceased . . . When adulterers increased, the bitter waters (Num. 5:12–31) ceased; and it was Rabban Johannan b. Zakkai who brought these to an end. For it is written, 'I will not punish your daughters when they commit whoredom nor your daughters-in-law when they commit adultery, for they themselves go apart with whores' (Hos. 4:14)." This latter is explained in the Talmud that the ordeal of the bitter waters can only be imposed on women when their husbands are beyond reproach.[172] Here, especially, the question of the historicity of the abolition remains a problem, as we have noted more than once in connection with Talmudic reports of very early legislation. For all that, the principle of change is accepted in this Mishnah and the right, even the duty, to change even a biblical law when conditions have changed is fully acknowledged.

NOTES

1. *Sanhedrin* 27a; SA, HM 34:12.

2. Responsa, no. 96.

3. HM 34:24. Another example of sinners whose status has changed is that of suicides. The SA, YD 345:1–3 rules that there is to be no mourning for a suicide because of the severity of his sin, but the later Halakhists tend to argue that the majority of suicides, nowadays, commit their act of self-destruction while they are of "unsound mind" and are to be treated no differently from other people; see *Baer Hetev* and *Pithey Teshuvah* to YD ad loc.; Shwardron, *Maharsham*, vol. 6, no. 123; Greenvald, *Kol Bo*, pp. 319–21.

4. *Hullin* 5a.

5. Responsa. *Binyan Tzion*, New Series, no. 23. On the wine of one who desecrates the Sabbath in public see the Responsum of *Rashba* quoted by Karo, *Bet Yoswf*, YD 119.

6. *Hatan Sofer*, no. 28.

7. *Tuv Taam va-Daat*, 3rd Series, part II, no. 16.

8. Melammed le-Hoil, part I, no. 29. Cf. Walkin, *Zekan Aharon,*, No. 12 on young men who are *kohanim* and who desecrate the Sabbath in public who may, nonetheless, recite the priestly blessing in the synagogue because one must be cautious in rejecting such folk and he refers to Ettlinger, though he is less inclined to be too permissive. The Responsum is dated 1926.

9. Mishnah, *Sanhedrin* 10:1.

10. *Avodah Zarah* 26b; Maimonides, *Yad, Akum* 10:1; SA, YD 158:2.

11. *Yad, Edut* 11:10.

12. *Hazon Ish* to YD 13:16, quoted in ET, Vol. 2, p. 137.

13. Quoted in ET, loc cit. from *Iggerot ha-Rayyah*, No. 15.

14. *Pesahim* 49a; SA, EH 2:8.

15. Responsa, *Avney Tzedek*, EH, no. 5. But see OP, vol. I, p. 50 for dissenting views.

16. Responsa, *Havvot Yair*, no. 70.

17. *Pesahim* 49a–b.

18. *Bava Batra* 8a; SA, YD 243:2.

19. *Bava Kama* 8:6 (6c).

20. Maimonides, *Yad, Talmud Torah* 6:12.

21. Yad, Hovel u-Mazik 3:5–6.

22. *Maharik, Shoresh* 163.

23. Responsa, no. 163. Actually (as Weiss, *Minhat Yitzhak*, vol. 3, no. 112 points out) there is only a single Responsum, that of Weil, not two. The editors of Colon add that this Responsum 163 is not Colon's own but is by "a disciple of R. Jacob Moellin (the *Maharil*)." Since Jacob Weil was a disciple of the *Hamaril*, this is, in fact, the same Responsum.

24. SA, YD 243:7.

25. YD 243:2.

26. *Teshuvot Maharit*, Part ii, HM, no. 47. Kamelhaar, *Dor Deah*, pp. 29–31, has a report, which may or may not be authentic, that R. Aryeh Laib Ginzberg, author of *Shaagat Aryeh*, once tried to encourage his pupils to become scholars by saying that things forbidden to an *am ha-aretz* are permitted to a scholar. He quotes R. Moses Kunitz who gives these examples: (1) a scholar is allowed to take revenge (*Yoma* 22b); (2) he need not restore a lost article to its owner if to do so will lower his dignity (HM 263); (3) he is exempt from taxation (*Nedarim* 62a); and (4) he may tell lies if the intention is to conceal his learning (*Bava Metzia* 23b). For another example of a change in the law with regard to scholars, see *Berakhot* 31b, where the Talmud forbids a disciple to render decisions in the presence of his teacher and to render any decisions until he has obtained permission from his master (*Sanhedrin* 5b). Maimonides (*Yad,*

Talmud Torah 5:2) records this as law, as does SA, YD 242:4. But Abraham di Boton (*Lehem-Mishnah* to *Talmud Torah* 5:4) remarks that he had heard a sage say that 'nowadays' these laws do not apply since we study from books and the books are our teachers. Samuel di Modina (*Maharashdam*, HN, no. 1) says the same thing at greater length. These two sources by Margaliot: *Margaliot ha-Yam*, vol. I, p. 15a. Cf. the important gloss of Isserles to YD 242:14 on the whole question of *semikhah*, "ordination," as an innovation and a *minhag* and the rules governing these.

27. Mishnah. *Hagigah* 1:1; *Hagigah* 3a; Maimonides, *Yad, Edut* 9:11.

28. Responsa, *Shevet Sofer*, EH, no. 21. Reference should also be made to the change in the law regarding the status of *kohanim* who "nowadays" are only doubtful *kohanim* or *kohanim* by presumption, *koheney hazakah*, as they are termed, see Maimonides, *Yad, Issurey Viah* 2:1; *Baer Hetev* note 2 and *Pithey Teshuvah* note 3 to SA, EH 6; Medini, *Sedey Hemed, Kelalim, kaf*, no. 92, vol. 3, pp. 183–88; Rubinstein, *"Kedushat Kohanim."* The question of whether it is permitted to be served by a *kohen* "nowadays" is duscussed by *Mordekhai, Gittin*, no. 401, who forbids it unless the *kohen* waives his rights. Isserles OH 128:45. Cf. David Oppenheim, *Nishal David*, OH, no. 4, vol. I, pp. 7–10.

29. *Terumot* 8:4.

30. *Yad, Rotzeah* 11:5–6.

31. *Avodah Zarah* 35a S. V. *Hada* AND *Betzah* 6a s.v. *ve-ha-iddana*, see sup., p. 140.

32. YD 116:1.

33. Nevertheless, some authorities hold that the original prohibition is still in force, see ET, vol. 6, p. 85.

34. See sup., p. 126.

35. To *Betzah* 6a.

36. Ibid. 6a.

37. *Ketubot* 77a.

38. See sup. p. 138.

39. *Teshuvot Ribash*, no. 15.

40. SA, EH 1:3.

41. For a fine account of the development see Sevin, *ha-Moadim ba-Halakhah*, pp. 245–55. On legal fictions and *haaremah*, "evasion," see ET, vol. 9, pp. 697–703; Silberg, "Evasion of the Law" in his *Talmudic Law and the Modern State*, chapter 3, pp. 22–41; and Atlas, "Legal Fictions in the Talmud" and his chapter in *Netivim be-Mishpat ha-Ivri*, pp. 265–304. Another very well-known example of a legal fiction is the sale of part of an animal in her first pregnancy to a Gentile so that the law of the firstling should not apply to the animal's offspring if it is a male, see SA, YD 320:6 and ET, vol. 3, p. 267.

42. *Pesahim* 5b.

43. Mishnah, *Pesahim* 2:1.

44. *Pesahim*, chapter 2, ed. Zuckermandel, p. 157.

45. *Tur*, OH 443.

46. *Bah* to *Tur*, OH 448.

47. For the whole question see Sevin, *le-Or ha-Halakhah*, pp. 85–97 and the very comprehensive account in Grunfeld, *The Dietary Laws*, vol. 2, pp. 94–155 and Appendix 2, pp. 177–229.

48. For Rabbi Kook's views see his *Shabbat ha-Aretz*, and for the opposing views of *Ridbaz* see his Commentary *Bet Ridbaz* to Israel of Shklov's *Peat ha-Shulhan*.

49. *Shabbat ha-Aretz*, introduction, par. 13, pp. 57–59.

50. *Avodah Zarah* 20a.

51. *Bava Metzia* 104b; cf. *Betzah* 32b. A fine study of the Renaissance Halakhists and how they managed to permit arrangements for the insurance of cargoes without offending against the laws of usury is that of S. Passamaneck, *Insurance in Rabbinic Law*.

52. No. 40. See the article "Usury" in JE, vol. XII, pp. 388–92 and in EJ, vol. 16, pp. 27–32. For a very clear account of the principles involved and for an example of the document to be drawn up for the *hetter iska*, see Ganzfried, *Kitzur Shulhan Arukh*, section 65.

53. *Kiddushin* 4:14.

54. *Gittin* 60a–b; *Temurah* 14a–b.

55. *Gittin* and *Temurah*, ibid.

56. See B. M. Lewin, *Iggeret de-Rav Sherira Gaon*; J. N. Epstein, *Mevuot le-Sifrut ha-Amoraim*, Appendix, pp. 610–15; Strack, *Introduction*, pp. 12–20, where a full account of the whole question is given; Elon, *ha-Mishpat ha-Ivri*, pp. 208–210; and especially J. N. Epstein, *Mavo le-Nusah ha-Mishnah*, pp. 629 ff. and Albeck, *Mevo le-Mishnah*, pp. 111–15.

57. *Tosafists Bava Kama* 3b s.v. *ke-de-metargem R. Yosef.*

58. For R. Nathan Adler's practice see S. Sofer, *Hut ha-Meshulash*, pp. 19–20.

59. *Sanhedrin* 25b.

60. *Yad, Sefer Torah* 7:1.

61. *Halakhot Ketanot, Sefer Torah*, beg.; see Kahana: *Mehkarim*, pp. 258–71.

62. *Tur*, YD 270.

63. YD 270:2.

64. *Nazir* 59a. On the question of men and women wearing one another's garments see Epstein, *Sex Laws*, pp. 66–67.

65. See *Tosefta Avodah Zarah* 3:5, ed. Zuckermandel, p. 463; *Avodah Zarah* 20a and *Tosafists* ad loc. s.v. *ha-mistapper.*

66. *Ran* to *Rif Avodah Zarah*, chapter 2, ed. Vilna, p. 9b.

67. YD 156:2 and 182:6.

68. YD 182:1.

69. Isserles to YD 156:2 and 182:1.

70. OH 696:8.

71. *Taz* to YD 182 note 4.

72. *Darkhey Teshuvah* 182 note 12.

73. YD 182:5.

74. On this subject see Norman Lamm, "Judaism and the Modern Attitude to Homosexuality."

75. Mishnah *Kiddushin* 4:14.

76. *Kiddushin* 82a.

77. *Yad, Issurey Viah* 22:2.

78. SA,EH 24:1.

79. *Bah* to *Tur* EH 24.

80. *Daat Kohen*, no. 3 and see OP, vol. 9, pp. 236–37.

81. *Bekhorot* 29a.

82. On the development of the professional rabbinate see Gaster, *The Rabbinical Degree* and the article, "Rabbi, Rabbinate" in EJ, vol. 13, pp. 1445–58.

83. *Bekhorot* 9a s.v. *mah ani.*

84. YD 246.

85. YD 246:5.

86. YD 245:22.

87. See the commentaries, especially *Shakh* note 15. Cf. the lengthy glass of Isserles to YD 246:21, quoting authorities who permit even a healthy person to receive a stipend in order to be able to devote himself to the study and teaching of the Torah and quoting Abarbanel who says, "Consequently, it is the custom in all places of Israel that the town Rabbi is supported financially by the townsfolk so that he should not be obliged to do work in the presence of others with the result that the Torah will be held in contempt by the masses." See the essay on the Rabbi's stipend and status by Solomon Ashkernazi in his *Dorot be-Yisrael*, pp. 74–75.

88. See, e.g., the remarkable contract of R. Ezekiel Landau drawn up by the Prague community, printed in his *Moda Biyhudan* and of Vol. II.

89. Quoted in *Pithey Teshuvah* to YD 245 note 11 from *Hatam Sofer*, YD 230.

90. *Cf.* on the question of whether the office of town rabbi is hereditary the sources quoted in ET, vol. 14, pp. 362–64 and *Hatam Sofer*, OH, nos. 12 and 13.

91. *Berakhot* 27b.

92. *Yad, Tefillah* 1:6; cf. Bertinoro to Mishnah *Berakhot* 4:1.

93. *Megillah* 1:8.

94. Maimonides, *Yad, Tefillah* 1:19; Bertinoro and *Tiferet Yisrael* to Mishnah *Megillah* 1:8.

95. *Yevamot* 121a.

96. The full statement of R. Eliezer of Verona is given by the editor in Herzog, *Hekhal Yitzhak*, EH, vol. I, no. 23, pp. 113–17.

97. *Hatam Sofer*, EH nos. 58 and 65.

98. *Beer Yitzhak*, no. 18; *Eyn Yitzhak*, 22:3, 20.

99. Mishnah, *Kilayim* 9:1, 2.

100. *Hilkhot Kilayim*, no. 7, printed after chapter 9 of the *Rosh* to *Niddah* in ed. Vilna, Romm.

101. *Tur*, YD 289.

102. YD 289:1. See *Pithey Teshuvah*, who raises the question of a later court not being able to set aside the decision of an earlier court and refers to *Tiferet Yisrael* to Mishnah, *Kilayim* 9, which discusses the question.

103. YD 289:2.

104. *Shakh* to YD 289 note 2.

105. SA,OH 276:5; Ganzfried, *Kitzur Shulhan Arukh* 90:18.

106. Mishnah *Sukkah* 2:1 and freq.

107. *Sukkah* 25b.

108. OH 639:2.

109. See *Mishnah Berurah* to OH 639:2 and Ganzfried, *Kitzur*, op. cit. 135:8.

110. *Shabbat* 16:1 and *Shabbat* 116a and further pages.

111. *Shabbat* 16:3 (15d).

112. *Mordekhai, Shabbat*, chapter 16, 393.

113. *Betzah* 30a.

114. *Terumat ha-Deshen*, No. 58.

115. *Bet Yosef* to *Tur*, OH 334.

116. OH 334:26. For a similar instance see the note of *Taz* to SA, OH 472 note 9 that "nowadays"—*Ha-iddana*—we do not use red wine at the Seder "because of the lies," i.e., the blood libel.

117. *Betzah* 5:2 (63a).

118. HM 5:2.

119. *Terumat ha-Deshen*, No. 237.

120. *Gittin* 88b; *Mekhilta, mishpatim* 1, ed. Weiss, p. 82.

121. See sup., p. .

122. *Yad, Sanhedrin* 26:7.

123. HM 26:1 Cf. Samuel Aboab, *Sefer ha-Zikhronot*, no. 10, section 3 and the commentary to this in Feldman, *Shimushah shel Torah*, pp. 39–44.

124. *ha-Mishpat ha-Ivri*, pp. 70–72.

125. *Keli Hemdah, mishpatim*, p. 226.

126. Note to vol. II of his *Eyn Mishpat* beg.

127. See, e.g., Feldman, *Shimushah*, pp. 39–44, where the author severely rebukes those who have resort to Gentile courts in defiance of the prohibition.

128. *Rosh ha-Shanah* 17a.
129. *Shabbat* 49a s.v. *ke-Elisha.*
130. *Shabbat* 130a.
131. See article "Tefillin" in EJ, vol. 15, pp. 898–904 and Zimmels; *Ashkenazim and Sephardim,* p. 252, and the literature cited by Zimmels in note 1.
132. *Semag, Aseh,* no. 3.
133. OH 37.
134. OH 37:2.
135. *Eruvin* 65a.
136. OH 98:2.
137. *Berakhot* 34b.
138. OH 101:1.
139. Mishnah *Taanit* 3:1; *Taanit* 22a.
140. OH 577:9.
141. *Pesahim* 74b.
142. YD 77:1.
143. Ibid., 57:18.
144. See *Horayot* 13b.
145. *Yoma* 8:4.
146. OH 616:2.
147. *Magen Avraham* ad loc., note 2.
148. *Ketubot* 110b.
149. *Ketubot* 110b s.v. *hu amar laalot.*
150. EH 75:4.
151. See *Pithey Teshuvah* to Eh 75 note 6 and the opinions of contemporary Halakhists in the booklet issued by "Mizrahi-Hapoel Hamizrahi," ed. J. Fried, *Hovat ha-Alyah le-Eretz Yisrael.*
152. *Bava Kama* 79b.
153. HM 409:1.
154. HM 409:3.
155. *Bava Kama* 83a. On this subject see the article by S. Turk, *"be-Inyan Giddul Kelavim li-Shemirah."*
156. Responsa, No. 133.
157. YD 114:12.
158. *Shakh* ad loc. note 21.
159. *Berakhot* 18a.
160. YD 367:4.
161. *Berakhot* 57b.
162. *Berakhot* 57b s.v. *ha-roeh merkulis.*
163. OH 224:1.
164. See Mishnah *Bava Kama* 6:6 and freq.
165. SA, OH 671:7.
166. *Bava Batra* 57b.
167. *Magen Avraham,* OH 2 note 1.
168. Ibid., OH 511 note 5.
169. *Berakhot* 16a.
170. OH 191:2.
171. Mishnah *Sotah* 9:9.
172. *Sotah* 47b. On this see Epstein, *Sex Laws and Customs in Judaism,* pp. 216–34.

11

New Inventions and Discoveries and the Halakhah

The Halakhah, as a complete guide to life, was obliged to take into account the problems for daily conduct posed by new inventions and discoveries. Obviously, no direct guidance could be forthcoming from the earlier Halakhic sources. For these the Halakhists resorted to the use of analogy, the earlier sources being carefully examined to determine the Halakhic principles involved, and these were then applied to the new situation. The trouble with any argument from analogy is its notorious inexactitude so that there was generally room for disagreements among the Halakhists; the actual needs of life often had a bearing, directly or, more frequently, indirectly, on the decisions.

It would be no exaggeration to say that the invention of printing brought about a complete transformation in Jewish life. Our concern here is with the question of how the impact of the new invention was felt in the Halakhah.[1] Before considering particular Halakhic problems in this area, we must note the influence of the printed word on Halakhah and Halakhic studies generally.[2]

The first complete edition of the Talmud was printed by Daniel Bomberg in Venice in the years 1500–1523. Not only did Bomberg's pagination become universally accepted, thus facilitating easy reference, but his printing of Rashi's Commentary side by side with the text, and, especially, that of the *Tosafists*, which was also universally adopted, set the pattern for centuries on how the Halakhah was to be studied. The legal casuistry and type of argumentation—*pilpul* in its best sense—which the *Tosafists* followed in their schools and which, for the first time became, as it were, part of the text, acquired such a close association with the Talmud that the conventional term for Talmud study was *gefat*—Gemara, *Pirush* ("Commentary," i.e., Rashi), *Tosefot.* Centuries later, when the printing house of Romm published the famous "Vilna Shas," the commentaries and supercommentaries contained in this edition of the Talmud became so closely identified with the text that few Halakhists could afford to ignore the Halakhic attitudes and observations of these commentaries, nor did they wish to do so. It is also no accident that the *Shulhan Arukh*, the first code to be widely disseminated after the invention of printing, became the most authoritative of the codes. When it is said that the House of Israel accepted the *Shulhan Arukh*, it is clear that the reason for the acceptance was the existence of thousands of copies of the work as a result of printed texts so that it became known far more widely than could ever have been possible for a code in manuscript.

The two main, particularly Halakhic problems to which the invention of printing gave rise were: (1) Does printing qualify legally as "writing" so that, for instance, a *get* or a Sefer Torah, which are required to be "written," are valid even if they are printed? and (2) do holy books that are printed enjoy the same sanctity as handwritten books? The two questions seem to be interconnected. It would appear to follow that if the first question were decided in the affirmative, printed books *are* "written" works and thus enjoy the same degree of sanctity, although it does not necessarily follow that if the first question were decided in the negative printed books would enjoy no sanctity. The printed work might not possess the same degree of sanctity as the written word but could enjoy a lesser degree of sanctity nonetheless.

The first recorded consideration of the question we have is a Responsum[3] of R. Menahem Azariah da Fano (1548–1620), the Italian Halakhist and Kabbalist who flourished one century after the invention of printing in Germany, at a time when Italy was the main home of Jewish printing, although the question on the subject, addressed to da Fano, came from one R. Abba of Candia in Crete. Da Fano remarks that he himself has been engaged in printing and is therefore thoroughly familiar with the process. The question addressed to da Fano was whether a printed *get* is valid. He first notes that a *get* must be written *lishmah*, "for her sake," i.e., for that particular woman. The typesetting must consequently be for this express purpose. But once the type has been set in this way, there is no objection to the *get* being printed since printing is, in law, "writing." As for the possible objection that printing is not to be construed as "writing" but as "engraving," da Fano quotes the Talmudic rule that a *get*, unlike a Sefer Torah, is valid even if engraved, provided the letters are embossed and not simply made to stand out by carving away the surrounds.[4] But he goes on to argue that printing is to be construed as "writing" since the ink on the type is impressed on the parchment or paper, i.e., so that even a Sefer Torah printed on parchment might be suitable for use.

Two standard commentators to the *Shulhan Arukh* discuss the question. David ha-Levi, the *Taz*, observes that he had heard some say that printed books have no sanctity but he takes strong issue with such a position.[5] Printing is not "engraving" but "writing" and printed books are, therefore, exactly the same as written books: "for what difference is there between pressing the pen on the paper or pressing the paper on the lead type?" However, the *Taz* holds that a *get* must be written by hand and not printed since printing "looks like" engraving, and although an engraved *get* is valid, as the Talmud states, it is the custom not to permit it. Abraham Gumbiner, in his *Magen Avraham*,[6] understands da Fano as saying that, since printing is "writing," strictly speaking, not only a printed *get* is valid but also a printed Sefer Torah, *tefillin*, and *mezuzot*. But Gumbiner introduces a new theory to invalidate printed *tefillin* and *mezuzot*. Unlike a Sefer Torah, these require to be written in order, i.e., letter after letter as in the sections in the Torah. In printing it is very difficult to avoid a letter, which appears later in the Torah text, being printed before a letter that appears earlier in the Torah text, because the letters in the typeface are frequently uneven.

Writing at the end of the seventeenth century, R. Jair Hayyim Bacharach[7] replies to a question concerning a scholar whose dwelling is so humble that he is obliged to use his book-lined study also as a bedroom. May he have marital relations in this room containing his sacred books? Bacharach states that he is unwilling to render an actual decision. At the most, he is only prepared to provide a theoretical discussion on the question of the sanctity of printed books. His main contention is that the sanctity of books, like that of a Sefer Torah, depends on the act of a human being. He understands da Fano as validating only a *get* not a Sefer Torah, *tefillin*, and *mezuzot*, and this is especially the case where the printer is not Jewish. Bacharach continues:

For this reason he also postulates and agrees that the sanctity of a Sefer

Torah derives from it having been written by a human being in whom there is the spirit of God and a portion of the divine from on high. Through the intentions of such a man and his forming of the letters, these acquire sanctity. Every Israelite can be presumed to be of this status for they are attached by their souls to the Lord our God. It is as a result of this that the sancity is drawn down to the Sefer Torah, *tefillin*, *mezuzot* and other books.

Thus, a mystical reason is introduced for demanding that the Sefer Torah, *tefillin*, and *mezuzot* be written by hand and not printed. It is the act of the Jew with intention that is alone capable of bringing down the sacred power which can alone endow the sacred books and so forth with the proper degree of sanctity. There can be little doubt that reasoning such as that of Bacharach is behind the unanimous decision in practice—whatever the Halakhic theoreticians may have said—never to use a printed Sefer Torah or printed *tefillin* and *mezuzot*. By a kind of instinctive reaction, on the part of both scholars and the masses, it was felt that for all the advantages of the new invention it should not be allowed to supersede the human effort and intention that are desirable if sanctity is to result.[8]

Hardly a work of practical Halakhah published during the twentieth century fails to deal with the Halakhic problems created by electricity and the use of electrical appliances. A typical Responsum on the permissibility of switching on electric lights on the Sabbath is that of David Hoffmann.[9] Hoffmann refers to the opinion of a rabbi, his name is not given, who argues, since the electric light filament burns in a vacuum and there is no combustion, to switch on an electric light does not fall under the head of, "ye shall kindle no fire throughout your habitations on the Sabbath day" (Exod. 35:3). Hoffmann first observes that in the year 1892 Rabbi Joseph Levy, in a monthly published by him, refutes the other rabbi's argument on the grounds that the creation of a complete vacuum is simply impossible. The light bulbs do wear out eventually and this means that each time the light is switched on there is a tiny amount of combustion and, since according to the Halakhah, there is no limit to the degree of combustion required to make the act a forbidden one, it is prohibited. In addition to the oxygen consumed, the filament itself is consumed little by little. Moreover, Hoffmann tentatively suggests, the prohibition is not that of *burning* but of *kindling*. Even if it were true that there is no combustion in the electric light and consequently no *burning*, there is *kindling* of the light. Hoffmann adds that it is forbidden to switch on the electric light even on a festival, when it is permitted to make fire for the purpose of providing warmth or light. The reason is that the Mishnah[10] forbids the production of fire on a festival by striking two stones together and the like, which the Gemara[11] explains because this is "to create (something new) on Yom Tov," and it is forbidden by rabbinic law. Despite occasional voices raised in favor of a more lenient attitude, the unanimous opinion, nowadays, among traditional Halakhists is that it is forbidden to switch an electric light on or off on the Sabbath, and many observant Jews have a time switch, set before the Sabbath, for this purpose. A different argument for permissiveness that has been advanced is that the turning of the switch is only an indirect cause of the kindling of the light so that, it can be argued, to turn on the switch is *gerama*, "indirect cause," not forbidden by biblical law in any event. This argument, too, is, nowadays, rejected by all Halakhists. As a result of the strict attitude that has prevailed, the use of electric appliances, such as microphones, telephones, phonographs, refrigerators (which have a light in them that goes on when the door is opened), radios, and television sets, has been severely curtailed.[12]

A widely discussed question is whether the obligation to hear the *shofar* on *Rosh ha-Shanah* or the reading of the Megillah on Purim can be fulfilled if these are heard over the radio. The principle involved, as Rabbi Ben Zion Uziel points out, is whether to hear something over the radio, or by telephone, is to hear the original sound or merely to hear a secondary sound.[13] If the latter, a rule of the Mishnah, as explained in the Gemara,[14] applies that it is insufficient to hear the sound of an echo of the original sound. If, for instance, the Mishnah states, one heard the *shofar* sounds in a pit or in a large barrel, then if the actual sounds are heard (i.e., when the people hearing them are also in the pit or the barrel) the obligation has been fulfilled. But if the sounds were heard by those standing outside, they would not have fulfilled their obligation because they would not have heard the actual sound, only the reverberations. (It has been noted that the question of hearing the *shofar* in a pit or barrel is not merely academic; in times of religious persecution this may have actually happened, the people hiding in order to avoid discovery).

The invention of machines resulted in the consideration of whether objects produced by machine qualify as objects produced by human agency since the machine is operated by a human being.[15] Specifically, the question was discussed with regard to *matzot* and *tzitzit* manufactured by machine. The *tzitzit* is required to be woven for that express purpose, and the *matzot* eaten at the Seder (when, according to the traditional law, it is a positive precept to eat an olive's bulk of *matzot*) has to be "guarded" from becoming leaven with the express intention of doing this for the purpose of the *mitzvah*. Many of the Halakhists argue that in both these instances the required intention is provided by the machine operator, a human being who is capable of having this intention, but other Halakhists cannot accept the operator's intention as sufficient since the machine operates on its own once the operator who tends it has set it in motion. The act of the machine is compared by these Halakhists to the act of a minor or an imbecile where there is insufficient intention in law. Against this the others argue that a minor or an imbecile does his act on his own, whereas the machine is operated by an intelligent human being whose intention is valid. The first recorded instance of a machine used to make *matzah* is in Austria in 1857. R. Solomon Kluger, rabbi of Brody, issued a stern warning against the use of this machine. His edict, banning the machine, was published in Breslau in 1859, together with the opinions of other rabbis who sided with him, under the title *Modaah le-Vet Yisrael*, "An Announcement to the House of Israel." The rabbi of Lemberg, R. Joseph Saul Nathansohn, published in Lemberg in the same year a permissive decision entitled *Bittul Modaah*, "An Annulment of the Announcement." A fierce controversy resulted in which leading Halakhists took part on both sides. Eventually, especially with the greater perfection of the machines, their use was accepted by the majority of Halakhists, but some traditionalists, even to the present day, prefer to use only handmade *matzot*.

Although R. Solomon Kluger advanced Halakhic arguments against the use of the machine (the question of valid intention and the fear that dough caught in the crevices of the machine might become leaven) his strongest reasons—judging by his own statements and by those of his supporters and opponents—were twofold. The first was the fear of innovative techniques at a time when the Reform movement was gaining strength in Germany. But the second reason, and, we can surmise the one that weighed most heavily with him, was that the introduction of the machine would obviate the need for many workers and the poor, who relied on the wages paid to them for helping make the *matzot*, would suffer greatly. Against this, the others argued that if the machine were to be accepted it would be of much benefit to the community as a whole, including the poor, by bringing down the heavy costs of

manufacturing. And in any event the poor could be provided with
an additional sum by the community.

The invention of the steam engine and other forms of speedy
travel also gave rise to Halakhic problems, particularly with regard
to the Sabbath laws. The reason given in the Talmud[16] for the
Mishnaic rule forbidding the riding of an animal on the Sabbath or
on a a festival is that this may lead to the breaking off of a shoot
from a tree to be used as a whip. The Talmud furthermore forbids
any use made of an animal on the Sabbath and festivals.[17] Consequently, Isserles rules that it is also forbidden for a Jew to travel on
the Sabbath in a cart with a non-Jewish driver because the animal is
being used by the Jew and because of the fear that the Jew might
cut the shoot from the tree.[18] Thus, there is no prohibition per se of
traveling on the Sabbath in a cart, and it might be argued that to
travel in a horseless carriage (to which Isserles' objections would
not apply) is permitted if the driver is not Jewish. Ben Zion Uziel
draws this conclusion to permit Jews to travel on the Sabbath in an
electric tram or steam train that runs in the town.[19] But he set
down the following qualifications: (a) both the driver and some of
the passengers must not be Jewish; (b) no money must be handled,
the fares being paid in advance; and (c) it must be for a religious
purpose, to attend synagogue, for example. Uziel refers to the
ruling in the *Shulhan Arukh*[20] that if a non-Jew makes a pathway or a
ramp on the Sabbath, it may be used by a Jew, even if the non-Jew
is a friend and intends the Jew to use it on the Sabbath, since there
is only a single act, permitted to the non-Jew, which the latter does
on his own accord, and there is no fear that extra effort be expended
specifically on behalf of the Jew. By the same token, the driver of
the tram or train operates his vehicle on behalf of his non-Jewish
passengers and for his own benefit so that there can be no objection
on the grounds that a non-Jew is doing work specifically on behalf
of the Jews. It is true, continues Uziel, that Nahmanides holds that
even acts which do not fall under the technical definition of "work"
are forbidden on the Sabbath if they are of a nature so as to disturb
the Sabbath rest, but a journey to the synagogue by tram or train
hardly offends against Nahmanides' principle.[21] A journey for
weekday pursuits does offend this principle and is, indeed, forbidden. Uziel quotes a Responsum of R. Moses Sofer[22] in which long
journeys by train are forbidden on these very grounds. But one
cannot compare a short journey for a religious purpose, by tram or
train within the town limits, to a lengthy, uncomfortable train
journey, usually only undertaken for business purposes. Uziel does

not refer to the Response *Bet Yitzhak* by R. Isaac Schmelkes (1828–1906), rabbi of Lemberg, who remarks that when the electric tram first began to run in Lemberg he was asked whether it was permitted to travel on it on the Sabbath.[23] Unlike Uziel, Schmelkes refuses to permit it, arguing among other considerations, that there *is* a prohibition of riding in a carriage even where the fear of cutting off a shoot does not apply.[24]

The two chief Halakhic questions occasioned by the discovery and use of tobacco are whether pipe (later cigar and cigarette) smoking is permitted on a fast day and on a festival. One of the earliest discussions is found in the Responsa collection: *Darkhey Noam* by R. Mordecai ha-Levi (d. 1684), Dayyan and Halakhic authority in Cairo for over forty years.[25] Work is permitted on a festival if it is for the purpose of food preparation (*okhel nefesh*, lit. "eating for life"). This was extended by the rabbis to include other essential needs such as the provision of light and warmth. R. Mordecai ha-Levi formulates the question:

> A consideration of the question whether or not it is permitted to imbibe the smoke drawn through hollow pipes, for this question is not found in the *Posekim* of blessed memory since it did not exist in their day. This smoke has only recently ascended but is now wide-spread throughout the world, there now being a majority who smoke. Is it permitted on Yom Tov or are there any objections on the grounds that it is not *okhel nefesh* and the Torah only permits *okhel nefesh*? Also to be considered is whether there is an objection on the grounds of putting out a fire or on other grounds. For there are many doubts in the matter. Some permit, others declare it to be forbidden, without any agreement having emerged in favour of either opinion. There is also an opinion that whoever does smoke on Yom Tov must not smoke on a fast-day since he treats it as *okhel nefesh*, and, conversely, whoever does smoke on a fast-day should treat it as forbidden on Yom Tov. It is necessary to examine whether there is anything to this theory in which the two are made interdependent.

In a lengthy and very erudite analysis, this scholar points out that the term *okhel nefesh* does not refer only to food but also to other physical pleasures. Consequently, it is permitted to smoke on Yom Tov. This disposes, too, of the argument that if it is *okhel nefesh* it should be forbidden on a fast day. Only eating and drinking are forbidden on a fast day, not other physical pleasures of this nature. Nevertheless, he concludes, it should not be permitted on *Tisha be-Av*, the fast commemorating the destruction of the Temple. On this day it is even forbidden to study the Torah so as to have the

mind concentrated entirely on the catastrophe. *A fortiori* it is forbidden to have to resort to such a distraction as smoking. He adds
an interesting note. Although, as he has stated, it is permitted to
smoke of the other fast days, it should only be done in the privacy
of the home not in public:

> But I can see no reason for forbidding it on the other fast-days but it
> should not be in the streets and squares lest the Gentiles witness it and
> there will be a profanation of the divine name, since they are of the
> opinion that it is wrong to smoke on a fast-day. It is improper to treat a
> fast-day so lightly in their opinion and to do it to their face is wrong
> since they think that we are very strict in all religious matters. Conse-
> quently, every religious person should take care not to smoke (on fast-
> days) in the presence of Gentiles.[26]

Abraham Gumbiner, on the other hand, forbids smoking on Yom
Tov because although work for the purpose of providing physical
pleasure is permitted on Yom Tov, it must be the kind of pleasure
enjoyed by the majority of people, which is not the case with
smoking.[27]

Another question discussed by the Halakhists in connection with
smoking is whether this requires a benediction beforehand of the
kind enjoined before eating and drinking, since the reason given in
the Talmud for these benedictions is that it is forbidden to enjoy
the things of the world without first thanking God for them.[28]
Abraham Gumbiner is inclined to hold that a benediction should be
recited before smoking,[29] although he finally leaves the matter un-
decided. Other Halakhists do not require a benediction to be recited, and this became the common practice.[30]

Advances in medical knowledge brought in their wake a host of
new and serious Halakhic problems.[31] Some of these are now
noted.

At the end of the eighteenth century, as a result of the work of
John Hunter, London had become the center for the study of
anatomy. At that time, the following question was addressed to
R. Ezekiel Landau of Prague.[32] A man suffering from a stone in the
bladder was unsuccessfully operated on in London and he had
died. The London physicians, eager to perfect the operation,
wished to conduct an autopsy in order to discover what had gone
wrong. Since the deceased was a Jew, they consulted the London
rabbis, who were divided in their opinion. This was a totally new
situation so that no direct guidance could have been forthcoming
from the classical Halakhic sources. The permissive rabbis resorted

to the biblical accounts of Jacob and Joseph being embalmed (Gen. 50:2–3; 26). Embalming involves the making of incisions in the corpse and yet it seems there was no objection to this being done in honor of the patriarchs. An autopsy with beneficial effects for society is an honor to the deceased on whom it is performed and ought, therefore, similarly to be permitted. These rabbis argued further that the *Shulhan Arukh*[33] rules, if a man decreed in his will that he was to be buried in a place other than that in which he was actually buried, it is permitted to disinter the corpse and accelerate decomposition by using quicklime, so that the skeleton can be taken to be buried in the place stated in the will. If even such a step may be taken in order to respect the wishes of the deceased, surely an autopsy, which can be of benefit to many sufferers, ought to be permitted. The opposing rabbis quoted a passage in the Talmud in which there is discussed the case of a boy who sold some property belonging to his estate and died shortly afterwards.[34] An attempt was made to invalidate the sale on the grounds that the boy was a minor at the time of the sale, with no power to sell property. The suggestion was made that the boy's body be disinterred in order to discover whether or not the signs of puberty were present. Rabbi Akiba ruled that it was forbidden to do this because of *nivvul ha-met* (desecrating the dead, i.e., mutilation of a corpse). Against this attempted proof was the counterargument that in the Talmudic case only financial loss was at stake, whereas an autopsy, which might bring relief and save human life, should be permitted even though it does involve *nivvul ha-met*, just as any other prohibition may be set aside where human life is at stake.

Rabbi Landau, in his reply, first observes that there can, indeed, be no doubt that where an autopsy will result in the saving of life it is permitted. The saving of life overrides much more serious prohibitions than the comparatively minor one of *nivvul ha-met*. But he adds a qualification, which, owing to his great reputation as a Halakhic authority of the first rank, became a real obstacle to progress whenever the question came up of the permissibility of autopsies to further medical knowledge. Landau's qualification is that there must be a direct connection between the otherwise prohibited act, in this case the mutilation of the corpse, and the saving of life, i.e., if someone else is suffering from the same disease as that which proved fatal to the man on whom the autopsy had been performed so that a life may be saved directly. But, Landau argues, autopsies cannot be permitted on the grounds that at a later date they may be the indirect cause of saving life, for if even indirect saving of life can render permitted an otherwise unlawful act it would follow (as a reductio ad absurdum) that a doctor may desecrate the Sabbath by preparing medicines because they may one day be required in order to save life. The analogy is obviously inexact and this cannot have escaped such an acute logician as Landau. There is no need for the doctor to prepare the medicines on the Sabbath; he can prepare them on days when there is no prohibition at all in him so doing. But if autopsies are permitted for the purpose of saving life, what difference does it make whether there is now present someone whose life will be saved or whether future lives will be saved as a result of the autopsy? Landau's real fear becomes evident from his concluding remarks:

> Far be it to permit this; even the Gentile doctors only use corpses for training in the performances of operations where the corpses are those of condemned criminals or of those who gave permission while they were still alive for this to be done to their bodies. If, God forbid, we permit these things then every corpse should be dissected in order to learn how the internal organs are distributed and thus cures be found for the living. There is, consequently, no need to elaborate on this and there is not the slightest possibility of permitting it.

In other words, Landau, writing at a time when the science of anatomy was in its infancy, is rightly apprehensive that a too permissive attitude may result in the corpses of Jews being used widely by the Gentile doctors since Jewish, unlike Gentile, religious attitudes permit it. In the State of Israel the problem assumed much larger proportions, especially since, as some of the bolder Halakhists argued, the state of medical knowledge and communications are now so much better than they were in Landau's day, that every autopsy considered necessary by the doctors can be said to benefit the living directly.[35]

When hypnotism (more specifically, magnetism) began to be used by some doctors, the question was discussed by Rabbi Jacob Ettlinger whether a pious Jew who had fallen ill may resort to this method of cure if so advised by his doctor.[36] Ettlinger states that he has consulted the experts from whom he has received contradictory replies. Some of them dismissed the method as sheer quackery but others said that there is something in it. Ettlinger eventually permitted hypnotism on the grounds that those who do use the method in practice consider it to be a perfectly normal and natural form of healing. As late as the twentieth century, R. Zevi Hirsch Shapira of Munkacs, in his compendium to the *Shulhan Arukh, Yoreh Deah*,

sees fit to discuss whether hypnotism is a legitimate form of healing, and he does so in his comments on that section of the Code
which deals with the prohibition of magical practices.[37] Natural
methods of healing are obviously permitted but is hypnotism such a
natural method or is it supernatural and so suspect? Shapira permits it on the basis of Ettlinger's ruling.

Artificial insemination is of two kinds: (a) AIH, where the donor
is the husband; (b) AID, where the donor is not the husband. With
regard to AIH the only Halakhic consideration is whether the production of the semen involves the prohibition of "waste of seed,"
i.e., masturbation. Many Halakhists permit AIH on the grounds
that since it is for the purpose of procreation the seed is not, in fact,
"wasted."[38] With regard to AID a number of serious Halakhic
questions arise. First, is it permitted? Second, if it is not permitted
would the children born of the insemination of a married woman
with the semen of a man who is not her husband be *mamzerim*?
Interestingly enough, there are precedents in the classical sources.
The Talmud records the possibility of a woman conceiving without
intercourse through bathing in a bath into which a man had deposited his semen.[39] There is also a curious legend to the effect that
Ben Sira was the son of the prophet Jeremiah[40] who had been first
forced to eject his semen into a bath and Ben Sira's mother bathed
there to become pregnant with him. In his compendium, *Pahad
Yitzhak*, the eighteenth-century scholar and physician Isaac Lampronti, poses the riddle: How is it possible for a man to have a son
by his daughter and yet that son be not a *mamzer*? Lampronti
replies to the riddle that in the legend the woman who bathed in the
bath into which Jeremiah had deposited his semen was none other
than the prophet's own daughter and yet Ben Sira was not a *mamzer*
(no one ever suggested that he was). The argument of the majority
of Halakhists is that it is the act of intercourse which constitutes
adultery or incest and it is from such an act that the resulting child
is a *mamzer* not where conception takes place without intercourse.
Consequently, AID is not adultery and the child born as a result of
it is not a *mamzer*. Nevertheless, all the Halakhists, with the notable
exception of Rabbi Moses Feinstein, do forbid AID on the grounds
that it may lead to incest (the same donor may be the natural father
of a boy and a girl who may meet and marry one another) and
because it is, in any event, morally dubious for a woman to have a
child from a man who is not her husband while she is still the wife
of her husband.[42]

Organ transplants belong to a very recent advance in surgery, but the Halakhic implications have been discussed in contemporary Halakhic literature.[43] With regard to corneal grafting the basic problem is that of *nivvul ha-met*, and the further question of whether it is permitted for the living to enjoy the benefits of the grafting since in the normal way it is forbidden, in Jewish law, to have any benefit from that which comes from a corpse. The majority of the Halakhists are permissive here. *Nivvul ha-met* and the other prohibition of deriving benefit from a corpse can be set aside in order to save life and, since the life of a blind man is more at risk than that of a man who can see, to save a man's sight can be construed as lifesaving. A further ingenious argument, first advanced by Chief Rabbi Unterman of Israel, is that the second prohibition is nonexistent in any event since the dead tissue becomes living tissue in the eye of the living man and no benefit is, in fact, derived from the "dead." Kidney transplants, too, are permitted by the majority of the Halakhists since the kidneys are taken from the living donors. The only possible Halakhic objection is that the donor places his own life at risk (there is, however, Halakhic precedence for a man placing his life at risk in order to save the life of another),[44] but the risk is not too high with developed techniques. Heart transplants are treated less sympathetically by the Halakhists chiefly because of the difficulty in determining the death of the donor and the general lack of success of the transplant.

A question discussed only by Rabbi I. Herzog,[45] who states that although the question was addressed to him by a notable medical authority, Professor Strauss, he sees no reason for strictness, is whether it is permitted to place some penicillin in a milk pail on the Sabbath in order to destroy the germs in the milk. Rabbi Herzog refers to the Talmudic discussion according to which it is permitted to kill lice on the Sabbath because lice are said to be generated from human perspiration, and the killing of living things on the Sabbath only applies when these are living organisms that are the result of generation from male and female.[46] Rabbi Herzog observes that although modern science does not acknowledge the possibility of spontaneous generation "yet in matters of Halakhah we must pay heed only to the words of our Sages of blessed memory." In any event, he concludes, science would hardly refer to the proliferation of germs as the result of "procreation" in any accepted sense of that term.

NOTES

1. On this see the excellent treatment in Kahana's essay, *"ha-Defus ba-Halakhah"* ("Printing in the Halakhah") in his *Mehkarim*, pp. 272–305. On the general subject of this chapter see Freehof, *The Responsa Literature*, chapter 6, pp. 227–42.

2. See Berliner's monograph, "Ueber d. Einfluss ersten hebr. Buchdrucks" in Hebrew translation in his *Ketavim Nivharim*, vol. 2, pp. 145–61. An important aspect of the influence of printing on the Halakha must also be mentioned here. The printers of Halakhic works used, not infrequently, inaccurate manuscripts and were guilty of printing errors. But the later *Posekim* at times relied on these corrupt texts. See the very interesting and important essay of Rabbi Weinberg, *Seridey Esh*, vol. 3, pp. 401–8.

3. Responsa, no. 93, pp. 171–72.

4. *Gittin* 20a.

5. *Tax*, YD 271 note 8.

6. OH 32 note 57.

7. Responsa, *Havvot Yair*, no. 184. Ben Zion Uziel, *Piskey Uziel*, no. 31, pp. 169–72 rejects the opinion of a rabbi who argued that a photocopy of a *mezuzah* is valid since it is a reproduction of a *written mezuzah*. According to Uziel photography can be considered "writing" far less than can printing and the photocopy *mezuzah* is invalid. Nevertheless, he says, it has the same degree of sanctity as have printed books and must not be treated disrespectfully. On the question of relying on a photograph for the purpose of identifying a corpse so that the wife can be permitted to remarry see OP. vol. 5, note 184:40, pp. 52–66. On the reliance on fingerprints for this purpose see Gad Navon in *Diney Israel*, vol. VII, Hebrew sec., pp. 129–41.

8. Rabbi A. I. Kook, *Daat Kohen*, no. 160 advances two further reasons for not treating printing as "writing"; (a) "writing" involves drawing the pen, whereas in printing it is all done at once; (b) printing by machine, as opposed to a hand press, is only indirect and cannot be considered as the direct act of a human being.

9. *Melammed le-Hoil*, part I, no. 49. For an account of the authorities who deal with this question see the lengthy note 5 in Braun, *Shearim*, vol. 2, pp. 103–5. Schwadron, *Maharasham*, vol. II, no. 246 uses the argument that since, according to the Talmudic principle, only the type of work used for the Tabernacle in the wilderness is forbidden by biblical law on the Sabbath (*Bava Kama* 2a and frq.), an electric light which is not consumed is neither the "burning" nor the "kindling" forbidden by biblical law since this kind of "work" was unknown in the time of the Tabernacle. Abraham Steinberg, *Mahzeh Avraham*, no. 42, refers to the argument that switching on of the electric light is only indirect because the power is already there and to switch on the light is merely to remove that which arrests the flow. Both these authorities, however, hold that there is a rabbinic prohibition but that it is, therefore, permitted to request a non-Jew to switch on the light if it is required for a religious purpose such as illuminating the synagogue for prayer. It should also be mentioned that Steinberg, No. 51, takes issue with Schwadron's contention that this type of light is different from "work" at the time of the Tabernacle.

10. *Betzah* 4:7.

11. *Betzah* 33b.

12. For an account of these see Braun, *Shearim*, vol. 2, Index *hashmal*, and Uziel, *Piskey Uziel*, nos. 6–17, pp. 40–74.

13. *Piskey Uziel*, no. 4, pp. 38–39.

14. *Rosh ha-Shanah* 27b.

15. There is a vast literature on this subject. See Sevin, *ha-Moadim ha-Halakhah*, pp. 247–48; Kahana, *Mehkarim be sfrut ha-Teshuvot*, p. 430; Freehof, *The Responsa Literature*, pp. 181–

89; Braun, *Shearim*, vol. 1, pp. 52–54 (note 2) and vol. 3, pp. 65–67 (note 23); Medini; *Sedey Hemed*, 13:12 (vol. 7, pp. 396–401); Halberstam, *Divrey Hayyim*, part I, OH, no. 25 and part II, OH, nos. 1 and 2; Kluger's *Modaah*, reprinted at the end of the New York ed. of his *Avodat Avodah*, Abraham Bornstein of Sochachov, *Avney Nezer*, OH 11. no. 537 in a Responsum, addressed to Ezekiel ha-Kohen, rabbi of Radomsk, as late as 1908, writes,

> My belly troubled when I heard that the making of *matzot* by machine has again come to the fore. The Geonim, the true Zaddihim, namely, His Honour our Master of Gur, of blessed memory; and the Holy Gaon of Sans, may his memory be for a blessing for the life of the World to Come and the Holy Gaon of Tehechenov, may his memory be for a blessing for the life of the World to Come, had bestirred themselves to forbid such *matzot* categorically for they are *hametz* and their contamination is in their skirts and the leprous plague-spot is underneath them. And many other great and righteous scholars have declared them to be forbidden. Some years ago they tried to reintroduce this in your town but it was immediately set at naught. And now they have revived it. The Hasidim went to the Rabbi of your community but he said that he does not wish to intefere one way or the other. He did show them, however, a letter from the Rabbi who permits it, namely, the Rabbi of Berzhan (Shwadron) who permits even such *matzot*. But of what use is this one's dispensation? Is he greater than the Rabbi of Lemberg, R. Joseph Saul (Nathansohn) of blessed memory? He did permit them and yet these great scholars, whose little finger is thicker than his loins in Torah and the fear of Heaven, declared that they are forbidden and his opinion was set at naught. It is well-known the extent to which our Master of Gur, of blessed memory, raised his voice loud in protest against the use of these *matzot*. And it is clear, he said, from the acts of those who are permissive that their real desire is to remove little by little something from each *mitzvah* with the intention of ultimately uprooting everything. So what is added by the Rabbi of Berzhan with his dispensation? Of what value is the squeaking of a mouse among the roaring lions? In our lands we have accepted upon ourselves the opinion of those who forbid them and in our land; it is a thing actually forbidden by the Torah. Consequently, we are obliged to stand firm in the breach, especially in this generation when if we are lenient with regard to forbidden things, especially with regard to the prohibition of leaven on Passover, the heart of the Torah, it is against the Torah that they stretch forth their hands."

16. *Betzah* 36b.
17. *Shabbat* 156b.
18. OH 305:18.
19. *Piskrey Uziel*, no. 13, pp. 55–56 and no. 14 end, p. 59.
20. OH 325:11.
21. Commentary to Levit. 23:24.
22. *Hatam Sofer*, part VI, no. 97 (in Uziel no. 93 is a printer's error).
23. *Bet Yitzhak*, YD II, in the index note to no. 31.
24. See Braun, *Shearim*, vol. 2, pp. 60–62; and on traveling in an airplane on the Sabbath Braun, p. 57 and an electrically operated lift, p. 62. Cf. Bronrot, "Travelling by Aeroplane on the Sabbath." On carrying spectacles on the Sabbath (these were known as early as the days of Karo) see Karo's *Bet Yosef* to *Tur* OH 301 and Isserles to SA, OH 301:11 who forbid it but Shapira, *Minhat Eleazar*, vol. 2, no. 4 argues that this was because in the days of Karo and Isserles people only wore spectacles for reading.
25. *Darkhey Noam*, OH, no. 9. On this whole subject see Kahana, *Mehkarim*, pp. 317–29.
26. On the *motif* of not appearing to be more lax than the Gentiles in religious observances see *sup.*, pp.
27. *Magen Avraham* to OH 514 note 4. See Ettlinger, *Tosefot Bikkurim*, end of his *Bikkurey Yaakov*, p. 54, that a man who does not smoke on Yom Tov must not handle the pipe.
28. *Berakhot* 35a.

29. *Magen Avraham* to OH 210 note 9.

30. See *Baer Hetev* to Oh ad loc. On the benediction to be recited before drinking coffee, tea, or chocolate, see Lampronti, *Pahad Yitzkah*, s.v. *kavvee* and *kikolateh*.

31. On the general question of Halakhic responses to medical challenges, see Zimmels, *Magicians, Theologians and Doctors* and Immanuel Jakobovits; *Jewish Medical Ethics*. On modern problems see Jakobovits, *Jewish Medical Ethics* Appendix 2, pp. 251–94; David M. Feldman, *Birth Control in Jewish Law*, chapters 12 and 13, pp. 227–48; J. David Bleich, *Contemporary Halakhic Problems*, chapter 5, pp. 92–128; Elon, "Jewish Law and Modern Medicine."

32. *Neda Biyhudah, Tinyana*, YD, No. 210.

33. YD 363:2.

34. *Bava Batra* 155a.

35. See Jakobovits, *Jewish Medical Ethics*, pp. 278–83.

36. Responsa, *Binyan Tzion* (Old Series), YD, No. 67.

37. *Darkhey Teshuvah* 179:6.

38. See the authorities quoted by Braun, *Shearim*, vol. 4, pp. 35–36 (note 2).

39. *Hagigah* 15a.

40. See Ginzberg, *Legends of the Jews*, vol. VI, pp. 400–402.

41. Vol. 2, letter *bet*, s.v. *ben bitto shel adam*, p. 30a.

42. See Feinstein, *Iggerot Moshe*, EH, no. 71; Schwarz, *Maaneh le-Iggerot* no. 166 (an attack on Feinstein). On the whole subject see Jakobovits, op. cit., Appendix: "Artificial Insemination," pp. 244–50; OP, vol. I, 1, note 42, p. 6a.

43. See the comprehensive survey in Jakobovits, op. cit., pp. 285–91.

44. See *sup.*, p. 38.

45. *Hekhal Yitzhak*, OH, no. 29.

46. *Shabbat* 107b.

12

Halakhah and Ethics

In a previous chapter we noted how ethical considerations influenced the Halakhah and how some of the Halakhists went so far as to formulate rules of ethical conduct in the style of the Halakhic codes. In this chapter we consider further the relationship between Halakhah and ethical principles. Since, as we have shown, the Halakhists did not normally operate in a compartmentlike fashion remote from life, and since Jewish law has the strongest religious dimension, the demarcation lines between Jewish law and ethics are finely drawn, the one discipline frequently invading the preserves of the other, despite the fact that, as in all legal systems, the law in itself, for all its ethical orientation, cannot always give expression to the highest ethical ideals. Law, by its very nature, is categorical and for all. It is down to earth, precise, and exact, whereas the ethical ideal is bound to be, to some extent, at least, individualistic and subjective. For this reason there is bound to be a degree of conflict between the Halakhah and ethical norms. And yet the Halakhists throughout the ages have sought to narrow the boundaries between law and ethics as we describe in this chapter.[1]

Precisely because there is a religious dimension to the law, there are instances in which a man who brings about loss to his neighbor indirectly, although he is not liable to compensate him by human law, is nonetheless obliged to compensate him "by the law of Heaven." The technical term for this is *patur mi-diney adam ve-hayyav be-diney shamayyim*, "exempt by the laws of man but liable by the laws of Heaven." The Talmud gives four examples in the name of R. Joshua.[2] The same statement, in the name of R. Joshua, is also made in the Tosefta but there the expression used is, "They are not liable to pay by law but Heaven will not pardon them until they pay."[3] The principle is the same: a wrong has been committed and there is a real obligation to compensate the victim but this cannot be enforced by the courts because of certain legal technicalities. Since a man is obliged to satisfy the ethical demands his religion makes on him, he cannot obtain pardon until he has redressed the wrong he has done. The "laws of Heaven" are also laws, and "Heaven" insists that these be obeyed.

The four examples given in the Talmud and the Tosefta are as follows. (1) A breaks down a fence belonging to B with the result that B's animal runs off through the breach and is lost. (2) A bends the standing corn of B in the direction of an approaching fire that then destroys B's corn. (3) A hires false witnesses to testify against B and their evidence is accepted by the court, who is unaware that they are false, with the result that B suffers financial loss. (4) A can give evidence in court that will save B from financial loss but A fails to testify. In all these cases A does not injure B directly, only indirectly, and the law does not enforce compensation for loss brought about indirectly. In example (1) the animal strays of its own accord, though it would not have escaped if A had not broken down the fence. In example (2) it is the fire that actually does the damage, and at the time the corn was bent in the direction of the fire it was only an approaching fire. In example (3) the loss is brought about by the testimony of the witnesses and only indirectly by A who hired them. In example (4), A's failure to testify is an offense of omission and the law can only enforce compensation when this is required for an offense of commission. But in all four cases an obvious wrong has been perpetrated by A and his ethical obligation is such that he must compensate B if he is to live up to the ethical standards his religion demands of him. The Talmud provides a number of subtle elaborations in its discussion of these four cases and then proceeds to record further examples of the same principle.[4] (1) A does some work with B's red heifer, thereby disqualifying the heifer (see Num. 19:2). The red heifer is extremely rare and can be sold for a very high price. Nevertheless, the courts cannot enforce payment since no actual mark of damage is evident on the heifer and it is the law of the Torah that renders it unfit. (2) A places poison in front of B's animal, who eats it and dies. The compensation due for the loss of the animal cannot be enforced by law since it was the animal's act of eating that caused the damage, A's contribution to it being indirect. (3) A hands a flaming torch to an imbecile who uses it to set B's haystack alight. Here, too, A has acted with the greatest irresponsibility but it was the act of the imbecile that brought about the actual damage. (4) A frightened B by giving a sudden shout and the like. There is no physical assault on B's person, although he suffered harm as a result of the shock. (5) A's jar broke in the public domain and he failed to remove the pieces, which later caused injury to B. Here again the offense is one of omission and payment cannot be enforced by the courts. The Talmud concludes that there are, indeed, many such instances in which there is no obligation enforcable by the human courts but where there is, nonetheless, an obligation if the perpetrator is to satisfy the demands of Heaven.

There are further discussions among the post-Talmudic Halakhists on the scope of this principle. For instance, some Halakhists go so far as to rule that whenever A has an obligation by the laws of Heaven to compensate B for a loss that A has brought about, there is a real legal obligation (albeit one that cannot be enforced by the courts) so that if B manages to seize some of A's property to the value of his loss he is empowered by the courts to keep it. Others disagree, holding that the human courts have no power at all in the matter so that if B does seize A's property A can obtain redress in the courts.[5]

Certain acts are valid in law but strongly disapproved of on ethical grounds. The Talmud gives three examples.[6] (1) A appointed B to be his agent to betroth to him a certain woman. B fell in love with the woman when he saw her and betrothed her to himself. B's betrothal is valid but he is said to have behaved "in a fraudulent fashion" (she-nahag bo minhaj ramaut). (2) A appointed B to buy a certain field on A's behalf. B took a liking to the field when he saw it and bought it for himself. The sale is valid but B has behaved "in a fraudulent fashion." (3) A is contemplating buying a field, the arrangements for the purchase having been made but no actual transfer has yet taken place. If B then intervenes and buys the field, securing it at a higher price ("gazumping" as it is now called) the sale is valid but is compared to "a poor man who is turning over a cake" (determined to acquire the cake that has been abandoned by its owner). One who takes the cake to himself is called "wicked" (rasha). In these cases the principle of liability according to the laws of Heaven does not apply, since, unlike in the cases referred to earlier, there is no actual loss to the victim. The woman from whom he has been deprived was not his, neither was the field nor the poor man's cake. Nevertheless, B's act is unethical and this statement is itself part of the law; i.e., the *law* declares the act to be unethical. It is part of the Halakhah and is recorded as such in the *Shulhan Arukh*.[7] The *Shulhan Arukh* extends this rule to cover the case of A in the process of obtaining employment as a hireling and B gets in first.

Another example of strong disapproval being given expression in the law to an act that does not involve even an obligation to pay by the laws of Heaven, is recorded in the Mishnah.[8] Movables are acquired by their actual removal into the possession of the buyer not by the payment of the purchase price. Thus if A gives B the money for his goods but the goods are still in A's possession no legal transfer has been effected and either party can retract. After stating this rule the Mishnah continues, "However, they (the sages) have said: 'He that exacted punishment *(mi she-para)* from the generation of the Flood and the generation of the Dispersion will exact punishment from him that does not abide by his word.'" Abbaye and Rava debate the meaning of the Mishnaic statement.[9] According to Abbaye the meaning is simply that the court must inform the party who wishes to retract that God punishes those who do not keep their word, but according to Rava the court must actually utter these words as a curse. The *Shulhan Arukh*,[10] following Rava's opinion, rules that the court actually curses the offender. Isserles quotes Mordecai b. Hillel that the curse is to be uttered in public. Where no money has exchanged hands and there is only a verbal agreement to the sale there is no *mi she-para* if either party wishes to retract. There is nevertheless a debate between Rab and R. Johanan, the latter holding, and his opinion followed, that where there has been a verbal agreement to a purchase it is "lacking in trustworthiness" if either party retracts.[11] This, too, is an ethical judgment that has been incorporated into the law. The one who retracts offends against the ethical "law" that a man's word should be his bond. Another expression used to denote ethical disapproval of the one who retracts is, "The spirit of the Sages is displeased with him."[12] This much softer expression than calling a man "wicked" or imposing a *mi she-para* or declaring that he is liable by the laws of Heaven, is also found in connection with the law that the victim of a robber, who wishes to repent of his misdeeds and restore his ill-gotten gains to their rightful owners, should refuse to accept the robber's repayment in order to afford encouragement for robbers to repent. If the victim does allow the robber to repay him, "the spirit of the Sages is displeased with him."[13] A remarkable instance of this formula being used is in the statement that a certain Tanna taught,[14] "Whoever kills snakes and scorpions on the Sabbath the spirit of the Hasidim ('saints') is displeased with him," whereupon Rava son of R. Huna retorted, "And the spirit of the Sages is displeased with those Hasidim."

The Hasidim obeyed a higher law of their own, not always, as in the previous example, with the approval of the sages. Generally, however, the Hasidic "higher law" not only met with the approval of the sages but it won their admiration and encouragement. Whether or not these laws of the Hasidim were ever actually recorded in codal form remains doubtful. What is not in doubt is that the Hasidim treated the higher standards they demanded of the members of their fraternity as actual laws, in the sense that these were categorically binding and not mere pious options. There are a number of references in the Talmudic literature to the "saints of old" (hasidim ha-rishonim). It is said that these would wait one hour before their prayers in order to direct their hearts to God;[15] they would insert the tzitzit in their garments as soon as three handbreadths of the garment had been woven, even though the law does not demand that the tzitzit be affixed until the garment is actually worn;[16] and they would only consort with their wives from Wednesday onwards in the belief that a conception during the earlier days of the week might result in a birth on the Sabbath, which involves some degree of Sabbath desecration, permitted by law but avoided by the Hasidim in obedience to their higher law.[17] These men are also said to have the same scrupulousness with regard to their social responsibilities. It was their habit to hide away their thorns and pieces of broken glass in the soil of their fields at a depth of at least three handbreadths so as to guard against anything of theirs possibly doing harm to others.[18] Although some of the details are undoubtedly later embellishments, there does seem to be behind these accounts an authentic tradition of pietists with special rules of their own according to which they conducted themselves with a scrupulousness extending far beyond the laws applicable to the generality of Jews in matters of prayer, of Sabbath observance, of ritual in general, and of social welfare.

In addition to the hasidim ha-rishonim, there are many references in the Talmudic literature to the hasid as a special type whose behavior was in accordance with the higher standards he had set himself. Of the four characters among men, the hasid is the one who says, "What is mine is thine and what is thine is thine."[19] Of the four kinds of temper, the hasid is the one whom it is hard to provoke and easy to pacify.[20] Of the four types of alms giving, the hasid gives himself and wishes others to give.[21] Of the four who frequent the House of Study the *hasid* goes there and also practices whatever he studies.[22] The ruling is given that the victim of a fraudulent change of money can return the deficient coins he received provided the return is made during a limited period in which he can discover their true value. If they are not returned within this period, it is assumed that the victim waives his right. But a ruling of the Mishnah is quoted from which it appears that the time limit is extended for as long as a year. R. Hisda suggests that the longer period is in accordance with "the saintly rule" *(mishnat hasidim)*.[23] Similarly, if a wealthy man, traveling from place to place and finding himself without money, is obliged to take poor relief, he has no legal obligation to repay on his return home since at that time he was, in fact, "a poor man." But another ruling is quoted in which it is stated that he is obliged to repay. R. Hisda replies that this latter rule is for the saints.[24] In these two examples the "saintly rule" is said to have been stated in the Mishnah. Whether or not this interpretation of the Mishnah is historically correct is beside the point. It remains true that according to R. Hisda the official code of conduct, while stating the minimum requirements of the law, occasionally offers guidance to those who wish to behave as do the saints. In other words, the "saintly rule," the *mishnat hasidim*, is more than an individual preference, it belongs to an actual code of conduct for the saints.

In this connection the following anecdote told in the Jerusalem Talmud is significant.[25] The Mishnah rules that a company of Jews attacked by heathens may save their lives by handing over one of their number if the heathens had specified that man by name; i.e., they declared that they wanted to kill him in particular, not *any* member of the company. R. Joshua b. Levi, following this rule, saved the lives of the inhabitants of his town by handing over a man specified by name, whereupon Elijah, who was a regular visitor to the saint, visited him no more. After R. Joshua b. Levi had fasted many days, Elijah did appear and rebuked R. Joshua b. Levi. R. Joshua defended his action by referring to the unambiguous rule of the Mishnah. "Yes," Elijah retorted, "but is that a *mishnat hasidim?*"

The distinction between the *tzaddik*, the formally righteous man, and the *hasid* is that the latter goes "beyond the line of the law"— *lifnim mi-shurat ha-din*. R. Huna contrasted the two halves of the verse, "The Lord is righteous *(tzaddik)* in all His ways and gracious *(hasid)* in all His works' (Ps. 145:17). At first God acts toward sinners in accord with their just deserts but in the end He is gracious to pardon, i.e., He goes beyond the line of the law.[26] But the obligation to go beyond the letter of the law was not only for saints (although for them it was presumably essential in all circumstances). R. Judah, commenting on the verse, "And thou shalt show them the way they must walk and the work which they must do" (Exod. 18:20) said that "the work" means the law while "which they must do" means that they should go beyond the line of the law.[27]

That for some persons in certain circumtances the obligation to go beyond the line of the law was itself held to be law is evidenced by the following narrative.[28] Rabbah bar Hanah hired porters to transport a cask of wine for him. The porters were not too careful and allowed the cask to be broken. As hired bailees they were liable to compensate their employer for the loss of his wine. Rabbah therefore seized their cloaks in payment. But Rav ordered Rabbah to give them back the cloaks. "Is this the law?" protested Rabbah. "Yes," replied Rav, "for it is written, 'That thou mayest walk in the way of good men' (Prov. 2:20)." The porters then demanded their wages and Rav ordered Rabbah to pay them their wages. "Surely this cannot be the law," Rabbah again protested. "Yes," replied Rav, quoting the end of the verse, "And the paths of righteousness shalt thou keep." The story implies, the law was as Rabbah held it to be but Rav quotes the verse to demonstrate to Rabbah that for a scholar such as he to act solely within the letter of the law is "illegal" or, at least, it offends against the principle stated in the verse.

Although excessive concern with the higher law was both admired and advocated in connection with interhuman relationships, with regard to religious obligation excessive zeal was generally frowned upon, unless it was displayed by a man otherwise noted for his great piety. For an ordinary person to display extraordinary religious zeal, when to do so did not suit his standing in the community, was considered to be an example of "showing off," of parading religious virtue. The term used for such a display is *yohara*, "pride," better understood as priggishness. The Talmud tells of Eliezer Zeira who wore black shoes in mourning for the destruction of the Temple.[29] The officers of the Exilarch put Eliezer in prison, declaring that he was guilty of *yohara*, until he demonstrated to them his skill in learning, implying that he was worthy of behaving more piously in this matter than ordinary folk. It is possible that there is another *motif* behind this story. For ordinary folk to mourn openly for the destruction of the Temple, in Babylon where the incident occurred, might have caused doubts to be cast by the authorities on Jewish loyalty to the Persian Empire. The Court of the Exilarch, as the Jewish representatives of the Babylonian aristocracy, would naturally have been especially sensitive on this issue. Other examples of *yohara* in the Talmud are refusing to work on Tisha be-Av, the anniversary of the destruction of the Temple, and a bridegroom reciting the Shema on the first night of his wedding, from which the law exempts him because, in his preoccupation, it is hard for him to concentrate.[30] Bertinoro, in his Commentary to the Mishnah states that some of his teachers ruled, "nowadays" the opposite is true.[31] The principle of *yohara* nowadays comes into operation when a bridegroom does not recite the Shema, implying that on all other nights he does concentrate adequately, whereas "in these days" we never concentrate as we should while reciting the Shema. The post-Talmudic authorities also invoke the *yohara* principle. Thus the *Shulhan Arukh* rules that only a man renowned for his piety may wear daily the *tefillin* of both Rashi and Rabbenu Tam.[32] But since the objection is to the display of excessive piety that is involved, in communities where ordinary worshipers do wear the two pairs of *tefillin*, there can be no fear of *yohara*. The followers of the Hasidic movement, for example, do wear both pairs.[33] It would appear that the *yohara* principle is never invoked with regard to purely ethical obligations. Nowhere is there any suggestion that it is priggish to be excessively generous or benevolent.[34] Thue, the Talmud lays it down as a rule that one should not give away to charity more than a fifth of one's total income, because this might lead to impoverishment and the burdening of the community with an additional mouth to feed.[35] But this is only applied to financial giving for the reason stated. It is nowhere suggested that practical help and concern, where no heavy financial loss is involved, can be in any way blameworthy when excessive or extraordinary. And even with regard to the rule that one must not give away more than a fifth, Maimonides adds "unless it be as a special act of piety" *(hasidut)*, and he makes no stipulation that this attitude of *hasidut* be limited to people otherwise noted for this quality.[36]

We noted earlier that where high ethical standards are held to be binding beyond the letter of the law the verse in Proverbs, "that thou mayest walk in the ways of good men" is quoted in support. The verse in the Pentateuch: "Thou shalt do that which is right and good in the eyes of the Lord" (Deut. 6:18) is quoted when the

higher ethical standard was incorporated into the law and could be
enforced by the courts. An example is the law of *bar mitzra* (literally, "son of the boundary"), that the first option to buy a field is to
be afforded to the owner of a field which borders on that being sold,
provided that he is willing to pay the asking price. This law is
enforceable, i.e., if the field had been sold to another, the owner of
the adjacent field can have the sale rendered null and void by the
courts. This rule was developed in the Amoraic period in Babylon
and is not found in the Palestinian Talmud.[37]

The interdependence of law and ethics was not allowed, however, to blur the distinction between the two, as Elon rightly remarks.[38] The verse, "neither shalt thou favor a poor man in his
cause" (Exod. 23:3) and the verse, "Ye shall do no unrighteousness
in judgment; thou shalt not respect the person of the poor, nor
favour the person of the mighty; but in righteousness shalt thou
judge thy neighbor" (Lev. 19:15) form the basis of the principle that
justice must be administered impartially. The *Sifra* states, " 'Thou
shalt not respect the person of the poor.'"[39] You should not say,
Since this man is poor and both I and this rich man are obliged to
support him, I shall decide the case in his favor so that he will find
his sustenance in a clean manner. That is why Scripture says:
"Thou shalt not regard the person of the poor.'" If the judge wishes
to help a poor man he should not do it by deciding unjustly in his
favor. If justice so demands the judge must decide against the poor
man and then compensate him out of the judge's own pocket.[40]

NOTES

1. On the subject of this chapter see the illuminating appendix, "Moral rights and duties
in Jewish Law" in Herzog, *The Main Institutions of Jewish Law*, vol. I, pp. 379–86; Elon, *ha-
Misphat ha-Ivri*, pp. 171–80; and the chapter "Law and equity" in Silberg, *Talmudic Law and
the Modern State*, pp. 93–130; and Federbush, *ha-Musar ve-ha-Mishpat be-Yisrael* devoted entirely to this subject. For the treatment by a Halakhist of the differences between the Torah
laws and secular laws in connection with ethical obligation see the introduction to Perlwut-
ter's *Dammecsek Eliezer*, pp. 2–7. Perlmutter notes extensions in a religiously orientated
ethical system such as that of the Torah. Only in the Torah is there a command to love the
neighbor; usury is prohibited; passive failure to save life is condemned; love for the neighbor
applies to aliens as well as the native-born; there is greater equality and rights for women; a
person has obligations to his own soul. To be further noted in connection with this whole
question of the relationship between Halakhah and ethics are the many rules and regulations
governing the practice of benevolence. The principle behind the practice of benevolence
(*gemillut hasidim*) is that of *Imitatio Dei* see *Sotah* 14a. *Gemillut hasadim* involves helping others
physically as well as financially (*Sukkah* 49b). There are no limits to *gemillut hasadim* (*Peah*
1:1). It is to be exercised on behalf of the rich as well as the poor and the dead as well as the

living (*Sukkah* 49b). Ethical offenses classified in Halakhic terms are the prohibitions of "wasteful speech" (*devarim betelim*) *Yoma* 19b; Maimonides, *Yad, Deot* 2:4; and of misleading others (*genevat daat*), *Hullin* 94a.

2. *Bava Kama* 55b.

3. *Shevuot* 3:1–3, ed. Zuckermandel, p. 449. For another example of liability by the laws of Heaven see *Mekhilta, mishpatim*, to Exod. 21:14, ed. Horovitz-Rabin, p. 263, where Issi b. Akiba states, although to kill a heathen is not a capital offense it cannot be other than an act of murder since it was so before the Torah was given and there are no greater leniencies only greater strickness now that the Torah has been given. Hence, he concludes, the murderer's law is "delivered to Heaven"—*dino masur la-shamayyim*.

4. *Bava Kama* 55b–56a. Another example recorded in the Tosefta, *Bava Kama* 6:17, ed. Zuckermandel, p. 355, is that of a skilled physician authorized by the court to practice his craft. If he caused injury to his patient while healing him he is not liable by the laws of men but "his law is delivered to Heaven." This is recorded as the law in SA, YD 366:1. A somewhat similar, but not identical, principle is, *latzet lidey shamayyim* "to satisfy the requirements of Heaven," e.g., if a man admits that he has robbed one of two men but does not know which of them, according to the strict law he need only deposit a single payment and leave it to them to sort it out. But if he wishes to satisfy the requirements of Heaven he must pay each of them. *Bava Metzia*, 37a. Here there is no *obligation*, not even by "the laws of Heaven," since he has, in fact, only robbed one of them. Nevertheless, he has the duty of restoring that which he hast taken illegally to its rightful owner, and in order to do this he must pay both of them and so make sure.

5. See ET, vol 7, s.v. *diney shamayyim*, pp. 382–96.

6. *Kiddushin* 58b–59a.

7. HM 237:1. Cf. the commentators to this section who remark that the offender is actually dubbed "wicked" in a public proclamation in the synagogue.

8. *Bava Metzia* 4:2.

9. Ibid. 48b.

10. HM 204:4.

11. *Bava Metzia* 49a; SA,HM 234:7. A similar expression used for certain legally valid acts that are nonetheless disapproved of as ethically dubious, is "there are only grounds for complaint' i.e., there are no legal grounds for redress but the victim is entitled to raise his voice in complaint; when, for example, a man hired laborers and then decided that he does not want the job done or where the workmen decided that they could do better with another employer, see *Bava Metzia* 76b (printed in error in Herzog, *Main Institutions*, p. 384 note 7 where the source is given as 75b).

12. *Bava Metzia* 48a.

13. *Bava Kama* 94b. Another example is that of the man who disinherits his own children in favor of strangers, *Bava Batra* 134b. The positive form of this is "the spirit of the Sages is pleased with him," found in connection with the year of release (Deut. 15:1). If, despite his release by the Torah, the debtor pays his debt, the sages are pleased with him, Mishnah, *Sheviit* 10:9.

14. *Shabbat* 121b.

15. Mishnah *Berakhot* 5:1; cf. *Berakhot* 32b.

16. *Menahot* 41a.

17. *Middah* 38a–b.

18. *Bava Kama* 30a.

19. *Avot* 5:10.

20. Ibid. 5:11.

21. Ibid. 5:13.

22. Ibid., 5:14.

23. *Bava Metzia* 52.

24. *Hullin* 130b.

25. *Terumot* 8:4 (46c).

26. *Rosh he-Shanah* 17b Cf. the statement of Maimonides, *Yad, Avadim* 9:8.

It is permitted to make a Canaanite slave work with rigor. But although this is the law, it belongs to the quality of saintliness *(middat hasidut)* and the ways of wisdom that a man be merciful and that he pursue righteousness, that he should not make his yoke heavy on his slave and should not cause him distress. He should give him to eat from every dish and give him to drink from every drink (he himself eats and drinks). The Sages of old used to give their slaves of every dish they themselves ate and would feed their animals and slaves before eating themselves. Behold Scripture says: 'As the eyes of servants look to the hand of their masters, and the eyes of a maidservant unto the hand of her mistress' (Ps. 123:2). He must offend him neither by striking him nor by insulting words. Scripture has permitted them to be used for service but not for humiliation. He must not shout at his slave or be very angry with him but should speak gently to him and listen to his complaints. So is it stated explicitly among the good ways of which Job boasted: "If I did despise the cause of my manservant or my maidservant. Did not He that made me in the womb make him?" (Job 31:13; 15). Cruelty and arrogance are only found among the pagan idolaters but the seed of our father Abraham, the Israelites, upon whom the Holy One, blessed be He, has bestowed the goodness of the Torah and to whom He has commanded just statues and laws, they have compassion for all.

27. *Bava Kama* 100a.

28. *Bava Metzia* 83b. Many of the later Halakhists, on the basis of this narrative, go so far as to argue that if the person can afford it he can be compelled by the court to go beyond the line of the law, see Elon, *ha-Mishpat ha Ivri*, pp. 176–80. Cf. *Bava Metzia* 33a that although ones own property has priority over all others yet whoever insists always on his rights in this matter will eventually become poor, see Rashi ad loc. who uses the expression *lifnim mishurat ha-din* and see Federbush *ha-Musar ve-ha-Mishpat, pp. 80–81.*

29. *Bava Kama* 59b.

30. Berakhot 17b.

31. To Mishnah *Berakhot* 2:8.

32. SA, OH 34:3. Another example is provided by the statement in SA, OH 3:1 that, "nowadays," we do not recite the formula mentioned in the Talmud (*Berakhot* 60b) imploring the angels who accompany us to forgive us when we enter the privy, because we are not sufficiently God-fearing to have angels accompany us (see *Taz* Note 1 and Epstein, *Arukh ha-Shulhan* 3:2, the latter using the term *yohara*).

33. See the discussion and defense of the Hasidic practice by Hayyim Eleazar Shapira, *Ot Hayyim ve-Shalom* to OH 34 notes 9 and 10.

34. But see *Bava Kama* 81b.

35. *Ketubot* 50a.

36. Commentary to Mishnah *Peah* 1:1.

37. See *Bava Metzia* 108a; Herzog *Main Institutions* pp. 385–86. Another example of the law demanding an ethical stance is the following. The Talmud (*Kiddushin* 32a) discusses whether a son is obliged to support his parents financially and the final ruling (see *Sheiltot, yitro,* end) is that he is not so obliged. Nevertheless the medieval authorities rule, on the basis of the Jerusalem Talmud, that if the son can afford it he is compelled to support his poor parents, see *Tosafists, Kiddushin* 32a, s.v. *oru leh* and SA, YD 240:5.

38. Elon *Ha Mishpat ha-Ivri*, p. 173.

39. *Sifra, kedoshim,* 4:4, ed. Weiss, p. 89a.

40. *Hullin* 134a.

13

Halakhah and Good Manners (Derekh Eretz)

In the previous chapter we examined the relationship between Halakhah and general ethical conduct. In this chapter we note how the Halakhah is related to a more particular type of conduct, that referred to in the Rabbinic literature as *derekh eretz*, literally "the way of the land," and denoting what might be described as good manners, etiquette, correct and decent behavior.[1] It has to be appreciated that this area is more tenuous and consequently less amenable to precise Halakhic formulation. Obviously, standards vary here. Attitudes that are offensive in one culture may be inoffensive or even quite acceptable and admirable in a different culture. Nevertheless, as the term *derekh eretz* implies, there are said to be universal norms belonging to man's essential nature. *Derekh eretz* is not solely a Jewish but a general human concept.

A whole minor tractate of the Talmud (though compiled in the post-Talmudic period, it contains much material going back to the Talmudic sages) is called *Derekh Eretz* (actually two tractates, *Rabbah* and *Zuta*), devoted to this theme. Although a good deal of the material in this tractate is Aggadic, it enjoys at least a quasi-Halakhic status. Similarly, a large portion of Maimonides *Hilkhot Deot*, in his *Mishneh Torah*, describes this aspect of behavior in Halakhic terms, especially with regard to the sage, the *talmid haham*, whose standards must be of the highest.[2] In Talmudic times, it appears, there was a collection of rules of conduct known as *Hilkhot Derekh Eretz* or, if there was no actual collection, the rules themselves existed and were known by this name.[3] These were held to be of a lesser order than *Halakhot* proper, so that a man who had had a seminal emission and was not allowed to study the Torah before his immersion could nonetheless rehearse these laws.

Many of the *derekh eretz* rules have to do with conduct at the table. A whole section of the *Shulhan Arukh* deals with this topic.[4] The Talmud states in the name of R. Johanan that it is improper to engage in conversation during a meal because the food may enter the windpipe and cause choking.[5] This is recorded as a rule in the *Shulhan Arukh*[6] but is a rule that is nowadays generally ignored.[7] According to Karo's understanding[8] of a Talmudic passage,[9] recorded in his *Shulhan Arukh*,[10] if two men are eating out of the same dish and one interrupts his meal to sip his wine, the other should wait until his friend has begun to eat again before continuing with his own eating. Two men need not wait, however, for a third and they may continue to eat while the third man sups. Here again the rule is ignored since we no longer eat from the same dish.[11] Maimonides rules that it is improper to gaze at the face of someone who is eating or at the portion he is eating because this will cause him to be embarrassed.[12] The *Shulhan Arukh*[13] records this *verbatim*.[14] Tractate *Derekh Eretz* states, "When a guest enters a house he should do whatever his host requests him to do."[15] The Talmudic version of the same rule is, "Whatever the host tells you to do that you must do."[16] This rule is recorded in the *Shulhan Arukh*, as is the further rule, also stated in tractate *Derekh Eretz*, that the host must not show any bad temper during the meal because this will embarrass the guests.[17] Further on etiquette at table, the Talmud states that to quaff a cup in a single gulp is to be a guzzler; in two gulps it is *derekh eretz*; and in three gulps it is to be overly fastidious.[18] This is recorded in the *Shulhan Arukh*,[19] but Isserles and the commentators naturally say that it all depends on the size of the cup and the strength of the drink. Some further details regarding table manners found in tractate *Derekh Eretz* are recorded in the *Shulhan Arukh*.[20] If two persons are seated at the same table the one of higher rank should reach for the food first. If the one of lesser rank does so, he is said to be a guzzler. When a guest enters a house he should not ask for food until he is invited to eat. Epstein observes that this would appear to be the rule only for a nonpaying guest but guests at an inn or boardinghouse who pay for their meals may call to be served without waiting until they are invited to eat "and such is the normal practice."[21] Quoting as his source a Talmudic passage,[22] Abraham Gumbiner says that it is *derekh eretz* for the host to pour out the wine for his guests.[23]

Two sections of the *Shulhan Arukh* are devoted, respectively, to the procedures to be followed when putting on one's clothes in the morning[24] and when visiting the privy.[25] Here, too, passages mainly of an Aggadic nature are given Halakhic status and are discussed in Halakhic terms by the codifiers. R. Jose, in the Talmud, boasts that the walls of his house never saw the seams of his shirt.[26] Rashi understands this to mean that he never turned up his shirt so as to leave his bare skin exposed. Although from the fact that R. Jose boasted of it, the implication is that the practice was unusual, yet the *Tur*, followed by the *Shulhan Arukh*, records it as a rule for all, "He should not put on his shirt while sitting up in bed but he should put it over his head and shoulders while still laying down (covered by the bedclothes) so that when he rises from his bed his body will be covered."[27] R. Johanan defines a scholar who can be trusted at his own word without further evidence that a lost article someone has found belongs to him, as one who puts on his robe the right way up when he finds that he has put it on with the seams showing outside, i.e., he is so concerned with avoiding causing distress to others that he never appears before them improperly dressed.[28] Here again a rule distinguishing scholars is codified in the *Shulhan Arukh* as a rule for all, "He should take care when putting on his shirt to wear it the right way up, not wearing it inside out."[29] David ha-Levi suggests that the *Tur*, followed by the *Shulhan Arukh*, holds that the rule is for all men in the first instance, the only difference being that the scholar will take his shirt off again if he had inadvertently put it on inside out.[30] The Talmud records a debate as to whether the right shoe should be put on first or the left shoe.[31] The claims of the right shoe to be put on first are based on the principle that right generally predominates, as, for example, in the Temple service which must be carried out with the right hand not the left. The claims for putting on the left shoe first are based on the fact that the *tefillin* are worn on the left hand not the right. It is said in the Talmudic passage that Ravina, "a God-fearing man," would satisfy both requirements. He would put on his right shoe first without tying it, then he would put on his left shoe, which he would tie up before he tied up his right shoe. R. Ashi, however, states that he had noticed that R. Kahana never bothered at all about the matter, which is no doubt why Alfasi, Maimonides, and other codifiers say nothing at all about the correct manner of putting on one's shoes.[32] The *Tur* and the *Shulhan Arukh* do state it: "He should first put on the right shoe without tying it, then he should put on the left shoe and tie it up, then he should tie up the right shoe."[33] thus, even in such a trivial matter as putting

on one's shoes, the symbolism of the right—justice and righteousness—is preserved, as is the reminder of the *tefillin*. In the same
Talmudic passage it is said that when removing the shoes the left
shoe should first be removed and this, too, is recorded as a rule in
the *Shulhan Arukh*.[34] The Talmud[35] expresses disapproval of one
who walks about with upright posture, i.e., in a haughty manner,
which Maimonides records as a rule for scholars.[36] The Talmud
similarly sees merit in having the head covered when walking although there is no reference to any prohibition of having the head
uncovered.[37] But again the *Shulhan Arukh* records as a rule for all,
"It is forbidden to walk with upright posture and one should not
walk four cubits with uncovered head."[38] Finally, Isserles states, in
the matter of correct dress, that a man's garment should cover the
whole of his body and that he should not go about with bare feet.[39]

The Talmud speaks of modesty in dress even when in the
privy.[40] Maimonides[41] records this, too, only as a rule for scholars
but the *Shulhan Arukh* records it as a rule for all, "He should be
modest when in the privy by not exposing himself until he is
seated."[42] Isserles adds, "Two men should not be there at the same
time and the door should be closed out of modesty." The Talmud
strongly advises against wiping with anything that can easily catch
fire in the belief that such material possesses a baneful, magical
power to injure the rectal glands.[43] The *Shulhan Arukh* records this
but Isserles adds that nowadays this rule is ignored and one should
follow the common practice.[44] The Talmud gives a number of
reasons why wiping should not be done with the right hand but
only with the left: the Torah was given by the right hand of God
(Deut. 33:2); one winds the *tefillin* with the right hand; and because
of hygiene since the food is conveyed to the mouth with the right
hand.[45] The *Shulhan Arukh* records this as the law.[46]

The intimacies of marital relations are also governed by rules of
decorum. The Talmud discusses which sex practices between husband and wife are proper and which are improper, and the *Shulhan
Arukh* has two lengthy sections on the subject.[47] Here, too, the
ideal for scholars is applied to all. For instance, the Talmud[48]
disapproves of scholars "being too much with their wives like
cocks" but in the *Shulhan Arukh* this becomes a rule for all.[49] Based
on a Talmudic passage[50] are the rules of the *Shulhan Arukh* that it is
forbidden for a man to be with his wife if she does not consent or if
he does not love her or where he intends to divorce her or if he has
another woman in mind during the act or where she takes the
initiative verbally.[51] The Talmud discusses whether certain unor-

thodox sex practices are permitted but arrives at the conclusion that "a man may do as he wishes when he is with his wife."[52] The *Shulhan Arukh* rules nonetheless that it is forbidden for a man to gaze at his wife's genital organs, *a fortiori* to kiss them, and that it is "brazen" for them to have intercourse with the wife on top or where they lie side by side.[53] Isserles, however, states,

> He can do as he wishes with his wife. He may have intercourse whenever he wishes and may kiss any part of her body he wishes and he may have intercourse either in the natural or the unnatural way or on other parts of her body provided there is no emission of semen. Others permit unnatural intercourse even where there is emission of semen provided it is only indulged in occasionally and no habit is made of it. But even though all these things are permited whoever sanctifies himself with regard to that which is permitted (i.e., by refusing to engage in these practices) will be hailed as a holy man.[54]

The Talmud[54] frowns on intercourse with the light on and this is recorded as a law in the *Shulhan Arukh*.[56] On the basis of a statement in the Talmud[57] that Imma Shalom attributed the handsomeness of her children to the fact that her husband only had relations with her in the middle of the night, not at its beginning or end, the *Shulhan Arukh* records it as a rule: "He should not have intercourse with her either at the beginning or end of the night, so that he should not hear the sound of people and thus perhaps have another woman in mind, but only in the middle of the night."[58]

From all of these examples we can see how the scope of the Halakhah was extended so as to embrace rules of conduct, dress, and deportment, which belonged originally to the *derekh eretz* concept. Because these found their ways into the codes, they acquired Halakhic status, their origin in *derekh eretz* being ignored.

NOTES

1. For the subject of this chapter see especially ET, vol. 7 s.v. *derekh eretz*, pp. 672–706, although the majority of the instances stated here are from Maimonides who generally does extend in any event the scope of the Halakhah, see supra, pp. 52–55; and Mordecai Fogelman: *Bet Mordekhai*, pp. 226–36. Fogelman, P. 226b, gives a complete list of the instances in the Mishnah and BT in which the term *derekh eretz* (or its Aramaic equivalent *orah ara*) is found and notes that the term is hardly ever found in JT.

2. Cf. Maimonides' opening remarks to the section of his Code dealing with proper behavior at the table (*Yad, Berakhot* 7:1): "There are many customs which the Sages of Israel adopted and they all belong to *Derekh Eretz*."

3. See *Berakhoh* 22a.

4. OH 170.
5. *Taanit* 5b.
6. OH 170:1.
7. See Epstein, *Arukh ha-Shulhan*, OH 170:2.
8. *Bet Yosef* to *Tur*, OH 170.
9. *Berakhot* 47a.
10. OH 170:2.
11. See Epstein, *Arukh ha-Shulhan*, OH 170:4.
12. *Yad, Berakhot* 7:2.
13. OH 170:4.
14. See Epstein, *Arukh ha-Shulhan*, 170:7 who remarks that he has been unable to discover any Talmudic source for Maimonides' ruling but that it is certainly reasonable to follow this ruling; i.e., Maimonides laid it down as a rule because of his own personal understanding of what is proper and what is improper.
15. *Derekh Eretz Rabbah*, chapter 7.
16. *Pesahim* 86b.
17. OH 170:5 and 6.
18. *Pesahim* 86b.
19. OH 170:8. A similar rule of *Derekh Eretz* is that one invited to lead the prayers should at first decline, then be hesitant, and at the third invitation accept the honor (*Berakhot* 34a).
20. *Derekh Eretz Rabbah* chapters 7 and 8; SA, OH 170; 12 and 13.
21. *Arukh ha-Shulhan*, OH 170:13.
22. *Kiddushin* 32b.
23. *Magen Avraham* to OH 170, note 21.
24. OH 2.
25. Ibid. 3.
26. *Shabbat* 118b.
27. OH 2:3.
28. *Shabbat* 114a.
29. OH 2:2.
30. *Taz* to OH 2, note 2.
31. *Shabbat* 61a.
32. Epstein, *Arukh ha-Shulhan*, OH 2:8.
33. OH 2:4.
34. Ibid. 2:5.
35. *Berakhot* 43b; *Kiddushin* 31a.
36. *Yad, Deot* 5:8.
37. *Shabbat* 118b; 156b; *Kiddushin* 31a.
38. OH 2:6.
39. Ibid. 2:6.
40. *Berakhot* 62a.
41. *Yad, Deot* 5:1.
42. OH 3:2.
43. *Shabbat* 82a.
44. OH 3:11; see Epstein, *Arikh ha-Shulhan*, OH 3:6.
45. *Berakhot* 62a.
46. OH 3:10.
47. Ibid. 240 and EH 25.
48. *Berakhot* 22a.
49. OH 240:1; EH 25:2.

50. *Nedarim* 20b.
51. OH 240:3; cf. EH 25:8–9.
52. *Nedarim* 20b.
53. OH 240:4 and 5; cf. OP to 5A, EH 25:2, notes 6–15, pp. 239–44.
54. EH 25:2.
55. *Niddah* 16b.
56. EH 25:5.
57. *Nedarim* 20a–b.
58. OH 240:7; cf. EH 25:3.

14

Halakhah and Psychology

The comprehensiveness of the Halakhic process is further evidenced by the numerous instances in which laws are formulated on the basis of human psychology, of how human beings normally respond rationally and emotionally in given circumstances. There is an abundance of material on this topic, especially in the Babylonian Talmud. It must be appreciated, however, that, as was demonstrated in the chapter on the Talmud as the source of the Halakhah, a good deal of the Talmud is purely theoretical. In the majority of instances, the psychological motivation suggested in the Talmud is not the starting point of the legal formulation but is rather an attempted explanation by the Amoraim of a law that has long been established. Nevertheless, this type of explanation becomes part of the Halakhic process so that one can still speak of this as evidence of Halakhic comprehensiveness. There are so many instances of this phenomenon in the Talmud that a separate volume would be required if they were all to be treated adequately. But all that need be done here is to list some of these instances, taken more or less at random.[1]

A particularly telling example is in connection with the disqualification of certain types of witnesses. The verse, "Put not thy hand with the wicked to be an unrighteous witness *(ed hamas)*" (Exod. 23:1) is interpreted to mean that the "wicked" *(rasha)* cannot act as a witness. A *mumar*, a man who habitually commits a certain sin, may do it either because he willfully rejects the law that states that the sin is forbidden or because, while acknowledging that he is committing a sin, he is overcome by his desire to commit the sin. In the former case he is known as a *mumar le-hakhis*, "a *mumar* who does it out of provocation." In the latter case he is known as *mumar le-teavon*, "a *mumar* who does it out of desire." On this the Talmud records a debate between Abbaye and Rava.[2] Does a *mumar* with regard to the law that prohibits *nevelah* (meat of an animal which has not been killed in the correct manner) become disqualified thereby from acting as a witness? Both Abbaye and Rava agree that if he is a *mumar le-teavon* (he will only succumb to the allure of the forbidden food when this is cheaper than permitted meat) he is disqualified. But if he does it *le-hakhis*, then Abbaye holds that he is disqualified but Rava holds that he is not disqualified. Abbaye's argument is that such a man is a *rasha* (since he transgresses a law of the Torah) and is therefore disqualified but Rava holds that the word *hamas* in the verse, translated as "unrighteous," means "robbery." According to Rava for a witness to be disqualified he must not only be a *rasha* but a *rasha* guilty of "robbery." In other words Abbaye and Rava debate whether the term *hamas* is given simply as an example or as an essential condition. From the point of view of religious law the *mumar le-hakhis* is obviously a more severe offender than the *mumar le-teavon* and yet in connection with this law of disqualification Rava holds that the *mumar le-hakhis* is not disqualified whereas the *mumar le-teavon* is. The reason is based on human psychology. The *mumar le-teavon* is a "robbery" *rasha*, that is, since he is prepared to do that which he acknowledges to be wrong for personal gain he may give false witness for personal gain. There is no evidence, on the other hand, that the *mumar le-hakhis* will commit a wrong for personal gain. He eats *nevelah* out of sheer spite, as it were, denying that the law has any significance. He is undoubtedly a *rasha* but not a "robbery" *rasha* and hence he is not disqualified according to Rava. Abbaye, too, seems to agree with the psychological principle. According to Abbaye, the reason why the *mumar le-hakhis* is disqualified is not because he is not to be trusted when he gives evidence but rather because the Torah disqualifies a *rasha* per se. It is as if the Torah does not wish such a person to participate in the administration of justice. Thus the psychological principle behind it all is that a man may be defiant of a religious law he does not acknowledge as binding and yet be entirely trustworthy in ethical matters which he does accept as binding.

The psychology of the *mumar* is behind another law laid down by Rava.[3] Rava states that a *mumar* who eats *nevelah le-teavon* may not be trusted to prepare the *shehitah* knife (because this is too bothersome for him) but if he is given a knife that is properly prepared he is trusted to perform the act of *shehitah* correctly. This is on the grounds that "he will not reject that which is permitted in order to eat that which is forbidden." Here Rava will agree that a *mumar le-hakhis* is not to be trusted since he will consciously refuse to avail himself of that which is permitted.

The analysis of states of mind and intention is prominent in the Talmudic discussions regarding the validity of a betrothal. For instance, the law is that for a betrothal to be valid the betrothal money must be given by the man to the woman and not by the woman to the man. But since the value of the betrothal money need be no more than a *perutah*, the smallest coin of the realm, there is an instance where the betrothal is valid even where the woman gives a sum of money or its value to the man. This is where the man is a person of high rank *(adam hashuv)*. It is a privilege to give a gift to such a person and to have it accepted. Thus, by accepting the present the man is, in fact, granting the woman a privilege and this is worth at least a *perutah*, so that her "giving" constitutes a "receiving" and it can be assumed that there is the intention for her to be betrothed in this manner. This rule is based on the psychological principle that in certain instances giving has the emotional effect of receiving.[4] Rava makes the following distinction.[5] If the man declares, "Be thou betrothed to half of me" it is a valid betrothal but if he declares, "Half of thee be betrothed unto me," it is invalid. The distinction is defended on the grounds that whereas there can be no valid betrothal of or by half a person, and hence the betrothal in the latter case is invalid, it is valid in the former case. Since a man can have more than one wife it can be assumed that when he declares, "Be betrothed to half of me" he does not mean this literally but merely wishes to stipulate that if he later wishes to take another woman also as his wife he may do so. In connection with betrothal, the Talmud discusses whether or not certain ambiguous declarations are valid, such as when the man uses expressions that may denote either that he wishes to betroth the woman or that he wishes her to work for him without becoming his wife.[6] The Talmud objects that even if no declaration were made at all the betrothal is still valid if it took place (i.e., if the betrothal money were handed over) at a time when the man and woman were both discussing the question of marriage so that it is obvious to both the two parties concerned and to their witnesses that their intention is for a betrothal to be effected. To this the reply is given; indeed, the betrothal is valid where no declaration at all is made but an ambiguous declaration, the wording of which does not necessarily denote an intention to betroth, is worse than no declaration at all since it introduces a doubt and this may have the effect of interfering with the requisite degree of consent demanded if a betrothal is to be valid.

With regard to contracts generally, the psychology of vendor and vendee is taken into account in determining whether or not there is a definite intention on the part of the one to sell and of the other to buy. For example, there is the case of a man who sold his estate because he wished to emigrate from Babylon to reside in the Holy Land, but at the time of the sale made no actual stipulation that the sale was conditional on his emigrating.[7] The man was unable to leave for the Holy Land because of circumstances beyond his control and he now wishes to revoke the sale. Rava rules that this is a case of *devarim she-be-lev*, "matters of the heart," that is, in the absence of an express verbal stipulation the sale is treated as an unconditional one and cannot therefore be revoked. The point here is not that there is really any doubt that the man only sold his property because he wished to emigrate. There is no such doubt since everyone knew that his desire to emigrate was the sole intention of his wish to dispose of his property in Babylon. But in the absence of an explicit verbal condition at the actual time of the sale, it is assumed that the mental reservation, albeit known to the two parties concerned, is too weak to qualify the act of selling. In reality, even a verbal condition is only valid normally when the condition that qualifies the sale is not only stated positively but also negatively; that is, 'If you will do this for me I sell you my field but if you do not do it for me I do not sell you my field,'[8] otherwise it is assumed that the qualification is not intended to be taken too seriously and is consequently too weak to disturb the sale. The *Tosafists* suggest that this double qualification is only required when it is not too obvious to all that there are reservations.[9] In the case of the man who sold his estate in order to emigrate, the sale would have been valid if he had stated the condition verbally and explicitly, even when he had not "doubled" it, simply declaring, "I sell you my estate provided I emigrate," since it is obvious to all that this is, in fact, his sole reason for selling.

Psychological analysis is also resorted to in order to determine the intention of a man who makes a documentary gift on his deathbed and then recovers. The question is whether the gift was made unconditionally or whether it was intended to be conditional on his dying of that illness, that is, can he revoke the gift if he recovers? A distinction is made between a gift of the whole of his estate and a gift of only a part of his estate. Where the man gave away the whole of his estate it can be assumed that it was only because he thought he would die and he can under these circumstances revoke the gift if he recovers. But where he gave away only a part of his estate, the very fact that he left some of it for himself shows that he did not have in mind that he would die but gave the part he stipulated as an unconditional gift.[10] A similar case is that of the father who assigned his estate to strangers on being informed that his only son had died. After the father's death it was discovered that the son had not died and the son now claims his inheritance. The ruling is that the father's assignment to the strangers is invalid since it can be assumed that had the father known that his son was alive he would not have disinherited the son in favor of strangers.[11]

The Mishnah states that if a man betrothed a woman on the understanding that he belonged to a particular social class (e.g., that he was a priest or a Levite) and it later became known that he did not, in fact, belong to that class, the betrothal is invalid, even if, in reality, he belonged to a superior class (e.g., he informed her that he was a Levite and it was later discovered that he was a priest).[12] This is based on the psychology of women. It can be assumed that a woman not only does not wish to be married to a man of inferior status but also to a man of superior status, "I do not want a sandal too large for my foot."[13] Similarly, if he betrothed her on the understanding that he had no maidservants and it transpired that he did have a maidservant who was skilled at hairdressing, the betrothal is invalid because, although it is to her benefit to have such a maidservant, it can be assumed that she could well do without a maidservant who might bear gossip about her mistress to the other women whose hair she dresses.[14] In the same context it is ruled that if a man betroths a woman on the understanding that he is a sage or powerful or rich, these are obviously relative terms and the validity of the betrothal must depend on the psychological understanding of these terms by normal people.[15] Thus, there is no need for the man who states that he is a sage to be of the caliber of a Rabbi Akiba, or the man who states that he is powerful to be a great warrior like Joab, or the man who states that he is rich to be as wealthy as R. Eleazar b. Azariah (the Croesus of the Talmud), but if he is familiar with all the subjects normally studied he is a sage for this purpose, and if he is feared by his contemporaries he is deemed to be "powerful," and if his townsfolk pay him honor because of his wealth he is deemed to be rich, i.e., it can be assumed that this is how the woman construed his declaration when she accepted the betrothal money. Even if a notorious sinner declared at the time of the betrothal that he is a righteous man the possibility must be taken into account that the betrothal is valid because he may have repented of his sins, and even if a great saint declared at the time of the betrothal that he is a sinner, the possibility must be taken into account that the betrothal is valid because he may have changed his status at the moment by entertaining idolatrous thoughts.

Throughout the Talmud, responsibility in law for sinful or criminal acts depends on the degree of awareness on the part of the one who commits these acts. There is a whole scale of diminishing responsibility, from *mezid*, intentional offense, through *shogeg*, unintentional offense (e.g., doing work on the Sabbath through forgetting that the particular act constitutes "work" or that the day is the Sabbath) to *ones*, an act committed which is beyond the power of the one who commits it to prevent. A married woman who cohabits intentionally with a man not her husband is forbidden to her husband but according to one opinion in the Talmud if a married woman was a victim of rape but consented during the act— even if she called off any would-be rescuers—it is treated as an act performed without her consent and she is not forbidden to her husband.[16] The reason given is that her passions became uncontrollable, i.e., human nature is such that an act in these circumstances, ostensibly carried out with intention is, in reality, an act carried out by *force majeure*, under the compulsion of the passions that have been aroused. The doctrine of diminished responsibility is used in the Talmud to exonerate an imbecile from any penalty the law otherwise attaches to an act and to free him from all obligation. There are discussions on the nature of an imbecile. In the most authoritative statement on the question an imbecile *(shoteh)* is defined as one who habitually goes out on his own at night, who stays overnight in the cemetery, and who rends his garments.[17]

There are many rules in connection with vows depending on how certain expressions are normally understood; i.e., the rule whether or not a particular expression covers a particular instance is determined by how people normally think. Thus if a man takes a vow not to enjoy anything belonging to seafarers, his vow does not cover land dwellers, and if he took a vow not to enjoy anything belonging to land dwellers, his vow applies to seafarers as well, since when people speak of land dwellers they do not intend to exclude seafarers. Furthermore, by "seafarers" people do not normally understand those who go for an occasional trip in a boat but real sailors, so that if a man made such a vow it would not embrace those who merely go for a casual trip from Acre to Jaffa.[18] If a man vows to have no enjoyment from meat he is permitted to enjoy a dish that has a meat flavoring. But if he took a vow not to drink a particular bottle of wine and some of that wine was mixed in a dish he may not eat that dish.[19] The distinction is clear. Where the vow was to abstain from wine in general it does not cover a dish with a wine flavor because people do not think of a dish containing meat flavor as "meat" or containing wine flavor as "wine." But where the vow covers some particular meat or wine, that meat or wine becomes forbidden and the admixture in a dish is treated like any other forbidden food mixed in a dish. The major portions of tractates *Nedarim*, *Shevuout*, and *Nazir* are concerned with psychological analyses of this kind.

An important principle of rabbinic jurisprudence—*miggo* ("since")—depends on psychological analysis.[20] The principle operates when someone presents an argument, essentially very weak in itself, which is nonetheless accepted by the court because the person presenting the weak argument had a perfectly acceptable argument he could have advanced. Since *(miggo)* he could easily have won his case by presenting the strong argument, why, unless he is honest and is telling the truth, should he have presented the weak argument? It is assumed that a fraudulent person would always prefer to present the argument he knows the court has no option but to accept rather than present one that is weak and questionable. Consequently, whoever presents this weaker argument thereby demonstrates that he is truthful. The following are examples of *miggo* found in the Talmud. A woman who has had intercourse with a man forbidden to her may not subsequently marry a priest. Supposing a woman was observed entering a private place with a man whose identity is unknown and she later admits that intercourse took place but she declares that the man was not one whose intercourse with her renders her unfit for the priesthood, e.g., he is an ordinary Israelite not a *mamzer* or a pagan. The woman could have denied that intercourse did take place at all and she would be believed in this in the absence of witnesses. Consequently, when she admits that intercourse did take place she is believed on the question of the man's identity, though this latter claim is not allowed and is weak where there are witnesses to the act of intercourse.[21] Another example: A has a claim on B's estate that A can prove B owes to him and B dies. The law is that A cannot collect his debt without first taking an oath. This rule was introduced as a special form of protection of the orphan heirs to the estate. But suppose A has had the land, which he admits belongs to B, but from which he has enjoyed the profits to the extent of his debt and he has been in possession of this land for three years, the rule being that undisturbed possession for three years gives a man the right to claim that the land is his (because he had bought it or been given it as a gift) without having to produce any further evidence. A is believed and is not required to take the oath since *(miggo)* if he were fraudulent all he needed to do was to claim that the field is his, i.e., that he had bought it from B. The fact that A admits that the field belongs to B's heirs is sufficient to demonstrate his trustworthiness and there is no need for him to take the oath.[22] In another case, A presents a document to the court, duly signed and validated, to the effect that B owes him a sum of money. There appears to be no reason to question that trustworthiness of the document, but when B declares that it is forged A admits it but claims that he had had a valid document which he had lost. According to one opinion, even here the rule of *miggo* applies. A could have kept silent, winning his case on the strength of the document. If he is sufficiently honest to admit that the document is forged, he establishes thereby his trustworthiness and is believed when he claims that he really did have a valid document.[23] In a further case, A has a document to the effect that B owes him a sum of money. B was observed by witnesses paying this sum to A. A cannot demand further payment on the strength of his document by arguing that the money B was observed to have paid to him was in payment of another debt. If, however, there were no witnesses that B had paid A any sum of money but A admits that he did so but claims that it was payment of another debt, then A's claim is accepted because of the *miggo* rule. If A were dishonest he could have denied that B had paid him any money at all.

The formula *"hazakah* no man . . .,"* "it is an established fact (by observing human psychology) that no man . . .," is a principle applied in a host of cases, only a few of which are noted here. A man divorced his wife and they were seen later to have had marital relations. A further bill of divorce *(get)* is required because it is assumed *(hazakah)* that no man will allow his act of intercourse to be one of fornication when he can make it legitimate, and they thus can be assumed, therefore, to have intended the act to be for the purpose of betrothal.[24] Another assumption *(hazakah)*, based on psychological norms, is that a man will not commit a sin for the sake of others without any personal gain. Thus, a shepherd who is suspected of allowing his animals to graze in the fields of others is a "robber" and thereby disqualified from acting as a witness in a court of law. But this only applies to one who shepherds his own flock. A shepherd hired to look after the animals of others does not become suspect because "no man will sin where it is not for his own personal gain."[25] Similarly, if A declares that all his property is given to the Temple and he then states that his gift did not include a certain sum of money because that sum does not belong to him but to B so that he has no right to donate it, his subsequent declaration has no validity since we suspect him of having come to a fraudulent arrangement with B from whom he will receive a portion of the money said to have been excluded. But if A makes such a declaration, that the sum belongs to B, on his deathbed, he is believed since here, if the statement is fraudulent, it is his heirs not he himself who will benefit and "no man will sin where it is not for his own personal gain." Again, if a woman states that a man she cannot identify has betrothed her and a man claims that it is he who has done so, he is believed to release her with a *get* he gives to her, although he is not believed to live with her as man and wife. In the latter case he might have fallen in love with her so that he may claim to be her husband even though he knows full well he is not. But in the former case he is believed since "no man will sin unless it is for his own gain," and he would not be guilty of releasing the woman to remarry unlawfully unless he really is the man who had betrothed her.[26]

An interesting example of the application of this type of *hazakah* is the following. A claims that B owes him a sum of money, but B denies it completely. In the absence of witnesses, A has no case at all and B is not even required to take an oath. But if B admits that he does owe a part of the sum A claims, then B has to take an oath that he does not owe A the remainder. But, it is asked, should B be released from the oath by the *miggo* principle since, if B is dishonest, he could have denied A's claim entirely? To this the reply is given "no man has the effrontery to deny outright to his creditor's face a sum he owes him," i.e., *miggo* does not operate here because no matter how dishonest he may be it is psychologically impossible for him to deny it completely. In other words, there is on the one hand the *miggo* principle, also based on an assessment of human psychology, but, on the other hand, there is the even stronger psychological principle to offset the *miggo*.[27] A similar *hazakah* operates in the case of a married woman who declares in the presence of her husband that he has divorced her but she is unable to produce the *get* to prove it. Although normally the *get* must be produced, she is here believed without the *get* because she makes her claim to the husband's face. The reason given is that it is psychologically impossible for her to state her denial, if it is untrue, to her husband's face, "it is a *hazakah* that no woman has the effrontery to do such a thing to her husband's face."[28] In an actual case, recorded in the Talmud in the same passage, a fornicator entered a house in order to seduce the mistress of the house but hearing her husband approaching he hid behind a curtain.[29] The husband was about to eat some food that contained poison but the fornicator called out to warn him not to eat. On the basis of this, Rava permitted the woman to remain with her husband because of the psychological principle that if her lover had succeeded in seducing her he would not have saved the husband's life. The Talmud asks, "Is this not obvious?" The reply is given that we might have invoked a different psychological principle, namely, that of "stolen waters are sweet," that is, because of the lure of the forbidden the lover might have preferred the husband to live so that his future relations with the wife will have the "sweetness" of the forbidden. This idea has, therefore, to be rejected by Rava whose ruling is consequently far from obvious.

Further rules are said to be based on psychological attitudes. The Mishnah[30] rules that if a man finds himself at a distance from his home at the advent of the Sabbath he may request a Gentile to carry his moneybag, although normally it is forbidden for a Jew to request a Gentile to do on his behalf that which he may not do himself on the Sabbath. The reason for the dispensation stated in the Talmud is that psychologically it is extremely difficult for a man to abandon his hard-earned money so that if no permission were given him to ask the Gentile to carry the moneybag for him he would carry it himself, rather than abandon it, and so be guilty of a more serious offense.[31] Here the psychological principle is that unless the lesser offense is made no offense at all, it would be expecting too much of human nature, where heavy financial loss is involved, to calculate soberly which offense is the greater. In his concern for his money a man is still capable of choosing between a permitted course of action and a forbidden one but he is not capable of preferring a lesser offense to a greater one. This same principle is invoked to explain the biblical law (Exod. 22:2) that if a householder surprises a thief breaking into his home and he kills the thief, the householder is not guilty of murder.[32] The thief is said to be fully aware of the psychological fact that a man loses his self-control when faced with the possibility of heavy financial loss and will defend his property by force if need be. The thief, knowing this and yet still prepared to break into the house, must therefore have steeled himself to engage in counterattack so that he can be said to have designs not only on the householder's property but on his very life. In that case the killing of the thief is an act of self-defense not of murder. An acute psychological note is then added. This law applies even if the thief is the son of the householder because a son may entertain the prospect of killing his own father. But if the thief is the father of the householder it is an act of murder for the son to kill him. No father ever has designs on the life of his son. The householder is therefore never in danger from his father and to kill the father cannot be considered an act of self-defense but of murder.

If A admitted that he owes B money, when B's claim was presented in the presence of witnesses, A can claim that he only admitted it in jest, unless A said to the witnesses; "You are my witnesses." But if A admitted to his debt on his deathbed, his heirs must pay the debt because of the psychological observation: "No man jests (on such matters) while he is dying."[33] Rava explains the law of *shohad*, that a judge must not take a gift from one of the parties to a lawsuit over which he is to sit in judgment (Deut. 16:19), on the basis of psychological observation.[34] Even if the judge intends to judge the case impartially he must not accept a gift from one of the parties since his acceptance of the gift makes him at one with his benefactor and since there is a *hazakah* that "no man sees liability in his own suit" the judge is bound to be partial even while imagining that he is impartial. The Talmud adds a pun on the word *shohad—she-hu had*, "that he is as one," i.e., the judge becomes as one with his benefactor.

Another Halakhic formula for a law based on psychological observation is, "A man knows that. . . ," i.e., everyone knows that act *a* is invalid so that if someone is observed apparently intending act *a* it can be assumed that he really intends act *b*. Thus, if a man gives betrothal money to his sister, declaring, "Be thou betrothed unto me with this money," he cannot possibly have really intended the money to be for the purpose of betrothal since everyone knows that a sister cannot be betrothed to her brother. Despite his declaration, therefore, it can be assumed that the money he gave to her was intended either as a gift or as a deposit (this is debated by Rav and Samuel) but cannot have been intended for betrothal.[35]

What is said to be normal female psychology is given expression in a number of laws. A girl attains her legal majority at the age of twelve but a boy reaches his majority at the age of thirteen because the female possesses greater powers of discernment than the male, i.e., her mental maturity comes at an earlier age.[36] If a man has divorced his wife the two must not live in the same courtyard. If the courtyard belongs to both of them, so that one of them must depart, it is the woman who must yield to the man because it is psychologically more difficult for a man to readjust himself to new surroundings than for a woman.[37] If a poor orphan boy and a poor orphan girl both require assistance and there is only enough for one of them in the charity funds, the girl must be assisted because it is psychologically more difficult for a female to go begging at doors than it is for a male.[38] If there is only enough money to provide for the marriage of one, the girl has preference because the embarrassment suffered by an unmarried woman is greater than that suffered by an unmarried man.[39] When a creditor collects his debt from real estate he can only claim, according to the original law, the worst quality land. But in order not to discourage people from lending their money to those in need, the sages introduced a new law that the creditor can claim his debt from average quality land. But the sages did not ordain this where the claim is by a widow or a divorcee on the strength of the debt her former husband owes her as her *ketubah*. Here there is said to be no fear that this will discourage women from marrying because "a woman wishes to marry more than a man."[40] R. Eliezer permits a woman to walk in the public domain while wearing the ornament known as "a golden city." The Talmud explains that the reason why women must not wear jewelry and ornaments in the public domain on the Sabbath is because they might forget it is the Sabbath and take them off in order to show them to their friends for their admiration and might be led to carry them in the public domain.[41] But, argues R. Eliezer, according to this explanation, only a woman of high rank *(ishah hashuvah)* wears "a golden city" and such a woman would never demean herself to show off her ornaments. We have here two psychological observations. Women tend to show their ornaments to their friends but aristocratic women consider such behavior to be beneath their dignity.

The post-Talmudic Halakhists are less prone to psychological interpretations since, unlike the rabbis of the Talmud, they did not normally see themselves as real innovators to formulate new laws on the basis of psychological observation. For all that, psychological motivation does appear occasionally in their deliberations as the following examples demonstrate.

Maimonides is fond of adding explanations of his own to the Talmudic rules. Some of these explanations are psychological. A particularly telling example is Maimonides' explanation, somewhat cautiously and tentatively advanced, for the rule in the Torah that if an animal is dedicated as a sacrifice in the Temple and an attempt is then made to change it for another animal, whether the second animal is superior or inferior, both become sacred, and for the rule that if a man redeems a house he has dedicated to the Temple he must add a fifth of its value to the redemption money. Maimonides writes:

> Even though all the laws of the Torah are divine decrees, as we have explained at the end of *Meilah*, it is proper to reflect on them and wherever you are able to suggest a reason for them you must do so. The Sages of old declared that King Solomon understood most of the reasons for the laws of the Torah. It appears to me that the law in the Torah: "then shall be holy both it and that for which it is changed" (Lev. 27:10) follows the same idea as the law which says: "And if he that sanctified it will redeem his house, then shall he add the fifth part of the money of thy valuation to it" (Lev. 27:15). The Torah penetrates to the limits of man's thoughts and his partial propensity for evil. For it belongs to man's nature to increase his possessions and care for his wealth so that even when he made a vow and given a donation to the Temple, he may later regret it and redeem it for less than its actual value. The Torah therefore says that if he redeems it for his own use he must add a fifth. And so, too, if he declares an animal to be sacred as a sacrifice, he may regret having done so. But since he cannot redeem it he may try to exchange it for another animal. If permission would have been given for him to exchange an inferior animal for a superior one, he will exchange a superior for an inferior, declaring that really it is superior. Consequently, the Torah closes the door to him, declaring that he can never exchange it, fining him if he did so by declaring: "then shall be holy both it and that for which it is exchanged." All these things are for the purpose of controlling his inclinations and improving his character. Most of the Torah laws are nothing else than "counsels from afar" (Isa. 25:1) from the "Great in counsel" (Jer. 32:19).[42]

Maimonides not only provides a psychological understanding of these laws but implies that such psychological motivation is behind the majority of the Torah laws, which provide "counsel" for the improvement of the human character.

Maimonides similarly observes with regard to the command to sound the *shofar* on Rosh ha-Shanah:

> Even though it is a decree of Scripture that the *shofar* be sounded on Rosh ha-Shanah, it contains a hint, as if to say: "Awake from your sleep, ye who sleep, arise from your slumbers, ye who slumber. Search your deeds, repent of your sins and remember your Creator. Ye who forget the truth in the vanity of time and spend all your years in the pursuit of vanity and emptiness, which neither helps nor profits, look to your soul, improve your ways and your deeds. Let each forsake his evil way and his thoughts that are not good.[43]

The sounding of the *shofar* is thus seen as the sounding of an alarm, as a psychological device for bestirring men to repent of their sins.

Maimonides sees fit to add, in the section of his code that deals with the laws of mourning over the death of near relatives, the psychological advantages, as he sees them, of mourning for the dead. One who mourns for too lengthy a period gives the impression that he grieves over "the pattern of life" *(minhago shel olam)* and not to accept the universe as it is in reality is to be a fool *(tippesh).*[44] On the other hand to fail to observe the laws of mourning is to be "cruel" unfeeling, insensitive to the loss. "He should be in a state of dread and anxiety and should scrutinize his deeds and repent of his sins."[45] Karo, in his commentary *Kesef Mishneh* to this passage remarks, "These words of our teacher are worthy of him." After recording the sex laws, Maimonides adds some reflections on the psychology of sex.[46] Man finds sexual gratification attractive so that nothing in the Torah is more difficult for the majority of people to observe than the laws which forbid illicit sex. No community in any period is ever found in which there is no breach of these laws. Maimonides concludes:

> Consequently, it is proper for man to subdue his inclinations in this matter, training himself in exceptional holiness and purity of thought and with firm will in order to be saved from these sins. He should take care never to be alone with a woman forbidden to him because that is the chief cause of sin. The great Sages used to say to their disciples: "Take care of me when I am with my daughter"; "Take care of me when I am with my daughter-in-law." They used to do this in order to teach their disciples not to be embarrassed in this matter and in order to keep far away from women forbidden to them. He should also accustom himself to keep far away from levity and drunkenness and from lewd topics for these, more than anything, lead to illicit sex relations. And he should not remain unmarried for the marriage habit is condu-

cive to exceptional purity. Most of all, the Sages say, he should direct himself and his thoughts to words of Torah and broaden his mind with wisdom. For illicit sexual thoughts only predominate in a mind empty of wisdom and it is of wisdom that Scripture affirms: "She is the loving hind and pleasant roe; let her breasts satisfy thee at all times; and be thou ravished always with her love" (Prov. 5:19).

We have here something not so very different from an anticipation of the Freudian doctrine of sublimation.

A number of examples, also taken at random, of how the post-Talmudic authorities invoke psychological observations for the determination of the law are now noted.

A good example is found in a Responsum of R. Joseph Colon, the *Maharik*.[47] In the case he considers, a woman married to a *kohen*, intended to become converted to Christianity and was discovered in the home of her Christian neighbor together with the Bishop, his assistant, and a number of other persons. The woman later regretted her attempt to become converted and she returned to the Jewish fold. Her husband wished to know whether his wife is permitted to him since, according to the Talmud, "the majority of the heathen are lax in matters of sexual morality."[48] They may, therefore, have had intercourse with the wife and since the husband is a *kohen* she would be forbidden to him even if the intercourse took place without her consent. Colon permits the woman to her husband. In the course of his Responsum he makes this observation:

> It goes without saying that one need have no fear because of the Bishop, his assistant and the priest, for it is well-known that, on the contrary, the majority of Gentiles like the Bishop, his assistant and the priest keep away from this, especially in public and in their church and *a fortiori* with a Jewess so that there is eternal shame for them if the faintest hint of scandal got out. Furthermore, according to their laws the penalty for the offense is burning at the stake. . . . But it can be said that there is no fear even because of the guests and the other Gentiles who were present at the time since the assistant and the priest, whose job it is to watch over these things, were also present. It is forbidden to them as a most serious sin, the penalty for which is burning at the stake. It is well-known that, on the contrary, they take the greatest care not to do such things if there is any risk that it will become known either to the bishop or to his assistant. This is as clear as can be and it is highly plausible to suggest that in such circumstances one cannot apply the maxim that the majority of the heathen are lax in matters of sexual morality.

Colon evidently feels free to set aside the Talmudic maxim regarding the sexual laxity of heathens on the grounds that the reference is only to the Gentiles of those days and the Talmudic "psychology" of heathen cannot be the psychology of a Bishop, his assistant, and those who are afraid of the penalties these meet out to wrongdoers.

Another example of a *hazakah* as stated in the Talmud being set aside by the later codifiers because of changes in psychological attitudes is in connection with the Talmudic rule, as noted, that if a woman declares in the presence of her husband that she has been divorced from him, she is believed because no woman would have the effrontery to deny to her husband's face that she is married to him if it were not true. A number of authorities rule, "she is not believed, nowadays, when there is so much effrontery *(hutzpah)* and loose living," i.e., what was psychologically true in Talmudic times is no longer true.[49] In this connection the commentators point to a similar *hazakah* derived by the authorities from the same Talmudic rule. According to some authorities, just as a woman is believed to declare that her husband has divorced her, because she does not have the effrontery to state to his face that which both he and she know to be untrue, a wife, by the same reasoning, is believed when she declares to his face that her husband is impotent and he must give her a *get*.[50] But here, Mordecai b. Hillel in the name of R. Meir of Rothenberg states that in these generations of effrontery and brazenness she is not believed.[51] A similar instance is the setting aside by some authorities of the *hazakah*, mentioned earlier in this chapter, that a *mumar le-teavon* is trusted with regard to *shehitah* because he would not reject that which is permitted to indulge in that which is forbidden. This is recorded as a rule in the *Shulhan Arukh*,[52] but later authorities argue that "nowadays" the psychological principle is no longer true and a *mumar* must not be trusted.[53]

The codifiers elaborate on the Talmudic definition, as noted, of a *shoteh*, "imbecile," as one who goes out alone at night, stays overnight in the cemetery, and rends his garments.[54] Maimonides,[55] after recording that a *shoteh* is disqualified from acting as a witness in a court of law, observes that in this context a *shoteh* is not only one who walks about naked or breaks vessels or throws stones but whoever is mentally disturbed.[55] Evidently, Maimonides understands the Talmudic definition to be in the nature of a general statement so that the term *shoteh* embraces anyone whose mind is disturbed in one matter *be-davar ehad min ha-devvrim).*[56] Maimonides continues:

> Those especially stupid in that they cannot note contradictions and
> cannot understand any matter in the way normal people do, and so,
> too, those who are confused and hasty in their minds and behave in an
> excessively crazy fashion, these are embraced by the term *shoteh*. This
> matter must depend on the assessment of the judge since it is impossible
> to state in writing an adequate definition of insanity.[57]

Thus Maimonides, perhaps because of his knowledge of medicine,
finds the notion of insanity too complicated and vague to be recorded as a precise legal definition so that the decision must be left
to the discretion of the judge in each particular case. The *Shulhan
Arukh* records this *verbatim* in connection with the laws of witnesses.[58] The Talmud[59] states that a *shoteh* cannot contract a valid
marriage and this, too, is recorded in the *Shulhan Arukh*,[60] to which
Isserles adds, in the name of earlier authorities, that here it all
depends on the degree of his insanity, but where a man's mental
capacity is merely weak it is necessary to take into account the
possibility that the marriage he contracts is valid and the wife
requires a *get* before she can remarry. Following the Talmudic
ruling, the *Shulhan Arukh* rules that if a man who is at times sane
and at other times insane divorces his wife the *get* is valid if it is
delivered during his sane period.[61] All these rules and the whole
definition of insanity became the subject of the *cause célèbre* in the
eighteenth century known as the Get of Cleves.[62] The debates and
the notes in Shor's edition of *Or ha-Yashar* are full of questions and
problems arising out of the definition of insanity. As can be seen
from the previous discussion, the basic problem does not lend itself
easily to precise legal definition, as Maimonides admits when he
leaves it largely to the discretion of the judges, who are almost
bound to differ especially when, as in the Get of Cleves case, many
of them were not familiar at first hand with the man whose state of
sanity was in doubt.

An area in which the *Posekim* have to rely on psychology is that of
betrothal. There are numerous discussions, for instance, on a man
who gives a ring or some other object of value to a woman in the
presence of witnesses, declaring, "Be thou betrothed unto me" and
then the man or the woman claims that it was only intended in jest.
Is a *get* required in these instances? Isserles quotes earlier authorities to the effect that, because of the severity of the matter, a
get is required even if the circumstances are such that there is a high
degree of probability that it was only intended in just.[63] Nevertheless, the majority of the later *Posekim* hold that it all depends on
the circumstances and that if it was really quite clear to everyone

that it was only in jest no *get* is required. All these discussions center around the psychological question.[64]

Another instance in which the Halakhists are concerned with psychology in connection with betrothal is when a woman is forced to consent to the marriage. The final ruling in the Talmud is that of Mar bar R. Ashi, that if a man tortured a woman physically until she agreed to marry him the sages invalidated that marriage.[65] "He did that which is improper therefore the Sages behaved improperly to him by invalidating the marriage." The meaning of this is that according to the strict law assent obtained under duress is construed as valid so that if A tortured B until he sold him his field the sale is valid. Nevertheless the Sages have the right to invalidate an otherwise valid marriage and they did this here, behaving "improperly" by the terms of the law because the man behaved "improperly." This ruling of Mar bar R. Ashi is recorded without dissenting voice in the *Shulḥan Arukh*.[66] But would psychological pressure be construed as duress, e.g., what if a man threatened to commit suicide unless a woman he loved agreed to marry him? This and similar questions are discussed by the *Posekim*.[67]

An important application of psychology to law is in the dictim, *batelah daato etzel kol adam*, "his attitude is set at naught in relation to the normal attitude, i.e., if a law is based on an assessment of normal human psychology, the law is operative even for a man who appears to have a psychological stance different from the norm. Thus the full grace is not recited after drinking wine because this form of grace must only be recited after a "meal." But what of the man who "makes a meal" of his wine? The reply is that his attitude is ignored because it is contrary to the norm.[68] The full prohibition of a non-*kohen* eating *terumah*, the portion given to the *kohen*, is not incurred if the man who eats the *terumah* does so while bowing down to eat *terumah* that is still growing in the field since this is not what is usually defined as "eating."[69] The full prohibition of carrying into the public domain on the Sabbath is not incurred if the object is carried out on the head. This is so even if in a particular place people do carry objects on their heads.[70]

NOTES

1. On this subject see Meir Berlin, *"Halakhot ha-Meyusadot Al Tekhunot ha-Nefesh"*; and K. Kahana, "The Connection between Law and other Branches of Knowledge," and on the use of psychology in the Courts see Gulak, *Yesodey ha-Mishpat ha-Ivri*, vol. IV, chapter 8, pp. 94–109.

2. *Sanhedrin* 27a.

3. *Hullin* 4a. On the psychological aspects of sin see *Yoma* 29a that sinful thoughts are "worse" than the sin itself on the analogy of the powerful smell of roasted meat that is more appetizing than the eating of the meat. On the other hand, a professional may carry out his professional duties even if this involves the performance of acts that are otherwise forbidden because they may lead to lustful thoughts since, as a professional, all his concentration will be on the task at hand, see *Avodah Zarah* 20b.

4. *Kiddushin* 7a.

5. Ibid. 7a.

6. Ibid. 6a.

7. Ibid. 49b.

8. Ibid. 61a–62a.

9. *Tosafits* to *Kiddushin* 49b s.v. *devarim she-be-lev.*

10. *Bava Batra* 146b.

11. Ibid. 132a.

12. *Kiddushin* 2:3.

13. Ibid. 49a.

14. Ibid. 49a.

15. Ibid. 49b.

16. *Ketubot* 51b. For another example of *ones* treated psychologically see *Shevuot* 26a: R. Kahana and R. Assi, after Rav's discourse, disagreed as to what Rav said and each took an oath that this is what Rav said. Rav later stated what he had actually said and the one whom he contradicted then asked him if he had taken a false oath, to which Rav replied; "Your heart forced you," i.e., at the time you were quite convinced that you were telling the truth! Cf. Maimonides' ruling (*Yad, Yesodey ha-Torah* 5:6) that if a person who is dangerously ill uses an idolatrous cure he is liable to the penalty of the court and yet in 5:4 he rules that there is no penalty if a man is compelled to worship idols or to commit a murder. The distinction is that here the sick person wants to be cured. His intention is not under compulsion only the reason for his intention (that he is sick). But in the latter case he has no wish to worship idols or to commit murder. The intention itself is under compulsion. See R. Meir Simhah Cohen, *Or Sameah* ad loc., who ingeniously compares this ruling to that of Shabbetai ha-Kohen, the *Shakh*, to SA, HM 388, note 2. If a man is forced by a robber to show where his fortune is hidden and he shows instead the fortune of his neighbor he is liable to compensate the neighbor for his loss. But if the robber threatens him that unless he shows his neighbor's fortune the robber will take his, he is not liable for showing the robber his neighbor's fortune. In the former case he willingly shows his neighbor's fortune in order to save his, whereas in the latter case he is compelled by the robber to have the wish to show his neighbor's fortune.

17. *Hagigah* 3b.

18. Mishnah, *Nedarim* 3:6.

19. Ibid. 6:7.

20. For *miggo* see Herzog, *Main Institutions of Jewish Law*, vol. I, pp. 117f.

21. *Ketubot* 16a.

22. *Bava Batra* 33a.

23. Ibid. 32b.

24. *Gittin* 81b.

25. *Bava Metzia* 5b.

26. *Kiddushin* 63b.

27. *Bava Metzia* 3a–b and see Rashi *ad loc.*

28. *Nedarim* 91a.

29. Ibid. 91b.

30. *Shabbat* 24:1.

31. Ibid. 153a.

32. *Sanhedrin* 72b.

33. *Bava Batra* 175a.

34. *Ketubot* 105b.

35. *Kiddushin* 46b.

36. *Niddah* 45b.

37. *Ketubot* 28a.

38. Ibid. 67a.

39. Ibid. 67b.

40. *Gittin* 49b.

41. *Shabbat* 59b, see Berlin, "Halakhot ha-Meyusadot", p. 212. Some further examples of the use of psychology in the Talmudic Halakhah may here be noted. (1) If a man is in the habit of casting slurs of *mamzerut* against others, he himself becomes suspect of being a *mamzer* and if he casts slurs that others are of slave descent he himself is suspect of being of slave descent. This is on the basis of Samuel's dictum: "Whoever goes about disqualifying others does so by imputing to them the defects he himself possesses"—*kol ha-posel be-mumo posel*—see *Kiddushin* 70b and Maimonides, *Yad, Issurey Viah* 19:17. (1) On the law in Deut. 21:11 "And seest among the captives a beautiful woman, and has a desire for her," the *Sifre*, ad loc., ed. Friedmann, 211, p. 112b, remarks that he is permitted to take her to wife even if she is not beautiful, since Scripture says "and he has a desire for her" (cf. *Kiddushin* 22a) i.e., it is possible for a man to fall in love with an ugly woman and the Halakhah acknowledges this. In *Midrash ha-Gadol* to the verse, p. 467, the reading is, "even if she is ugly." (3) *Sanhedrin* 29a, "Two scholars who hate one another must not sit together as judges in the same case." Maimonides, *Yad, Sanhedrin* 23:7, "For such a thing brings about a perverted judgment; because of the hatred they bear for one another each one will be inclined to prove the other wrong." (4) The law of *boshet*, compensation for putting another to shame, is stated as the damages are assessed according to the rank and social standing of both the offender and his victim, *Bava Kama* 86a.

42. *Yad, Temurah* 4:13.

43. *Yad, Teshuvah* 3:4.

44. *Yad, Avel* 10:11.

45. Ibid. 10:12.

46. *Yad, Issurey Viah* 22:17–21.

47. *Teshuvot Maharik, Shoresh* 160.

48. *Ketubot* 13b.

49. *Bet Yosef* to *Tur*, EH 17; SA, EH 17:2; and see OP, vol. 3, p. 14 note 15.

50. *Tosehists* to *Yevamot* 65a s.v. *she-beno le-verah*, and SA, EH 154:7.

51. Isserles to EH 154:7.

52. YD 2:2.

53. See *Baer Helev* to YD 2, note 4 and Shapiro, *Darkhey Zeshuvah* note 13.

54. *Hagigah* 3b.

55. *Yad, Edut* 9:9.

56. See *Bet Yosef* to *Tur*, EH 121.

57. *Yad, Edut* 9:10; see Karo, *Kesef Mishneh* ad loc. that Maimonides relies on a gaonic source.

58. HN 35:10.

59. *Yevamot* 112b.

60. EH 44:2.

61. Ibid. 121:3.

62. On the Get of Cleves see Freehof, *The Responsa Literature*, pp. 159–61.

63. EH 42:1.

64. For all the sources and authorities see OP, vol. 14, pp. 12–26 note 11.

65. *Bava Batra* 48b.

66. EH 42:1.

67. See OP, vol. 14, pp. 1–4 note 3.

68. *Berakhot* 35b. On this see ET, vol. 3, pp. 94–97 and the astonishingly erudite collection of material in Joseph Engel, *Bet ha-Otzar*, vol. 2, *Kelal* 17, pp. 64–66.

69. *Menahot* 70a.

70. *Shabbat* 92a–b.

[15]

Halakhah and the Customs of the People

We have seen in several of the previous chapters how the practice of the people is decisive in Halakhic matters in certain circumstances. In this chapter we examine the question of *minhag*, "custom," when it is explicitly acknowledged that *vox populi vox Dei*, or, in the later Hebraic formulation,[1] "the custom of our fathers is Torah" (in variant form, "the custom of Israel is Torah").

Minhag, "custom," in the Halakhic sources, is of three kinds: (1) procedural; (2) local custom as binding, (3) folk practices that come to acquire Halakhic status. As a matter of procedure, where the law is uncertain, the actual practice of the people has a decisive voice.[2] In a much-disputed passage in the Jerusalem Talmud[3] it is said that even if Elijah would come to tell us that *halitzah* cannot be performed with a sandal we would pay no heed to him since the people do it with a sandal and *minhag* overrides the law.[3] Even though the custom of the people is allowed to decide the law when the matter is debated by the authorities, none of the Halakhists allow the practice of the people to be decisive when it is contrary to the unanimous opinion of the Halakhists. No one ever thought of interpreting the cryptic saying of the Jerusalem Talmud as a blanket permission for legal anarchy.[4] As R. Solomon b. Simeon Duran (d. 1467) states, "For if we were to abolish laws prohibiting certain things as a result of the (contrary) *minhag*, then one by one all prohibitions will be permitted and the whole of the Torah set at naught."[5] That local custom is binding is obviously the case with regard to legal contracts, as stated in the Mishnah.[6] This is because, in the absence of an express stipulation to the contrary, it is assumed that the

221

contract is entered into with both parties agreeing to abide by the local custom. But also in connection with religious law, local customs are binding according to the law, whether these originated because in a certain district particular authorities are generally followed or because of local traditions regarding extensions of the law. The fourth chapter of tractate *Pesahim* in the Mishnah discusses the binding character of such local customs as those that prohibit work on the eve of Passover or on Tisha be-Av. Purely local customs also found their way eventually into the Halakhah, the rationale for this being the mystical idea that customs adopted by the "holy people" are "Torah" almost in the sense of a divine revelation.

The earliest collection of local customs is the *Sefer ha-Manhig* by the Provençal scholar R. Abraham b. Nathan of Lunel (d. 1215).[7] Some of these customs are mentioned here for the purpose of illustration. It is the custom in France to recite the hymn *Ein Kelohenu* after the prayers and to recite the Talmudic account of the preparation of the incense on Sabbath morning after the prayers and in the Provence when the Sabbath departs. It is now the custom among all Jews to recite the benedictions on rising from the bed in the synagogue, not, as in Talmudic times, when actually rising (in the name of R. Natronai Gaon). In France and the Provence it is the custom to recite the Sabbath psalms on Hoshnah Rabbah; Psalm 100 is not recited on Sabbaths and Festivals in France but it is recited in the Provence and Spain. In the Provence and France it is the custom to recite the Aramaic Targum to the Haftarot of Passover and Pentecost and it is the custom not to pray with the head uncovered; it is good to follow the custom of all people in Spain never to walk about with uncovered head. One should sway while praying as is the custom of the rabbis and saints of France. The *Sefer ha-Minhag* also states, "I have seen in France that many people raise themselves upwards when reciting the *kedushah*." The author similarly remarks that it is the custom for the priests to open the fingers when they recite the priestly benediction and it is the custom of the people that they do not gaze at the priests when the latter are reciting the blessing. It is the custom in France and the Provence to make up the quorum for prayer, the *minyan*, with a boy under age who holds a *Sefer Torah* in his hands.

With regard to the Sabbath, the *Sefer Ha-Minhag* continues, it is the established custom to send letters by post even on the eve of the Sabbath (i.e., even though this may mean that they will be sent out for delivery on the Sabbath). It is the custom in Spain and the Provence to recite the *kiddush* in the synagogue on Sabbaths and

Festivals and it is the custom in France and the Provence not to call to the reading of the Torah two brothers or a father and son one after the other. It is the custom in Spain and the Provence to partake of the special third meal of the Sabbath in the afternoon and this is correct, not that of the French Jews who partake of the third meal during the morning.

Another custom, of a more general nature, recorded in the *Sefer ha-Minhag* is that it is the universal custom in France, the Provence, and Spain for a woman, after the period of her separation, to undergo immersion in a *mikveh* where no natural spring is available. The custom that women have of dipping themselves three times in the *mikveh* is not because this is really mandatory but because the sages of former times suggested that it should be done so as to make sure that there has been a total immersion. It is the universal custom at a circumcision to place on the lips of the infant a little of the wine over which the benediction has been recited, and it is similarly the custom to give the bride and bridegroom a sip of the wine over which the marriage benedictions are recited. It is the custom in all the borders of Israel to have at a circumcision a special chair for Elijah the prophet. In the majority of places it is the custom to have a festive meal on the day of the circumcision. It is the custom in Spain not to eat bread baked by non-Jews. In Spain Jews do not object to drinking wine touched by a Muslim because Muslims never use wine for idolatrous purposes since they are not idolators. It is the universal custom to have the *get* written out in twelve lines, neither more nor less (the numerical value of the word *get* is twelve).

The majority of the differences in ritual between Ashkenazim and Sephardim stems from the different local customs of the two communities, and these, in turn, are usually the result of the different opinions of the authorities acknowledged by the two communities.[8] The author of the *Shulhan Arukh*, R. Joseph Karo, follows, on the whole, the Sephardi practice, whereas Isserles, in his glosses to the *Shulhan Arukh*, records the Ashkenazi practice when this differs from the rulings of Karo. It was said[9] that the post-*Shulhan Arukh* Sephardim applied the verse, "Go unto Joseph; what he saith to you, do" (Gen. 41:55) to R. *Joseph* Karo, whereas the Ashkenazim applied the verse, "For the children of Israel went out with a high hand" (*be-yad ramah*, Exod. 14:8) to Isserles—*Rama* = R. *Moshe Is*serles. In this way the local customs of the two communities became legally binding on each, with the result that in some respects there is a different Halakhah for Sephardim and

Ashkenazim. Where Halakhic differences existed between Sephardim and Ashkenazim, it was no longer possible to debate which practice is correct and no longer possible to argue the case by the normal canons of Halakhic discussion. Each community was "correct" and authoritative for its own members. The members of each community now had to abide by what had now become the overriding principle, that of loyalty to its own *minhag*, its own local custom. This was itself seen as a general rule that was binding upon all. No Ashkenazi, for example, could henceforth argue that the Ashkenazi custom of refraining from eating rice on Passover did not accord with the statement in the Talmud and that the practice is therefore "wrong" and without binding power. It was the duty of the Ashkenazi to follow the custom of his fathers and this, too, is a law. By refraining from eating rice on Passover the Ashkenazi was not offending a Passover law at all but the different law that requires the acceptance of local custom. This is especially significant in that the aim of both the *Tur* and Karo in his *Bet Yosef* was avowedly to provide a uniform law that was binding equally upon all Jews.

In these instances the *minhag* is a matter of Halakhic procedure. Where local custom accepts the authority of a particular teacher or school that becomes the rule. The matter is somewhat more complicated with regard to folk practices that have no basis in the Halakhah. The general tendency can be observed among the Halakhists to defend such practices and even to endow them with Halakhic status unless they are held to be of heretical, idolatrous, or superstitious origin. But it is futile to look for complete consistency here. Even dubious practices that had become too deeply rooted among the people to be banned by a simple Rabbinic edict were accepted by many of the Halakhists who then tried hard to discover some warrant for them in the Halakhah. Maimonides, naturally, in view of his rationalistic stance, is especially strict in rejecting customs he believed had their origin in heretical or pagan views. Thus, Maimonides refers to the custom in some places, a custom mentioned in the gaonic writings, of a woman who has given birth to a boy abstaining from marital relations for forty days after the birth and for eighty days if she gave birth to a girl. Maimonides dubs this "an heretical way."[10] They have learned this, he says, from the Sadducees (i.e., the Karaites) and the custom should be abolished, by force if necessary. Similarly, he rejects vehemently the custom followed by some people of writing in the *mezuzah* the names of angels and the like, on the grounds that "these fools" turn such an elevated *mitzvah* into an amulet.[11]

The custom of *kapparot* on the eve of Yom Kippur, of waving a cock over the head and then killing it as a *kapparah*, "atonement," for humans, is mentioned in gaonic sources and is recorded in the *Tur*, where detailed rules are given for the observance of the rite.[12] But Karo, in his *Bet Yosef* on the *Tur*, quotes R. Solomon Ibn Adret, the *Rashba*, who objects, in the name of his teacher, Nahmanides, on the grounds that the custom is pagan and Karo writes in his *Shulhan Arukh*, "Regarding the custom of *kapparot* on the eve of Yom Kippur, when they take a cock for every male child and recite Scriptural verses over it, the practice should be stopped."[13] Isserles, however, comments, "Some of the Gaonim recorded this custom as did many of the later scholars and it is the custom in all these lands which should not be changed since it is a worthwhile custom." Isserles then gives the details of the rite and adds that it is also customary to give the *kapparot* or their value to the poor. Isserles, in the same note, records the custom of visiting the cemetery on the eve of Yom Kippur and of giving much charity and adds that all this is extremely worthy. Attempts were later made to abolish the *kapparot* custom on the grounds that the slaughterers, with so many cocks to kill, were in danger of performing the *shehitah* incorrectly and thus causing people to eat *terefa*. The efforts of these authorities were frustrated because the custom had become deeply rooted in the life of the people. Revealing are the remarks of Epstein, writing in the nineteenth century:

> All this is with regard to the matter itself but, for our sins, we notice how the *shehitah* is adversely affected because there are so many *kapparot* and so much pressure that the *shohetim* are unable to take proper care, they are so worn out, and they allow many *terefot* to go out of their hands. It is also impossible for them to examine the knife properly and their hands are heavy. Nowadays, therefore, it is a religious duty to keep them few in number so as not to enter into the sacred day with a possibility that *terefa* may have been eaten. They tried hard in previous generations to abolish this custom but without success since the masses are as addicted to the custom as to the *mitzvah* of the *etrog* and even more so.[14]

Another eve of Yom Kippur custom, originally German but later very widely adopted, is that of *malkut*, of flagellation in the synagogue as a penance. The *Shulhan Arukh* records this as, "All the members of the congregation are given 40 lashes after the Minhah service so that each will set his heart to repenting of his sins."[15] Isserles gives further details from the *Minhagim* produced in the Middle Ages as well as from the best-known source for the customs recorded by Isserles, Jacob Moellin (d. 1427), the famous German authority known as *Maharil*. *Maharil's* customs were collected by his pupil Zalman of St. Goar and first published, in Sabionetta, in 1556. In connection with procedures on the eve of Yom Kippur, Isserles also quotes Maharil on *kapparot*, on begging forgiveness from one's neighbor,[16] and on bathing and immersion by a mourner on the eve of Yom Kippur.[17]

The verse generally quoted as demanding obedience to local custom is "Forsake not the teaching of thy mother" (Prov. 1:8). This verse is quoted in the Talmud in connection with the question of whether the testicles of an animal lying loose in the scrotum while the animal was alive are permitted when the animal is slaughtered or whether they are forbidden because they are like a piece of flesh cut or removed from a living animal.[18] The matter is debated by the Amoraim, the Babylonian teachers taking the strict view. It is said that the Palestinian Amora, R. Johanan, declared to the Babylonian, R. Shamen b. Abba, "They are permitted but you must not eat them because of 'Forsake not the teaching of thy mother.'" The point here is that R. Johanan is quite convinced that the testicles are permitted. If R. Shamen were to eat them it would not be an offense against the law forbidding the eating of flesh that comes from a living animal. But he would have offended against the general rule, implied in the Proverbs verse, of obeying local custom. Eventually, the principle was extended to cover customs that have no direct connection with ritual law but are simply folk practices.

Many of these folk practices have to do with the observance of the festivals. Isserles records, for instance, the custom of having plants and flowers in the synagogue and home on Shavuot to commemorate the giving of the Torah, as well as the custom of eating dairy dishes on that day. As in all such instances, various reasons were later advanced to explain the custom.[19] Isserles[20] quotes *Maharil* that in some places it is the custom to visit the cemetery and offer supplication there on the eve of Rosh ha-Shanah. Other Rosh ha-Shanah customs recorded by Isserles are eating an apple dipped in honey and eating pomegranates, fat meat, and sweet things on Rosh ha-Shanah as symbolic expression of the hope for a sweet and good year;[21] in the name of *Maharil*, not eating nuts on Rosh ha-Shanah (because the word for nut *"egoz,"* has the same numerical value as *het*, "sin," and because they produce phlegm, making it more difficult to recite the prayers); the custom of *Tashlikh*, of going to a river on Rosh ha-Shanah to "cast away" sins there;[22] and, again, in the name of *Maharil*, the custom of prolonging the prayers and hymns until midday.[23] Of particular interest are Isserles' remarks regarding the celebration of Purim, a feast around which a number of folk customs grew up. Isserles writes that originally it was the custom on Purim for children to draw a picture of Haman or to write Haman's name on sticks and stones and beat these so as to fulfill the injunction to blot out the name of Amalek (Exod. 17:14; Deut. 25:19).[24] Isserles quotes Abudraham to the effect that out of this custom the further custom developed of "smiting Haman," i.e., of banging or knocking whenever Haman's name is mentioned during the reading of the Megillah. On this Isserles adds, quoting Karo's *Bet Yosef*, "One must never abolish any custom or scoff at it for it was not fixed without a purpose." This latter statement served as a springboard for the discussion by the Halakhists of the whole question of when a *minhag* is binding.[25]

Death and mourning attracted to themselves a large number of customs, some of them of great antiquity. The whole institution of the mourner's *kaddish* originated in folk custom. The generally accepted opinion among historians is that the custom of a son reciting the *kaddish* during the first year after his father's death originated in Germany in the thirteenth century at a time of persecution by the Crusaders. The custom is certainly not found before this date and is not mentioned at all by the *Shulhan Arukh*. Isserles, however, has a lengthy gloss on the mourner's *kaddish* in which he discusses the procedures.[26] Out of this a whole new branch of the Halakhah developed.[27] In the same gloss, Isserles refers to *Maharil* who says, "some say" that when people return from attending a funeral they should sit down seven times to drive away the ghosts that accompany them from the cemetery but that "in these lands" it is the custom to sit only three times after washing the hands. It is also the custom, again quoting *Maharil*, to take care not to enter a house before washing the hands and sitting down. It is in this connection that *Maharil* states "the *minhag* of our fathers is Torah." The *Shulhan Arukh* states that it is the custom *(minhag)* to pour out all the drawn water in the vicinity when a person has passed away.[28] Isserles[29] states that when the corpse is washed beaten eggs are smeared on its head to symbolize death which comes around to all sooner or later, eggs being oval-shaped. Isserles states that according to some authorities there is to be no mourning by the parents

after their first child to die or after the death of their firstborn.[30]
Isserles describes this as a custom based on error; the parents are
obliged to mourn. Nevertheless, he continues, it is the custom "in
our city" (Cracow) that parents do not accompany the body of their
first son to die to his resting place. In the same gloss *Maharil* is
quoted to the effect that there is to be no mourning when people die
during an epidemic because it might lead to panic, and Isserles
states that he has noticed some few people who follow this practice.

As Chajes has shown, the principle of *minhag* operates not only in
connection with the introduction of new laws but also, occasionally, by the abolition of established laws.[31] There are instances of
laws that simply fell into abeyance because the people no longer
observed them. Total recognition by the Halakhists was rarely
accorded for this neglect by the people. As in other legal systems,
such laws still remained in the statute books but they had become a
dead letter. The idea that the teachers of the law should leave well
enough alone if they know their protests will be ignored is found in
the Talmud where the formula is found, "Leave Israel alone.[32] It is
better that they sin unwittingly rather than that they should sin
intentionally," i.e., if they are informed that it is wrong they will
not give it up so it is better that they be left in blissful ignorance.
This principle, since it is found in the Talmud, became itself a law
so that in certain circumstances, discussed by the Halakhists, it is
positively forbidden for the teachers of the law to rebuke the people
for its neglect.[33] Among the examples referred to by Chajes are the
following: The Talmud states that when the hands are washed the
right hand should be washed first, and when bathing the whole
body the head should be bathed first.[34] But Gumbiner[35] quotes
Isserles, in the latter's *Darkhey Moshe*, who observes, "I have never
seen anyone take any notice of this." The Talmud rules that there
must be a ritual washing of the hands before eating anything
dipped in liquid.[36] This is the accepted rule and is recorded in the
Shulḥan Arukh.[37] David ha-Levi offers a stern rebuke to those who
do this at the Passover Seder but fail to do it during the rest of the
year.[38] They are inconsistent, he says, and should mend their
ways, especially during the period from Rosh ha-Shanah to Yom
Kippur. Gumbiner[39] again quotes Yom Tov Lippmann Heller who
remarks that people no longer observe this law and can find authority for their neglect in the *Tosafists*.[40] "Go out and see what the
people do,"[41] adds Heller, thus giving Halakhic support for the
neglect. The Talmud rules that one is to have a constant reminder
of the destruction of the Temple, leaving, for example, a portion of

the house near the door undecorated.[42] This rule is recorded in the *Shulhan Arukh* without dissenting voice.[43] Yet very few people, says Chajes, keep this law. He refers to the comment of his teacher, R. Ephraim Zalman Margaliot, who cannot find any reason for tolerating this neglect of the law and hints that it may be because to mourn openly in this way for the destruction of the Temple might awaken the hostility of the governmental authorities.[44]

When the early Reformers at the beginning of the nineteenth century began to introduce changes in the liturgy, they were faced with the question whether long-established customs and traditions can legitimately be abolished. At this early period the arguments on both sides of the debate were on the legitimacy of change within the traditional framework. The Reformers claimed that the principle "the *minhag* of Israel is Torah" cannot be invoked to deny the right to introduce liturgical changes. The Hamburg Temple, opened in 1817, sought to justify, on traditional grounds, the comparatively modest innovations of German prayers, a sermon in German, choral singing, and organ music as well as the omission of some of the traditional prayers.[45] It comes as no surprise, therefore, to find that the Orthodox rabbis in this period tended all the more to elevate the binding force of custom. The foremost leader in the battle against Reform, R. Moses Sofer, always seeks in his Responsa to defend even those customs that had no basis in the Halakhah and even those which in themselves were very insignificant.[46] In a Responsum addressed to the Haham of Triest[47] he writes that custom supposedly based on ignorance can be shown to well forth from the springs containing the living waters of the Torah and that he is accustomed to declare, "Whoever casts doubts on our laws and customs requires to be investigated" (i.e., examined for heresy).[47] Especially worthy of note in this connection is the book, *Elleh Divrey ha-Berit*, published in Altona in 1819 by the Hamburg rabbis as a counter-attack to the Hamburg Reformers. Many words and phrases in the book are printed in large type to serve as italics. The following are some of these words and phrases from the replies of the Orthodox rabbis published in the book in connection with the question of the changing of established custom, "the *minhag* of Israel is Torah";[48] "It is forbidden to change either content or form (of the liturgy) and whoever does so offends against, "Forsake not" (the Torah of thy mother)";[49] the Ashkenazi liturgy has "spread to all of them without exception and the Sephardi to the Sephardim;"[50] "even Elijah the prophet cannot abolish it";[51] "they (the Reformers) have invented their own custom" and they are "neither Jews nor Christians";[52] "it is absolutely forbidden to change any of our fathers' customs";[53] "we must never introduce any false innovation to permit that which our fathers and their fathers have been accustomed to treat as forbidden";[54] "we have no power to skip over or to change that which is ordained in the Talmud, not even by an hairbreadth";[55] "a certain sect has arisen among the congregation to breach the fence and the wall created by the sages of old, to uproot that which is planted, to destroy that which is firmly fixed";[56] "we obey the laws of the King and they must neither be diminished nor added to";[57] "God forbid that we should ever change anything at all";[58] " 'Forsake not the Torah of thy mother' ";[59] "who is this and what is he who has the effrontery to do such a thing, to change the order of prayers accepted by our fathers and their fathers."[60] These words are italicized in the original; in all probability they were so printed by the rabbinic editors, the Hamburg rabbis who published the book. The whole debate is unusual not only for its content but also because the Halakhists now function as polemicists who are anxious to defend tradition and are more concerned with winning their case than with Halakhic argumentation pure and simple.

Writing at a slightly later period, Chajes[61] made a more sustained and systematic defense of the traditional Halakhah against the attacks of the Reformers. (Chajes is also far more historically sophisticated. Chajes was not only a distinguished Halakhist but also a pioneer of the new historical approach to Jewish studies known as Jüdische Wissenschaft). After noting the various heretical sects that sprang up among Jews in the past, Chajes continues:

Also in our times we see breaches and lack of order in Israel brought about by those who invent new laws and compose vain epistles. With all their might they try to destroy the old construction, each one building a high place for himself by introducing innovations in his city and community, changing the order of the prayers and the customs of the synagogue. These men are sages in their own eyes and righteous in their self-opinion. They see themselves as if they are the Supreme Court in Jerusalem to whom the gates of understanding are open and to whom permission has been granted to diminish and change the laws of Israel just as they please and they imagine that the Torah has been given to them as sages to do with it all their heart desires and that they alone are the true builders who want and care for the good of their people. They imagine that faith is the girdle of their loins and the fear of God the girdle of their waists and that they are superior and more talented in understanding and the fear of God than all the other Rabbis and Gaonim of the age who devote themselves entirely to Torah and testimony and who hold fast with a strong hand to the customs of our fathers as recorded for us in the *Shulhan Arukh* of the two pillars of the Exile and the foundations of all legal decisions—our master the *Bet Yosef* and R. Moshe Isserles.[62]

Chajes continues further that the Babylonian Talmud has always been the basis for Jews everywhere of every legal decision with the exception of the Karaites and the few Samaritans on Mount Gerizim who have separated themselves from our people and no longer see themselves as Jews. It has never before been heard of that a handful of men have the sheer effrontery to teach the Torah in a way contrary to the Halakhah by openly declaring that the laws and regulations which stem from the authors of the Talmud are not in accord with the *Zeitgeist* and so are no longer binding upon our people. It is perfectly true that for a long time now there has been the split between the Ashkenazim and the Sephardim but this concerns only a number of peripheral matters. Ashkenazim and Sephardim do not differ regarding the basic laws of the Written and Oral Torah or about matters which, though only in the nature of *Takkanot* and fences around the Torah, are based on the Talmud and the words of the great *Posekim*. A fortiori there has been no dispute regarding the thirteen principles of the faith as laid down by Maimonides. The Reformers treat the *mitzvot* of the Torah as if they were like women's fashions to be changed whenever the latest craze demands it.

At first, says Chajes, when all the Reformers wished to do was to change a few of the customs, the rabbis realized that in these times it did no good simply to hurl anathemas at these Reformers and it became imperative to demonstrate to them that their understanding of the Halakhah in the matter of change was at fault. But now that they have gone so far as to deny the whole authority of the Halakhah, there is no point in arguing with them at all. They are to be treated as the rabbis of old treated the Samaritans and the Karaites and other heretical sects. The difference between them and us is no longer in connection with this or that law or custom but on fundamental matters of faith, and here there is no room for any compromise.

Subsequent Jewish history proved Chajes' analysis to be substantially correct. From the rise and growth of the Reform movement to the present day the question of change is no longer one of this or that detail being altered or abolished but has to do with the far more basic question of how far the Halakhah in its totality is binding upon Jews. The leading thinkers of the Conservative movement from Zecharias Frankel and Solomon Schechter down to the present have tried to work out a philosophy of Halakhah in which this, the most significant aspect of Judaism as traditionally conceived, is preserved as authoritative but with the dynamism that, so they claim, has been typical throughout the ages, even though, perhaps, this dynamism has been less consciously acknowledged in the past. This book has sought to examine in some detail the dynamic spirit and creativity of the traditional Halakhic process. What is really new on the contemporary scene is the nonfundamentalist, historical approach to the Halakhah. This has certainly created new problems hitherto unknown but it has also shown the way for the emergence of a strong, viable approach to the Halakhah for the future. The task of the theologian who is anxious to develop a philosophy of the Halakhah today is to try to pursue the question of a nonfundamentalist Halakhah in detail. Some important beginnings have been made and there is good reason to hope that increasingly the *minhag* of Israel, with the dynamism implied in this designation, will continue to be the Torah of Israel.

NOTES

1. See Isserles' gloss to YD 376:4. On this subject see the comprehensive account by Elon, *ha-Mishpat ha-Ivri*, pp. 726–47 and in his article in EJ, vol. 12, pp. 4–26 (see bibliography at end of this article); Kahana, *Mehkarim be Sifrut ha-Teshuvot*, pp. 108–116; Tchernowitz, *Toledot ha-Posekim*, vol. 3, pp. 332–61; Medini, *Sedey Hemed, Kelalim mem*, nos. 37 and 38, vol. 4, pp. 74–108; Eisenstein, *Otzar Dinim u-Minhagim* Sperling; *Taamey ha-Minhagim*; and especially Chajes, *Kol Kitvey*, vol. 1, pp. 217–42.

2. See supra., p. 26.

3. *Yevamot* 12:1 (12c); cf. the statement in BT *Yevamot* 102a where the same rule is laid down but with the omission of "*minhag* overrides the law." Cf. Alexander Sender Schor (d. 1737'; *Simlah Hadashah*, par. 35, *Tevuot Shor*, note 47, in connection with kinds of *terefa* not mentioned at all in the Talmud. Schor argues that R. Ashi, when he edited the Talmud, did not record all the laws and customs stated in the later (literature) but these do go back, nonetheless, to the Amoraim and even earlier and are binding. Schor's descendent, Menahem Manish Babad of Tarnapol (1865–1938) quotes his ancestor in order to adopt the most extreme view with regard to the binding character of *minhag*. Thus he refuses to countenance any departure from the traditional method of teaching children the alphabet, e.g., *kametz alef = oh* and so forth (*Havatzelel ha-Sharon* vol. 3 *(Tinyana)*, no. 12); and with regard to the placing of the tombstone of the head, not the foot, of the grave (*Havatzelel ha-Sharon* vol. 2, *Yoreh Deah*, no. 94) he quotes a saying attributed to *Rashba* that not even six hundred thousand proofs can succeed in persuading us to reject any custom observed by the old women of Israel.

4. See the discussion in Elon, Kahana, and Medini.

5. Response, *Rashbash*, nos. 419 and 562, quoted by Kahana *Mehkarim*, p. 115.

6. *Bava Metzia* 7:1.

7. See the full list of these customs drawn up by Rafael in his edition of *sefer ha-Manhig*, Introduction, pp. 43–66. An example of a *minhag* that became a very widely accepted practice for the devout Jew is the giving of a tenth of ones income to charity annually, see *Pithey Teshuvah* SA, YD 331, note 12, for the sources that it is a *minhag*.

8. The best treatment of this question is Zimmels, *Ashkenazim and Sephardim*.

9. Ibid., p. 57 and notes.

10. *Yad, Issurey Viah* 11:15.

11. Yad, Tefillin 5:4.

12. *Tur*, OH 605.

13. OH 605:1. Cf. the much-discussed case of the hen that crowed like a cock. In the Will of R. Judah the Saint (beginning of the Margaliot ed. of *Sefer Hasidim*, pp. 26–27) No. 50 it is said that the hen must be killed at once but the Talmud (*Shabbot* 67b) states explicitly that to do this belongs to "the ways of the Amorites." The *Maharil* (see the note of Margaliot) argues that the correct reading in the Talmud is, "it is *not* the ways of the Amorites." The SA, YD 179:3 declares it to be forbidden but Isserles comments, "But some say that if he does not state the reason why he orders the hen to be killed but simply says, "Kill it," it is permitted to kill it when it crows like a cock. And this is the custom." See the note of the gaon of Vilna, ad loc. *Biur ha-Gra*, note 8, who defends the reading "it is *not* the way of the Amorites." R. Joseph Engel, *Ben Porat*, vol. II, no. 11, with a degree of oversubtlety, suggests that R. Judah the Saint, when he saw that people did this, ordered it to be done in obedience to his will and not in order to follow the ways of the Amorites. Historically, Engel is correct that this is precisely how *minhagim* based on superstitions came to be law on the basis of "if you cannot beat them join them."

14. *Arukh ha-Shulhan*, OH 605:5.

15. OH 607:6.

16. Ibid. 606:1.

17. Ibid. 606:4. On the whole question of Ashkenazi folk creativity see Freehof, "Ceremonial Creativity Among the Ashkenazim." Among other customs originating in German Jewry, Freehof, p. 251f. lists the breaking of a glass at weddings and *Bar Mitzvah*. Karo refers to the custom of breaking a glass at weddings in his *Bel Yosef* to *Tur*, OH 560 but has no reference to it in his SA, whereas Isserles (OH 560:2 and EH 65:3) does record the custom. Neither the *Tur* nor Karo make any mention of the *Bar Mitzvah* ceremonies, but Isserles refers to these in his *Darlchey Mosleh* to *Tur*, OH 225 and in his gloss to SA, OH 55:10. Freehof sees as the reason for the special creativity of the Ashkenazim in this area of ceremonial custom the fact that life in the medieval Ashkenazi communities was less centrally organized than in Spain, thus allowing to a greater extent the emergence of folk customs. Another reason is because of the German emphasis on *hibbub mitzvah*, "love of the precepts," see Zimmels *Ashkenazim and Sephardim*, pp. 279ff. Zangwill remarks somewhere that whereas medieval potentates would offer a reward to anyone who invented a new pleasure, the Jews of the Middle Ages would offer a reward to anyone who invented a new *mitzvah*. An example of Jewish creativity in the matter of ceremonies at an earlier period is the special festival of *Simhat Torah*. An interesting example of a recent new *minhag* is the introduction in Eretz Yisrael of *zekher le-hakhel*, the ceremony of a reminder of the ancient law that once every seven years the people were to assemble to hear the king read from the Torah (see Deut. 31:10–13). On this see Herzog, *Hekhal Yitzhak*, OH, Nos 58–60. Another example is the introduction of a special celebration for *Yom ha-Abzmaut*, "Israeli Independence Day." See the articles by Zevi Neriah and N. Z. Friedmann in Israeli, *ha-Torah ve-ha-Medinah*, pp. 103–124.

18. Hullin 93b.

19. OH 494:3; Gumbiner, *Magen Avraham*, note 6. Cf. Isserles, OH 619:1 in name of *Maharil* that no one should depart from the customs of his town even with regard to the melodies used on Yom Kippur. On this see David Oppenheim (1664–1736) in his *Nishal David*, OH, no. 2, vol. I, pp. 3–6. Oppenheim refers to *Arakkin* 10a–b that it was forbidden for the Levites in the Temple to make any alterations to their musical instruments and the same applies to the synagogue melodies handed down by tradition. Cf. the editor's note in his introduction to vol. II of *Mishal David*, pp. 29–30.

20. Ibid. 581:4.

21. Ibid. 583:1.

22. Ibid. 583:2.

23. Ibid. 584:1.

24. Ibid. 690:17.

25. See *Baer Hetev* note 15 and *Mishnah Berurah* note 59.

26. YD 376:4. Karo in his *Bet Yosef* to *Tur*, YD 403 discusses the details of the *kaddish*, but as Freehof, *Ceremonial Creativity* p. 212 notes, all the authorities he quotes are Ashkenazim. Freehof, pp. 214–15 also notes that the custom of observing the Yahrzeit is Ashkenazic and was at first resisted by the Sephardim.

27. See, e.g., Ganzfried, *Kitzur* 24, with the heading, "The *Laws* of the Mourner's Kaddish."

28. YD 339:5. On these customs and the ideas behind them see Trachtenberg, *Jewish Magic and Superstition*, chapter 5, "The Spirits of the Dead," pp. 61–68.

29. Ibid. 352:4.

30. Ibid. 374:11.

31. *Kol Kitvey*, pp. 230–31.

32. *Betzah* 30a.

33. See SA, OH 608:2 and Isserles ad loc.

34. *Shabbat* 61a.

35. *Magen Avraham* to OH 2, note 4 quotes Isserles' *Darkhey Moshe*, "I have never seen anyone taking notice of this."

36. *Pesahim* 115a.

37. OH 158:4.

38. *Taz* to CH 473, note 6.

39. *Magen Avraham* to OH 158, note 8.

40. *Pesahim* 115a s.v. *kol she-tibbulo be-mashkeh*.

41. See sup., p. 221.

42. *Bava Batra* 60b.

43. OH 560.

44. *Shaarey Teshuvah* to OH 560, note 1.

45. On this see Plaut, *The Rise of Reform Judaism*, pp. 31–42. See especially Plaut's quote (p. 33) from Aaron Chorin, the Reform leader, who states explicitly that the question is whether the liturgical innovations are forbidden because of "*minhag* of Israel is Torah."

46. See e.g., *Hatam Sofer*, YD, no. 191.

47. *Hatam Sofer*, OH, no. 51.

48. Ibid. p. 1.

49. Ibid. p. 4.

50. Ibid. p. 8.

51. Ibid. p. 8.

52. Ibid. p. 17.

53. Ibid. p. 25.

54. Ibid. p. 32.

55. Ibid. p. 47.

56. Ibid. p. 70.

57. Ibid. p. 70.

58. Ibid. p. 78.

59. Ibid. p. 79.

60. Ibid. p. 89.

61. *Minhat Kenaot* in his *Kol Sifrey*, vol. 2, pp. 975–1036. On Chajes and his attitude see Hirshkovitz, *Maharatz Hayot*, especially chapter 13, pp. 300–40.

62. *Kol Sifrey*, p. 977.

[16]

Toward a Non-Fundamentalist Halakhah

This book has dealt with the diversity, flexibility, and creativity of the Halakhah. The question that immediately concerns the reader who is committed to the Halakhah when such a presentation is offered, is what of the future? As we observed at the end of the previous chapter, much work has been done in a consideration of this question, especially by the leading thinkers of the Conservative movement (chiefly in the United States), the avowed aim of which is to preserve and foster the Halakhic process as essential to Judaism but with full awareness of the need for a more dynamic approach than is provided by Orthodoxy.[1] On the whole, the weight is given to the tradition. Change is never engaged in for its own sake and there is a proper appreciation of the great caution that is required if continuity is to be preserved. But where the Halakhah, as it is at presently practiced, results in the kind of injustice that reasonable persons would see as detrimental to Judaism itself, a frank avowal is called for that there must be changes in the law. In Appendix II we examine at length a typical problem, that of *mamzerut*, in which no amount of legal tampering will succeed in removing injustice and where, consequently, a radical change in the law becomes imperative.

Although, as we have seen, the great Halakhists of the past refused to allow the Halakhah to become fossilized, they did not have to confront the problems that the moderns have had to confront. Zunz's famous remark is sound, that for Jews the "Middle Ages" did not come to an end until around about the time of the

236

French Revolution. No blame is to be attached to teachers who either lived in this precritical age or whose background, training, and cultural environment compelled them to operate as if nothing serious had happened to present any challenge to the medieval world view. Not even the most farseeing of men is able to get out of his own skin. Among the German and German-influenced Halakhists such as Ettlinger and Chajes there is, to be sure, a real awareness of the new challenges, but whereas this awareness may have influenced their approach they, too, would bound by what we would today call a fundamentalist attitude. None of the traditional Halakhists ever dared, or, judging by their writings, ever thought, to take issue with, for them, the basic doctrine upon which the Halakhic structure is reared, namely, the infallibility of Scripture in its rabbinic interpretation and the infallibility of the Talmudic rabbis as the sole and final arbiters of the Halakhah. The Halakhists virtually refused even to mention nontraditional thinkers except for the purpose of refuting their heretical ideas. When Hayyim Hezekiah Medini, in his *Sedey Hemed*, quoted Zechariah Joseph Stern, who made a casual reference to the *Biur* of Moses Mendelssohn and saw no harm in it, Medini received a sharp reprimand from Rabbi Shalom Mordecai Schwadron, the *Maharsham*, for mentioning such a person in an Halakhic context.[2] Medini referred the rebuke to Stern and he records Stern's reply. (Rabbi Stern was an outstanding Halakhist of the nineteenth century and the rabbi of Shavul in Lithuania.) First, Stern remarks, he quoted the *Biur* in a personal letter to Medini and did not imagine that Medini would print it. Secondly, the *Biur* to Leviticus he had quoted is by Wessely and contains no heresy, whereas the report that R. Moses Sofer, the *Hatam Sofer*, had ordered his children, in his last will and testament, never to look into the works of Mendelssohn, referred only to the latter's writings. It is true that the particular note to the *Biur*, which Medini quotes, is by Mendelssohn himself but there is no harm in quoting even Mendelssohn himself, as other Halakhists have done, provided that he and others like him are never relied on in matters of Halakhah. The whole passage in Medini deserves further study. In any event, it is quite unknown for any of the traditional Halakhists, down to the present day, to quote unorthodox Halakhic theories except, as we have seen, for purposes of refutation. When, for instance, Saul Berlin's *Besamim Rosh* is quoted this is because many of the Halakhists accepted uncritically the claim of the book to contain the opinion of R. Asher b. Yehiel, the

Rosh. Moreover, when the Halakhists of a later period do quote the book they generally add a rider to the effect that the work is suspect.[3]

The real difference, and one that cannot be ignored, between the traditional Halakhists and modernists such as the thinkers referred to at the beginning of this chapter, is on the question of how the Halakhah came to be and how it developed. The basic question is the historical one, from which the practical consequences all stem. Indeed, the very notion that there is a *history* of the Halakhah and that it *developed* is anathema to the traditional Halakhist who operates on the massive assumption that the Torah, both in its written form, the Pentateuch, and its oral form, as found in the Talmudic literature, was directly conveyed by God to Moses either at Sinai or during the forty years of wandering through the wilderness. Furthermore, the traditional Halakhists accept implicitly that the Talmudic literature contains the whole of the Oral Torah and that even those laws and ordinances called rabbinic are eternally binding and that, as we have seen, the Talmud is the final authority, which can never be countermanded. All this, at least, is the theory, the philosophy behind the Halakhah. If, nevertheless, the post-Talmudic Halakhists did succeed, as we have shown in preserving the dynamism of the Halakhah, this speaks volumes for their humaneness and liberality. These men were truly geniuses of the spirit, capable of adapting a law they believed unquestioningly to be divinely revealed and yet defending their adaptations not as real innovation but as inherent in the very idea of a law revealed by God to be interpreted by humans.

The traditional picture has grandeur and compelling power. It can be argued that a thorough familiarity with the Halakhah, the result of the most assiduous application, is only possible for those who accept the dogmas to which we have alluded and so are prepared to devote laborious years to the undivided study the discipline demands. At the very least it can be said that Halakhists of note today who did not begin and pursue their studies in a precritical attitude (only becoming aware of the critical view at a later stage) can be counted on one hand, if they exist at all. Unfortunately, the precritical attitude is untenable. However many conflicting hypotheses have been advanced by the higher critics, one basic fact that emerges from modern biblical studies, is that the Pentateuch is a composite work produced at different periods in the life of ancient Israel. I have surveyed elsewhere the overwhelming evidence for this contention and there is no point in repeating the argument here which is, in any event, taken for granted even by the most conservative biblical scholars.[4] We need only refer to the marvelous book of Deuteronomy which, for anyone with a sense of history, is different in style, content, and background from, say, the book of Leviticus. The Code of law in Deuteronomy reflects a different age from that in which were produced the Covenant Code in Exodus and the Holiness Code in Leviticus. Even such a conservative Jewish scholar as M. H. Segal, Professor of Bible at the Hebrew University from 1926 to 1949, after coming to the conclusion that the discourses in Deuteronomy really were addressed by Moses to Israel before his death, goes on to say that this does not imply that the whole of our Deuteronomy is the work of Moses.[5] In fact, Segal remarks, the book contains a fair amount of material that is certainly not Mosaic. The expression "a fair amount of material" is a giveaway of Siegel's position. The extent of this post-Mosaic material according to Segal—the additions in the final chapters of the book, portions of the legislative section, and the repeated amplification in chapter 28, including "a quotation from Jeremiah" [*sic*]—makes Deuteronomy itself a composite work and the difficulty remains of the strong resemblances in style between the original discourses and the "additions."

Revelation is a matter of faith rather than historical scholarship. Scholarly investigation into the authorship of the biblical books cannot by its nature make any pronouncement on whether the author or authors of a biblical book were inspired. What it can do and has succeeded in doing is to demolish the idea of verbal inspiration, of God conveying information to purely passive human recipients. For if, as scholarly investigation has established, the Pentateuch was produced by a series of human authors, albeit, from the point of view of faith, inspired authors who were influenced in their work by the conditions which obtained in their day, then revelation must be understood as a far more complicated and complex process of divine–human encounter and interaction and quite differently from the idea of direct divine communication of infallible laws and propositions, upon which the traditional theory of the Halakhah depends. And all this is to say nothing about the history of rabbinic interpretation of the Torah and the way this has developed, as the massive researches of the modern scholars to whom we have referred demonstrate.

Putting the whole matter in different words, it can be said that traditional Judaism is based on the three tremendous ideas of God, the Torah, and Israel.[6] In the traditional scheme—which, it must

not be overlooked is itself the product of history—God gives the
Torah to Israel and through Israel to all mankind. But what is
meant by God *giving* the Torah to Israel? From the days of Philo of
Alexandria there has been much discussion concerning the difficult
concept of God "speaking" to man. God does not have vocal organs, but the problem for moderns is not that of communication
but of content. A medieval thinker like Maimonides is quite prepared to acknowledge that the nature of the divine communication
is a mystery beyond human grasp, although insisting that the scope
of such communication covered the whole of the Pentateuch together with the interpretations of its laws found in the Talmudic
literature. On this view, and it is one held virtually without exception throughout the Talmudic and medieval periods, God dictated
(Maimonides would agree that this is merely an attempt to describe
the unfathomable in intelligible human terms) the whole of the five
books to Moses, word for word and letter by letter, together with
the Oral Torah, that is, the detailed expositions of the Torah laws
as found in the teachings of the rabbis. Modern concepts such as
the development of ideas, laws, and institutions under social, economic, historical, and political influences, are entirely foreign to
this way of looking at revelation. The great rabbis, without doubt,
did introduce new legislation on comparatively rare occasions (that
is, in theory; in practice it was far from rare, as we have seen) but
their chief role was that of transmitters of laws reaching back without break to the days of Moses. The idea that King David, Elijah,
and the Hebrew prophets wore *tefillin*, for example, differing in no
essential detail from the *tefillin* that observant Jews now wear, may
offend the historical sense of moderns as anachronistic but there is
little doubt that such was the traditional view as stated clearly in
the Talmud and recorded with the same lack of ambiguity by
Maimonides.

On this view, God imparted to Moses a series of laws, narratives,
religious and moral doctrines, and sublime mysteries regarding the
divine nature in its creative activity, these being imparted in turn to
Joshua and, through the "chain of tradition," to the present-day
teachers of Judaism. On this view it is hard to know the Torah, but
all the difficulties are the result of the limited powers of comprehension of its students. Infallible, divine truth is there to be discovered
and to serve as life's safe and sure guide. Here, in propositional
form, is God's truth, ready to be assimilated by the diligent students of the Torah, albeit that the task is never-ending, since the
Torah is itself a reflection of the Infinite.

Why have most moderns been compelled to reject this conception? The new picture of the Bible, and this includes the Pentateuch, which has emerged as a result of the researches of a host of dedicated scholars since the sixteenth century, is a collection of works produced by many hands over a long period, during which the influence of diverse ancient civilizations were brought to bear on the language, style, and thought patterns of the authors. The Pentateuch itself is now seen as a composite work, bearing all the indications of compositeness such as different strata, varying historical and geographical backgrounds, and changes of style. Although containing much early material, the Pentateuch is now seen as a work put together at a comparatively late stage in Israel's history. Many modern scholars are far less confident than those of the nineteenth century in our capacity, after twenty-five hundred years, to disentangle in neat sequence the three main strands that have been detected, but there is no biblical scholar of repute, whether Jew, Catholic, or Protestant, who, having studied the evidence of compositeness, is not convinced by it. Moreover, the findings of the physical sciences with regard to such matters as the age of the earth, and anthropology with regard to the age of man upon earth, make it clear that, whatever its marvelous value for religion and ethics, there can no longer be any question of a divinely dictated book, infallible in all the information it conveys. Then again, new archeological discoveries have made us aware of the religion, culture, and myths of Egypt, Babylonia, Canaan, and Sumeria, demonstrating that many of the biblical ideas have their roots in these civilizations. This is not to say that the biblical narratives, for example, are identical with the ancient myths. For all its striking parallels in ancient mythologies, nay, rather because of them, the story of Noah's ark, to quote only one example, stands out as a glorious testimony to the power of ethical monotheism to transform a soulless, immoral myth of the gods into a vehicle for the transmission of truths by which men may live. For all that, it is now very difficult,to say the least, to believe that the story of the Deluge is historical, still less that it was divinely dictated.

Dr. John Baillie, in his 1961 and 1962 Gifford Lectures sums up the modern attitude when he writes:

It is now agreed by responsible theologians that for our knowledge of such things as are perceived by the senses, for our knowledge of "things seen," we are dependent alone on the evidence of these senses and the scientific reflection that builds on such evidence. Needless to say this does not mean that faith has nothing to say about the corporeal world. It has much to say.

For a Jew this last sentence would be reworded "very much, *indeed*, to say." The whole of the Halakhah is a mighty attempt at bringing holiness into the detailed affairs of life in this corporeal world.

In the face of the new evidence brought to light by the scientific investigation into the classical sources of Judaism, three attitudes are possible. The first ignores the new knowledge altogether, asserting, with a vast contempt for the whole science of the "Goyyim," that the world is only five thousand seven hundred and forty years old and God, for reasons unknown to us, planted the fossils (perhaps to give the appearance of growth just as Adam presumably had a navel); or, on the more sophisticated level, tries to come to grips with the new knowledge by interpreting Scripture in a nonliteral fashion, "days" representing millions of years and so forth. The infallibility of Scripture and its divine dictation are preserved with the implication that without a belief in these there is neither meaning nor value in the whole concept of Torah.[7] The second attitude draws the conclusion from the new knowledge that the whole concept of revelation must be discarded. The Bible is seen as an all too human work, replete with errors, so that if we are to speak of inspiration at all we can only say that the Bible is inspired in the sense in which Shakespeare or Beethovan is inspired. The third attitude, the one adopted by the thinkers we have mentioned and which is followed in this book as the nearest to the truth, is that what is called for is not an abandonment of the concept of revelation but its reinterpretation (in reality, a return to the claims the Bible makes about itself). On this view, it can no longer be denied that there is a human element in the Bible, that the whole record is colored by the human beings who put it down in writing, that it contains error as well as eternal truth, but that it is in this book or collection of books that God was first revealed to mankind and that here, and in the subsequent rabbinic commentary, including and especially through the Halakhah, He speaks to us today. Revelation is now seen as a series of meetings or encounters between God and man. The Bible is seen as the record of these encounters, as is the Torah throughout Israel's generations. It is not the actual words of the Bible that were revealed. These belong rather to the faltering human attempts at putting down what it signified for men to have felt themselves very near to God and how they reflected on the nearness to God of their ancestors.

This is to state baldly an extremely complex position. Many attempts have been made and are now being made by Jewish thinkers to work it all out in greater detail and with greater precision, especially in its implications for Jewish practice, for the Halakhah. The issue involved is one of accepting or rejecting the facts discovered by modern scholarship and this cannot be prejudiced by appeals to the question-begging term "Orthodoxy." This, incidentally, is not a Jewish term at all, and its use might qualify Halakhically as *"hukkot ha-goy"!* If the facts are so, then this interpretation is right and hence "orthodox."

A pseudo-sophisticated critique of this position is sometimes put forward by thinkers determined to uphold intact the traditional–medieval position on the nature of Scripture and of Torah as a whole. The argument runs as follows. There are no scientific facts, only scientific hypotheses based on the facts observed. Such hypotheses are, in the nature of the case, only tentative. They are advanced as an attempt to explain the facts observed and are to be tested through further investigation. The history of science informs us that all scientific progress is made by abandoning hypotheses which no longer explain the facts in favor of those which do, and these are in turn abandoned in favor of more refined hypotheses which explain more than the earlier ones do. It follows that all scientific explanation is tentative. All the scientist can be certain of are the basic facts of observation. Any interpretation that the scientist may place on the facts is subject to revision whenever new facts emerge. Newtonian physics, for example, served adequately to explain the known facts about gravitation until the more effective hypothesis was advanced by Einstein and this, in turn, may also be revised in the future. It can be seen, therefore, how precarious it is to reject the certain truth of tradition in favor of what is termed scientific scholarship. Even the most plausible suggestions as to the authorship and date of the biblical books are no more than brilliant guesses, which it is sheer folly to prefer to the sure truth of tradition. It is only misguided Jewish theologians, dazzled by the achievements of the physical sciences, in whose methods they have had no training and whose nature they do not understand, who swallow biblical criticism whole in the false belief that they are being 'scientific' and up to date.

The fallacy here is so blatant that no response seems to be called for. From Hume and Kant onwards (and reaching back to Greek thought in its late period) subtle theories have been advanced regarding the tentativeness of all human knowledge but these offer cold comfort to the traditionalist. On their own showing these theories themselves are only tentative. If, as may well be the case, the most we can hope for from hypotheses based on an examination of the observable facts is a very high degree of plausibility, never complete certainty, this would apply a fortiori to theories found in the traditional literature. If, for example, the verdict of modern scholarship is that the book of Ecclesiastes could not possibly have been written in its present form by King Solomon, a verdict based on philological, stylistic, and historical evidence, it will not do to assert as true the traditional view, that it was written by King Solomon, on the grounds that all the evidence amounts to no more than a hypothesis, which, by definition, is only tentative. For if there is no certainty in any human knowledge, there is surely no certainty in prescientific traditions that are themselves part of human knowledge. The only reply to this is that traditional knowledge is not human at all but divine and therefore guaranteed to be free from error. Apart from the absurdity and untraditionalism of the view that not only the Pentateuch but everything in the traditional sources is divine and consequently infallible, the human recognition that this is so is surely a part of human knowledge and hence subject to the same objections put forward against the verdict of scholarship.

A variation of this critique is to admit, at least by implication, that the verdict of scholarship is to be preferred to that of tradition, but to deny that the nonfundamentalist views are based on the verdict of the best modern scholarship. This critique scorns any reliance on, say, the Documentary Hypothesis—that there are in the Pentateuch four documents of different ages put together by a series of editors—expounded at length by the anti-Semitic Wellhausen, whose views are rejected by present-day biblical scholars. (A further twist is sometimes given: What can one expect from nineteenth-century scholars from Germany, a country that produced the Nazis in the twentieth-century)? But no serious student today ever dreams of claiming that Wellhausen's is the final word in biblical scholarship. Our contention is that whether Wellhausen is to be accepted or rejected is a matter not of faith but of scholarship. Present-day biblical scholars who believe Wellhausen to be wrong arrive at their conclusions, as did Professor Segal mentioned earlier in this chapter, by the exercise of scholarly methods, not by an appeal to dogma. Moreover, modifications of the documentary Hypothesis, or even its complete overthrow, in present-day scholarship takes place in favor of other equally untraditional hypotheses. The conclusion that the Pentateuch is, in part at least, post-Mosaic, and that it is a composite work, is accepted by every biblical scholar of note today who does not dismiss as erroneous the scholarly enterprise itself. This is based on the strongest evidence and is extremely unlikely to be overthrown. It is, of course, a conclusion that is only "tentative" in the sense in which all human knowledge is tentative, but to invoke the principle of tentativeness in defense of tradition leads, as we have seen, to illogicality. The only remaining course open to the fundamentalist is to admit that the scholarly picture of how it all came to be is convincing but that, nevertheless, our faith in the Torah compels us to reject that picture. The belief implicit in such a position is that God has planted false clues, it is very hard to believe that our faith calls in desperation for this kind of belief.

All this is in the realm of theory. But how does it work out in practice, how is our attitude to the living Halakhah affected? If there is such a vast gulf between us and the traditional Hakakhists in the theory of the Halakhah, can there be any continuity in practice? Part of the answer is that the traditional Halakhists were inspired by their theory but were not in thralldom to it. They did adopt a fundamentalist stance but when they did it was quite a respectable stance to adopt. Before the rise of modern scholarship and without any anticipation of its achievements, the doctrine of verbal inspiration and the rest did not offend reason and did not call into compromise the intellectual integrity of the Halakhist. It provided the background to all his activity because no convincing rival theory ever presented itself to his mind. And the Halakhists never understood the theory in a way that would have inhibited them from making their own original contribution. On the contrary, the whole area of *Rabbinic* law, of the right to issue ordinances and to interpret the Halakhah so as to make it conform to as well as to guide and direct the life of the people, was itself seen as having biblical sanction. It is but a step—a vast one to be sure—from this to Halakhah based on nonfundamentalist premises.

It is neither illogical nor cowardly for a non-Fundamentalist Jew to be loyal to the Halakhah. The ultimate authority for determining which observances are binding upon the faithful Jew is the historical experience of the people of Israel, since, historically perceived, this is ultimately the sanction of the Halakhah itself, which, as we have seen, originated and developed as a result of Israel's experi-

ences. But this requires some elaboration. It is possible to take the
view, and some have taken it, that traditional practices are binding
in themselves, that, as has been said, it is possible to have *mitzvot*
("commands") without a *metzavveh* ("one who issues the commands") or with the people of Israel being the *metzavveh*. The old
slogan, "Believe what you like as long as you keep the *mitzvot*" is
the slogan of some even today, and even among the Orthodox,
perhaps, especially among the Orthodox, who sometimes tend to
place all the emphasis on what Heschel has called "pan-
Halakhism." Such an attitude is a theological monstrosity. Ancestor worship is a form of idolatry. The religious appeal to history is
that, whatever their origins, Jewish observances have come to be
the most effective vehicles for the worship of God.

An obvious example is *Yom Kippur*. If scholarship is to be trusted
at all, it is clear that this institution did not fall down from Heaven
in its entirety but is the product of gradual growth from early,
possibly even from primitive and pagan, beginnings, reaching its
biblical development late in biblical history, and receiving fresh
embellishments through the ages. (Even according to the most Fundamentalist interpretation, the majestic liturgy of Yom Kippur is a
human and comparatively very late innovation.) But although this
is an untraditional way of looking at how Yom Kippur came to be,
it is really irrelevant to the question of the religious value of Yom
Kippur observed in the traditional way and of its consequent binding force for Jews today. In theological language, God really did
command Jews to keep Yom Kippur but the command has to be
seen as conveyed through the divine-human encounter in Jewish
history. But it is not history that is being worshiped, it is the God
who reveals His will through history.

In summary, there are many religious Jews who see supreme
value in the vocabulary of Jewish worship provided by the
Halakhah in all its ramifications and for this reason have not the
slightest desire to embrace that interpretation of Reform Judaism in
which the Halakhah is relegated to very much a secondary place.
But these same Jews cannot bring themselves to compromise their
intellectual integrity by accepting traditional theories, as opposed
to traditional practices, which seem to them untenable. They have
no need to despair when they appreciate that the Halakhah has
always possessed the vitality to assimilate new knowledge. As we
have demonstrated, the Halakhah is a living corpus whose practitioners were far more than mere transmitters of a noble heritage.

They were creative thinkers, responding both intellectually and emotionally to the challenges and needs of the age in which they lived, with their quota of human temperament and failings, as well as being highly gifted leaders who tried to pursue the truth objectively as a divinely ordained task.

As we have already remarked, and it is really an impertinence even to state it, this book offers no blueprint for the future. The problems are many and stubborn: of the rights of women; of dialogue and relationships with non-Jews; of life in a technological society; and, in the State of Israel, the needs of a modern democratic state in which religious coercion is neither possible nor desirable and for which the methods adopted by the great Halakhists are no longer applicable. But faith in the Almighty who guides His people through their own efforts to be nearer to Him is still our confidence and our trust. If this book ends on a theological note this is not necessarily a bad thing. The question of how the Halakhah can function in the contemporary world is, when all is said and done, a theological question.

NOTES

1. The literature on this is so vast that it is impossible to list it all. In this note some of the more important writings are referred to. First, there are the continuing discussions in both the *Proceedings of the Rabbinical Assembly* and in the journal *Conservative Judaism*. Louis Ginsberg's essay on Zecharias Frankel in *Students, Scholars and Saints*, pp. 195–216, is an excellent treatment of the thought of a pioneer of the movement. Solomon Schechter's *Studies in Judaism* and especially his *Seminary Addresses* contain a good deal of material on the subject by another pioneer and follower of Frankel. Louis Finkelstein's essay "Tradition in the Making" and his *The Pharisees* discuss, respectively, the practical and the theoretical aspects of the question. Among more recent writers reference should be made to Robert Gordis, *Judaism for the Modern Age;* his "A Dynamic Halakhah" and, especially, his *Understanding Conservative Judaism;* Jacob B. Agus, *Guideposts in Modern Judaism;* M. Davis, *The Emergence of Conservative Judaism;* M. Sklare's sociological study, *Conservative Judaism;* J. J. Petuchowski, *Ever Since Sinai;* Herbert Loewe's introduction to A Rabbinic Anthology, pp. 1v–cvi; and the good popular account by Israel H. Levinthal, *Judaism: An Analysis and Interpretation.* The two works of "Conservative" Halakhah by Isaac Klein are important: *Response and Halakhic Studies* and *A Guide to Jewish Religious Practice.* There is also the collection of essays edited by Mordecai Waxman, *Tradition and Change* and its successor edited by Seymour Siegel, *Conservative Judaism and Jewish Law.*

2. *Sedey Hemed, Kelalim, alef,* no. 64, vol. I, pp. 188–89.

3. See my *Theology in the Responsa,* Appendix I: "Saul Berlin and the *"Besamim Rosh,"* pp. 347–52.

4. Principles of the Jewish Faith, chapter 9, pp. 216–301.

5. *The Pentateuch*, chapter 3, section 5, pp. 75–102.

6. I repeat here my survey in the now unobtainable journal *Quest* I, published by the New London Synagogue.

7. For a critique of Christian fundamentalism from the scholarly point of view see James Barr, *Fundamentalism*. It is important, however, to appreciate that the problem for Jews is more complicated because of the doctrine of the Oral Torah, which, on the one hand, tends to aggravate the problem but which, on the other hand, paves the way for its solution in that, rightly understood, the doctrine calls attention to the human element in revelation.

Appendix A

The Literary Form of the Halakhah

Related to the theme of this book, that the Halakhah is not a self-contained system but has its roots and expression in the whole life of the community, is the fact that a good deal of the Halakhah is presented in literary form. Many of the great Halakhists were literary stylists who were not content with bare juridical arguments and formulations but endeavored to express their views and enhance them by skillfully attractive presentation. We are not thinking solely of the Introductions of Hakakhic works and the flowery prefaces to individual Responsa, which were obviously written as literary compositions. But even the actual debates and rulings of the Halakhists frequently appear in a form in which close attention is paid to the aesthetic as well as to the purely legal aspects.

We do not find in the Talmudic literature, or for that matter in the post-Talmudic, any attempt at praising the Bible for its literary quality. Indeed, the opposite tendency is to be discerned, evidently because to hail Scripture as good writing was to denigrate its sacred character. The Bible is divinely inspired for the rabbis and it would have been ridiculous to imply that God has a good literary style. Revealing is the exposition of Rava (*Sotah* 35a) on why King David was punished by the death of Uzzah who touched the holy ark (I Chron. 13:9), "Why was David punished? Because he called words of Torah 'songs,' as it was said, 'Thy statutes have been my songs in the house of my pilgrimage' (Ps. 119:54). The Holy One, blessed be He, said to him: Words to Torah, of which it is written, 'Wilt thou set thine eyes upon it? It is gone' (Prov. 23:5), thou callest 'song.' I will cause thee to stumble in a matter which every schoolboy knows. For it is written, 'But unto the sons of Kohath he gave none, because the service of the sanctuary etc.' (Numb. 7:9); and David brought it in a wagon." The meaning of the passage is clear. To refer to the Torah as "songs," to call attention to its aesthetic qualities, to treat it merely as great literature, as we would say, is to lesson the awe men should feel for the sanctity of the Torah. David's attitude caused him to place the ark on a wagon and for Uzzah to touch it. The remoteness required if the numinous is to make its impact had gone.

The nearest we get in the rabbinic literature to the recognition of what might be termed literary style in the Bible is the maxim (*Sanhedrin* 89a) that whereas the same signal *(signon)* is given to all the prophets, no two prophets, if they are true, give expression to their prophetic message in exactly the same style *(signon)*. What is being stressed in this passage is that where two or more prophets all use exactly the same words this shows that their message is "made up," that they had prearranged it, much as false witnesses will be careful to use the same words so as not to contradict one another when giving their false testimony. In any event this passage refers only to the prophets not to the Torah itself. At a much later period, the Zohar (III, 152a), obedient to its understanding of the Torah as a mystical text, goes even further to state, "Woe to the man who says that the Torah merely tells us tales in general and speaks of ordinary matters. If this were so we could make up even nowadays a Torah dealing with ordinary matters and an even better one at that. If all the Torah does is to tell us about worldly things there are far superior things told in worldly books so let us copy these and make up a Torah from them. But the truth is that all the words of the Torah have to do with the most elevated themes and with the highest mysteries."

The oft-quoted maxim, "The Torah speaks in the language of men" (*Borakhot* 31b and very freq.) suggests that even the divine Torah uses customary human speech but this idea is only applied in a very limited sense, e.g., that no legal rules can be derived from the use of the infinite absolute together with the verb and even this is a matter of debate. Maimonides (*Guide*, I, 26) extends the maxim to cover the use of anthropomorphic expressions in Scripture. *CF.* Heschel, *Torah min ha-Shamayyim*, pp. 3–19. But this is a far cry from the acknowledgment that the Torah strives for literary effect.

All this, however, only refers to the Torah itself. The *teachers* of the Torah not only had no objection to the use of a good literary style for the expression of their views, this was encouraged once the

"Oral Torah" began to be recorded in writing. In the chapter on the Talmud examples were given of how the editors of the Babylonian Talmud used such things as literary devices so that even the Halakhic portions of the Talmud, constituting its major part, are in a calculated literary form. The literary style of the Mishnah is self-evident. (On the language and style of the Mishnah see Albeck, *Mavo la-Mishnah*, chapter 8, pp. 128–215). Perhaps influenced by Muslim praise of the Koran's literary beauty, Judah ha-Levi (*Kuzari*, III, 67) bestows his praise on the literary style of the Mishnah claiming that no human being could have compiled a work of such literary excellence without divine assistance. Among other literary devices used in the Mishnah are biblical expression or direct quotes from the Bible for the sake of literary effect, not in order to support a particular law. Some of these are *Peah* 2:2, "And on all hills that are digged with the mattock" (Isa. 7:25); *Bikkurim* 3:3 "captains and rulers" ((Ezek. 23:6); *Ketubot* 1:11, "She went down to draw water from the well" (based on Gen. 24:13, 16); *Sotah 8:7, "let the bridegroom go forth from his chamber, and the bride out of her closet" (Joel 2:16); Sanhedrin* 9:5: "the bread of adversity and the water of affliction" (Isa. 30:20); *Avodah Zarah* 2:3, "the sacrifices of the dead" (Ps. 106:28); *Avodah Zarah* 3:5, "high mountains and elevated hills" (Isa. 30:25). Both the Mishnah and the Gemara have "happy endings" appended to them (see e.g., the ending of *Yadaim* and the last "Mishnah" of *Uktzin*, the ending of the whole six orders, and, possibly, the words "and the Sefer Torah that he possessed" in *Yevamot* 16:7; and the famous saying of R. Haninah at the end of the Gemara in *Berakhot; Yevamot; Nazir; Tamid* and *Keritut*). The great codes follow the same pattern. Maimonides begins his *Mishneh Torah* with four Hebrew words the initial letters of which form the Tetragrammaton, and he concludes the work with a paragraph on the Messianic Age that is virtually a poem (see Kaufmann's Introduction to his edition of the *Guide*, p. xxxvii, where this passage is arranged as a prose poem). The *Tur* opens with the word *Yehudah*, the name of the sage he quotes, because the word contains the letters of the Tetragrammaton. The author of the *Tur* similarly has gone out of his way to add the passage about "Peace" to the end of *Yoreh Deah*, which deals with the laws of death and mourning. The conclusion of *Hoshen Mishpat*, and thus of the *Tur* as a whole, is similarly contrived, although there the ending is really a quote from Maimonides (*Yad, Rotzeah* 1:16) who no doubt ended his chapter in this way for the same reason. The *Shulhan Arukh* has a similar addition and for the same purpose at the end of *Hoshen Mishpat*.

Rashi, the author of the greatest Commentary to the Talmud, the major portion of which is of a Halakhic nature, is also the greatest stylist among the commentators. (See Aviniri, "Rashi's Style"). Rashi has the uncanny ability of anticipating the difficulties a student of the text will find and he supplies the solution in a few, well-chosen words that were exactly right for the purpose. For instance (*Betzah* 2b), the Talmud states that preference is given, when formulating a Halakhic debate, to the opinion of the teacher who is permissive rather than to that of the teacher who is strict. The reason given is that "the power to permit is greater." Rashi, evidently, finds it hard to understand this to mean that it is always better to be permissive (why should it be?) and, in any event, what is the significance of the term "the power"? Rashi, therefore, adds the brief comment, making it all clear, "It is better to inform us of the words of the one who is permissive, that is, the one who relies on his opinion and is not afraid to be permissive. But there is no evidence of any power among those who are strict since anyone can be stringent even when something is really permitted." Another example is from Rashi's commentary to *Bava Metzia* 33a on the law of helping a man whose animal is crouching under its heavy load (Exod. 23:5). The statement is here made that since the Torah uses the word *rovetz* for "crouching" the law only applies to a *rovetz* not to a *ravtzan*. Rashi neatly describes the difference: "*rovetz:* it is occasional with the animal, which crouches on a single occasion under its burden; but not *ravtzan*, an animal which does it regularly."

The *Tosafists* to the Talmud are far more than bare records of the debates and discussions in the French and German schools. They are presented in literary form so as to convey to the various statements something of the flavor of the argumentation as if the student were present when these took place (cf. Urbach, *Baaley ha-Tosafot* pp. 523–25). The form, "If you will say . . .fl" 'one can reply . . .' is found throughout. When a problem is presented to which there is no apparent solution the term *temah*, "surprise" or "astonishment," conveys exactly the right tantilizing note. Moreover, as in the Babylonian Talmud itself, a lengthy series of arguments or solutions to problems by various teachers is presented in such a manner that one leads to another to a kind of climax to the whole discussion. See e.g., the *Tosafists* to *Kiddushin* 70b s.v. *kashim gerim*, on the saying of R. Helbo that converts to Judaism are as harmful to Israel as a scab, which is contradicted by other sayings in praise of converts. The *Tosafists* present all the various solutions so as to lead up to the best solution of all and include the interpretation that the converts "show up" Israel by their zeal for the *mitzvot*, and this interpretation is given in the name of Rabbi Abraham the convert!

There are even Halakhic treatises that are in actual poetic form; legal poems with rhyme and meter (see the article in JE, vol. X, pp. 98–99). Joseph Bonfils (eleventh century) wrote a lengthy poem— *avo ve-hil*—on the laws of Passover (now recited during the morning service on *Shabbat ha-Gadol*, see Baer, *Siddur*, pp. 715–718). The poem is referred to in the *Tosafists* to *Pesahim* 115b s.v. *lamah okerin*. Poems are found on the laws of *shehitah*. The earliest of these is by R. Eliezer b. Nathan *(Raban)* of Msinz (ca. 1090–ca. 1170) published from a manuscript by Israel Davidson in the *Sefer ha-Yovel* for R. Simeon Shkop, pp. 81–88. A poem on the laws regarding the examination of the animal's lungs after *shehitah* by David Vital is published in the popular little book *Meah Berakhot*, Amsterdam, 1687, end. B. M. Toledano's *Rinah u-Teffilah* is a digest, by a contemporary Halakhist, of parts of the *Shulhan Arukh* in rhyme. R. David Abudraham (fourteenth century), author of the famous compendium on the liturgy *(Sefer Abudraham)*, frequently uses rhymed prose in his formulations. Apart from his use of this in his Introduction, he resorts to it in parts of the work itself (see Wertheimer's note to his edition of Abudraham, p. 396). At the beginning of *Shaar* II, for example (ed. Wertheimer, p. 5) Abudraham quotes Maimonides' rulings on the laws of prayer but paraphrases these in rhymed prose.

Prominent among the codifiers for his exquisite literary style is Maimonides, the author of the greatest code of all, the *Mishneh Torah*, where this giant of the Halakhah breathes life into the driest of laws by his stately presentation, lucid Hebrew, logical arrangement of the material, and fine poetic asides. Among the more recent codifiers, R. Shneor Zalman of Liady in his *Shulhan Arukh (ha-Rav);* R.Y.M. Epstein in his *Arukh ha-Shulhan;* and R. Solomon Ganzfried in his *Kitzur Shulhan Arukh* are notable stylists.

Each of the medieval commentators to the Talmud has his own style, so much so that the well-known Rosh Yeshiva, R. Elhanan Wassermann was able to add an interesting, critical note (*Kovetz Hearot* to *Yevamot*, beg.) in which he skillfully detects the various styles of the *rishonim* and shows that certain attributions must be false on grounds of style and usage.

All of Menahem Meiri's monumental works display literary talent of a high order. Meiri's coinage of special terms for the Halakhists he quotes tends to introduce a grandeur of its own to the legal discussions, *aharoney ha-Rabbanim*, "the later Rabbis" (generally referring to Rabbenu Tam); *gedoley ha-dorot she-lefanenu*, "the great ones of the previous generations" (Nahmanides); *gedoley ha-mehabberim*, "the great authors" (Maimonides); *gedoley ha-posekim*, "the great Codifiers" (Alfasi); *gedoley ha-Rabbanim*, "the great Rabbis" (Rashi); *hakhmey ha-aharonim*, "the later Sages" *(Rashba)*. Typical of Meiri's forceful style is his statement (*Bet ha-Behirah, Avodah Zarah*, p. 3) that, nowadays, the older regulations, which banned all business dealings with Gentiles on the days preceding their festivals, are no longer followed, "Nowadays no one pays any attention whatsoever to these matters even on the actual day of the festival, neither Gaon nor Rabbi nor Sage nor Disciple nor Saint nor one who presumes to be a Saint *(mithassed)*." Examples of Meiri's literary elegance are to be found on virtually every page of his works. We need here refer only to one further example taken at random. At the beginning of his Commentary to the fifth chapter of *Berakhot* (*Bet ha-Behirah, Berakhot*, p. 110) he writes: "Some of the great Sages used to adorn themselves with their finest clothes for their prayers as it is said in the first chapter of tractate *Shabbat*. Although this is not given to everyone, it is nevertheless fitting that a man should not stand during his prayers in a common manner but it is proper for him to adorn himself with whatever is to hand."

In connection with the literary style of the Halakhists is the interesting correspondence between R. Solomon Luria and R. Moses Isserles (*Teshuvot Rama*, nos. 6 and 7). Luria rebukes Isserles for his ungrammatical Hebrew, in which he confuses the genders, singular and plural, first and third persons, and the like. Isserles admits the fault but avers that "every great man in Israel," when he concentrates on the subject about which he writes, cannot at the same time bother with the niceties of grammar. See on this Medini, *Sedey Hemed, Kelaley ha-Posekim*, no. 16:65, vol. 9, pp. 205–6, who quotes Maimonides' Commentary to the Mishnah (*Gittin* 6:7) that it does not follow that the Supreme Court in Jerusalem was necessarily composed of people who could write since it was essential for the members of this court to be sages not great writers.

Clever puns are frequently used by the Halakhists. An early example is in the famous poem attributed to Saadia Gaon but unlikely to be quite so early (see OY, vol. XI, p. 215 and Waldinberg, *Tzitz Eliezer*, vol. 12, no. 66, pp. 176–78). Discussing Rabbinic attitudes to the Karaites (see sup. p. 13) a pun is made on the rule that when garments are rent over the death of a parent they must never be stitched together again, thus yielding the pun: *ha-Karaim* (for *ha-keraim*) can never be put together (with the Jews) again. R. Ezekiel Landau in his polemic against the recital by the Hasidim of the Kabbalistic formula: *le-Shem Yihud,* "for the sake of the unification of the Holy One, blessed be He" (*Noda Biyhudah, Yoreh Deah,* No. 93) writes, "To this generation I apply the verse: "The ways of the Lord are right, and the just *(tzaddikim)* do walk in them; but the *Hasidim* do stumble in them" (Hos. 14:10)." Landau has substituted the word *Hasidim* for the word *posheim* ("transgressors") in the original (see my Hasidic Prayer, pp. 140f.). The meaning is presumably that the *tzaddikim* are the traditional, anti-Hasidic Kabbalists who do use this formula. But it is possible that Landau's pun is more subtle, intending to convey the thought that whereas the *tzaddikim,* the Hasidic masters (the Hasidic master is called the Zaddik) themselves are perfectly entitled to use this mysterious formula, because they know what it signifies, the *Hasidim,* i.e., the followers of the Zaddik, have no right to use it because they have no inkling of its meaning; this, at any rate, is how Landau's aphorism is understood by Gottleber, *Zikhronot,* vol. I, pp. 146–47.

We noted earlier (sup. p. 13) R. Moses Sofer's use of a pun in connection with the need for Halakhic reasoning to be "untainted" by Kabbalah or philosophy. Another of this author's puns did more for his battle against the Hungarian Reform rabbi, Aaron Choriner, than all the massive arguments he marshaled against Choriner. R. Moses Sofer (*Teshuvot Hatam Sofer,* vol. 6, no. 96) refers to Choriner's notepaper that had the heading, *Aaron Choriner Rabbiner,* the initial letters of which, R. Moses Sofer remarks, form the word *Aher,* "that other one," the name given to Elisha b. Abuya, the apostate referred to in the Talmud. No pun of R. Moses Sofer has had a greater influence, not always a beneficial one, than his famous *hadash asur min ha-Torah,* "anything new is forbidden by the Torah." In the polemics of both Orthodoxy and Reform this maxim is quoted repeatedly by the former in support of extreme conservatism and by the latter as evidence of the reactionary nature of the rabbinic attitude. R. Moses Sofer first uses this pun in a Responsum dated 1819 (*Hatam Sofer, Yoreh Deah,* no. 19), in which he defends Jewish customs even when they tended toward greater leniency, i.e., where Halakhic arguments can be advanced to suggest that the custom is somewhat dubious (see sup. p. 229). As an illustration Sofer refers to the fact that the authorities try hard to justify the neglect by the people of the law forbidding new produce *(hadash)* harvested before the *omer* (Lev. 23:9–14). The defense is on the grounds that the Mishnaic rule (*Orlah* 3:9), "*hadash* (i.e., new corn) *asur min ha-Torah*" does not refer to produce outside the Holy Land, which according to many, but not all, authorities is permitted even by rabbinic law. Punning on the word *hadash*, R. Moses Sofer continues that *hadash* (i.e., innovations) is forbidden everywhere by the Torah, and the older a thing is the better. Thus, originally the *Hatam Sofer* invented his pun *in connection with the law of hadash* and, moreover, he uses it there to condemn innovations that are in the direction of greater stringency not only those which result in leniency. Later on he appears to have been captivated by his own pun and employs it as a maxim to state his attitude to all reformist tendencies. In a Responsum dated 1830 (*Hatam Sofer, Orah Hayyim*, No. 28) Sofer uses this maxim against the attempts by the Reformers to remove the *bimah* from the middle of the synagogue to a place near the Ark, and in a Responsun dated 1831 (*Hatam Sofer, Even ha-Ezer* II, no. 29) against changing the name of a town for the purpose of a *get*. In R. Moses Sofer's contribution to *Elleh Divrey ha-Berit*, the collection of Orthodox rulings against the innovations of the Hamburg Temple, he does not use the maxim even though it would have been apt, because in 1819, when the work was published, he had not yet coined the phrase, certainly not in the general sense of opposition by the Torah to any innovations on principle. Because of his great authority, the maxim of the *Hatam Sofer* helped to mold attitudes toward changes in the law until, for some, the maxim became a virtual dogma of Judaism. And yet it all began as a literary pun.

Appendix B

The Problem of the Mamzer

The most stubborn and embarrassing problem traditional Jewish law has to face is that of the *mamzer*, the offspring of an adulterous or incestuous union, upon whom and upon whose descendants there is a marriage ban. First we must note the background and then proceed to examine the problem and the solutions that have been put forward by the traditional Halakhists.

THE BACKGROUND

The law of *mamzer* occurs in the book of Deut. (23:3) in the section in which are listed the persons to be excluded from the community of the Lord. AV, translating *mamzer* as "bastard," renders the verse: "A bastard shall not enter into the congregation of the Lord; even to his tenth generation shall he not enter into the congregation of the Lord." NEB renders the verse, "No descendant of an irregular union, even down to the tenth generation, shall become a member of the assembly of the Lord." The new Jewish translation, *The Torah*, renders it, "No one misbegotten shall be admitted into the congregation of the Lord; none of his descendants, even in the tenth generation, shall be admitted into the congregation of the Lord"; the footnote adding, "Meaning of the Hebrew *mamzer* uncertain; in Jewish law, the offspring of adultery or incest between Jews." The Septuagint renders *mamzer* in Deuteronomy as "offspring of a harlot," perhaps by substituting *nun* for *resh*, *mamzen* = *me-im zonah*. The Targum

257

renders the verse, "A *mamzer* shall never become pure (*lo yidkey mamzera*) so as to enter the community of the Lord; even in the tenth generation he shall not become pure so as to enter the community of the Lord." Geiger's famous suggestion that the word *mamzer* is an abbreviation of *ma-am zar*, "belonging to a foreign nation," is brilliant but untenable since not all foreigners but only those mentioned in the other verses are excluded (see Aptowitzer in HUCA, vol. 5 [1928], pp. 271–72). The only other reference to the *mamzer*, in the Bible, is in Zech. 9:6: "And a bastard shall dwell in Ashdod, and I will cut off the pride of the Philistines" (AV). NEB: "Half-breeds shall settle in Ashdod, and I will uproot the pride of the Philistines."

What does the word *mamzer* mean in these two passages and what precisely is to be understood by the *mamzer's* exclusion from the community in the Deuteronomic verse? In the rabbinic sources the *mamzer* is understood to be the offspring of a forbidden union (though opinions differ as to which type of forbidden union), and by exclusion from the community of the Lord these sources unanimously understand a ban on the *mamzer's* marriage into the community. BDB gives the etymology of *mamzer* as from the root *mzr*, "to be bad," "to be foul," and renders the word as "bastard" but specifically a child of incest. Driver, *Deuteronomy*, pp. 260–61, remarks that the word is of uncertain origin but that probably the rabbinic tradition is right in supposing the term to denote not generally one born out of wedlock but the offspring of an incestuous union, or of a marriage contracted within the prohibited degrees of affinity. Among the medieval commentators, Abraham Ibn Ezra connects the word *mamzer* with *zar*, "a stranger," and follows the rabbinic understanding of the word. However, both in his commentary to Deuteronomy and to Zechariah (here in the name of Judah Ibn Balaam) Ibn Ezra quotes an opinion that the term *mamzer* denotes a certain tribe. Nahmanides (*Commentary to the Pentateuch*, ed. Chavel, p. 455) understands *mamzer* as from *muzar*, i.e., one estranged from his kith and kin. The meaning of the verse in Zechariah is that Ashdod will be so desolate that only passing strangers will be found there. Hence the rabbinic understanding of the term, since the offspring of an adulterous or incestuous union is bound to become estranged from his parents who do not wish to acknowledge him as their child. Nahmanides quotes the opinion of R. Abbahu (JT *Kiddushin* 3:12, 64c) that *mamzer* has the meaning of *mum zar*, "strange blemish." (Cf. *Sifre*, Deuteronomy 248, ed.

Friedmann, p. 119b, and BT *Yevamot* 76b that since Scripture says *mum zar* the law applies to females as well as to males, i.e., to whomsoever the taint applies.) Kimhi in his comment to the verse in Zechariah quotes the view that *mamzer* refers to a non-Israelite tribe but also to Israelite offspring of incestuous unions, as well as to the view that it means one estranged, i.e., only Israelites will be at home in Ashdod; the Philistines who remain there will be as foreigners in their own land. As for the original meaning of exclusion from the community of the Lord, the Rabbinic interpretation certainly cannot be ruled out and is, indeed, very plausible in the context. The verse in Zechariah might seem to lend support to the view that the original meaning of *mamzer* was a member of a certain non-Israelite tribe, as does the juxtaposition in Deuteronomy of the *mamzer* with Ammon and Moab (23:4) and the permission granted to the Edomites and the Egyptians (verses 8–9). Against this, however, stands the Rabbinic tradition as well as the narrative in Gen. 19:30–38 in which the origins of Ammon and Moab are traced to the incestuous union of Lot and his daughters.

The rabbinic view is summarized in both the *Sifre* and the Mishnah. The *Sifre* (Deut. 248) first remarks that although the word *mamzer* is in the masculine, the law applies also to a female (*mamzeret*) who may not be taken in marriage by a Jewish male. The *Sifre* proceeds to define the term *mamzer:*

Who is a *mamzer?* (The offspring of) any union of near relationship (*sheer basar,* affinity or consanguinity, as in Leviticus 18:6) to which the expression *he shall not come* (to cohabit with) applies. These are the words of Rabbi Akiba. For it is said (Deut. 23:1) "A man shall not take his father's wife nor discover his father's skirt." Just as the case of a father's wife is one of near relationship to which the term *he shall not come* applies and the offspring is a *mamzer* (since the prohibition of the *mamzer* is placed in juxtaposition with that of a father's wife) so in every case of a union involving near relationship to which the term *he shall not come* applies the offspring is a *mamzer.* Simeon of Teman says: The offspring of any union for which the penalty is extirpation (*karet*) at the hand of Heaven. R. Joshua says: The offspring of any union for which the penalty is death at the hand of the Court. For it is said: "A man shall not take his father's wife. . ." and it goes on to say: "A *mamzer* shall not come. . ." Just as in the case of the father's wife it is one for which the penalty is death at the hand of the Court and the offspring is a *mamzer* so in the case of every union for which the penalty is death at the hand of the Court the offspring is a *mamzer.*

The formulation of the matter in the Mishnah (*Yevamot* 4:13 ; cf. Mishnah *Yevamot* 8:3, where it is also stated that the law of *mamzer* refers to females as well as males) obviously bears a very close resemblance to that found in the *Sifre*:

> Who is a *mamzer*? [The offspring of] any union of near relationship to which the term *he shall not come* applies. These are the words of R. Akiba. Simeon of Teman says [The offspring of] any union for which the penalty is extirpation at the hand of Heaven. And the *Halakhah* is in accord with his words. R. Joshua says [The offspring of] any union for which the penalty is death at the hand of the Court. Said R. Simeon b. Azzai: "I found a family register (*megillat yohasin*) in Jerusalem, in which it was recorded: *So-and-so is a mamzer because he is the offspring of a married woman*, which confirms the words of R. Joshua."

The proof-texts of the *Sifre* are absent from the Mishnah, and the Mishnaic glosses that the *Halakhah* is in accord with Simeon of Teman and that R. Simeon b. Azzai found the family register are absent from the *Sifre*. Otherwise, apart from insignificant variants, the Mishnah and *Sifre* are parallels. The difference between the opinion of Simeon of Teman and that of R. Joshua is clear. There are forbidden unions, such as that of a married woman and a man not her husband, for which the penalty is death at the hand of the court, and there are others, such as that of brother and sister, for which the penalty is extirpation. But what is R. Akiba's view and how does it differ from that of R. Joshua since the union with a father's wife carries the penalty of death at the hand of the court? The Babylonian Talmud (*Yevamot* 49a, cf. JT *Yevamot* 4:15, 6b–c) suggests that R. Akiba understands the second part of the verse, "nor discover his father's skirt" as referring to a woman his father had raped. She is forbidden to the son on grounds of affinity but the penalty is neither extirpation nor death by the Court but involves only a negative prohibition ("to which the term *he shall not come* applies"). Whether or not this is the difference between R. Akiba and the others is historically important but irrelevant to our inquiry since all the later masters of the law naturally accept this interpretation of the Talmud without question. (The suggestion that R. Simeon b. Azzai's "So-and-so" is a reference to Jesus and is thus a polemic against Christianity, as Dalman, *Jesus Christ*, pp. 30–33, would have it, is extremely farfetched and is not

nowadays accepted by scholars even as a conjecture; see Lauterbach: *Rabbinic Essays*, pp. 539–40).

It would thus appear that in the first half of the second century it was the unanimous opinion among the Tannaim that the
mamzer is the offspring of a forbidden union, but they still debate which type of forbidden union. Since the Mishnah states
that the *Halakhah* follows the opinion of Simeon of Teman, this
became the accepted rule in the post-Mishnaic period and, indeed, the rule is treated in an anonymous Mishnah (*Kiddushin*
3:12). Here it is also stated that the marriage of a *mamzer* to an
ordinary Jewish woman or of a *mamzeret* to an ordinary Jewish
man, though forbidden, is nonetheless valid. This does not mean
that the two may henceforth live together as man and wife, only
that the wife requires a *get* before she is free to marry another
(*kiddishin tofesin*). Thus from the end of the second century onwards in Rabbinic law a *mamzer* is considered the offspring of an
adulterous or incestuous union, and the prohibition extends to
females as well as to males. The children of a *mamzer* or a *mamzeret* are *mamzerim*, as are their children "for ever," which is said
to be the meaning of "even unto the tenth generation" (*Sifre*,
Deuteronomy 248 and frequently in the Rabbinic literature without any dissenting voice. See JT *Kiddishin* 3:12, 64a, and BT
Yevamot 78b that if either of the parents is a *mamzer* the child is
also a *mamzer*).

Further statements regarding the *mamzer*, which became standard rules in the Codes, are the following. There is no objection
whatsoever to a *mamzer* marrying a *mamzeret* (Mishnah *Kiddushin*
4:1). The second century Tannaim, R. Jose and R. Judah, debate
whether a *mamzer* may marry a female proselyte and a *mamzeret* a
male proselyte (*Kiddushin* 72b), but the final ruling is given (*Kiddushin* 73a) that such a marriage is allowed. (Cf. *Kiddushin* 67a that
the offspring of such a marriage is nonetheless a *mamzer*, and see
Baruch Epstein, *Torah Temimah* to Deut. 23:3, p. 328 note 21).
Even in those instances where a *mamzer* may marry (i.e., a *mamzeret*
or a female proselyte) the children are, as noted, *mamzerim;* the
taint being carried down throughout all the generations. There is
much debate as to whether the offspring of a Gentile and a Jewess is
a *mamzer* but the final ruling (*Yevamot* 45a–b) is that the child is not.
According to the accepted rabbinic view (e.g., in Mishnah *Kiddushin* 3:12), the offspring of a Jewish father and Gentile mother is
not Jewish. The child requires conversion to Judaism before he can

marry a Jewess, but once he has been converted he bears no taint of
mamzerut and is free to marry an ordinary Jewess. Conversely, the
offspring of a Gentile father and a Jewish mother is a Jew and, as
has been noted, is also free to marry an ordinary Jewess since he is
not a *mamzer*. It should be noted that nowhere in the rabbinic
literature is there the slightest suggestion that a child is a *mamzer*
merely as a result of his being born out of wedlock. The translation
of *mamzer* as "bastard" is consequently inaccurate so far as rabbinic
Judaism is concerned, nor is it correct to describe the *mamzer* as an
"illegitimate child"; there is no such concept in rabbinic Judaism.
The *mamzer* is the legitimate heir of his natural father and is considered to be his son for all purposes of the law (*Yevamot* 22a–b).
Although *yihus*, "good ancestry," counted for much in rabbinic
times, and in this respect the *mamzer* occupied a much lower rank in
society than other Jews, to say nothing of priests and Levites (Mishnah *Kiddushin* 4:1), the Mishnah (*Horayot* 3:8) can still rule that a
mamzer who is a scholar takes precedence over a high priest who is
an ignoramus. (On this question of the *yihus* of a *mamzer* see the
megillat yohasin, "family register," in Mishnah *Yevamot* 4:13, and in
Midrash Genesis Rabbah 98, ed. Theodor-Albeck, p. 1299. Cf.
Kiddishin 28a that one who calls his neighbor a *mamzer* is liable to a
flogging. Isserles to SA, HM 420:38 record this but it is not found
in the SA itself nor is it found in Maimonides. According to the
Tosafists to *Kiddushin* 28a s.v. *ha-kore* the reason the penalty is a
flogging is by the principle of measure for measure, since if the
victim of the insult is a *mamzer* he is liable to a flogging if he marries
an ordinary Jewess. Commenting on the Mishnaic rule about the
mamzer taking precedence over the high priest, JT *Horayot* 3:8, 48a,
observes that at first it was thought that by taking precedence is
meant only that the *mamzer* who is a scholar must be rescued from
captivity and so forth before the high priest, but that if both are
sitting together at a banquet the position of honor must be given to
the high priest; it was, however, later concluded that even here the
mamzer takes precedence if he is a scholar. For another example of
the high priest as the exact opposite of the *mamzer*, see *Yevamot*
37a). The main, but obviously very serious disability under which
the *mamzer* suffers is that he is unable to marry anyone other than a
mamzeret or a female proselyte and even then his children are *mamzerim* and their children "for ever" will suffer from the same disability.

The codes follow the Talmudic rules regarding the *mamzer* as
well as adding further rules that were either derived from Talmudic

sources by inference or were the result of medieval custom and practice. Maimonides (*Yad, Issurey Viah* 15:2) rules that the full penalty (of flogging) is only incurred if the *mamzer* both marries and cohabits with an ordinary Jewess. Cohabitation of a *mamzer* and an ordinary Jewess, though forbidden, does not alone incur the penalty. In other words, Maimonides understands the prohibition to be that of the *mamzer* marrying an ordinary Jewess and then cohabiting with her and not as a prohibition of intercourse alone. The sages of Lunel addressed a letter to Maimonides expressing their astonishment at his ruling but when Maimonides explained his opinion to them they became convinced of its correctness (see *Maggid Mishneh* ad loc. and the full reply in *Teshuvot ha-Rambam*, ed. Blau, no. 345, vol. II, pp. 617–20). On the other hand both Maimonides' critic, Abraham Ibn David, and Nahmanides take issue with Maimonides' ruling, holding that the penalty is incurred for intercourse alone even without prior marriage (*Raabad* and *Maggid Mishneh* ad loc.). The *Tur* (EH 4) records an interesting difference of opinion between Maimonides and the author of *Halakhot Gedolot* regarding a married woman who became pregnant while her husband was away overseas. According to the famous ruling by Rava Tosfaah (*Yevamot* 80b) in a case of this kind, the child is not a *mamzer* even if the husband had been absent for twelve months, since it is possible for a woman to carry a child for as long as this so that the pregnancy can be attributed to her cohabitation with her husband before he left on his voyage. Maimonides (*Yad, Issurey Viah* 15:19) declares that a fetus cannot possibly remain in its mother's womb for longer than this period so that if the husband has been away overseas for over twelve months the child is a *mamzer*. The *Halakhot Gedolot*, however, rules that even if the husband has been absent for more than twelve months the child is not a *mamzer* since it should be assumed that the husband did, in fact, return home to his wife surreptitiously during this period and the child is his. The *Shulhan Arukh* (EH 4:14) records both views and rules that since the authorities disagree the child is a doubtful *mamzer*. The view of the *Halakhot Gedolot* is, evidently, that in the case of Rava Tosfaah both husband and wife admit that the husband had not returned home during the period in question, but if it is claimed that he did return home the claim is accepted rather than have the child branded as a *mamzer*. A curious interpretation of the ruling of the *Halakhot Gedolot* (see *Rosh* to *Kiddushin*, chapter 4, beg. and *Tosafists* to *Kiddushin* 73a s.v. *mai ikka*) is that the child is assumed to be the husband's because he may have visited his wife by means of a "divine name" and then used the same magic to return swiftly from whence he came without anyone knowing of it!

Although the *mamzer* is disbarred from marriage, he is not disbarred from occupying positions of trust in the community. He can serve as a judge in civil cases (*Sanhedrin* 32b; *Kiddushin* 76a). Maimonides (*Yad, Sanhedrin* 2:9) holds that this applies even if all three judges are *mamzerim* and in this he is followed by the *Shulhan Arukh* (HM 7:2). There appears to be no objection whatsoever to a *mamzer* serving as a rabbi. However, Isserles remarks in a Responsum (*Teshuvot Rama*, No. 24) that to appoint as a Rabbi a man whose parentage is in doubt *(shetuki)* is a disgrace to the Torah. R. Moses Sofer (*Hatam Sofer* EH, Part II, No. 94; see sup., p. 15) concurs with this ruling, arguing that whereas the rabbis do say that a *mamzer* who is a scholar takes precedence over an ignorant high priest, to appoint such a man as a rabbi would only result in disrespect for the Torah since, because of the base origins of the *mamzer* people will refuse to abide by his decisions—"how much more so in our generation when, for our sins, the glory of the Torah has departed so that people say even to those of aristocratic birth, 'Remove the beam from thine own eye' how much more so to one of base parentage." (It is obvious that all this is far more a matter of expediency than of legal decision. The *Hatam Sofer* continues that there is no objection whatsoever to granting *semikhah* to a *mamzer*. He can be ordained, and it may be declared in the ordination certificate that the *mamzer* is fit to be a rabbi if he has the necessary qualification, but one should stop short of actually appointing him to serve as a rabbi. Cf. the hair-raising case in Oshri, *Teshuvot Mi-Maamakim*, vol. III, no. 9, pp. 73–86, about a woman who had escaped during the Holocaust and, believing her husband to have been murdered by the Nazis, had remarried in a foreign country. She had a child from her second husband who became a rabbi, only to learn later that her first husband was still alive. The first husband threatened to expose the *mamzer* status of the rabbi. Oshri, relying on Isserles and *Hatam Sofer*, urged the rabbi to relinquish his post, not because a *mamzer* is intrinsically disqualified from serving as a Rabbi but because of *hillul ha-shem*, "profanation of the divine name"!)

The *Shulhan Arukh* (YD 265:4 and see the standard commentaries) rules that a *mamzer* is to be circumcised and the benedictions recited as at the circumcision of any other child, but that the usual prayer for the child to grow up and be well is not recited. This goes back to R. Jacob Moellin (d. 1427), the *Maharil*, who also states that the child should be circumcised at the door of the synagogue so as to make a clear distinction between him and other Jewish children. In some places it was, and still is, the custom to add to the name given to the *mamzer* at his circumcision the additional name of *Kidor* (based on *Yoma* 83b), after the verse: "For they are a very froward generation" (Deut. 32:20)—"for a generation" = *ki dor* in Hebrew. Extremely odd and inhumane is the ruling of Ishmael ha-Kohen of Modena (1723–1811), who is otherwise considered to be something of a moderate (see EJ, vol. 9, p. 83), that it is permitted to have the word *mamzer* tattooed on the forehead of the child [*sic*] so that people will know of his base status and will not allow him to marry their daughter, the name *Kidor* being no real guarantee since he will not use it (*Zera Emet*, vol. III, no. 111). Although rabbinic law forbids the instruction of a Gentile to make a tattoo on the skin of a Jewish child, here it is permitted in order to guard against the more severe, since it is a biblical, offense of a marriage by a *mamzer*. R. Zevi Hirsch Shapira of Munkacs (*Darkhey Teshuvah* 190:1) quotes this ruling with evident approval though obviously for him the question is purely academic. The authorities disagree on whether it is the duty of a *mamzer* to engage in procreation, i.e., whether he is obliged to marry (a *mamzeret* or a female proselyte). On the one hand, the *mamzer* is still a Jew and therefore obliged to carry out all religious duties, of which the command to procreate is one. On the other hand, however, it can be argued that the Torah "whose ways are ways of pleasantness" (see sup., p. 38) would not demand the performance of a religious duty that will result in an increase of "disqualified persons"—*pesulim* (see OP, vol. I, 1 note 1). According to one reading in the minor tractate *Soferim* (I:13) a scroll of the Torah written by a *mamzer* is unfit for use in the synagogue (see SA, YD 281:4, *Pithey Teshuvah* ad loc. and Abraham B. Zevi, *Mishnat Avraham*, on the laws of the *Sefer Torah*, 18:16–18, p. 38a).

THE PROBLEM

The problem arising out of the *mamzer* law is obvious. Through no fault of his own the *mamzer* and even his remote descendants acquire the taint that prevents them from marrying except in the rare instances where marriage is permitted (to a *mamzeret* or a female proselyte), and even in these instances the children are still *mamzerim*. This is the only instance in Jewish law where children suffer for the sins of their parents, and even though the law does not necessarily see it as a penalty the fact remains that it is a disability of the most serious nature, intolerable within a legal system that prides itself on its passion for justice. That the law does not necessarily see it as a penalty can be inferred from the fact that the child is a *mamzer* even where no sin at all was committed by the parents, e.g., where the adulterous union took place without either party knowing that it was adulterous, such as when it was thought that the woman's *get* from her former husband was perfectly valid and it was later discovered that, through an error of the court, the *get* turned out to be invalid. Cf. Mishnah *Yevamot* 3:10 and 10:1; Maimonides, *Yad, Issurey Viah* 15:1. Mishnah *Hagigah* 1:7 states, "R. Simeon b. Menasya said: What is the meaning of: 'That which is crooked cannot be made straight' (Eccles. 1:15)? It refers to one who had connection with an *ervah* and begat by her a *mamzer*." It is somewhat strange that in *Yevamot* 22b, quoting this Mishnah, it seems to be taken for granted that the parents of the *mamzer* must have been guilty of sin (see note of Strashun in Vilna edition ad loc.). In a nonlegal context, however, it is occasionally suggested that the base status of the *mamzer* and his descendants was intended as a penalty and was there as a deterrent to the adulterers, see, e.g., Maimonides, *Guide*, III, 49, who adds another reason for the law of *mamzer*, that the noble people of Israel has to be protected from any adulteration of its purity. Cf. *Sefer ha-Hinakh*, no. 560, "The very conception of the *mamzer* is exceedingly evil, having been brought about in impurity, abominable intention and counsel of sin and there is no doubt that the nature of the parent is concealed in the child. Consequently, God, in His love, has kept the holy people away from him (the *mamzer*) just as He has separated us and kept us far away from all that is evil." The strange status of the *mamzer* is also discussed in a semilegal context by Rabbi Ben Zion Uziel (*Mishpetey Uziel*, EH, no. 3). Uziel was asked what would happen if the natural parents of the *mamzer* repented of their sin and did so, moreover, out of the love of God, which would have the effect, so the rabbis say, of converting their sin into merit. The innocent child should then no longer be considered to be the fruit of a sinful union. The sinners themselves would now bask in their newly won glory and yet the poor child would still be branded a *mamzer*. Uziel replies that repentance, even when performed out of love, only has the effect of purifying the sinful soul, not the sinful act itself. The *mamzer*'s base status should not be seen as a punishment for the sin of his parents but is rather a quasi-physical taint. The sinful act taints automatically the child born of it. The child is, indeed, innocent but such is life that the innocents do suffer for the guilty as when an innocent victim of a vicious assault is maimed for life. (For contemporary Orthodox attempts at justifying the *mamzer* law see I. Freilich in the journal *Or ha-Mizrah*, vol. 20 (1970–1971), pp. 265–70 and D. Mazeh in the same journal vol. 21 (1971–1972), pp. 198–200.)

In a late Midrash (Levi. Rabbah 32:8 and, in much shorter form, Eccles. Rabbah 4:1) there is found this startling comment on the verse: "But I returned and considered all the oppressions that were done under the sun; and behold the tears of such that were oppressed, and they had no comforter; and on the side of their oppressers there was power, but they had no comforter" (Eccles. 4:1). "Daniel the Tailor interpreted this verse as referring to *mamzerim*. 'And behold the tears of such that were oppressed.' The parents of these have sinned, why should these poor folk be obliged to suffer? So the father of this one has cohabited with an *ervah*, what sin has he (the child) committed and why should he suffer? 'And they had no comforter; and on the side of their oppressors there was power,' on the side of the Great Sanhedrin of Israel who come against them with the power of the Torah and keep them afar because Scripture says, "A *mamzer* shall not enter into the congregation of the Lord." 'And they had no comforter.' The Holy One, blessed be He, says, It is up to me to comfort them. For in this world they are unfit (to marry) but in the World to Come. . . ." (Daniel Hayyata is only mentioned in one other place, Genesis Rabbah 64:7, where he seems to be protesting against the institution of slavery! He was not evidently a rabbi. It is possible that this was originally an antirabbinic polemic that has somehow slipped into the Midrashic texts?) This idea that the *mamzer* will automatically become pure in the Messianic age is said to have been debated by R. Meir and R. Jose, the former holding that there is no purification for the *mamzer* in the Messianic age, the latter holding that in the future age the *mamzerim* will again become pure (*Tosefta, Kiddushin* 5:4, ed. Zuckermandel, p. 342). The debate is referred to in both the Palestinian Talmud (JT *Kiddushin* 3:13, 64d) and the Babylonian (*Kiddushin* 72b). In the former, R. Huna says in the name of R. Joseph that the ruling does not follow R. Jose, but in the latter R. Judah says in the name of Samuel that the ruling does follow R. Jose and the *mamzerim* will become pure in the Messianic age and here R. Joseph (!) accepts this ruling. (Rabbi Z. E. Michaelson, *Tirosh ve-Yitzhor*, no. 123, raises the question of how this can be squared with the normative rabbinic view that the Torah is immutable. The same question is discussed by Margaliot, *Nitzutzey Or*, pp. 132–33. Possibly, the meaning is that the law of *mamzer* was only *given in the first instance* for the pre-Messianic age so that it is not a question of any law being abolished. Michaelson refers to *Rashba* who deals with the question in his Novellae to *Kiddushin* 72b. *Rashba* here advances the theory that the *mamzerim* who will be born after the Messiah has come will not become pure again. It is only for those who were born before the Messianic age that a special, and thus only temporary, dispensation will be granted.)

There are also a number of indications in the Talmudic literature that the rabbis sought whenever possible to minimize the baneful effects of the *mamzer* legislation. Although there are numerous references to the *mamzer* and detailed discussions regarding his status, these are largely academic, of the same order as discussions concerning the sacrificial system in the period long after the destruction of the Temple. There are comparatively few references to actual cases of *mamzerut*. (Cf. *Yevamot* 20b where it is taken for granted that a woman is rarely a *mamzeret*). In the case of a woman known to be unfaithful to her husband the child she bears is still ruled not to be a *mamzer* because "the majority of acts of intercourse are those of the husband" (*Sotah* 27a; cf. *Hullin* 11b; Maimonides, *Yad, Issurey Viah* 15:20; SA, EH 4:15). This ruling, which is the accepted one, means that there can be only a few cases in which the child can be known to be a *mamzer*. (It is generally agreed that in a case of artificial insemination by a donor—AID—the child is not a *mamzer* since there has been no act of forbidden intercourse, see OP, vol. I, to EH 4:13, note 39:3, pp. 129–30.) There is even an opinion (JT *Kiddushin* 3:12, 64c) that a *mamzer* who is not known to be definitely such will not be allowed by God to live for more than thirty days, i.e., so that except in notorious cases there need be no fear of contracting a marriage with a *mamzer* or *mamzeret*. Even if it is known that at one time a *mamzer* had married into a family, that family does not become tainted since "a family that has suffered an admixture has suffered an admixture," i.e., there is no longer any need to do anything about it. This is said to be the meaning of: "Silver purifies *mamzerim*" i.e., *mamzerim* use their money to buy their way into the best families and thus their taint is gradually absorbed and becomes nonexistent (*Kiddishin* 72a and Rashi ad loc.; *cf. Kiddushin* 76a and *Ketubot* 26a). It also appears that no investigation was normally made into the family background of one who wishes to marry (*Yevamot* 46a and *Tosafists* ad loc. and *Tosafists* to *Yevamot* 47a s.v. *be-muhakek*). In another Talmudic passage (*Gittin* 89a) it is implied that if there is a mere rumor that a woman is a *mamzeret* it must be completely ignored. (On the question of an unknown *mamzer* see BT *Yevamot* 78b where a distinction is made between a completely unknown *mamzer*, whom God does not allow to survive at all; a known *mamzer*, who is allowed to survive in the normal way, and one who is "known and not known," whose taint is only allowed to be continued for three generations. Is there some confusion here between the *three* generations of BT and the *thirty* days of JT? Cf. the narrative in BT *Yevamot* ibid. about R. Ammi who issued a proclamation that a man is a *mamzer* in order that the man should be allowed by God to survive because his status would no longer be in doubt.) The medieval authorities (see *Tosafists* to *Zevahim* 45a) hold that the practical consequences of the ruling, as noted, that *mamzerim* will become pure in the Messianic age, are that even now there is no need to keep apart from families whose genealogy is unknown. Isserles (to EB 2:15) formulated it as follows: "If one who is unfit has become mixed in a particular family, then once it has become mixed it has become mixed and whoever knows of the disqualification is not permitted to disclose it and must leave well alone since all families in which there has been an admixture will become pure in the future."

It is relevant here to note how the laws regarding the doubtful *mamzer* were interpreted leniently. The two types are *asufi*, the foundling, and *shetuki*, the child who knows his mother but not his father (Mishnah *Kiddushin* 4:1 and 2). The *asufi* is held to be pure and not a *mamzer* if the circumstances in which he has been found are such as to indicate that his parents wanted him to survive, see *Kiddushin* 73a–b. In the case of the *shetuki*, the mother's declaration that the father was pure or, for that matter, a non-Jew, suffices to render the child pure and no *mamzer*, see *Kiddushin* 74a. (For two illuminating examples of how the post-Talmudic authorities sought to confine the taint of *mamzerut*, see S. M. Passamaneck, "Some Mediaeval Problems in *Mamzerut*".)

The post-Talmudic authorities follow the Talmudic principles in order to free suspicious cases from the taint of *mamzerut* even where the grounds for suspicion are extremely strong, e.g., Benjamin Zeev of Arta (sixteenth century), Responsa, *Binyamin Zeev*, vol. I, EH, no. 136, where a mother confesses that her son was not her husband's; Samuel di Medina of Salonika (1508–1589), Responsa *Maharashdam*, EH, no. 138, where a single witness testifies that a man is a *mamzer*; Mordecai ha-Levi of Egypt (d. 1684), Responsa, *Darkhey Noam*, EH, No. 43 who remarks that the Talmudic teachers removed the taint of *mamzerut* by resorting to "strange things remote from nature"; R. Akiba Eger, Responsa, two cases, Nos. 123 and 128; *Hatam Sofer*, EH, No. 10, in the case of a woman who had a child many years after her sick husband had left her. In this last case R. Moses Sofer decides that the child is not a *mamzer* because of the principle of *safek safeka*, "double doubt," i.e., the father may have been a Gentile and even if the father was a Jew the husband may have died before the woman conceived. This author stresses the need to find means of freeing a person from the taint of *mamzerut* and compares it to the urgency with which the tradition treats cases of *agunah*. Rabbi A. I. Kook, *Ezrat Kohen*, no. 8, pp. 11–26, deals with a similar case and is similarly lenient, and Rabbi Moses Feinstein, *Iggerot Moshe*, EH, part III, no. 8, pp. 424–25, rules that a mother is not believed to declare that she had been previously married so that her son from her second husband is a *mamzer*. The same lenient attitude as adopted by Rabbi Aaron Walkin, *Zekan Aharon*, no. 65. (Cf. the very interesting Responsa of Obadiah Hadayya: *Yaskil Avdi*, vol. 2, EH, No. 3 and Mayer Lerner: *Hadar ha-Karmel*, vol. 2, EH, no. 1.)

The *mamzer* problem has become especially acute in recent years. In the State of Israel the marriage laws are administered entirely by the rabbinic courts. There is no civil marriage and consequently no way in which the *mamzer* can disregard the law that bans him from marrying. In addition, records are, according to rumor, kept by the rabbinic courts of known *mamzerim* (e.g., where a woman had been divorced from her husband in other countries without receiving a *get* so that any children she has afterwards are *mamzerim*) so that it is extremely difficult, if not impossible, for the *mamzer* to slip through the net of the law. In countries outside Israel in which civil marriages and divorces are available, women not infrequently are divorced without receiving a *get* and then remarry, especially when the husband refuses to give the *get*. Under these conditions, her children from her second husband would be *mamzerim*. The Reform *get*, even when it is resorted to, as well as, increasingly, the conservative *get*, even though the latter is drawn up according to the full requirements of the Halakhah, are both considered to be invalid by the Orthodox. As noted, once the taint of *mamzerut* has been established it is carried on from generation to generation. There is thus a frightening proliferation of technical *mamzerim* on a scale that is completely unknown or even envisaged in the classical period of the Halakhah. In addition to the terrible hardships for the individuals concerned, there is now a real danger of a group emerging in Jewry with whom the Orthodox cannot intermarry. The very last thing Judaism now needs is the emergence of a caste system. It is only fair to remark that the Orthodox Halakhists are keenly aware of the problem and that various remedies have been suggested within the framework of the traditional Halakhah. We now examine these proposed remedies.

REMEDIES

Four remedies have been suggested or acted upon by Orthodox rabbis in an attempt finally to solve the *mamzer* problem. These are recorded in turn.

The Silberg Proposal

(For this proposal see the paper *Panim el Panim*, issues Iyar 5 and Sivan 4, 5731, 1971). We have seen that according to Maimonides (*Issurey Viah* 15:2) the offense of *mamzerut* is only incurred if there is both a formal marriage (*kiddushin*) and intercourse. In that case why does Maimonides still rule that intercourse on its own is forbidden? The answer (see *Maggid Mishneh* and *Kesef Mishneh ad loc*) is that Maimonides follows here another ruling of his (*Yad, Ishut* 1:4) that a concubine (*pilegesh*) is only permitted to a king, not to a commoner. Nahmanides (see *Kesef Mishneh* to both passages) disagrees with both rulings. According to Nahmanides, the prohibition of *mamzer* applies to intercourse on its own even without prior *kiddushin*, but a *pilegesh* is permitted even to a commoner. On this basis, the late Judge Silberg, a jurist and Halakhist of note in the State of Israel, put forward his solution to the *mamzer* problem. The *mamzer* can take his partner as a "common-law wife," living with her as man and wife but without any formal *kiddushin*. According to Nahmanides this is permitted so far as the *pilegesh* question is concerned and according to Maimonides it is permitted so far as

the *mamzer* question is concerned. But the Silberg proposal was
really a nonstarter. In the present climate of opinion, the Orthodox rabbis were not prepared to allow any form of civil marriage, even of this limited kind for the few couples concerned.
Moreover, there would still remain the problem of the children
of the union who would still be *mamzerim*. But even from the
purely legal point of view, the Silberg proposal is dubious and
was rejected by the rabbis. Although one does find occasionally
in Jewish law that grounds for leniency are based on the views of
two different authorities, each contributing a reason for permissiveness, this cannot be applied here. Both Maimonides and
Nahmanides would reject the Silberg proposal: Maimonides on
the grounds of *pilegesh*, Nahmanides on the grounds of *mamzer*.
How, then, can one think of invoking the authority of
Maimonides on the *mamzer* question and that of Nahmanides on
the *pilegesh* question? An attempt to do this is to try to have one's
cake and eat it too, or, in the conventional language of the
Halakhists (based on *Pesahim* 78a), to produce a bond which gives
the right to both parties in a dispute.

Nullification of the First Marriage

Cases of *mamzerut* from incestuous unions are extremely rare.
If, say, a brother and sister lived together the problem of the
paternity of the child would probably be solved so as to free the
child from the taint of *mamzerut*, i.e., that the father was not the
brother but a stranger. In cases of suspected incest this is the
line the Halakhists generally take; see, e.g., the Responsum of
David Hoffmann, *Melammed le-Hoil*, vol. III, No. 2, pp. 1–3, in
a case in which there was strong circumstantial evidence that a
child had been born as a result of intercourse between a man and
his wife's sister while the wife was still alive, and the Responsa
of R. Yitzhak Elhanan Spektor, *Eyn Yitzhak*, EH, no. 8 (and see
nos. 6 and 7 where this famous Russian authority finds adequate
grounds for refusing to declare a child to be a *mamzer* even
though there were strong grounds for suspicion). Since, therefore, all cases of actual *mamzerut* arise from adulterous unions,
the obvious legal remedy is to seek to invalidate the first marriage. If the Halakhist can succeed in this the woman concerned
is seen retrospectively to have been no married woman and,
therefore, not guilty technically of the sin of adultery with the
consequence that her children from the second union would not
be *mamzerim*. Examples of marriage invalidation by the Halakh-

ists for the purpose of removing the taint of *mamzerut* are where it can be reasonably supposed that the first husband was insane at the time of his marriage but did not disclose it to his bride; where the first marriage was only a civil marriage or a Reform marriage; and where it can be shown that in the first marriage the husband was a convert to Judaism who had not been converted according to the Halakhah. This latter procedure was adopted by Chief Rabbi Goren in the Langer case. Rabbi Goren declared the Langer brother and sister not to be *mamzerim*, and he officiated himself at the wedding. His argument was based on the demonstration that their mother's first husband, who had been converted to Judaism in Poland, was never properly converted. Thus, when the marriage took place he was still a non-Jew and the marriage was invalid in Jewish law. Rabbi Goren's ruling occasioned much fierce debate and received vehement condemnation, but he staunchly defended his ruling in a learned treatise composed specially for the purpose *(Pesak Din be-Inyan ho-Ah ve-he-Ahot)*. (Contemporary Halakhists are divided on whether a *get* is required where there has only been a civil marriage, see the references in "Appendix on Civil Marriage" in Boaz Cohen, *Law and Tradition in Judaism*, pp. 239–43. Cf. I. England, "The Relationship Between Religion and State in Israel." England, p. 187, points to the dangers of schism in the Jewish nation as a result of prohibited *connubium* because of the *mamzer* laws: "Such a schism, by definition permanently irreperable, would be a national disaster which even the secular view cannot ignore." He states that if civil marriage is held not to be valid in the eyes of the Halakhah the schism can be avoided by the State recognizing civil marriage. He continues, "The result of such a situation would be that the State would be interested in the religious authorities *not* recognizing the institution of civil marriage." Cf. Feinstein, *Iggerot Moshe*, EH, part II, no. 19, p. 322, who observes that even if a *get* should be demanded in order to dissolve a civil marriage there is no question that in the absence of a *get* the children of the second marriage are not *mamzerim*. For a similar ruling, see the same author's *Iggerot Moshe*, EH, part I, No. 80, pp. 190–92, where he argues for the invalidation of a marriage on the grounds that the husband was insane and did not disclose it at the time of the marriage, and see *Iggerot Moshe*, EH, part II, nos. 45 and 46, pp. 489–90. On the invalidation of Reform marriages see Feinstein, *Iggerot Moshe*, EH, part I, nos. 76 and 77, pp. 177–80 and EH, part III, no. 25, p. 447; I. J. Weiss, *Minhat Yitzhak,* vol. II, no. 66, pp. 132–33. However,

the famous Galician Halakhist Shalom Mordecai Schwadron
takes it for granted that Reform marriages are valid and categorically rejects as absurd the notion that no *get* is required for them
to be dissolved, see Responsa *Maharsham*, vol. II, nos. 110 and
167. Cf. M. Steinberg, "*Siddur Kiddushin* by a Reform Rabbi".)

Obviously, however, extreme remedies of this kind are only
available in the minority of cases where there are reasonable
grounds for invalidating the first marriage. No solution is offered
in those many cases in which the first marriage cannot really be
questioned as to its complete validity.

Purification of the Mamzer

A remedy for the *mamzer* to "purify" his seed from the taint of
mamzerut is mentioned in the Mishnah (*Kiddushin* 3:13). According to R. Tarfon the *mamzer* can take a Canaanite slave girl (with
whom he is allowed to live, this being permitted to him but not
to a "pure" Jew) and have children from her. The children of a
Canaanite slave girl (i.e., a Gentile girl converted to Judaism but
not to the full status of a Jewess, only to the partial status enjoyed by "Canaanite" male and female slaves) have the status of
Canaanite slaves but are not *mamzerim;* this taint only applies to
full Jews. The owner of the slave-girl is also the owner of the
children she bears and he has the right to set them free. If he
does set them free, the children become full Jews. Thus, the
mamzer can arrange in this manner to have slave children who
have no taint of *mamzerut* and if the owner (he can be the "husband" himself) cooperates by freeing the children they become
full Jews and free not only from their state of bondage but also
from the taint of *mamzerut*. The Talmud (*Kiddushin* 69a) argues
that R. Tarfon intended his remedy to be applied even *ab initio*
and the law follows this ruling. This remedy is quoted by
Maimonides (*Yad, Issurey Viah* 15:3–4) and accepted as law in the
Shulhan Arukh (EH 4:20). Thus, in order to "purify" his seed the
mamzer (there is no way out for the *mamzeret* since if she marries
a Gentile slave the children are Jewish and hence remain tainted)
can live with a Gentile girl who is willing to be formally
"bought" as a slave-girl and converted to this status. The *mamzer*
can then live with her and have children by her. The formal
owner (this can be, as noted the "husband" himself) can then set
the children free and the taint of *mamzerut* will have gone. The
later authorities debate, however, whether this remedy can be resorted to in lands in which slavery is illegal. The principle here

is that the rule "the law of the kingdom is law" (*dina de-malhuta dina*, see sup., p. 91) might invalidate the whole procedure (see OP, vol. I, to EH 4:20, note 85, p. 158). This bizarre remedy was advocated as a distinct possibility in the case of a number of young men in Hungary whose mothers had remarried in the belief that their first husbands had been murdered by the Nazis, only to discover later that the previous husbands were still alive so that the young men born from the second marriages were *mamzerim*. The remedy was discussed by the Halakhists and some of them proposed its formal adoption (assuming that girls would be found willing to become formal "slaves"), but nothing came of it and it is unlikely to find any advocates now (see the discussion in Breisch, *Helkat Yaakov*, vol. 3, nos. 91–93 and in Weiss, *Minhat Yitzhak*, vol. 5, nos. 46–52, pp. 142–152). This says nothing of the ethical question involved; such a cure would be worse than the disease.

Allowing the Mamzer to Be "Lost"

As we have seen earlier there is ample Talmudic warrant for a refusal to investigate too closely into the antecedents of applicants for marriage. Since the majority of Jews who wish to marry are not *mamzerim* the rule of probability can and should be relied upon. There are even rumors, quite persistent, that in prewar days some Orthodox Rabbis would drop broad hints to known *mamzerim* that they should emigrate to a community where they were not known and marry there. It is not possible to pin down these rumors and it is doubtful whether Orthodox rabbis would ever have done this since the *mamzer* himself knows that he is tainted and for him the prohibition still applies, apart from the moral question of whether it is right to trick the brides involved. Nevertheless, a very good case can be made out for at least avoiding any investigation the purpose of which is to uncover the identity of *mamzerim.* This is certainly the norm among the Orthodox in most parts of the United States where cases of *mamzerut* hardly ever occur because the Orthodox rabbis are intentionally perfunctory in their investigations. The keeping of registers of *mamzerim* certainly seems to be in complete variance with the whole tendency of Talmudic and medieval legislation in this matter.

List of Abbreviations

AV	Authorized Version of the Bible
b.	son of, *ben*
Bah	*Bayit Hadash*, Joel Sirkes
BDB	Brown, Driver and Briggs
BH	*Baer Hetev*
BT	Babylonian Talmud
DS	*Dikdukey Soferim*, Rabbinovics
EJ	*Encyclopedia Judaica*
ET	*Encyclopedia Talmudit*
HUCA	*Hebrew Union College Annual*
JE	*Jewish Encyclopedia*
JJS	*Journal of Jewish Studies*
JLA	*Jewish Law Annual*
JQR	*Jewish Quarterly Review*
JT	*Jerusalem Talmud*
KS	*Kiryat Sefer*
Maharik	Joseph Colon
NEB	New English Bible
OP	*Otzar ha-Posekim*
OY	*Otzar Yisrael*
PT	*Pithey Teshuvah*
R.	Rabbi
Rabad	Abraham ibn David
Radbaz	David Ibn Abi Zimra
Rama	Moses Isserles
Ran	Nissim of Gerona
Rashba	Solomon Ibn Adret
Rashbash	Solomon Duran

Ribash	Isaac Perfet
Rid	Isaiah Di Trani
Rif	Isaac Alfasi
Ritba	Yom Tov Ishbili
Rosh	Asher b. Yehiel
SA	*Shulhan Arukh*
	OH *Orah Hayyim*
	YD *Yoreh Deah*
	EH *Even ha-Ezer*
	HM *Hoshen Mishpat*
Semag	Moses of Coucy
Shakh	Shabbetai ha-Kohen
Shelah	Isaiah Horowitz
ST	*Shaarey Teshuvah*
Taz	David ha-Levi
Yad	Maimonides' *Mishneh Torah*

Bibliography

TALMUDIC SOURCES

Mishnah, ed. Warsaw, 1882.

Babylonian Talmud, ed. Romm. Vilna 1933.

Jerusalem Talmud, ed. Romm. Vilna 1933.

———. ed. Krotoschin, 1886.

Tosefta, ed. Zuckermandel. Pasewalk, 1881.

Mekhilta, ed. Weiss. Vienna, 1865.

———. ed. Horovitz-Rabin. Frankfurt, 1931.

Sifra, ed. Weiss. Vienna, 1862.

Sifre, ed. Friedmann. Vienna, 1864.

———. ed. Horovitz. Leipzig, 1917.

Tractate Makkot of Babylonian Talmud, ed. Friedmann. Vienna, 1865.

Pesikta de-Rav Kahana, ed. B. Mandelbaum. New York, 1962.

Midrash ha-Gadol to Genesis, ed. M. Margoliot. Jerusalem, 1975; to Deuteronomy ed. S. Fisch. Jerusalem, 1975.

Minor tractate Derekh Eretz, ed. M. Higger. New York, 1935.

Minor tractate *Kutim*, ed. M. Higger. New York, 1935.

SECONDARY WORKS

Abohab, Samuel. *Sefer ha-Zikhronot*. New York, 1979.

Abraham b. Nathan of Lunel. *Sefer ha-Manhig*. Edited by Y. Rafael. Jerusalem, 1978.

Abraham b. Zevi. *Mishnat Avraham*, Zhitomer. 1868.

Abraham Ibn David. Strictures to Maimonides' *Yad*, various eds.

Abudraham, David. *Sefer Abudraham*. Edited by Wertheimer. Jerusalem, 1963.

Adret, Solomon Ibn. *Teshuvot ha-Rashba*. Lemberg, 1811.

———. *Hiddushey ha-Rashba*. Lemberg, 1860.

Agus, Jacob B. *Guideposts in Modern Judaism*. New York, 1954.

Agush, H. H. *Marheshet*. Bilgoraj, 1931.

Albeck, Hanoch. *Mavo le-Mishnah*. Jerusalem, 1939.

Alfasi, R. Isaac. in Babylonian Talmud. Edited by Romm. Vilna, 1933.

Alfasi, Y. *Toledot ha-Hasidut*. Tel-Aviv, 1959.

Allon, Gedaliah. *Mehkarim be-Toledot Yisrael*. Tel-Aviv, 1958.

Amiel, M. A. *Derashot el-Ammi*. Warsaw, 1929.

———. *ha-Middot le-Heker ha-Halakhah*, 3 vols. Jerusalem, 1972–73.

Appel, Gersion. *A Philosophy of Mitzvot*. New York, 1975.

Arik, Meir. *Imrey Yosher*, Responsa, I. Munkacs, 1913; II, Cracow, 1925.

Arzi, A. "The Interweaving of Aggadah into the Halakhah" (Hebrew) in the Jubilee Volume for Albeck, pp. 41–51. Jerusalem, 1963.

Asher b. Yehiel. *Rosh* in Babylonian Talmud. Edited by Romm. Vilna, 1933.

———. *Teshuvot ha-Rosh*. Jerusalem, 1971.

Asher ha-Kohen. *Orhot Hayyim*, printed at end of *Siddur Ishey Yisrael*. Tel-Aviv, 1968.

Ashkenazi, Bezalel. *Shitta Mekubbetzet*, var. eds.

Ashkenazi, Judah. *Baer Hetev* to *Shulhan Arukh*, var. eds.

Ashkenazi, Solomon. *Dorot be-Yisrael*. Tel-Aviv, 1975.

Ashkenazi, Zevi. *Haham Tzevi*, Responsa. Amsterdam, 1712.

Atlas, Samuel. "Legal Fictions in the Talmud" in Louis Ginzberg Jubilee Volume. New York, 1945, Hebrew section.

———. *Netivim be-Mishpat ha-Ivri*. New York, 1978.

Avineri, I. "Rashi's Style' (Hebrew). In *Rashi: His Teachings and Personality* (Hebrew), edited by Federbusch, pp. 75–112. New York, 1958.

Azulai, Hayyim Joseph David. *Shem ha-Gedolim*. Warsaw, 1921.

Babad, Joseph. *Minhat Hinnukh*, var. eds and with *Sefer ha-Hashlamah*. New York, 1952.

Babad, Menahem Manish. *Havatzelet ha-Sharon*. Bilgoraj, 1931–1938.

Bacharach, Jair Hayyim. *Havvot Yair*, Responsa. Frankfurt am Main, 1699.

Baer, I. F. *"Yesodot ha-Historiim shel ha-Halakhah." Zion*, 17 (1951–52): 1–55.

———. *Yisrael ba-Amim*. Jerusalem, 1955.

Baer, Seligmann. *Siddur Avodat Yisrael*. Rödelheim, 1868.

Baneth, Mordecai. *Parashat Mordekhai*, Responsa. Marsighet, 1889.

Baron, S. W. *The Jewish Community*. Philadelphia, 1945.

———. *A Social and Religious History of the Jews*. New York 1951–.

Barr, James. *Fundamentalism*. London, 1977.

Benjamin Zeev of Arta. *Binyamin Zeev*. Jerusalem, 1969.

Berlin, Meir. *"Halakhot ha-Meyusadot al Tekhunot ha-Nefesh."* In *Azkarah*, Memorial Volume for Rav Kook, vol. IV, pp. 209–220. Jerusalem, 1937.

Berlin, Saul. *Besamim Rosh*. Cracow, 1881.

Berliner, Abraham. *Ueber d. Einfluss ersten hebr. Buchdrucks auf d. Cultus v. Cultur d. Jüden*. Frankfurt am Main, 1896.

———. *Ketavim Nivharim*, Jerusalem, 1969.

Bertinoro, Obadiah. Commentary to the Mishnah, var. eds.

Bleich, J. David. *Contemporary Halakhic Problems*. New York, 1977.

———. "Settlement in Egypt." *Tradition* 17, no. 2 (Spring 1978): 99–104.

Blidstein, Gerald. *Honor Thy Father and Mother: Filial Responsibility in Jewish Law and Ethics*. New York, 1975.

Bloch, Abraham. *"Halakhah ve-Aggadah" Peri Etz Hayyim* (1938): 59–64.

Bloch, Joseph L. *Shiurey Daat*. New York, 1949.

———. *Shiurey Halakhah*. Tel-Aviv, 1958.

Bloch, Joseph S. *Israel and the Nations*. Berlin and Vienna, 1927.

Bornstein, Abraham, of Sochachov. *Egley Tal*. Pietrikow, 1921.

———. Avney Nezer, Responsa. Tel-Aviv/Jerusalem, 1964–.

Braun, Solomon. *Shearim ha-Metzuyanim ba-Halakhah*. New York, 1949; *Supplementary Volume*. New York/Jerusalem, 1978.

Breisch, T. *Helkat Yaakov*. vol. 3. Bene Berak, 1966.

Bronrot, H. M. "Travelling by Aeroplane on the Sabbath" (Hebrew). *Sinai* 8 (January–February 1944): 129–35.

Brown, F. Driver. S. R., and Briggs, C. A. *Hebrew and English Lexicon of the Old Testament*. Oxford, 1906.

Carmilly-Weinberger, M. *Censorship and Freedom of Expression in Jewish History*. New York, 1977.

Chajes, Zevi Hirsch. Notes to the Talmud in Romm Edition of the Babylonian Talmud, Vilna, 1933.

———. *Kol Sifrey Maharatz Chajes*. Jerusalem, 1958.

Cohen, Boaz. *Law and Tradition in Judaism*. New York, 1959.

———. *Kuneros ha-Teshuvot*. Budapest, 1930; Jerusalem, 1970 (photo-copy).

Cohen, Gerson D. "Esau as Symbol in Early Medieval Thought." In *Jewish Medieval and Renaissance Studies*, edited by A. Altmann, pp. 19–48. Cambridge, Mass.: Harvard University Press, 1967.

Cohn, H. H., ed. *Jewish Law in Ancient and Modern Israel*. New York, 1971.

Colon, Joseph. *Teshuvot Maharik*. Lemberg, 1789.

Copperman, Judah. *Bal Tosif: The Immutability of the Torah*. Jerusalem, 1962.

Da Fano, Menahem Azarish. *Teshuvot*, Responsa. Jerusalem, 1963.

Dalman, G. *Jesus Christ in the Talmud. Midrash cod Zohar*. Cambridge, 1893.

Da Silva, Hezekiah. *Peri Hadash* to *Shulhan Arukh*, var. eds.

David ha-Levi. *Turey Zahaz* to *Shulhan Arukh*, var. eds.

David Ibn Abi Zimra. *Teshuvot Radbaz*. Warsaw, 1862.

Davidson, Israel. *"Hilkhot Shehitah be-Haruzim le-ha-Raban"* in *Sefer ha-Yovel* for R. Simeon Shkop, pp. 81–88.

Davis, M. *The Emergence of Conservative Judaism*. New York, 1963.

De-Friess, Benjamin. *Mehkarim be-Sifrut ha-Talmud*. Jerusalem, 1968.

Delmedigo, Joseph Solomon. *Matzref le-Hokhmah*. Edited with notes by D. Torsh. Odessa, 1865.

Dembitzer, H. N. *Kelilat Yofi*. Cracow, 1888.

De Vidas, Elijah. *Reshit Hokhmah, Shaar ha-Ahavah*, Tel-Aviv, n.d.

Di Boton, Abraham. *Lehem Mishneh*, Commentary to Maimonides' *Yad*, var. eds.

Dichowsky, S. "Rescue and Treatment—Halakhic Scales of Priorities." In Dine Israel. Vol. VII. Hebrew section; pp. 45–66.

Di Medina, Samuel. *Teshuvot Maharashdam*. Salonika, 1797–8.

Domb, I. *The Transformation*. London, 1978.

Dressner, Samuel H. *The Zaddik*. New York, n.d.

Driver, G. R. *A Critical and Exegetical Commentary on Deuteronomy*. Edinburgh, 1951.

Duchinsky, C. "May a Woman Act as Shoheteth?" In *Occident and Orient: Gaster Anniversary Volume*, edited by B. Schindler and A. Marmorstein, pp. 96–106. London, 1936.

Duran, Solomon b. Simeon. *Teshuvot Rashbash*. Leghorn, 1742.

Eger, Akiba. *Tosefot* to Mishnah. Warsaw edition, 1882.

———. Responsa. Warsaw, 1892.

Ehrenfeld, Samuel. *Hatan Sofer*, Responsa. Paks, 1912.

Eisenstadt, Abraham. *Pithey Teshuvah* to *Shulhan Arukh*, var. eds.

Eisenstein, J. D. *Otzar Dinim u-Minhagim*. New York, 1919.

Elbogen, I. *ha-Tefillah be-Yisrael*, trans. of *Der Judische Gottesdienst*. Edited by I. Adler, A. Negev, J. Petuchowski, H. Schirmann. Tel-Aviv, 1972.

Eleazar of Worms. *Rokeah*. Edited by B. Schneerson. Jerusalem, 1967.

Eliezer of Metz. *Sefer Yereim*. Vilna, 1881.

Elijah Gaon of Vilna. *Biur ha-Gra* in *Shulhan Arukh*, var. eds.

Elleh Divrey ha-Berit. Altona, 1819.

Elon, Menahem. "*Takkanot*" in *EJ*, vol. 15, pp. 712–28.

―――. "Jewish Law and Modern Medicine." In *Jewish Law in Ancient and Modern Israel*. Edited by H. H. Cohn, pp. 131–42. New York, 1971.

―――. *ha-Mishpat ha-Ivri*, 2d ed. Jerusalem, 1978.

Emden, Jacob. *Sheilot Yaavetz*. Lemberg, 1884.

Engel, Joseph. *Lekah Tov*. Warsaw, 1892.

―――. *Tziyonim la-Torah*. Pietrikow, 1906.

―――. *Bet ha-Otzar*. Pietrikow, 1903–1908.

―――. *Ben Porat*, Responsa. Pietrikow, 1907-Cracow, 1912.

England, I. "The Relationship Between Religion and State in Israel" in *Jewish Law*, edited by H. H. Cohn, pp. 168f. New York, 1971.

Epstein, Baruch. *Torah Temimah*. Tel-Aviv, 1956.

Epstein, J. N. *Mavo le-Nusah ha-Mishnah. Jerusalem, 1948*.

―――. *Mevuot le-Sifrut ha-Tannaim*. Jersualem, 1957.

―――. *Mevuot le-Sifrut ha-Amoraim*. Jerusalem, 1962.

Epstein, Kalonymos Kalman, *Maor va-Shemesh*. Tel-Aviv, 1965.

Epstein, Louis M. *The Jewish Marriage Contract*. New York, 1927.

―――. *Sex Laws and Customs in Judaism*. New York, 1948.

Epstein, Y. M. *Arukh ha-Shulhan*. Pietrikow, 1903.

Ettlinger, Jacob. *Bikkurey Yaakov*. Altona, 1836.

―――. *Binyan Tzion*, Responsa, Old Series. Altona, 1868; New Series, Vilna, 1878.

―――. ed. *Shomer Tzion ha-Neeman, 1846–1857*. New York, 1963.

Falk, Z. and Kirschenbaum, A., eds. *Diné Israel*, vol. VII. Tel-Aviv, 1776.

Falk, Z. W. *Jewish Matrimonial Law in the Middle Ages*. Oxford, 1966.

Federbusch, S. *ha-Musar ve-ha-Mishpat be-Yisrael*. New York, 1943.

————. *bi-Netivot ha-Talmud.* Jerusalem, 1957.

————. *Hikrey Yahadut.* Jerusalem, 1965.

Feinstein, Moses. *Iggerot Moshe,* New York, 1959–1963.

Felder, Gedaliah. *Sheilot Yeshurun,* Responsa. New York, 1944.

Feldman, David. *Shimushah shel Torah.* London, 1951.

Feldman, David M. *Birth Control in Jewish Law.* New York, 1968.

Feldman, Leon. "Nissim ben Reuben Gerondi" in EJ, vol. 12, pp. 1185–86.

Finkelstein, Louis. *Jewish Self-Government in the Middle Ages.* New York, 1924.

————. "Tradition in the Making." In *The Jewish Theological Seminary of America. Semi-Centennial Volume,* edited by Cyrus Adler, pp. 22–34. New York, 1939.

————. *The Pharisees.* Philadelphia, 1955.

Fleckeles, Eleazar. *Teshuvah me-Ahavah,* Responsa. Kassa, 1912.

Fogelman, Mordecai. *Bet Mordekhai.* Jerusalem, 1970.

Frankel, Zecharias. *Darkhey ha-Mishnah.* Warsaw, 1923.

Freehof, Solomon B. "Ceremonial Creativity Among the Ashkenazim." In *Seventy-Fifth Anniversary Volume of the JQR,* edited by Newman and Zeitlin, pp. 210–24. Philadelphia, 1967.

————. *The Responsa Literature* and *A Treasury of Responsa.* 2d joint ed. New York, 1973.

Fried, J. ed. *Hovat ha-Aliyah le-Eretz Yisrael. Jerusalem, 1972.*

Friedman, S. Perek ha-Ishah Rabbah. Jerusalem/New York, 1978.
————. *Mivneh Sifruti be-Sugyot ha-Bavli."* In *Proceedings of the World Congress of Jewish Studies* (Hebrew), vol. 3, pp. 389–402. Jerusalem, 1977.

Ganzfried, Solomon. *Kitzur Shulhan Arukh,* var. eds.

Gaster, Moses. *The Rabbinical Degree.* Reprinted from the Jewish Chronicle. London, 1900.

Gerondi, Jonah. *Shaarey Teshuvah.* Vilna, 1927.

Gershom of Mayyence. *Teshuvot Rabbenu Gershom.* Edited by Eidelberg. New York, 1955.

Ginzberg, Louis. *Mekomah shel ha-Halakhah be-Hokhmat Yisrael.* Jerusalem, 1931.

————. *Legends of the Jews.* Philadelphia, 1946.

————. *Jewish Lore and Law.* Philadelphia, 1955.

————. *Students, Scholars and Saints.* New York, 1958.

Goitein, Baruch Benedict. *Kesef Nivhar.* Prague, 1827–1828; Jerusalem, 1974.

Gold, Y. M. *Measef le-Khol ha-Mahanot.* Munkacs, 1939.

———. *Darkhey Hayyim ve-Shalom.* Jerusalem, 1974.

Gordis, Robert. *Judaism for the Modern Age.* New York, 1955.

———. *Understanding Conservative Judaism.* New York, 1978.

———. "The Dynamics of Halakhah: Principles and Procedures." *Judaism* 28, no. 3 (Spring 1979): 263–82.

Goren, S. *Pesak Din be-Inyan he-Ah ve-he-Ahot.* Jerusalem, 1975.

Gottlober, A. B. *Zikhronot u-Masaot,* Edited by R. Goldberg. Jerusalem, 1976.

Greenvald, J. J. *Kol Bo Al Avelut.* New York, 1956.

Grunfeld, I. *The Jewish Dietary Laws.* London, 1972.

Grünwald, Moses. *Arugot ha-Bosem,* Responsa. Szalyva, 1912.

Gulak, Asher. *Yesodey ha-Mishpat ha-Ivri.* Berlin, 1923.

Gumbiner, Abraham. *Magen Avraham* to *Shulhan Arukh,* var. eds.

Guttmann, Y. M. "*Sheelot Akademiot ba-Talmud.*" In *Dvir,* vol. I. pp. 38–87; Berlin, 1923; vol. II, pp. 101–164. Berlin, 1924.

———. *Behinat ha-Mitzvot.* Breslau, 1931.

———. *Behinat Kiyyum ha-Mitzvot.* Breslau, 1931.

———. Photocopy of both, *Makor.* Jerusalem, 1978.

Haddaya, Obadiah. *Yaskil Avdi,* Responsa. Jerusalem, 1976.

ha-Hinnukh, attributed to Aaron ha-Levi of Barcelona. var. eds., ed. Chavel. Jerusalem, 1957.

Halberstam, Hayyim. *Divrey Hayyim,* Responsa. New York, n.d.

Halevy, Isaak. *Dorot ha-Rishonim.* Frankfurt, 1915–Berlin/Vienna, 1922.

Hartman, David. *Maimonides: Torah and Philosophic Quest.* Philadelphia, 1976.

Hayyim of Volozhyn. *Nefesh ha-Hayyim.* Jerusalem, 1973.

Hayyim, Yosef of Baghdad. *Rav Pealim,* Responsa. Jerusalem, 1961.

Heinemann, I. *Taamey ha-Mitzvot.* Jerusalem, 1949.

Heller, Aryeh Laib. *Ketzot ha-Hoshen* in var. eds. of *Shulhan Arukh, Hoshen Mishpat.*

———. *Shev Shematata.* Lemberg, 1805 and var. eds.

———. *Avney Milluim.* Lemberg, 1813.

Heller, Yom Tov Lippmann. *Tosefot Yom Tov* to Mishnah. ed. Warsaw, 1882.

———. *Divrey Hamudot* to the *Rosh,* Romm, Vilna ed. of Talmud.

Hertz, J. H. Authorised Daily Prayer Book. London, 1967.

Herzog, Isaac. *Hekhal Yitzhak,* Responsa. Jerusalem, 1960–1972.

———. *The Main Institutions of Jewish Law.* London and New York, 1965.

Heschel, Abraham Joshua. *Torah min ha-Shamayyim*. London, New York, 1962–1965.

Hillel, J. M. *Ahavat Shalom*. Jerusalem, 1977.

Hillman, D. Z. *Iggerot Baal ha-Tanya u-Veney Doro*. Jerusalem, 1953.

Hirschensohn, Hayyim. *Malki ba-Kodesh*, Responsa. Hoboken, 1918–1923.

Hoffmann, David Zevi. *Melammed le-Hoil*, Responsa. New York, 1954.

Horowitz, Isaiah. *Sheney Luhot ha-Berit*. Jerusalem, 1963.

Isaiah b. Mali di Trani. *Teshuvot ha-Rid*. Edited by J. Wertheimer. Jerusalem, 1967.

Ishmael ha-Kolen. *Zera Emet*. Rigio, 1815.

Israel, of Shklov. *Peat ha-Shulhan*. Jerusalem, 1912.

Israeli, Saul, ed. *ha-Torah ve-ha-Medinah*, 2. Tel-Aviv, 1950.

Isserlein, Israel. *Terumat ha-Deshen*. Bene Berak, 1971.

Isserles, Moses. *Mappah*, glosses to *Shulhan Arukh*, var. eds.

———. *Darkhey Moshe* to *Tur*, var. eds.

———. *Teshuvot Rama*. Amsterdam, 1711.

Jackson, B. ed. *The Jewish Law Annual*, vol. I. Leiden, 1978.

Jacob of Marvège. *Sheelot u-Teshuvot min ha-Shamayyim*. Edited by R. Margaliot. Jerusalem, 1957.

Jacob Weil. Responsa. Jerusalem, 1959.

Jacob b. Asher. *Turim (Tur)* var. eds.

Jacobs, Louis. *Principles of the Jewish Faith*. London, 1961.

———. *Studies in Talmudic Logic and Methodology*. London, 1961.

———. "Are There Fictitious Baraitot in the Babylonian Talmud?" HUCA 42 (1971): 185–96.

———. *Hasidic Prayer*. London, 1972; Littman Library of Jewish Civilization.

———. *Theology in the Responsa*. London, 1975; Littman Library of Jewish Civilization.

———. "How Much of the Babylonian Talmud Is Pseudepigraphic?" JJS no. 1 (Spring, 1977): 46–59.

———. *Jewish Mystical Testimonies*. New York, 1977.

———. "The Doctrine of the Zaddik in the Thought of Elimelech of Lizensk" (Rabbi Louis Feinberg Memorial Lecture in Jewish Studies). Cincinnati, February 9, 1978.

———. "The Responsa of Rabbi Joseph Hayyim of Baghdad." In *Perspectives on Jews and Judaism* (Essays in Honor of Wolfe Kelman), pp. 189–214. New York, 1978.

Jakobovits, Immanuel. *Jewish Medical Ethics*, 2d ed.. New York, 1975.

Jastrow, Marcus. *A Dictionary of the Targumim, the Talmud Babli and Yerushalmi, and the Midrashic Literature*. New York, 1950.

Judah Ha-Leui. *Kuzari*, ed. Laufmann. Tel-Aviv, 1972.

Kagan, Israel Meir. *Sefer Hapetz Hayyim*. Vilna, 1873; New York, 1952.

———. *Mishnah Berurah*. *New York, 1943*.

Kahana, I. Z. Mehkarim be-Sifrut ha-Teshuvot. Jerusalem, 1973.

Kahana, K. "The Connection Between Law and Other Branches of Knowledge." In *Essays Presented to Chief Rabbi Israel Brodie on the occasion of his seventieth Birthday*, edited by H. J. Zimmels, J. Rabbinowitz, and I. Finestein, English vol., pp. 219–29. London, 1967.

Kamelhaar, Y. A. *Dor Deah*. Pietrikow, 1935; 2d ed., n.p., 1970.

Kaplan, Zevi. *me-Olamah shel Torah*. Jerusalem, 1974.

Karl, Zevi. *Mishnayot: Pesahim*. Lemberg, 1925.

Karlin, Aryeh. *Lev Aryeh*. Tel-Aviv, 1938.

Karo, Joseph. *Shulhan Arukh*, var. eds.

———. *Bet Yosef* to *Tur*, var. eds.

———. *Kesef Mishnah* to Maimonides' *Yad*, var. eds.

Kasher, M. M. *Mefaneah Tzefunot*. Jerusalem, 1976.

Katz, Jacob. *Exclusiveness and Tolerance*. Oxford, 1961.

———. "Though He Sinned, He Remains an Israelite" (Hebrew). *Tarbiz* 28, nos. 2–3(January 1958): 203–217.

Katzenellenbogen, Y. L. *ha-Talmud ve-Hokhmat ha-Refuah*. Berlin, 1928.

Kimhi, David. *Commentary to the Bible*, var. eds.

Kirschenbaum. A. "The 'Good Samaritan' in Jewish Law" in *Diné Israel*. vol. VII, pp. 7–86.

Klein, Isaac. Responsa and Halakhic Studies. New York, 1975.

———. *A Guide to Jewish Religious Practice* New York, 1979.

Kluger, Solomon. *Modaah le-Vet Yisrael*. Breslau, 1859.

———. *Tuv Taam va-Daat*, Responsa, 3d Series, Part II. Podgorze, 1900.

———. *Avodat Avodah*. New York, 1962.

Kohen, Meir Simhah. *Meshekh Hokhmah*. Riga, 1927.

———. *Or Sameah*. New York, 1946.

Kook, A. I. *Etz Hadar*. Jerusalem, 1907.

———. *Shabbat ha-Aretz*, 2d. ed. Jerusalem, 1937.

———. *Iggerot ha-Rayah*. Jerusalem, 1943.

———. *Daat Kohen*, Responsa. Jerusalem, 1969.

———. *Ezrat Kohen*. Jerusalem, 1969.

Kook, S. H. *Iyyunim u-Mehkarim*. Jerusalem, 1959.

Krochmal, Nahman. *Moreh Nevukhey ha-Zeman*. Edited by S. Rawidowicz. London, 1961.

Lamm, Norman. *Torah Lishmah*. Jerusalem, 1972.

———. "Judaism and the Modern Attitude to Homosexuality." In Yearbook of EJ, pp. 194–205. 1974.

Lampronti, Isaac. *Pahad Yitzhak*. Jerusalem, 1970.

Landau, Ezekiel. *Noda Biyhudah*, Responsa. Jerusalem, 1969.

Lauterbach, J. Z. *Rabbinic Essays*. Cincinnati, 1951.

Lerner, Meir. *Hadar ha-Karmel*, Responsa, vol. I. London, 1970; vol. 2, 1975.

Levi Ibn Habib. Responsa. Lemberg, 1865.

Levinthal, Israel H. *Judaism: An Analysis and Interpretation*. New York, 1935.

Levitats, Isaac. "Takkanot Ha-Kahal" in EJ, vol. 15, pp. 728–37.

Lewin, B. M. *Iggeret de-Rav Sherira Gaon*. Haifa, 1921.

———. *Otzar ha-Geonim, Kiddushin*. Jerusalem, 1940.

Lieberman, Saul. *Hellenism in Jewish Palestine*. New York, 1950.

———. "How Much Greek in Jewish Palestine?" in *Biblical and Other Studies*. Edited by A. Altman. pp. 123–41. Cambridge, Mass. Harvard University Press, 1963.

Lipshutz, Israel. *Tiferet Yisrael* in Mishnah ed. Vilna, 1913.

Loewe, H., and Montefiore, C. G. *A Rabbinic Anthology*. London, 1938.

Lorberbaum, Jacob. *Netivot ha-Mishpat* to *Shulhan Arukh, Hoshen Mishpat*, var. eds.

Löw, Immanuel. "Hā-'Iddānā" HUCA 11 (1936): 193–206.

Lowy, S. "Polygamy." In JJS, 9, 1958, pp. 115–38.

Luria, Solomon. *Teshuvot Rashal*. Fuerth, 1768.

Maimonides, Moses. *Mishneh Torah (Yad ha-Hazakah)*. Amsterdam, 1702.

———. *Kovetz Teshuvot ha-Rambam*. Leipzig, 1859.

———. *Moreh Nevukhim*, Lemberg, 1866. Edited by Kaufmann. Tel-Aviv, 1935. (English trans. S. Pines, *The Guide of the Perplexed*. Chicago and London, 1963).

———. *Sefer ha-Mitzvot*. Warsaw, 1883 (English trans. by C. B. Chavel, *Maimonides and the Commandments*. London, 1967).

———. *Rambam la-Am*. Edited by S. T. Rubinstein. Jerusalem, 1967.

———. *Teshuvot ha-Rambam*. Edited by Freimann. Jerusalem, 1934. Edited by Blau, Jerusalem, 1960.

———. Commentary to the Mishnah in Babylonian Talmud, Romm, Vilan 1933.

Malachi ha-Kohen. *Yad Malakhi*. Jerusalem, 1976.

Margaliot, Reuben. *Margaliot ha-Yam*. Jerusalem, 1958.

———. *Nitzutzey Or*. Jerusalem, 1965.

Margoliot, Ephraim Zalman. *Shaarey Teshuvah* to *Shulhan Arukh*, var. eds.

Meah Berakhot. Amsterdam, 1687.

Medini, H. H. *Sedey Hemed*. Edited by Friedmann. New York, 1962.

Meir ha-Kohen. *Haggahot Maimoni* to Maimonides' *Yad*, var. eds.

Meiri, Menahem. *Hibbur ha-Teshuvah*. Edited by A. Sofer. Jerusalem, 1976.

———. *Bet ha-Behirah : Berakhot*. Edited by S. Dickman. Jerusalem, 1976.

———. *Eruvin*. Edited by M. Hirshler. Jerusalem, 1965.

———. *Pesahim*. Edited by J. Klain. Jerusalem, 1966.

———. *Horayot*. Edited by A. Sofer. Jerusalem, 1970.

———. *Hullin*. Edited by A. Liss. Jerusalem, 1970.

———. *Avodah Zarah*. Edited by A. Sofer. Jerusalem, 1971.

———. *Bava Kama*. Edited by K. Schlesinger. Jerusalem, 1973.

———. *Shavuot*. Edited by A. Liss. Jerusalem, 1973.

Menahem Mendel of Lubavitch. *Tzemah Tzedek*, Responsa. Vilna, 1872.

Menahem Mendel of Vitebsk. *Peri ha-Aretz*. Jerusalem, 1965.

Michaelson, Zevi Ezekiel. *Tirosh ve-Yitzhar*. Warsaw, 1936.

"Mishneh Torah Studies." In *The Jewish Law Annual*. Edited by B. Jackson. pp. 3–176. Vol. I. Leiden, 1978.

Moore, G. F. *Judaism in the First Centuries of the Christian Era*. Cambridge, Mass.: Harvard University Press, 1927–30.

Mordecai b. Hillel. *Mordekhai* in Babylonian Talmud, Romm. Vilna.

Mordecai ha-Levi. *Darkhey Noam*. Venice, 1697.

Moses of Coucy. *Sefer Mitzvot Gadol*.

Nahmanides, Moses. *Hiddushey ha-Ramban*. Jerusalem, 1928.

———. *Pirush ha-Ramban al ha-Torah*. Edited by Chavel. Jerusalem, 1959.

———. *Teshuvot ha-Ramban*, edited by Chavel. Jerusalem, 1975.

———. *Milhamot ha-Shem*, to Alfasi in Babylonian Talmud, Romm. Vilna.

Nathansohn, J. S. *Bittul Modaah*. Lemberg, 1859.

———. *Shoel u-Meshiv*, Responsa. Lemberg, 1868.

Neusner, Jacob. *The Rabbinic Traditions About the Pharisees Before 70*. Leiden, 1971.

———. *A History of the Mishnaic Law of Purities*. Leiden, 1974–1977.

Newman, J. *"mi-Diney ha-Halom ba-Halakhah."* *Hadarom*, no. 28 (Tishri 5729):64–68.

Nissim of Gerona *Hiddushey ha-Ran*. Jerusalem, 1975.

———. Commentary to *Nedarim*, Babylonian Talmud, Romm. Vilna.

———. Commentary to Alfasi, Babylonian Talmud, Romm. Vilan.

Oppenheim, David. *Nishal David*, Responsa. Edited by J. Feld, vol. I, Jerusalem, 1972; vol. II, Jerusalem, 1975.

Oshri, E. *Teshuvot Mi-Maamakim*. New York. 1968.

Otzar ha-Geonim. Edited by B. M. Lewin, vol. 7, *Yevamot*. Jerusalem, 1936; vol. 9. *Kiddushin*. Jerusalem, 1940.

Otzar ha-Posekim. Jerusalem, 1970–

Palaggi, Hayyim. *Kol ha-Hayyim*. Izmir, 1874.

Passamaneck, S. M. "Some Mediaeval Problems in *Mamzerot*." HUCA, 37 (1966):121–45.

———. *Insurance in Rabbinic Law*. Edinburgh, 1974.

Perfet, Isaac b. Sheshet: *Teshuvot Ribash*. New York, 1944.

Perl, Joseph. *Megalle Temirin*. Lemberg, 1864.

Perla, K. A. *Otzar Lashon Hakhamim*. Jerusalem, 1947.

Perlmutter, Abraham Zevi. *Dammesek Eliezer*. Pietrikow, 1905.

Petuchowski, J. J. *Ever Since Sinai*. New York, 1961.

Pineles, H. M. *Darkah shel Torah*. Vienna, 1861.

Plaut, W. Gunther. *The Rise of Reform Judaism*. New York, 1963.

Plotzki, Meir Dan. *Keli Hemdah*. Pietrikow, 1927.

Quest. London, 1965.

Rabbinovicz, R. *Dikdukey Soferim: Variae Lectiones in Mischnam et in Talmud Babylonicum*. New York, 1960.

Rabbinowitz, Joseph. *Mishnah Megillah*. London, 1931.

Rapoport, Abraham ha-Kohen. *Eitan ha-Ezrahi*, Responsa. Ostrow, 1796.

Rapoport, Albert, A. "Confession in the Circle of R. Nahman of Bratzlav." *Bulletin of the Institute of Jewish Studies*. 1 (London, 1973):65–96.

Rapoport, S. J. *Erekh Millin*. Prague, 1852.

Rashi Commentary to Babylonian Talmud, Romm, Vilna:*Teshuvot Rashi*. Edited by Elfenbein. New York, 1942.

Rawidowicz, S. *Sefer ha-Madda*. Berlin, 1922.

Reines, Jacob. *Hotam Tokhnit*, Vol. I, Mainz, 1880; Vol. 2, Pressburg, 1881.

———. *Sefer ha-Arakhin*. New York, 1926.

Reisher, Jacob. *Solet le-Minhah*. Dessau, 1696.

Rivkes, Moses. *Baer ha-Golah* to *Shulhan Arukh*, var. eds.

Rosenbaum, Zevi Hirsh. *Raza de-Uvda*. New York, 1976.

Rosenthal, J. "Karaim and the Karaite Faith in Western Lands" (Hebrew). In the H. Albeck Jubilee Volume. pp. 425–44. Jerusalem, 1963.

Rubinstein, A. Review of Wertheim's *Halakhot ve-Halikhot ba-Hasidut*. KS 36, no. 3, (June 1961):280–86.

Rubinstein, S. T. *"Kedushat Kohanim bi-Zeman ha-Zeh." Sinai* 52, nos. 4–5, (January–February 1963):161–66.

Samuel b. David Moses ha-Levi. *Nahalat Shivah*. Berlin, 1763.

Schachter, Jacob. *Sefer Mishli be-Divrey Hazal*. Jerusalem, 1963.

Schatz Uffenheimer, Rivka. *ha-Hasidut ke-Mistika*. Jerusalem, 1968.

Schechter, Solomon. *Studies in Judaism*. Philadelphia, 1945.

———. *Seminary Addresses*. New York, 1959.

Schick, Moses. *Teshuvot Maharam Shik*. Lemberg, 1884.

Schmelkes, Isaac. *Bet Yitzhak*, Responsa. New York 1960.

Scholem, Gershon. *Major Trends in Jewish Mysticism*, 3d. ed.. London, 1955.

———. *"Demuto ha-Historit shel Rabbi Yisrael Baal Shem Tov"* In *Molad*, Nos. 144–45, pp. 3–24. Av-Elul, 1960.

———. *The Messianic Idea in Judaism*. New York, 1971.

———. *Shabbetai Zevi*, Tel-Aviv, 1957. English trans. London, 1973. *Kabbalah*. Jerusalem, 1974.

Schor, Alexander Sender. *Simlah Hadashah*. Sudlikow, 1820.

Schwadron, Shalom Mordecai. *Sheelot u-Teshuvot Maharsham*. Jerusalem, 1974.

Schwarz, J. *Maaneh le-Iggerot*. New York, 1973.

Sefer Hasidim. Edited by J. Wistinetzki. Frankfurt, 1924. Edited by R. Margaliot, Jerusalem, 1973.

Sefer ha-Minhagim. Minhagey Habad. New York, 1978.

Segal, M. H. *The Pentateuch*. Jerusalem, 1967.

Sevin, S. J. *le-Or ha-Halakhah*. Jerusalem, 1946.

———. *ha-Moadim ba-Halakhah*. Tel-Aviv, 1949.

———. *Ishim ve-Shittot*. Tel-Aviv, 1952.

Shabbetai ha-Kohen. *Siftey Kohen* to *Shulhan Arukh*, var. eds.

Shapira, Hayyim Eleazar. *Nimmukey Orah Hayyim*. Jerusalem, 1968.

———. *Ot Hayyim ve-Shalom*. Jerusalem, 1965.

———. *Minhat Eleazar*, Responsa. New York, 1974.

———. *Hamishah Maamarot*. Jerusalem, 1962.

Shapira, Zevi Hirsh. *Beer Lahai Roi.* Jerusalem, 1964.

———. *Darkhey Teshuvah.* Jerusalem, 1967.

Sheiltot. Edited by N.Z.J. Berlin. Jerusalem, 1975.

Shiloh, S. *Dina de-Malkhuta Dina.* Jerusalem, 1975.

Shkop, Simeon. *Shaarey Yosher,* Warsaw, 1928; 3d ed. n.p., n.d..

———. *Sefer ha-Yovel* (in honour of R. Simeon). Vilna, 1936.

Shneor Zalman of Liady. *Seder Tefillot.* New York, 1965.

———. *Shulhan Arukh.* New York, 1976.

Shobet, D. M. *The Jewish Court in the Middle Ages.* New York, 1931.

Shor, Y. Z. ed. *Or ha-Yashar.* Lemberg, 1902.

Shrock, A. T. *Rabbi Jonah ben Abraham of Gerona.* London, 1948.

Siegel, Seymour. "The War of the *Kitniyot* (Legumes)." In *Perspectives on Jews and Judaism* (Essays in Honor of Wolfe Kelman), edited by A. A. Chiel, pp. 383–408. New York 1978.

———, ed. *Conservative Judaism and Jewish Law.* New York, 1977.

Siev, Asher. "*ha-Rama ke-Fosek u-Makhria.*" *Talpiot,* vol. VI. pp. 321–35. New York, 1953.

Silberg, M. *Talmudic Law and the Modern State.* New York, 1973.

Singer, J. D. *Ziv ha-Minhagim.* Jerusalem, 1971.

Sirkes, Joel. *Bayit Hadash* to *Tur,* var. eds.

Sklare, M. *Conservative Judaism.* New York, 1965.

Sofer, Moses. *Teshuvot Hatam Sofer.* Pressburg, 1859.

———. *Hiddushey Hatam Sofer. Nedarim.* Jerusalem, 1947.

Sofer, Simhah Bunem. *Teshuvot Shevet Sofer.* Jerusalem, 1974.

Sofer, Solomon. *Hut ha-Meshulash.* Tel-Aviv, 1963.

Solomon, Norman. "Hilluq and Haqira: A Study in the Method of the Lithuanian Halakhists." *Diné Yisrael,* 4, (1973): LXIX–CVI.

———."Definition and Classification in the Works of the Lithuanian Halakhists." *Diné Yisrael,* 6, (1975): LXIII–CIII.

Soloveitchik, Hayyim. *Hiddushey Rabbenu Hayyim ha-Levi.* Brest-Litovsk, 1936.

Soloveitchik, Joseph Dov. "*Ish ha-Halakhah.*" In *Talpiot,* 1944, pp. 651–735.

Sorski, A. *Rabbi Shimeon ve-Torato.* Bene Berak, 1971.

———. *Marbitzey Torah u-Musar.* New York, 1977.

Spektor, Isaac Elhanan. *Eyn Yitzhak,* Responsa. Vilna, 1888–1895.

———. *Beer Yitzhak,* Responsa. Königsberg, n.d.

Sperling, A. T. *Taamey ha-Minhagim*. Edited by J. S. Weinfeld. Jerusalem, 1957.

Steinberg, Abraham Menahem. *Mahazey Avraham*, Responsa. Brody, 1927.

Steinberg, M. "*Siddur Kiddushin* by a Reform Rabbi" in *Hadarom*, No. 29. Nisan: 5729, p. 528.

Strack, Hermann L. *Introduction to the Talmud and Midrash*. Philadelphia, 1945.

Strauss, Leo. "The Literary Character of the Guide for the Perplexed." In *Essays on Maimonides: An Octecentennial Volume*, edited by S. W. Baron, pp. 37–91. New York, 1941.

Talmage, Frank E. *David Kimhi: The Man and His Commentaries*. Cambridge, Mass.: Harvard University Press, 1975.

Tamar, David. "Hints of the Shabbetai Zevi Movement in the Responsa of Hayyim Bevenisti" (Hebrew). In *Sefer Margaliot*. Edited by Y. Rafael. pp. 149–52. Jerusalem, 1973.

Tchnerowitz, Chaim. *Toledot ha-Halakhah*. New York, 1935–1950.

———. *Toledot ha-Posekim*. New York, 1946–1947.

———. *Pirkey Hayyim* (Autobiography). New York, 1954.

Teitelbaum, Yekutiel Judah. *Avney Tzedek*, Responsa. Lemberg, 1888.

Tenenbaum, Malkiel. *Divrey Malkiel*, Responsa. Vilna, 1891–. Jerusalem, 1976.

Toledano, B. A. *Rinah u-Tefillah*. Jerusalem, 1973.

Tosafot (Tosafists). To Babylonian Talmud, Romm. Vilna, 1933.

Trachtenberg, Joshua. *Jewish Magic and Superstition*. New York, 1939.

Trani, Joseph. *Teshuvot Maharit*. Lemberg, 1861.

———. *Hiddushey Maharit* to *Kiddushin*. Jerusalem, 1976.

Trani, Moses. *Bet Elohim*. New York, 1972.

Treves (Dreifuss), Menahem Abraham. *Orah Mesharim*. Jerusalem, 1969.

Turk, S. "*be-Inyan Giddul Kelavim Li-Shemirah*. *Hadarom*, 30 (1970): 55–61.

Twersky, Isadore. *Rabad of Posquières*. Cambridge, Mass.: Harvard University Press, 1962.

———. "Some Non-Halakic Aspects of the *Mishneh Torah*." In *Jewish Medieval and Rennaissance Studies*, edited by A. Altmann. Cambridge, Mass.: Harvard University Press, 1962.

Urbach, E. E. *Baaley ha-Tosafot*. Jerusalem, 1955.

———. *The Sages: Their Concepts and Beliefs* (Hebrew *Hazal*). Jerusalem, 1969.

Uziel, Ben Zion. *Mishpetey Uziel*. Jerusalem, 1964.

———. *Piskey Uziel*. Jerusalem, 1977.

Vital, Hayyim. *Peri Etz Hayyim*. Koretz, 1788.

———. *Etz Hayyim*. Tel-Aviv, 1960.

———. *Shaar ha-Mitzvot*. Tel-Aviv, 1962.

Waldinberg, E. *Tzitz Eliezer*. Responsa, vol. 12. Jerusalem, 1976.

Walkin, Aaron, *Zekan Aharon*. Responsa. New York, 1977.

Wasserman, Elhanan Bunem. *Kovetz Hearot* to *Yevamot*. Tel-Aviv, 1967.

Waxman, Mordecai, ed. *Tradition and Change*. New York, 1958.

Weinberg, Y. J. *Seridey Esh*, Responsa. Jerusalem, 1977.

Weiner, M. *Hadrat Panim-Zakan*. New York, 1977.

Weingarten, Jacob. *Helkat Yoav*, Responsa, 3d ed. Israel, n.p., n.d.

Weiss, I. H. *Dor Dor ve-Doreshav*. Berlin, 1924.

Weiss, J. J. *Minhat Yitzhak*, Responsa, vol. 3. London, 1962.

Weissberg, J. D. *Otzar ha-Hayyim*. Jerusalem, 1978.

Wertheim, Aaron. *Halakhot ve-Halikhot ba-Hasidut*. Jerusalem, 1960.

Wilensky, M. *Hasidim u-Mitnaggedim*, Jerusalem, 1970.

Willowsky, Jacob David. Responsa, Jerusalem, 1908.

Yitzhak Eisik of Komarno. *Notzer Hesed*. New York, 1954.

———. *Shulhan ha-Tahor*, Edited by A. A. Ziss. Tel-Aviv, 1963.

Yom Tov Ishbili. *Teshuvot ha-Ritba*. Edited by J. D. Kapah. Jerusalem, 1959.

———. *Hiddushey Ritba*, var. eds. and to *Nedarim*. Edited by A. Yafin, Jerusalem, 1977; to *Yoma*. Edited by E. Lichtenstein. Jerusalem, 1976.

Yosef, Obadiah. *Yabia Omer*, vol. IV. Jerusalem, 1964.

Yuter, Alan J. "Mehitzah, Midrash and Modernity: A Study in Religious Rhetoric." *Judaism* 28 Spring 1979: 147–59.

Zalman of St. Goar. *Sefer Maharil*. Sabionetta, 1556.

Zechariah Mendel *Baer Hetev* to *Shulhan Arukh*. var. eds.

Zemah, Jacob *Nagid u-Metzavveh*. Venice, 1712.

———. *Shulhan Arukh ha-Ari*. Jerusalem, 1961.

Zevi Hirsh of Zhydachow. *Sur me-Ra va-Aseh Tov*. Pest, 1942.

Zimmels, H. J. *Magicians, Theologians and Doctors*. London, 1952.

———. *Ashkenazim and Sephardim*. London, 1958.

———. "*Inyaney Hukkot ha-Goyyim be-Sheelot u-Teshuvot*." In H. Albeck Jubilee volume. Jerusalem, 1963, pp. 402–424.

Zohar, var. eds.

Zohar Hadash, var. eds.

Tikkuney Zohar, var. eds.

Zucrow, S. *Adjustment of Law to Life in Rabbinic Literature*. Boston, 1928.

Index

Aaron of Barcelona (Aaron ben Joseph Ha-Levi), 34
Abarbanel (Abravanel Abrabanel), 163
Abba of Candia, 167
Abbahu, R., 258
Abbaye, 44, 52, 64, 97, 185, 201
Aboab, S., 164
Abolition of laws, 228–29
Abrabanel, Abravanel. *See* Abarbanel
Abraham (patriarch), 192
Abraham (the convert), 253
Abraham ben Nathan, 222–23
Abraham ben Zevi, 265
Abraham Ibn David, *(Rabad)*, 50, 79, 111, 126
Abraham Ibn Ezra, 65, 258
Abudraham, 49, 227, 253
Academic study, 24, 25, 28–29, 31, 32, 58–64, 111, 138, 263, 268
Achilles, 28
Acquisition, simultaneous, 58
Acre, 206
Adam, 242
Adler, N., 146, 163
Adultery, 45, 106, 160, 257, 258, 261, 266, 268, 272
Aesthetics, 46–47
Agency, 58, 67, 184
Aggadah, 9–19, 27, 33–34, 53, 62–63, 67, 101, 138, 193, 195
Agunah, 46, 150–51, 270
Agus, J., 247
Agush, H. H., 66
Ahad ha-Am, 10

Aharonim, 11, 59, 132–33. *See also Rishonim*
Airplane, 180
Akiba, R., 204, 259–60
Albeck, H., 30, 119, 163, 251
Alexandria, 103, 240
Alfakar, Judah, 64
Alfasi, Isaac, 19, 30–31, 57, 66, 101, 195, 254
Alfasi, Y., 89
Algiers, 97, 140
Allon, G., 30
Alphabet, 230
Altona, 135, 229
Amalek, 227
Amen, 117
America, 136, 275
Am ha-aretz, 137–38, 140. *See also* Scholars
Amiel, A., 63, 65–66
Ammi, R., 105, 269
Ammon and Moab, 99–100, 259
Amoraim, 12, 16, 18–19, 25, 27–28, 30–31, 35, 143, 190, 200, 226, 232
Amorites: ways of, 80, 94–98, 233. *See also* Superstition
Amulets, 54, 225
Analogy, 30, 166
Analysis, 25, 56–64
Anatomy, 174–76
Angels, 44, 88, 131, 192, 225
Animals, 95–96, 98–99, 111, 158, 172, 226, 252
Aphrodite, 91

294